The Matthean Community and the World

Studies in Biblical Literature

Hemchand Gossai
General Editor

Vol. 111

PETER LANG
New York • Washington, D.C./Baltimore • Bern
Frankfurt am Main • Berlin • Brussels • Vienna • Oxford

James P. Grimshaw

The Matthean Community and the World

An Analysis of Matthew's Food Exchange

PETER LANG
New York • Washington, D.C./Baltimore • Bern
Frankfurt am Main • Berlin • Brussels • Vienna • Oxford

Library of Congress Cataloging-in-Publication Data

Grimshaw, James P.
The Matthean community and the world: an analysis
of Matthew's food exchange / James P. Grimshaw.
p. cm. — (Studies in biblical literature; v. 111)
Includes bibliographical references and index.
1. Food in the Bible. 2. Sociology, Biblical. 3. Bible. N.T. Matthew—
Social scientific criticism. 4. God—Biblical teaching.
5. Bible. N.T. Matthew—Theology. I. Title.
BS2575.6.D56G75 226.2'067—dc22 2007026671
ISBN 978-1-4331-0083-3
ISSN 1089-0645

Bibliographic information published by **Die Deutsche Bibliothek**.
Die Deutsche Bibliothek lists this publication in the "Deutsche
Nationalbibliografie"; detailed bibliographic data is available
on the Internet at http://dnb.ddb.de/.

The paper in this book meets the guidelines for permanence and durability
of the Committee on Production Guidelines for Book Longevity
of the Council of Library Resources.

29 Broadway, 18th floor, New York, NY 10006
www.peterlang.com

Printed in the United States of America

To Cindy, Savannah, and India,

with whom I share food every day

Table of Contents

Part III: Food Exchange Outside the Community

Part IV: Food Exchange Inside and Outside the Community

Editor's Preface

More than ever the horizons in biblical literature are being expanded beyond that which is immediately imagined; important new methodological, theological, and hermeneutical directions are being explored, often resulting in significant contributions to the world of biblical scholarship. It is an exciting time for the academy as engagement in biblical studies continues to be heightened.

This series seeks to make available to scholars and institutions, scholarship of a high order, and which will make a significant contribution to the ongoing biblical discourse. This series includes established and innovative directions, covering general and particular areas in biblical study. For every volume considered for this series, we explore the question as to whether the study will push the horizons of biblical scholarship. The answer must be *yes* for inclusion.

In this volume James Grimshaw explores the foundation for the relationship between the Matthean community and the surrounding community and other groups. He challenges the scholarly convention which has routinely argued that for the most part the relationship between these groups was adversarial. While there is certainly some evidence for this, Grimshaw proceeds in a different direction and predicates his argument on the presupposition that the relationship between these communities is best understood through the lens of food exchange. The author makes two significant advancements in the manner in which essential themes and trajectories of this particular book might be studied, but also presents a hermeneutic of socio-economic engagement for the contemporary world that is enlightening.

Here is a study that scholars will find fresh and sophisticated, and the ideas and arguments generated here will certainly extend the discussion in unavoidable ways particularly in light of the ever increasing challenges of food distribution, inequity of food resources, division between rich and poor communities, and the manner in which the text and world of the Bible comes to bear in practical and concrete ways on our society. This is an important and wide-ranging addition to the already well established body of scholarly work on this text, and it is one that I believe must be reckoned with.

The horizon has been expanded.

Hemchand Gossai
Series Editor

Acknowledgments

This project is a revision of my dissertation. It would not have been possible without the support and encouragement of my teachers in the Graduate Department of Religion at Vanderbilt University. I wish to thank Professors Daniel Patte, Amy-Jill Levine, Fernando Segovia, John Fitzmier, Beth Conklin, and Patout Burns. I am especially grateful for my advisor Professor Patte, whose encouraging and constructive feedback at each step of the process kept my spirits up and convinced me I could finish the project.

I am thankful for the Vanderbilt Divinity School library and the Central library for their excellent resources and cooperative staffs. To the Disciples Divinity House for its hospitality—it is there where I often took refuge from my time in the library to eat lunch and visit with the Disciples community, a community which has a history of reaching out beyond its boundaries.

I would like to thank Luther College for the many ways they supported me in this project. Luther College provided me with EndNote software and funds for a student research assistant, Amber Ingalsbe, who spent many hours on various research tasks and kept me working on the project when teaching pressures were mounting. Thanks Amber. Several other Luther College students also helped me with footnotes and bibliography. Much thanks to Janelle Ott, Adnan Shaikh, and Britta Schaffmeyer for their good and attentive work. The Luther College library was a good resource for my research and the Interlibrary Loan service was very prompt and efficient. I am thankful to the Anthropology faculty, especially Lori Stanley, whose conversations over lunch helped me to make sense out of the anthropological research on food exchange. I am especially grateful for the members of the Religion and Philosophy Department, for the supportive environment they created for both teaching and research and the many tangible ways in which they helped me make progress while I was there.

I am also grateful for the support of Carroll College. To my Dean, Lelan McLemore, I am thankful for support and resources. The library opened up office space for me during the summer before I was able to move into my permanent office, which allowed me to continue working on the project. Its Interlibrary Loan program was very responsive and staff always helpful in so many ways. Much thanks to ITS for providing updated EndNote software to my computer and for helping me figure out Word 2007. A big thank you to two student workers, Corrie Christiaansen and Sam Bister, for their good work with proofreading. I am very grateful for my Carroll College colleague, Emily Askew, who put in an enormous amount of effort to help me finish this work. I do not know how anyone can wrap up a project like this without a friend like Emily. Thank you, Emily, for your gracious generosity. I hope I can pass it forward some day.

There are many others who helped me with this project. I wish to thank my students at Luther and Carroll Colleges for teaching me as much as I have taught them. The Raynor Memorial Libraries at Marquette University and the Nashotah House Library provided access to valuable resources. And for many colleagues I discussed this project with as I was working on it.

I appreciate those with Peter Lang who provided so much support: for Heidi Burns, Senior Editor, who encouraged me to submit my manuscript and was patient and helpful with many initial questions; for Richard Atkins and Jackie Pavlovic in production supervision who addressed many questions along the way; and for Hemchand Gossai who edits this wonderful series.

For my family, I continue to be grateful for the support and understanding and encouragement they gave me, an extension of what they have always done for me. To my parents and siblings and their families, my wife's parents and sister and her family, thank you for hanging in there with me, for practical and emotional support, for believing in me when I stopped believing, and for celebrating with me when I finished. And finally, to my wife Cindy, and our two beautiful daughters, Savannah Grace and India Ruth, you are the joy of my life. Thank you for your patience, for your unwavering support and love, and for never giving up. You have taught me so much about hope, about the gift of life, and about strength and endurance.

Part I

Introduction

Chapter 1

The Problem

Matthean Community and the World

The Matthean community did not get along very well with the rest of the world. This is what I discovered as I began a deliberate reading of scholarship on the Matthean community, paying attention to the relationship between the community and outside groups. I was surprised. The community was "competing with," "differentiated from," "in heightened opposition," or "withdrawing from" various other groups in the larger society and world. In addition, the God of this Matthean community had similar relationships with those outside the community. There was certainly a substantial collection of textual, historical, and sociological evidence to support these claims, and I concurred with much of it, but it seemed odd to me that a community and its God would not have any cooperative or reciprocal relationships with outside communities. At this same time, I was interested in the study of food exchange and decided to study food exchange within the Matthean community and between the community and outside groups. As I proceeded, I found evidence of a different relationship.

This study explores the Matthean community's relationship with the world through the lens of food exchange. In my reading of Matthew's narrative, the Matthean community integrates itself into the world in order to envision itself as part of the larger world beyond its community as a people of a God of all creation. I consider this reading clearly based on textual evidence and more relevant and compelling to those who live in and are concerned about today's socially and economically stratified and ecologically disrupted and deteriorating world.

This study contends that portrayals of the community's relationship with the world and of God are elucidated when Matthew's passages on food exchange are considered. From this perspective

Matthew's God is interpreted as the heavenly Father and nursing Mother who creates and provides for all the world (i.e. the human and natural world of the earth) and the members of Matthew's community are shown to be engaged in reciprocal and mutually beneficial interactions with a wider realm than their own community. This is in contrast with the many studies which focus on how the Matthean community differentiates itself with various segments of the wider society (e.g. the Jewish community, Pharisees and other Jewish leaders, Gentile world, patriarchal society, and Roman authorities). While the purpose of these studies is to better define the identity of the Matthean community as distinct from other communities in society, my study seeks to better identify the place of the Matthean community within society and the natural world as a whole.

Previous Studies

Three general models best depict, for Matthean scholars, the relationship between the community and its wider environment: Matthew's community as a household in a patriarchal society, as a sect or deviant group of Judaism, and as an independent church separated from Judaism. In these models, scholars focus on confrontation between leaders, communities in conflict, and polemical interpretations of the law. As I review one representative study in each model, I analyze the images of God and the views of the relationship between community and world which scholars presupposed in their interpretations.

Household

Crosby provides an example of the household model. The Matthean community's relationship with the world is as a household in conflict with other households in a patriarchal society. Matthew's God is a ruler who reigns over a particular household. Household (*oikos/oikía*) is the root metaphor in the Matthean text and the social, economic, and theological relationships within the household depict the model of community.[1] Matthew's community follows the Roman egalitarian *collegia* (or voluntary association) model, which allows for the free association of people (4:22, 18:18), democratic relations, and an equal sharing of *exousía*.[2] This model is differentiated from the patriarchal family model of the house of Israel and patriarchal Roman society. The community in this latter model is hierarchically ordered with wives, children, and slaves submitting to the father as authority.[3] A pattern of dependence and subordination is established between man-woman, master-slave, and father-child. According to Crosby, the Matthean community as *collegia* is more inclusive than the Roman patriarchal family model and does not acknowledge submission to the father of the household, only submission to the household/*ekklesía* itself.[4]

The task of the Matthean community is to reorder the economic and social resources within its house. Crosby suggests that Matthew's household is responsible for right order in the *oikouméne* (which he defines as the inhabited world, and more nearly the Roman Empire) and implies the household is a part of the *oikouméne*. Yet Crosby's emphasis is on the right order within Matthew's household and the distinction between his community's right order and the lack of order in the patriarchal Roman society and the patriarchal house of Israel. The faithful elect are those inside the Matthean house or those who gather to be with Jesus. The traditional patriarchal family is outside the house.[5] The Matthean household is responsible to the *oikouméne* in that it brings persons from outside the house to live rightly inside the house.

Crosby's image of God reflects the relationship of the community with the world. Crosby makes the sweeping statement that the "prevailing Jewish practice" was to refer to God's work as a reign in terms of royal notions about God and people.[6] Matthew's household, however, perceives God properly as Father. On the basis of general theological comments by Jeremias and Schneider, Crosby underscores that Matthew's God as Father is paternal, even maternal, and is therefore not experienced as a patriarch. Despite his theological assertions, Crosby's evidence points more to a ruling patriarch than a nurturing parent as he interprets the image of God in Matthew's text. He describes God as one who reigns over a particular house-based social grouping, as one to whom the house church is obedient, and as the one under whose will and loving authority the house church lives.[7]

God's control is indeed limited to a particular area—it is discovered and celebrated in the Matthean household, where the goods of salvation are available and received. The household is the social location for the realization of God's reign.[8] God reigns over Matthew's new household of faith, not over the house of Israel or patriarchal Roman society.

Sectarian

Sectarian or deviant models characterize a sectarian God whose community relates to the world around it with heightened opposition or tension. Sectarian interpretations pay particular attention to the conflicts among leaders and disputes over the interpretation of the law. Overman is among recent interpreters using sectarian or deviant models to describe Matthew's community. Overman names the Matthean community as Matthean Judaism and identifies it as a sect within Judaism, a minority that claims to be the true righteous group chosen by God and rejected by its parent body and primary opponent, formative Judaism.[9] The interaction between Matthean Judaism and formative Judaism is contentious as the leaders of the groups compete for control and influence within Jewish society. In response to the conflict, Matthean Judaism withdraws from formative Judaism and from the equally hostile civil realm and constructs and maintains its own world where the law is accurately interpreted and enacted, the community life is ordered by the standards of righteousness and discipline procedures (18:15–18), and social roles are reassessed and particular ones reinforced (e.g. disciple as teacher).[10] Community formation, not world transformation, is the priority.

Overman does not indicate Father as Matthew's primary image of God nor does he explicitly refer to God as king. Rather, he uses the language of covenant, law and inheritance to explain the relationship of God to God's people. God has chosen the Matthean community as the covenant people (i.e. the "true Israel") and has given them the Kingdom as inheritance.[11] Covenant and inheritance imply the role of God as king/lawgiver/liberator[12] who brings the Israelites out of Egypt, establishes a covenant with them as a king with his vassal, and promises the inheritance of the land of Canaan. Overman emphasizes not the role of liberator with the Matthean community but that of lawgiver. The faithful remnant (i.e. true Israel) obeys God's commandments and is rewarded with the inheritance. God is lawgiver who orders, controls, gives the law, and demands obedience.

To understand the image of God for Overman, one can look to the community's embodiment of God's activity—Matthean Judaism reflects heavenly society. The paradigmatic text is 6:10, "Your will be done on earth as it is in heaven." The community is the new kingdom on earth. As such it possesses God's authority and power to forgive sins, to judge, to bind and loose, to expel persons from the community, and to enact legal procedures formerly executed outside the community. The language of authority and power and the types of activity Overman describes frames God as a divine ruler and lawmaker/judge.

The activity of God turns to the sectarian community. God judges and rejects the false leaders/current leadership of the Jewish community and vindicates the sectarian community.[13] God turns to the leaders of Matthean Judaism and its people to carry God's will and message forward (21:43), "God is truly on their side."[14] Although not stated explicitly, Overman implies the former "people," in addition to the leaders, are judged and rejected. While the main problem is with the Jewish leadership, Overman admits that the confrontation is with the Jewish community and he identifies the opponent as formative Judaism which includes persons other than the leadership.[15] Both God and the Matthean community withdraw from the world and set up their own kingdom.

Church

Graham Stanton represents interpretations of Matthew's community as an independent church separated from Judaism.[16] This interpretation marks the clearest and most defined division between community and world. Stanton contends that Matthew's cluster of Christian communities exists *extra muros* in relation to the synagogue. The Matthean communities stand as a separate religious entity from its non-Christian Jewish parent body after a prolonged hostility and a recent and painful parting. The cluster, as a new people, exhibits a sectarian character yet it also has distanced itself (as a minority community) from its parent body, Judaism, and does not consider itself a part of the Jewish community.[17]

As a new people with a new story, Matthew's communities are over and against both the Jewish community and the Gentile world at large. While Stanton recognizes some blurred boundaries between Matthew's ἐκκλεσία and the synagogue, and individual Jews are still pursued as possible converts, Israel as a people or group is considered a separate community and is not expected to be a part of the Matthean cluster. This cluster is also over and against the Gentile world.[18] Matthew's beleaguered sect continues to experience hostility from the Gentiles (10:18, 22). Gentiles are referred to regularly in a derogatory light (5:46, 24:9, tax collectors) and the heightened apocalyptic theme confirms the hostility of the Gentile (and Jewish) world at large.[19] Matthew's cluster as "salt of the earth" and "light of the world" intimates that the cluster is a minority group over and against the world at large, both Jews and Gentiles. The cluster has high community boundaries and the boundaries are partially open only to recruit Gentiles and individual Jews in order to survive. Matthew's community boundaries are tightening and the group is developing greater cohesion within to maintain its distinct identity.

Stanton minimally treats the question of God's role and realm, but his limited discussion matches that of other scholars who share his position on the community's split with Judaism. God transfers God's kingdom and promises to God's true people. God's heir was Israel until its evil leaders, the Pharisees, led Israel astray. The Pharisees were never planted by the heavenly Father and will be uprooted. Now, Israel is under Satan's sway. But God does more than allow Israel to go astray; God takes an active role and rejects God's former people, finally and completely.[20] God has taken the initiative, then, to part the ways between Matthew's sect and Israel and to transfer God's promises and kingdom to a new people, Matthew's communities.[21] Referring to 21:33–46, which is a paradigmatic passage for Stanton and this group of scholars, Hare sums up God's role well as the sovereign one who elects God's people.

> The "Kingdom of God" is used here in an unusual way. It refers not to the age to come but to a special relationship to God's sovereignty, that is, divine election, including the privileges and responsibilities of being God's elect people...Israel is now to be "decommissioned"; its elect status as "light to the Gentiles" is to be taken over by the church.[22]

God functions as sovereign King, distant and swift with decisions for God's obedient servants.[23]

God's realm is limited to this new people of God as a distinct group. They are not a true Israel or even a new Israel but a third race with clear entrance rites as seen in its form of baptism and definitive worship acts as reflected in the liturgy of the Lord's Supper.[24] While a new people, Matthew's communities have deep roots and are clearly the true heirs to God's promises and kingdom. Neither does God's realm include the Gentile world. As with Israel, the Gentile world is judged because the (non-Christian) Gentiles show hostility, not hospitality, to the least of these my brethren, who are members of the Matthean community.[25]

Conclusions of Studies

While the conclusions in these three models slightly differ, their interpretations of Matthew's image of God surprisingly agree upon the monarchical model, that is, God as a king who relates exclusively to and controls a particular human community. God governs the Matthean household, sect, or church with domination and benevolence and the human subjects, in return, submit to God's will and loving authority.[26] God does not interact with the human or natural world outside the Matthean community but defends the community against the outside human world and legitimates its authority.

The Matthean community's relationship with the world corresponds to this image in terms of unilateral/asymmetric control. Scholars interpret the relationship between community and world as being only antagonistic. The community is depicted as being in one of three adversarial relations with the world. The community either withdraws from the wider world or is in constant conflict with groups in the world or, again, engages in conversion-oriented mission to draw people away from the world into the community. Relationships of reciprocity or cooperation are given little attention. Attention to the relationship between community and the world is merely for the purpose of further identifying the contours of the Matthean community itself and its distinction from the world. The community is not seen as part of or oriented toward that world. It competes with opposing communities and their religious leaders for power and disciples. The Matthean community relates to the world through struggle and conflict, and aims at controlling and manipulating the world for its own advantage. These portrayals of community and of God are related to one another and are both problematic. A representation of the community separated from the world implies and conveys a troubling theological vision, and a God who relates exclusively to one human group suggests a disturbing vision of community.

Addressing the Problem

In contrast to the previous scholarship, this study will consider an alternative community model which takes into account an alternative view of God's role and realm. The community model and image of God emerge as the study examines Matthew's passages on food exchange instead of the confrontation between leaders and communities and conflicting interpretations of the law. In particular, attention is given to passages that present "real" or material food, as opposed to passages that treat food as a metaphor or symbolic object (i.e. food as teaching, 16:12). That food is essential and urgent for all of life, and therefore more necessarily shared, makes food acquisition a valid indicator of a community's relationship with the world and God's relationship with the created order.[27]

It is my thesis that the Matthean text's presentation of food exchange can be read as evidence for the relationship between the Matthean community and the world—a relationship also reflected by the text's theology. My interpretation reveals that the literary text constructs a community which is necessarily connected to the world in a way that is reciprocal and mutual. This view of community coincides with the text's image of God as heavenly Father, a cosmic creator, who actively provides for and relates to all creation, not as a ruling monarch who controls a particular community. This model of the Matthean community posits an active interaction with the world as reflected by collaborative food exchange presented in the text.

My social location affects how I read these previous studies and how I interpret the Matthean community and its relationship to the world in the narrative. I consider these previous studies problematic, in part, because they have been influenced by a view of relationship which has become unacceptable for me. I also critique them because the readers have not acknowledged their textual, contextual, or theological choices nor have they considered the ethical implications of their conclusions. I interpret the Matthean community in a way that supports my view of community and world relationships, but I also acknowledge my choices and make clear the implications of my interpretation.

It is critical, then, that I make explicit my methodology and the way in which I will proceed in this study. I continue Part I in the next chapter as I clearly set forth my methodology. Part II begins the analysis of Matthew's narrative as I focus on the first thematic unit (i.e. Matthew 4:1–11, 6:1–21, 6:25–34, 7:7–11) where food distribution occurs primarily within the Matthean community. In Part III, I address the second thematic unit in the narrative (i.e. Matthew 10:5–11, 12:1–8) where food exchange involves those outside the Matthean community and includes those in the larger Jewish community. Part IV analyzes the third and final thematic unit (i.e. Matthew 14:13–22 and 15:29–39) where food exchange includes the larger Jewish and Gentile worlds outside the Matthean community. I conclude by tracking the development of the key ideas of the study and explaining why this project's interpretation is more relevant and compelling for today's world.

Chapter 2

Methodology

Introduction

I support my thesis with a contextual and socio-literary approach that involves three interrelated features: life context, theological perceptions, and textual features. All three must be made explicit in the critical study of the text.[1] My education and experience has taught me that it is essential to include all three features in an interpretation of a biblical text. The postmodern paradigm has brought to an increased awareness the role of the reader's life situation in interpretation.[2] By surveying the many different interpretations of a particular biblical text through time and cultures, it becomes clear (to me and others) that readers' life contexts influence the method used, the particular features of the text focused upon, and the conclusions reached.[3] I have also become increasingly more concerned with the ethical effects of an interpretation. In particular, I am troubled with how interpretations, lived out by many interpreters and by those who read or hear these interpretations, adversely affect marginal groups including the environment and benefit dominant cultural groups.[4] Being aware of how one's life context influences an interpretation, making it explicit, and assuming responsibility for an interpretation and its effects are ethical steps in a critical, self-conscious interpretation.[5]

Following the methodological approach by Grenholm and Patte, and informed by Segovia and O'Connor, I support my thesis with these three interrelated poles: life-context, theological perceptions, and textual features.[6] A greater consensus has formed around the proposal that biblical critics move away from the use of one pole, the text itself, which often results in a positivistic, objective analysis that promotes triumphalism, sexism, and racism.[7] While the first and last poles (life context and textual features) have been more common in biblical interpretations,[8] the addition of the third pole (theological perceptions) allows for a reading to be clear on the religious perception that is brought to the reading and moves away from a hierarchical and unidirectional use of the other two poles.[9] The use of the three poles also makes apparent what it is that is being interpreted: the text certainly but also the life context and a reader's religious experience.[10] The three poles are interdependent and influence one another. I now explore these three poles.

Life Context

My family life, education, work, and life experiences as a privileged part of the dominant culture (e.g. white, male, heterosexual, middle-class, U.S. citizen, Protestant) have deeply influenced me. While part of the majority, I have also learned to critique it. As a way to explain my context that is both succinct and relevant, I discuss my experiences and views on food exchange. My participation in Community Supported Agriculture and my study of the growing and distribution of food for U.S. consumption has led me to think that U.S. food policies have placed a strenuous demand on the land and the poor in the U.S. and in developing countries. Transnational corporations have dominated the "agro-food sector" and have established a "food regime."[11] Rainforests in Brazil, and communities of poor settlers, are being destroyed to produce beef.[12] In a *New York Times* article on February 26, 2002, Tim Weiner reports that subsidized U.S. corn exports, enabled by NAFTA, displace unsubsidized Mexican farmers like Lorenzo Rebollo. As I purchase food in the U.S., I participate in this colonizing that robs the earth and the working poor. I also believe in participating with others to resist this exploitation through local interdependent food relationships.[13] As I read the Matthean narrative as a citizen and food consumer in the United States, I choose passages that highlight food exchange and identify relationships between the community and the world.

The main concern in my interpretation, which emerges out of my life context, is the contemporary community's lack of vision for its shared life in the larger world. More specifically, many individuals and communities in the United States see their lives and actions as unrelated to—not affecting or being affected by—the rest of the world, yet their materialistic and consumer-centered lifestyles posit a high demand for the earth's resources. I experience U.S. communities that culturally isolate themselves and are unaware of their destructive economic interaction and impact on other communities. I see rampant individualism in the Western world. The created world is seen as compartmentalized and treated as separate, autonomous pieces.[14] Similarly, I read Matthean scholarship that focuses on Matthean communities as either withdrawing from or in adversarial interactions with other communities. I perceive the conclusions of these studies on Matthew's community as problematic because I see them as influenced by a view of relationship which has become problematic for me.[15]

I envision all of life as intimately connected and interdependent. Individuals depend upon and contribute to social groups and social groups need and are integral to other social groups with which they interact. The human world relies on the natural world but also must be in relationship with it for mutual survival. Communities in the United States are indeed connected to and make a significant impact on the broader world as they share the earth's limited resources (e.g. food). There are many ways the U.S. and other communities in the world could benefit if U.S. communities were open to a more balanced and reciprocal interaction and drastically changed their consumer lifestyles. Communities, for example, which use local food supply and exchange food with local growers spend less money on fuel to transport food and chemicals to prepare foods for transport, take better care of the earth's resources, and form tighter, connected local communities often across family, race, ethnic, and religious lines.[16] In addition, recent scholarship on Jewish, Christian, and Greco-Roman communities in the first century demonstrates the complex and sustained interactions among these groups.[17]

Theological Perceptions

Two theological views of God's relationship with the world which are popular in the United States culture corroborate this individualistic view of relationship that I experience in my life context. The first is best described by the dialogic model. God and world are viewed in a dialogic, interpersonal relationship.[18] The relationship is between God and an individual human being in the present moment. The "world" is the "human world" and, more accurately, the world of only one human being at a time.[19] God and human encounter not in the social or political or ecological world but in the private, inner world of personal human experience. The second view, best summarized by the monarchical model, demonstrates the notion of distance from and control over others inherent in the individualistic relationship. God's relationship with the world is depicted as a king who rules over his subject people. God governs from a distant throne with domination and benevolence. All the asymmetric power is on God's side—God acts on the world not in it. God's subjects, limited to humans, respond passively with obedience and reverence to their king.[20]

A model of God relating to the world that supports the view of life as intimately connected and interdependent is one offered by McFague that combines the procreation and emanation models. In the procreation model, the world comes out of God, out of the material of God, and is formed by God. Rather than creation as production in which God constructs the world, the world being external to God and static, creation emerges from God as a body that is ongoing and continuing. The mother generates life from her being and that life grows and develops.[21] The emanation model adds an agential component to the procreation model and contends that God continues to be a source of life even after procreation. Not only does God body forth life, but there is a continuing connection between this life and God, a continuing dependence of the new life on God as a divine source of power. The life brought forth by God does not "grow away from God" but continues its bond and reliance on God.[22]

My life context, with experiences in the social, political, ecological, and economical arenas of life, has shaped my theological views. I claim for myself a view of God as one who is intimately connected with all of life, who continues to be immanent and active in working with creation, and who encourages humans to recognize that all of life is interdependent and valued and to be responsible in all of its interactions. These perceptions lead me to read the Matthean text in particular ways such that I limit and focus the dialogue with the text on theological topics concerning the community's image of God and how that image affects the community's relationships with the larger world. This is necessary to do because interpretation for me is a theological process. As a person with a particular religious perception, I approach the text as a theological product. Interpretation is a conversation between my theological world and that of the text.[23] I do not extract information from the text but enter into its world to exchange ideas. My own perceptions, as influenced by a dialogue with the text, have led me to identify those theological topics which are the subject matter of the conversation. I now discuss the textual features of the text but will return to the implications of these textual choices on my religious perceptions toward the end of the chapter.

Textual Features

My life context and theological perceptions have focused my reading of the biblical text toward the theme of food exchange in the Matthean narrative and toward a socio-literary critical method. The experiences I have encountered in my context regarding isolated or conflicted communities, the ways I have seen food exchange between local groups form more integrated communities, and my interest in highlighting how communities cooperatively interact has guided my reading of the Matthean text. My attention was drawn, then, toward food distribution and exchange (i.e. the movement, sharing, giving/receiving, and allocation of food among God, humans, and communities).

Selection of Texts

Given the focus on food exchange among God, humans, and communities, I narrowed the corpus of food passages in Matthew to those texts that met three criteria. First, I chose texts that address how food is requested and/or acquired. This criterion fits with my interests in how food is transferred from one person, entity, or group to another and provides a marker of relationship. Jack Goody refers to this phase of commensality as distribution.[24] Passages that primarily discuss production (the first phase of commensality; e.g. 13:3–9, 20:1–16, 21:28–32, 21:33–46) or focus on preparation and/or consumption (the third and four phases; e.g. 9:9–13, 26:17–29) are not included. Second, I selected texts that discuss "real," material food with nutritional value, that is, food as substance, which is meant to be eaten.[25] This eliminates passages that refer to food for the primary purpose of its symbolic value (e.g. fruit as works in 3:8; 16:5–12) or as a lesson for teaching (e.g. 13:3–9, 18–23, 24–30, 36–43). The third criterion is an expression of need for material food. This follows but completes the first two criteria. A person or group asserts a need for real, material food, requests food, is hungry for food, or expresses a need to acquire food. The need may or may not be solely a biological need—it could also be social or political—but there is a need to get food. This criterion minimizes, then, any guesswork as to whether or how food was acquired or transferred from one person or group to another and asserts that food is necessary and must be accessed.

The passages selected for this study are grouped into three units. The first unit (6:1–21, 6:25–34, 7:7–11) emphasizes the exchange of food between God and the Matthean community as family. Food moves in one direction, from God to the community. In the second unit (10:5–11:1, 12:1–8) food continues to be received by the Matthean community but is given through those outside the Matthean community—the larger Jewish community and the natural world. In the third unit (14:13–22, 15:29–39), food is given by the Matthean community to the crowds, who represent the larger Jewish and Gentile worlds outside the community.

Social Texture

As I address these passages, the two textual features I consider are the social and literary textures. The social texture of the socio-literary approach explores the social and cultural nature of the narrative text.[26] Anthropological studies of food exchange and the cultural script for kinship form the foundation of my particular social approach in this study, which considers two main issues: what motivates the action of reciprocity in the narrative and what is the interaction between practice and the system.[27]

Anthropological Studies. As I interpret food exchange in the Matthean narrative, I draw on anthropological theories of food exchange (i.e. Malinowski, Mauss, Lévi-Strauss, Harris, Sahlins, and a recent study by Gudeman). The larger anthropological field that food exchange best fits under is economic anthropology, an anthropological approach to various types of economic systems that "describes the ways in which people produce, distribute, and consume goods…(and) how these systems are organized."[28] I will hone in on the distribution of goods. In Jack Goody's representation of the five stages of commensality (i.e. production, distribution, preparation, consumption, and disposal) food exchange would best fit under the second category of distribution.[29] Distribution may refer to transfer or sharing (i.e. getting the products to people) and I will extend it to include both giving and receiving, that is, the overall exchange of food. I set the exchange of food in the larger anthropological area of exchange (also called reciprocity and includes gift giving), which also includes the exchange of other goods, services, and people (i.e. clothes, armshells, blankets, wives, etc.).[30] Food exchange, then, can be located under the field of economic anthropology and in the specific area of exchange.

In addition to the studies on food exchange, I draw from anthropological studies of kinship that focus on family and hospitality. The model of kinship, used by some scholars to read the New Testament, is derived from cultural anthropological studies and is used as an interpretive tool when reading an ancient text.[31] This model approximates part of the social context embedded in the narrative text and complements the analysis of narrative criticism.

The cultural model of kinship helps explain food exchange in the Matthean narrative. Kinship relations and household imagery are present throughout the passages in this study. Food exchange in 6:1–21 is situated within an inner room of the house (6:6) between a Father and his children (6:9b). In 7:7–11, a father gives bread and fish to his child. Household imagery is present in 10:5–11:1 and hospitality themes are emphasized in 10:5–11:1 and Matt 14 and 15.

Kinship, the primary category for social organization in Mediterranean societies in the first century, included the relationships regarding families and incorporated the elements of marriage, genealogy and descent, child raising, and inheritance and property.[32] Other institutions (e.g. politics, economics, and religion) interacted and were ordered by the kinship social domain.[33]

Kinship relationships in the household included several family and nonfamily members and each member fulfilled a particular role. Beyond the nuclear family of father, mother, and children were other generations and extended family members. Besides blood family were those related by marriage and beyond family ties day laborers, sojourners, and slaves might be included.[34] Although critiqued for being set too rigidly, roles were generally divided along gender lines. Roles for males included work in the public spaces, political activities, agricultural labor, formal education, and patronage, with the father having primary authority.[35] Women's roles revolved around the private domain or household and included economic management of the household, childcare, education of children, and midwifery.[36]

The household was a base for three main areas of social relations: those within the household, those outside of the household but within the community, and those beyond the boundaries of the community.[37] While a certain system of roles might be assumed in each of these areas (i.e. those within the household mentioned above), the expectations of relationships within and among families may vary according to the cultural setting or the type of good exchanged. In Athens, for example, the political system developed in such a way that relationships between friends, in some cases, replaced those between kin.[38] Sahlins argues that the exchange of food may not follow typical kinship roles in the setting of hospitality or when wealth or rank distinctions are taken into account.[39]

Hospitality is situated in the last two areas of social relations: those relationships between the household and community and those beyond the community. Hospitality is an expected role of the household and is "rooted in kinship."[40] The family is to host those strangers who need a place to stay and food to eat, particularly if they are traveling. Hospitality also intersects with the cultural models of honor and shame and patron and client.[41] Honor is gained or lost depending upon how a host treats a guest. If a guest is of a higher social status, honor can be gained not only by the host but by the whole community.[42] The male head of the family also demonstrates honor as a patron when he provides for and protects a stranger.[43] The stranger is without identity or status but becomes a fictive kin when welcomed through hospitality.[44]

A "law of hospitality" existed in the Mediterranean world as a social necessity. These rules made it possible for people to travel across the harsh landscape and it also regulated community relations with outsiders, a "form of foreign policy…to determine whether strangers were friends or enemies; whether or not they would improve distribution of resources, labor, and goods, prevent war, and keep the peace."[45] A guest was to honor his host, act like a guest and not usurp the role of host, accept the food offered him, and stay for the agreed upon time. A host was to honor his guest, provide food and protection for him, and always offer him the best that was possible.[46] The characters and setting that participate in food exchange are often situated in kinship, and hospitality roles in the Matthean narrative and the inclusion of the cultural script of kinship better takes into account the divine, human, communal, and natural relationships that are shaped by food exchange.

First Main Issue. Two main issues are addressed in this social approach: what motivates the action of reciprocity in the narrative and what is the interaction between practice and the system. Gudeman addresses the first main issue as he claims that reciprocity is complex and a variety of motives may be present as a community engages in reciprocity.[47] I recognize three primary motivating actions for exchanging food in the Matthean narrative that each addresses certain needs in the community: material or biological needs, political needs, and social needs.

While I limited my choice of passages in Matthew's narrative to those where a need for acquiring food was expressed, this need is not necessarily or exclusively biological. Several of the passages do, however, mention that characters are "hungry" (4:1–11, 12:1–8, 15:29–39) and the evidence suggests they are hungry for material food to satisfy biological needs. Other passages do not state that the characters are hungry but they can certainly be read as implying that characters are asking for material food, that food is necessary for biological survival, or that there is a need for food (6:11, 6:25–34, 7:7–11, 10:10, 14:13–22). The Matthean community needs to acquire material food to survive biologically and the acquisition of food often comes from those outside this community. Food was not always grown by one's own community in the first century, especially if situated in an urban setting.[48] When this is coupled with the interpretation that Matthew's community was not composed only of wealthy people but probably reflected a cross-section of society who might have a greater urgency to acquire daily food,[49] it suggests that at least some in the Matthean community were hungry due to a lack of available food. Food, then, was acquired from both those inside and outside the community.

The works of Malinowski, Sahlins, and Harris particularly bear out this motivation to exchange food. Malinowski established a theory of functionalism that differed from A. R. Radcliffe-Brown's structural functionalism. Structural functionalism focused on how different parts of society work to maintain the social structure of society, the integration of society as a whole. The emphasis is on maintaining the system.[50] By contrast, Malinowski's functionalism began with the needs of persons within a society and how the different parts of society function in order to meet people's biological, social, and symbolic needs.[51] While Malinowski emphasized the social needs met by food sharing, he also recognized that food is necessary for meeting physical needs.

For Sahlins as well, the giving of food is based, at least in part, on biological need. Giving flows from those with higher status or kinship rank to those with lower status based on biological need. The gift satisfies basic needs, although it also creates a response from those who receive it.[52] Similarly, those with wealth recognize the material need of those who are poor and provide for them. This particularly happens in communities where everyone might, from time to time, be in a situation of need.[53] The object of exchange, in this case food, clearly affects how one considers reciprocity according to Sahlins. He claims that food "is more readily, or more necessarily, shared"[54] than other objects of exchange primarily because "food is life-giving, urgent, ordinarily symbolic of hearth and home, if not of mother."[55] Food plays a delicate role in food sharing due to its need for survival.

Finally, Marvin Harris and other materialists also focus on the practical and biological aspects of eating. Harris entitled one of his books *Good to Eat* to counter Lévi-Strauss' emphasis that food is "good to think."[56] One of the motivations for exchanging food, then, is overcoming physical hunger for the sake of biological survival.

A second motivation for exchanging food in the Matthean narrative is to address political needs. The Matthean community, at least to some degree, understands the reciprocity of food in terms of maintaining and expressing its power and independence in relation to other communities. The Matthean community here differentiates itself from other communities, a dynamic more predominate early in the narrative. The exchange of food with God (4:1–11, 6:1–21, 6:25–34, 7:7–11) establishes God, not Satan, as the one who is the source of food and who has authority over the community's life and those in all of creation. Jesus, as an agent of God, is also seen as one who expresses power in relation to Satan (4:1–11), the priests (12:1–8), and the towns (14:13–22). While political needs are clearly not the only motivating factor, it is one dynamic present through the narrative.

While giving for Sahlins can be based on biological need, it also can carry with it a political impulse. Giving often flows from those with higher status (e.g. a chief or leader) to those with lower status. While the gift satisfies basic biological needs, it also creates a followership when an equal gift cannot be returned, thus compelling those with lower status to demonstrate loyalty to this particular leader.[57] The exchange indicates a status relation.[58] Likewise, those with wealth might have a certain obligation, a *richesse oblige*, to provide for those in need, an obligation influenced by empathy and compassion or other social pressures to avoid being the object of envy.[59]

For Mauss, the cycle of giving, receiving, and repaying is caught up in relationships of rivalry. The obligation to give maintains a person's authority within the social and political network of relations. The generosity shown through giving suggests the person is a good leader. The receiver of the gift is obligated to accept it in order to maintain his own dignity and place in society. Finally, the obligation to repay also determines one's place and rank within the social relationships.[60]

Reciprocity expresses and extends a community to others and can express dominance over and independence from other communities, according to Gudeman.[61] Reciprocity is the sign of relationship but not the sign of equality and not always the sign of mutuality. Reciprocity is an exchange of inequivalents, "a gesture of commensality not commensuration, yet filled at times with countervailing impulses of competition."[62] Competition can be seen when the extension of a community through reciprocity identifies the existent and giving community as a separate, self-sufficient unit, distinct from outside communities.[63]

The third motivating factor for giving and receiving food, the one emphasized in this study, is the need for social relations. Exchanging food establishes and solidifies social relationships within and outside the family, sustains societal structures beyond the family unit, and addresses emotional needs. The Matthean community sees itself as a part of the world and as participating in the world. This social motivation focuses on unity by contrast with the political motivation which focuses on separation. Through reciprocity, the Matthean community strengthens internal ties and also moves toward greater social interaction with human and natural communities outside their borders as the narrative progresses.

Early in the Matthean narrative, social bonds are coalesced within the Matthean family as God gives food to the community (6:1–21) and community members exchange food with each other (7:7–11). Food addresses the social needs of its community as children who depend on their father and mother for intimacy and a place to belong (6:1–21, 7:7–11) and as people in crisis whose anxiety is alleviated (6:25–34).

As the narrative progresses, the Matthean community forges social ties through food exchange with those in the larger world: the wider Jewish community (10:5–11:1), the Pharisees (12:1–8), and the Gentile world (14:13–22, 15:29–39). Social and emotional needs are addressed through these interactions: those who suffer are comforted (10:5–11:1, 14:13–22, 15:29–39), a place to live is secured (10:5–11:1).[64]

Malinowski, Sahlins, and Lévi-Strauss underscore how reciprocity functions to meet a community's social needs. In Malinowski's study of the kula, a ceremonial exchange in the Trobriand Islands, he concluded that the community's life was "permeated by a constant give and take," that there was a "deep tendency to create social ties through the exchange of gifts," and that there was a "fundamental human impulse to display, to share, to bestow."[65] Food exchange strengthens a community's social ties.

Sahlins arranges reciprocity according to space, most clearly seen as a series of concentric circles. He argues that generalized reciprocity, the sustained one-way flow of goods and services from the haves to the have-nots with little expectation of return, operates primarily within the innermost circle, the kinship sphere.[66] Generalized reciprocity is personal and dependent upon social relations such that "material flow is sustained by prevailing social relations."[67] While this type of reciprocity most often occurs in kinship relations, other factors like rank, wealth, and food as the object of exchange all have the effect of extending "generalized exchange beyond the customary range of sharing" that might be expected with kinship distance alone.[68]

Claude Lévi-Strauss, a French anthropologist, particularly emphasized the role of reciprocity in creating social ties beyond a smaller community, of guaranteeing the priority of society over family, and preventing the larger social group from fragmenting into isolated family units.[69] Lévi-Strauss develops his theory of reciprocity in his work *The Elementary Structures of Kinship*, a book that tackles the case of intergroup exchange of women in marriage as a way to make sense of incest prohibition. The function of gift exchange is not to "promote solidarity within social groups but to forge alliances between groups, thus widening the network of sociality to include those who had been potential enemies."[70] Matthew's generalized reciprocity is used to solidify internal communal ties but it also reaches out to other communities to entertain intercommunal social relationships.

Second Main Issue. The second main issue addressed from this social approach is the interaction between daily practices of exchange and the larger cultural system.[71] Two dynamics are present in the Matthean narrative, as well as in many societies. First, the cultural system shapes the giving and receiving of food in the narrative and, second, the regular, ordinary practice of reciprocity reproduces and, to some extent, changes the system.[72] Beginning with the first dynamic, larger social forces noticeably guide and perhaps even determine, at times, food exchange in the narrative. Several examples are seen in references to the obligations inherent in life centered around family relations (see especially 7:7–11) and the Jewish traditions regarding the understandings of God's provision (cf. 6:25–34), the hospitality afforded to strangers (10:10, "a worker is worthy of his food"), and demands for justice and mercy (12:7, Hosea 6:6). A sense of duty and moral obligations come out of a cultural system that guides reciprocity.

Mauss argued that exchange is based not on voluntary or spontaneous giving but on social obligations. The obligatory cycle of giving, receiving, and repaying is created by a type of force or essence called the *hau* and this also creates relationships of rivalry. Reciprocity is institutionalized and obligatory.[73] Lévi-Strauss contended that reciprocity is more than an external force; it is a universal rule or principle of society. That is, reciprocity is not a social norm that emerges from society or is derived from an institution of society but a fact, a rule that creates the possibility of society.[74] As a regulating principle, reciprocity guarantees the priority of society over family.[75]

Considering the second dynamic, the system is also shaped by the ordinary and repetitive practices of food exchange, practices that are offered up not simply as enactments of social norms but out of choice, of interest, or upon reflection.[76] In the narrative, the Matthean community is asked to be deliberate and to make daily decisions about food: to pray "give us this day our daily bread" (6:11), "to seek first the kingdom of God and his righteousness" (6:33), and to ask, seek, and find (7:7–11). Jesus reinterprets the tradition in order to feed himself and the disciples (12:1–8). These choices are intentional but not necessarily made out of "pragmatic rationality."[77] Inner and emotional needs are also part of the motivation.[78] Jesus makes choices out of his emotional connection to those who follow him: he is moved by compassion to feed the crowds (14:14, 15:32).

Gudeman argues that gifts and reciprocity are not the "primary building block of community," but "tactical acts that extend the base to persons outside a community."[79] In line with Bourdieu, and within a stream of scholars who, since the 1980s, have focused on the idea of practice,[80] Gudeman situates himself against Lévi-Strauss and formalists when he identifies reciprocity not as "a rule or norm of social life…a function of self-interest, or an essential foundation of society," but as "part of a system of practices in which participants express, conserve, lose, and gain position in the sphere of social value."[81] Gudeman understands reciprocity as expressing and extending a community to others and mediating borders but always by means of trial and error that results in uncertainty and vulnerability.

Literary Features

Along with the sociocultural methods of food exchange and kinship relations, I use literary methods in order to address my interests about food exchange and community in Matthew. I focus on the represented world within the text with an emphasis on the sociocultural and theological relations and networks inscribed in that narrative world.[82] This approach follows the lead of several scholars who combine literary and social criticisms.[83] Vernon Robbins, for example, argues that the New Testament texts are "highly interactive and complex" and "richly textured" and recommends "a well-tuned interdisciplinary approach" that can better explore new meanings relevant for today's issues.[84] He adds that the use of multiple interpretive strategies by different interpreters can help raise important issues and lead to greater cooperation and understanding among scholars, even when they continue to disagree.[85] The approach used in this study considers literary, sociocultural, and contextual methods in order to attend to the complex text in Matthew and to work in cooperation with other scholars in interpreting the Matthean community.

Because my context has guided my reading of food passages that deal with exchange, I focus on the theme of food exchange and its development from the beginning of the narrative to the end and address how the interaction of characters and settings participate in that theme. What are the dynamics of social and theological relations formed through food exchange in the narrative?

Narrative and Reader-Response Criticism. While the literary and social approaches are intertwined in my analysis of the Matthean text, I discuss them separately in this chapter to be clear about each piece of the method. The literary approach pays attention to the formal literary features of the text. Different from historical criticism, which generally focuses on the external world and communities the text refers to, literary criticisms generally focus on the world, communities, characters, setting, plot, and other formal aspects within the text. The text is conceived as a literary whole, an end in itself, and thus its final form and unity is the object of study as opposed to the stages it might have gone through to reach this finished form.[86]

The literary approach in this study employs a combination of narrative and reader-response criticisms.[87] I use a linear, sequential reading of the text that follows the development of the story from beginning to end. I consider the interrelationship of the parts (i.e. characters and setting) within the narrative, as well as the relationship of these parts to the whole story. In addition, I pay attention to the type of inner texture that is represented in the different passages studied.[88] For example, repetitive-progressive texture is predominate in the passages in Matt 6, 7, 10, and 12.

The use of narrative criticism in this study assumes neither that the story reflects a particular author's intention nor that the story is without connection to elements outside of the narrative.[89] I keep in mind that other phenomena influenced the writing of the text. History and culture obviously influenced the writing of the narrative and this study will use anthropological studies and cultural scripts in reading the text.[90] Outside literature influenced the narrative; the implied audience has knowledge of what is now referred to by some as the Hebrew Bible, of Mark, and of oral stories, and these writings are used to interpret the narrative.[91] The story world was not created in a vacuum and I do not interpret it in a vacuum.

The narrative is examined from the point of view of a reader who follows the story from beginning to end, interacts with the text, and has a temporal, cumulative experience of the reading process. It is here that "narrative criticism shades over into reader-response criticism."[92] Reader-response criticism focuses on the reader or audience[93] that reads the text, the definition of the audience, the role of the audience in creating meaning and the dynamics of this reading process.[94]

The reader in this study is, in part, an ideal, implied audience presupposed in the text.[95] This is not a real, flesh-and-blood reader, but a hypothetical construction created by the ideal author and "produced by the text as its ideal interpreter."[96] In this case, the view of the reader is the "reader *in* the text" and the text, not the reader, determines the reader's response.[97] Yet, in this study, as the author of this study and an interpreter, I also shape the implied audience. My own interests, ideology, and religious convictions affect how I construct the implied audience. Iser's implied reader comes closest to a description of the reader in this study, both a creation of the text and therefore ideal and yet a real individual and therefore of flesh and blood. For Iser, the reading of the text is affected by the reader's "own characteristic selection process. For it is not given by the text itself; it arises from the meeting between the written text and the individual mind of the reader with its own particular history of experience, its own consciousness, its own outlook."[98] Because of this hybrid reader, meaning is not determined solely by the text but is clearly influenced by the real reader, the author of this study. In this case, then, the view of the reader is the "reader *with* the text."[99]

While the reader does follow the text from beginning to end in a linear, sequential reading, the reader is not a first-time reader nor is the reading done in a strict, consecutive process that follows every portion of the text. The reader has some familiarity with the whole text and may jump back and forth in the text from time to time. The reader is reading the text for the second or third time, with some but not complete memory of what is to come and still with anticipation and an evolving interpretation as the text is followed from beginning to end.[100] The reader is specifically engaged with the theme of food exchange, and its implications for social and theological relations, and interprets this theme as the reader moves through the narrative.[101]

Characters and Setting. Characters and setting are the two primary formal features considered in this narrative study. Characterization is a process in which characters are identified and described in the narrative.[102] This study's discussion of characters in the Matthean narrative includes a description of their traits as well as an understanding of characters as ambiguous, changing, and unresolved entities.[103] For example, the Matthean community is a round character, with a variety of traits. It is both dependent (i.e. acted upon by others) and independent (i.e. acts upon others). The community also develops in a moderately steady way through the narrative from a dependent to interdependent entity. Yet, it is also in flux and unresolved. While portrayed as a child who is dependent upon others in Matt 6–7, the community is first described in Matt 10 as "the twelve" who boldly proclaim to the lost sheep of the house only to then become laborers who need food later in the chapter. Then, it is not clear that they ever receive the food.

Characters in this study include mostly groups (e.g. Matthean community, disciples, crowds, lost sheep of the house of Israel, Pharisees), a few individuals (e.g. Jesus, God), several anonymous characters (e.g. hypocrites, everyone, whoever, crowds), and animals (e.g. birds of the air).[104] I do not primarily consider characters as plot functionaries; rather the main focus of this study is upon the characters and their settings as they participate in the theme of food exchange.[105]

Settings provide context for the action of characters; they set the stage "against which" actions emerge.[106] Settings, in this narrative study, operate to better understand the narrative world itself. In particular, setting influences how food exchange between characters reveals social and theological relations.[107] The setting of food exchange shapes the nature of subsequent social relations.[108]

I consider two main types of settings in the Matthean narrative: spatial and temporal.[109] The spatial setting relates to the physical environment (e.g. wilderness, city, sea, home).[110] In this study, the change in spatial setting through the narrative parallels a change in social relations as a result of food exchange. The settings in the narrative move from architectural settings (i.e. one of Malbon's categories that refers to artificially enclosed spaces) that focus on inside, private, family, and internal Matthean community locations to topographical settings (i.e. natural and human-made physical features of the earth) that focus on outside, public, communal, and natural Matthean community locations.[111] The change in locations represents an ever-widening reach for food exchange, from a central location to the surrounding world.[112] The inclusion of architectural and topographical space but not geopolitical space (i.e. areas of the earth defined by human-made political boundaries) implies that the giving and receiving of food takes place in social and natural settings, which emphasize relations with social groups and the natural world and deemphasizes political relations.

The second category of setting, temporal settings, is divided into two types: chronological and typological.[113] The references to time in this study involve mostly typological references, "the kind of time within which an action transpires."[114] Instead of "when" an event occurs (e.g. chronological references), typological references pinpoint a certain type of time that is in contrast to other types of time (e.g. today as opposed to tomorrow, Matthew 6:11, 30, 34).[115]

Understanding the nuances of the temporal settings in Matthew can help explain food exchange. First, these settings have connotative significance. That is, the settings have connections to ideas that emerge out of history and culture and these ideas cling to the reference and are then given further meaning in the narrative context.[116] Sabbath in Matthew 12:1–8, for example, is connected to the ideas of God as creator and God's work to meet human need through food.[117] Second, in the first century, present orientation was the preference with the past and future being less significant.[118] Peasants and the non-elite especially experienced time as present and as related to their daily life.[119] The Matthean community, for example, requests food for today ("give us today our daily bread," 6:11).

Third, time was also comprehended as social and procedural. Social time emphasizes the relations with people and the completion of social interactions instead of a strict adherence to timetables and schedules that put less priority on social life.[120] Related to social time is procedural time, which refers to the completion of tasks "at the right time." That is, one travels to festivals during the dry seasons and stays at home and makes plans during the rainfall and winter seasons.[121] Procedural time is rooted in the biological and ecological processes of life.[122] In Matthew, Jesus and his disciples are hungry and pluck heads of grain and eat them on the Sabbath "at that time" (12:1), exemplifying social and procedural ideas of time.

Back to Theological Perceptions

I return now to the implications of these textual choices on my religious perceptions. While my theological views inform my reading of the text, the engagement with the text also shapes my theological views. According to my religious perception, human communities are intimately connected with all creatures in social, ecological, and political ways. This includes relationships among various human communities and between human and nonhuman communities. As I read the Matthean text, I am most interested in, and thus highlight, the Matthean community's reciprocal relationships with the larger Jewish community, the natural world, the crowds, and other groups (e.g. ἄνθρωπος, πᾶς). My in-depth encounter with the text convinces me even more that these relationships are present. At the same time, the text clearly alerts me to the power differences and struggles between the different parts of life, and I recognize the Matthean community's own efforts to define itself as an independent entity in relationship to other parts of life.

As I focus my conversation with the text on the view of God, my understanding of God is as a creator and provider who relates to all creation, not simply to one human community or even solely to the human community. In the text, God relates to the birds of the air and lilies of the field, the larger Jewish community that hosts the disciples in Matt 10, and the crowds in Matt 14 and 15. God acts *in* the world through guidance, care, and nurture, which is different than acting *on* the world as a monarch who rules and demands obedience. God has an interdependent relationship with humans and encourages humans to act responsibly as well.[123] As I read the text carefully, I indeed see this view of God. At the same time, my engagement with the Matthean world shows me that God is without a doubt the God of the Matthean community and the community experiences God as a king and a distant judge who acts on the world. The power of God is exercised in acts of sovereignty over all of creation. The view of God and the Matthean community's relationship with the world in the text is complex and nuanced and my encounter with the text confirms this.

Much of the Matthean scholarship that explores the community and its relationship with the world emphasizes some form of the monarchical model. From my perspective, this reflects the popular culture of the United States and the view of many Christians who understand God as a ruling monarch over his obedient subjects. This model focuses on personal or political dimensions but not on social or ecological dimensions. The Matthean scholarship that reflects this model certainly reflects this culture but, in many ways, it is a legitimate interpretation of the text. What has received much less attention, however, are interpretations that perceive God as creator and provider whose relationship with the world includes personal, social, political, and ecological dimensions and encourages reciprocal relationships among human and natural communities. A few examples of Matthean scholarship investigate this view of God and community relations.[124] This study is committed to continuing this latter type of scholarship.

Part II

Food Exchange Within the Community

Chapter 3

The Family (6:1–21)

Introduction

First Thematic Unit

The first thematic unit of Matthew encompasses 4:1–11, 6:1–21, 6:25–34, and 7:7–11. A close examination of these passages will show that the exchange of food is primarily between God the Father and the Matthean community as children. Food moves primarily in one direction, from God to the community. God feeds his son Jesus in 4:1–11; the Matthean community requests bread from its heavenly Father in 6:1–21; the heavenly Father assures that his children will receive food just as the birds of the air are fed in 6:25–34; and the heavenly Father will respond to his children when they ask for bread or fish in 7:7–11. Further, the location of food exchange remains in the household and primarily within the Matthean community, although the birds of the air are fed outside and in 7:7–11 there are subtle references to those beyond the Matthean community who are to receive food. God is seen as the heavenly Father who feeds in secret in 6:1–21 but who begins to take on the image of creator whose work is manifest in public in 6:25–34 and 7:7–11. The Matthean community becomes progressively more active in seeking out and participating in food exchange yet it is still clearly dependent upon God as the central actor in providing food. Finally, the provision of food satisfies biological needs and reinforces social ties within the family but also expresses independence from the world as the community identifies itself as the place where God, not Satan or any other source, feeds the Matthean community. Even though the first unit officially starts with 6:1–21, 4:1–11 provides a broad introduction to this unit.

God as the spirit, an anonymous Father, distributes food to Jesus the son in 4:1–11.[1] The exchange encapsulates the focus in the first thematic unit on food exchange between parent and child. This Father-Son relationship, as Saldarini puts it, is the center of the web of relationships in Matthew, or at least in this first part of Matthew.[2] The food distribution in 4:1–11 is the beginning of distributions that will later expand and involve more public relationships between Matthew's community and the world.

Matt 4:1–11 also flags majors issues that I propose to pursue as they unfold in the three thematic units of Matthew. First, food is a real, material item that serves biological needs but also has implications for social, theological, and political relationships. Jesus needs real food to survive—the lack of and need for food is highlighted at the beginning, "Jesus fasted and afterwards was famished" (4:2) and at the end, "the angels served him" (4:11).[3] Yet with whom one exchanges food, and where and how it is exchanged, has consequences regarding theological, social, and political relationships (4:4, 4:6, 4:8–11).

The second major issue is the question: who provides the food? Is it God? The devil (4:1–11)? A parent (6:1–21, 6:25–34)? A family member (7:7–11, 14:13–21, 15:29–38)? An extended relative (10:10)? If it is acquired from God, what kind of provider is he? Does God provide like a distant king who commands and demands obedience? Or as one who creates, provides, and delivers by acting in the world with humans? In 4:1–11, the devil is an example of the former as he commands Jesus to act out certain practices in order to show him obedience.[4] God, however, is an example of the latter. God is spirit, an image that recalls the first creation story (Gen 1:2) and the work of God during the exodus and the wanderings in the wilderness.[5] Furthermore, the allusions to the Hebrew Bible in 4:1–11 pinpoint the exodus and wilderness travels as well, which further support the view of God as provider.[6]

Third, I ask how humans participate in food acquisition. Do they receive it passively by simple devotion to a demanding power/monarch? Or do they actively participate because they are encouraged to do so from their relationship with the divine? In the second temptation, the devil expects God to protect Jesus whether or not Jesus is acting responsibly and faithfully.[7]

Fourth, how is food shared among parties? Is it an isolated nutritive object that is distributed without any connection to community, nature or God?[8] Is it given by elite leaders from a centralized location or shared generously from those who have little expectation of a return gift? Jesus replies to the devil in the first temptation that humans do not live by bread alone (i.e. an isolated nutritive object) but by every word that proceeds through the mouth of God (4:4).

Fifth, I examine the location of food exchange. The general movement of the place for exchanging food in the narrative progresses from the private household to the households of extended family (i.e. the larger Jewish community outside the Matthean community) to the natural world to the larger human world outside the Matthean community. The progression in the three temptations appears to follow this movement, from a first private encounter between the devil and Jesus to the Temple, representing the larger Jewish community, to the larger world. The settings in 4:1–11 are also represented in the subsequent narrative, a wilderness (15:29–38), the Temple (12:1–8), and a mountain (15:29–38).

A sixth issue focuses on how the world or public space is perceived. Is the world corrupt or is it God's good world?[9] Can a person move out into the world and relate to it having some confidence it will be safe? Is public space dangerous or a place of God's provision or both? The "kingdoms of the world" (4:8) appear to be controlled by the devil at this point in the narrative. Finally, I consider the dynamic present in food passages of the theme of encouragement and compassion in the midst of conflict and danger. The degree of conflict increases through the narrative yet food exchange continues to be present as a means of encouragement and divine help. Despite the testing in 4:1–11, for example, the devil leaves and angels serve Jesus (4:11). Matthew 4:1–11 provides a general entrée into this first thematic unit, but it is in 6:1–21 that the implied audience first encounters in the Matthean narrative the theme concerning food exchange.

Matthew 6:1–21

Matthew 6:1–21 is the first passage of the first thematic unit which emphasizes the distribution of food from God the Father to the Matthean Community as children. After determining the scope of 6:1–21, we will see that the father image is clearly stated, the recipient of food is the broader audience, and the setting is the household. The Matthean community is instructed on how to begin to receive food as it learns how to integrate itself into the larger world while maintaining its independence.[10]

A detailed study of 6:1–21 will show that the Matthean community is instructed not to practice its righteousness before humans (ἀνθρώποις) in public places, which would distinguish it from the larger society and would set the community over and against the world. Rather, the Matthean community is to practice righteousness in a way that does not emphasize the act of righteousness nor draw attention to the one practicing righteousness in relation to the world outside the community. For now righteousness is to be practiced in secret so one does not stand out in the larger world. Over the course of the narrative, however, the Matthean community must learn how to practice righteousness in the context of a larger world so it may be integrated into the world.

As we shall see, the community commences this learning process in 6:1–21 with lessons for a young community in training about how to view God and how to find food. Two images of God are juxtaposed in 6:1–21: the more obvious image of God as authoritative Father and the less evident view of God as nursing Mother. As God is seen as creator of and provider for the Matthean community, so God will relate to the larger world. Food exchange and the relationship between God and the world in 6:1–21, however, is focused within the family as father feeds children. The community primarily receives the food passively and does not participate in any other way in the food distribution beyond asking and praying. Seeking, accessing, distributing, and exchanging food is a way of practicing righteousness and 6:1–21 begins to teach this to the Matthean community.

Matthew 6:1–21 is shaped by a repetitive-progressive texture as language and ideas are repeated yet the pattern develops through the repetition.[11] I hone in on two particular phrases or ideas that repeat themselves. The first is a similar structure in the four passages (vv. 2–4, 5–6, 16–18, 19–21) which includes four components: (a) whenever...(b) do not...as the hypocrites...(c) in the...(d) so that...[12] The second is the description of the Father who sees in secret and is in secret. The first repetition is a phrase that instructs the audience: whenever (you practice righteousness), do not (do it as hypocrites do who interact with the world in a destructive way) in the (increasingly public arena where interaction with the world takes place) so that (those practicing in public in this destructive way may be glorified or seen or appear before humans). The repetition looks like this:

whenever	you give alms (v. 2) you pray (v. 5) you fast (v. 16) you store up treasures, v. 19
do not...as the hypocrites	
	sound a trumpet before you as the hypocrites do (v. 2) be as the hypocrites (v. 5) be as the gloomy hypocrites (v. 16) store up treasures (v. 19)
in the	synagogues and the streets (v. 2) the synagogues and on the corners of the streets (v. 5) upon the earth (v. 19)
so that	they may be glorified by humans (v. 2) seen by humans (v. 5) they may appear to humans (v. 16) where moth and rust destroy and where thieves break in and steal, v. 19

The progressive nature of the repetition demonstrates the increasingly public setting of the interaction with the world and the final destruction in v. 19 that occurs.

The second repetition describes God as "your Father who sees in secret" (v. 4, 6, 17) and "your Father knows what things you need before you ask him" (v. 8) "your Father who is in secret" (6, 18). The heavenly Father sees in secret, he also knows what things you need, and he is in secret and hidden for now although he will be manifest in the world as the narrative continues. The image of the Father evolves in this passage and will continue to evolve in the narrative.

I now turn to examine the characters, setting, and theology in 6:1–21 and then discuss the food distribution in 6:11 in the remainder of this chapter. Characters, setting, and the view of God are essential indicators of social relations in food exchange. Both the characters and the setting of the exchange or distribution indicate the primary mode of operation (e.g. gift, reciprocal exchange, market exchange, centric transfer), which influences the nature of subsequent social relations. Who gives food to whom in what location affects the contours of the relations. Since God is one of the main characters, who feeds the Matthean community, an in-depth look at this character is justified.

Practicing Righteousness

How Not to Practice Righteousness

The Matthean community is not to practice righteousness, as hypocrites do, before humans (ἀνθρώποις) in the synagogues, or on the streets and street corners. Neither is it to store up treasures on the earth. The settings where one is not to practice righteousness become more and more public through 6:1–21. Hypocrites act in public in ways that do not engender constructive relationships with the larger world. The Matthean community is not to act in public in ways that might inhibit cooperative relationships with the larger world.

In 6:1–4,[13] the audience is not to give alms "as the hypocrites do in the synagogues and in the streets, so that they may be praised by others."[14] In 6:1–4, the synagogue should primarily be seen as a type of setting, a type of architectural space which is an artificially enclosed area used by a specific Jewish community.[15] It is a public space, set apart for a particular function—whether it is a building of its own or a home used for religious purposes—where alms should not be distributed and righteousness should not practiced for public scrutiny.[16]

The hypocrites also practice righteousness in the streets. The streets are a location that includes even more of a public aura than the synagogues and, used with the synagogue, highlights the use of the streets as a public setting. While the synagogue refers to a specifically religious and more particularly Jewish gathering place, the streets refer to space that is not explicitly Jewish, not necessarily religious, and furthermore not inside. "In the streets" is an outside public space shared by all those who live in that area.[17] More, it carries connotations of the "world," particularly the Gentile human world. Giving alms in the streets and the synagogue, then, is seen not only by fellow Jews, more intimate companions, but also by those in the world who are not Jews.[18] The synagogue and the streets together imply all public, human space. The synagogue refers to Jewish public space and the streets to Gentile (and Jewish) public space.

In 6:5–8, the hypocrites pray on the street corners. A corner, depending on whether one looks at it from the inside or outside, suggests either a more concealed place or a more open area.[19] Its use with street certainly leads the audience to picture an open area, an intersection where a person is visible in several directions[20] and where people tend to gather. The street corner is a place where more people can see the hypocrite, a more public location than the streets or synagogues.

One is not to disfigure one's face in 6:16–18 for the same criterion as almsgiving on the street corners; one attracts attention to oneself in a made-up, false way. The imperative already sets up the hypocritical act, "Do not become sullen/dismal/sad," that is, do not act or pretend in this way, do not become something you are not. The hypocrites disfigure (ἀφανίζουσιν) their faces; they make themselves unrecognizable. By changing their body to become unrecognizable, ironically, the hypocrites are recognized by others. The concern about practicing righteousness in public in 6:1–21 is being seen by humans, appearing before humans, being glorified by humans. A public place is where one is seen, where one appears before humans. By disfiguring one's face, one draws attention to one's true face, and one is more recognized by others.

Finally, in 6:19–21, one is not to practice righteousness on the earth. As mentioned earlier, "beware of practicing your righteousness before others" in verse 1 parallels "do not store up for yourselves treasures on earth" in verse 19. Earth now becomes the setting that one is not to practice righteousness. In terms of how public a place is, the earth would seem to be the most public of places, the location where one can be seen by the most people.[21] The earth is the place where one appears before all humans and the natural world. The further description of the earth in v. 19 gives the full range of settings in the public world—from the household which has just been opened up (i.e. where thieves break in and steal) to the natural world (i.e. where moth and rust/worm consume).[22] The earth extends the type of public places in 6:1–21 from all human public places (the synagogues and the streets) to all human and nonhuman public places. The type of setting where one is not to practice righteousness, then, has evolved in 6:1–21 from a less public place (the synagogue) to places which could be characterized as more and more public (i.e. streets, street corners, earth).

While these locations set off limits for practicing righteousness, the synagogue, streets, and street corners do not carry negative connotations at this point in the narrative. They are visible, public spaces where alms and prayers are not to be given. The synagogue is not associated with opposing religious leaders[23] and the streets and street corners are not dangerous places.[24]

How to Practice Righteousness

Those in the Matthean community are to practice righteousness so as not to be seen by humans (ἀνθρώποις) and, in fact, should not even be seen by themselves. The community is to withdraw into a room and close the door. They are not to draw attention to themselves but to do works that draw attention to others, and thus sustain the lives of others. This is the first step toward learning how to build cooperative relationships with those beyond the community.

The directives from vv. 1–4 and 16–18 are a good beginning point for how to practice righteousness because of their similar nature: "Do not let your left hand know what your right hand is doing so that your alms may be done in secret" (v. 3) and "when you fast, put oil on your head and wash your face, so that your fasting may be seen not by others" (v. 17). Both instructions underscore what persons are to do with their bodies.[25] There is a sense of self-forgetfulness, keeping the act even from oneself.[26] One is not to recognize even one's own body.[27]

The instructions in vv. 16–18 confirm this denial of self-recognition, although it is ironic in its presentation. At first glance, there appears to be a directive to make oneself recognizable. "Do not make your face unrecognizable like the hypocrites." But the result of making one's face unrecognizable is to be recognized. So, one is to put oil on his head and wash his face. The purpose of this practice is not so much to look like yourself and make yourself stand out, but rather to become unremarkable to others. Again, one is to forget the self and blend in with the rest of the community. There is a movement away from identifying yourself (e.g. making yourself stand out in a crowd, having yourself recognized by others around you).

The instruction on prayer of how to properly practice righteousness goes even farther regarding the public and private realms and directs the practitioners to isolate themselves, to withdraw from public places, even from the world. In vv. 5–6 the audience is directed to "go into your room and shut the door and pray to your Father who is in secret." This is the space where the audience is to ask the Father in heaven for daily bread. The space is a room in an inhabited home behind a closed door.[28] The room is an enclosed space within an enclosed space.[29] Two boundaries are present between the one praying and the world outside the house.[30]

Finally, the setting for prayer is considered inhabited space. Inhabited areas are generally associated with security and promise while isolated areas are associated with danger and threat.[31] The room behind a closed door, then, would be a place of security and promise. In Matthew's narrative, however, this is not always the case. The wilderness, as an isolated area, is a place where God's providence is revealed and Jerusalem, as an inhabited place, becomes a place of considerable threat and death as the narrative unfolds.[32] The synagogue, as well, becomes a place of opposition later in the narrative (i.e. beginning with 10:17). In 6:6, however, the home is more clearly a place of security and promise than a place of threat. It is an inhabited place where prayer to God is rewarded. The audience only later will recognize private and inhabited locations as places of isolation from the world around it, which will serve as a threat to the audience's survival in that world.[33]

Finally, in 6:20, the right practice of righteousness is to "store up for yourselves treasures in heaven."[34] To store up treasures in heaven is contrasted with storing up treasures on earth. The problem with storing up treasures on earth is the accumulation of valuable material goods, the excessive valuing of material goods this implies, and the potential for loss of these goods. To store up is to draw in, to bring material wealth to oneself in order to save and keep for oneself, with the consequence of taking away material goods (a limited commodity)[35] from others. Furthermore, the earth is the most public of places and to store up treasures on earth is to practice one's righteousness before all others, to be seen by all.[36]

While storing up treasures in heaven uses the same image of "storing up," it has a different purpose than accumulating material goods for oneself. To store up material goods is a practice that seeks to draw the attention and giving of others toward you, to be recognized by others, to receive praise from others. This practice means one will eventually be consumed by others and have their life stolen by them (v. 19). To store up treasures in heaven is to store up heavenly rewards for the appropriate type of practice—practice that works to sustain the lives of others, that moves out toward others in giving but does so in secrecy.[37]

The proper practice of righteousness in 6:2–18 follows this type of secret self-giving. One is to give alms to others but to do so without drawing attention to oneself. Prayer includes the type of requests that provide for others—God's will be done, bread given to "us," debtors forgiven, and deliverance for "us." And fasting, while not explicit, would be associated (for Matthew's audience) with righteousness in terms of loosening the bonds of injustice, undoing the thongs of the yoke, letting the oppressed go free, sharing bread with the hungry, bringing the homeless poor into the house, and covering the naked (Isa 58:3–14; cf. Jer 14:12, Sir 34:31, Zech 7:5–7).[38]

In summary, then, this study is interested to discover how Matthew's community is related to the world. As I examine 6:1–21 and the practice of the three types of righteousness (alms, prayer, and fasting), I concentrate on how these practices (and here, the constructions of the settings and characters) situate the community in light of the world around it.[39] The section sends out ambivalent messages regarding the relationship with the world. In one respect, the greatest impression left with the reader is to withdraw from the world into an inner room, where self and the Father in heaven communicate. The setting for the improper practice of righteousness becomes more and more public (i.e. from synagogue to streets to street corners to the earth) and for the appropriate practice more and more private (i.e. from privacy out in public to a private room to heaven). One is not to be seen by others or even by oneself. Furthermore, private places are considered places of security and promise while public places are mostly undistinguished but begin to take on an increasingly negative character (i.e. the earth as a place of decay and danger and the later narrative moves in this direction). Persons practicing righteousness are to relate directly to the Father and draw away from world.

Yet, public places are not decidedly dangerous or off limits. Those who practice righteousness are to relate to and reach out to others: giving alms and forgiving debts. Public places are generally neutral. The synagogue is not a hostile place and is not identified as an "other." The Jewish leaders are not connected with the hypocrites in this passage. The streets are not inhospitable. While those who practice righteousness are not to be seen practicing by others, they are to be such a part of the world that, with head oiled and face washed, they fit right in. The audience is not to separate from others but to blend in with them.

The practice of righteousness before others is critical to the Matthean community because of their sense that they were part of the larger world.[40] Persons in the first century understood themselves as part of a larger group. Instead of considering themselves "individuals," they saw themselves as embedded in a larger body.[41] This pertained not only to a family or kinship group but even to larger communities—village and nation. The Matthean community had a need to participate in the larger world and the way they went about practicing righteousness was critical to that need. Matthew's narrative is constructed to teach that lesson slowly to its audience. At this early stage in Matt 6, the emphasis remains on the identity of the group and its internal practices. But the understated references to relating to the larger world point to a movement in the later narrative toward that type of association. The audience is learning through the narrative how to be in public, how to relate to the world. But the pace is slow and deliberate in order to introduce the community to the proper way of relating.

The extensive use of hypocrite in this passage supports my conclusion that one is to act in public in a way that encourages reciprocally beneficial relationships. Hypocrite referred initially to those who acted or played a part in the Greek theaters, but it later came to be used pejoratively as a negative stereotype for a godless person or someone playing a role.[42] Its use in 6:1–21 is as a foil to how the Matthean community should act in public. According to Hans Mol, hypocrisy makes it difficult to establish strong and binding relationships among people.[43] It reduces commitment and predictability in relationships. Hypocrisy is therefore a destructive social quality because it makes it difficult for persons to be public figures. Hypocrites do not live in public in a way that engenders constructive and cooperative social relations between Matthew's community and world. They "play" a public role, they "act" at being in public, but they do not properly live with people in the public realm. Matthew's narrative is teaching its audience how those in the community, unlike hypocrites, are to practice in public.

God as Authoritative Father

As the study of characters and setting revealed an ambivalent message about the community's relationship with the world, so the characterization of God reveals a Father who is hidden and works in secret rewarding a few of the righteous yet will not remain hidden throughout the narrative. He is also a cosmic Father who sees all, knows all, and is impartial to his creatures. The image of God as authoritative Father communicates to the Matthean community that its God observes and knows their needs and will provide for them yet will also provide for those outside its community. Several images of God (i.e. the Father, the heavenly Father, the Father who sees, the Father who knows, the Father who creates, and the Father who rewards) are integrated and point to a God who creates, provides and delivers. The Matthean community's view of God and food exchange will enable it to build cooperative relationships with the world yet maintain its own identity.

God as Father

God is the Father (πατήρ). More than in any other thematic unit, there is a predominant use of "Father" and "child" (or child-like) language in this first unit (chs. 4–7).[44] The first explicit reference to God as Father in Matthew's narrative is in 5:16. Chapters 5–7 have seventeen references to God as Father, all of which occur in Jesus' words. Not until 7:21 is it explicit that God is Jesus' Father. In 6:1–21, the audience hears that God is the Father of the disciples, representing the Matthean community, not the Father in a special relationship with Jesus.

Of the seventeen references in chapters 5–7, the first sixteen refer to the Father with the pronouns "your (s.)," "our," or "your (pl.)." It is only with Father that the personal pronouns "our" and "your" are used extensively. They are never used with the reference to God as "lord" (κύριος), and only three times with God (θεός; 4:4, 4:7, 22:37).[45] This use of Father with personal pronouns reinforces the social and relational link between God and the Matthean community. It also suggests a dependency model between God as Father and the Matthean community as children. God is an authoritative Father yet he cares and provides for his children and gives them their daily bread.[46]

God is the Father in heaven. As such he continues to relate personally to the Matthean community, yet he is also the cosmic Father who relates to all creatures and is primarily generous in disbursing rewards. The phrase linking Father with heaven, τὸν πατέρα ὑμῶν τὸν ἐν τοῖς οὐρανοῖς and ὁ πατὴρ ὑμῶν ὁ οὐράνιος, occurs in 5:16, 5:45, 5:48, 6:1, 6:14 in this first thematic unit. All five texts use "your" to describe the Father in the heavens or the heavenly Father, reflecting a similar use with πατήρ by itself. Again, this reinforces the personal tie between the Father and children. The first three uses of this composite phrase in Matthew's narrative (5:16, 5:45, 5:48) are instructive in understanding its meaning and its use in 6:1–21. One clear aspect of the meaning of heaven in relation to the Father is as a place of residence, the Father's abode. Heaven is where the Father dwells. This conveys a transcendent view of God.[47] Second, the Father in heaven is the creator who deals impartially with his creatures. With God as creator, there are two divine and cosmic activities; the heavenly Father causes the sun to rise[48] and rains on the righteous and unrighteous.[49] The image of cosmic Fatherhood—God as creator of the natural world and the one who daily and directly causes the natural processes (*creatio continua*)—is not new in Matthew's first-century world and would be a familiar image to Matthew's audience.[50] In addition to sun and rain, the cosmic Father/God gives to the wind its weight, makes it snow and hail, controls the clouds and stars, feeds the lions and raven (Job 38:12–41) and has control over when and to whom God wields these creative forces.

The cosmic Father deals without favor with his creatures. The Father in heaven shines the sun on the bad and good and rains on the righteous and unrighteous. The reference appears to be to humanity yet one must not miss the later reference in Matthew's text to good and bad fruit, good and bad trees (7:17–18, 12:33). One might draw from this, then, that God's cosmic activities affect both humanity and the natural world. The Father's justice, as Betz points out, is "revealed in the beneficence of nature."[51] Notice that the world is divided up into two groups: the good and evil, the righteous and unrighteous. The adjectives, however, do not refer to particular groups in Matthew's narrative world.[52] Only in a few passages are good and evil (or righteous and unrighteous or mixed) divided into two groups (7:17, 7:18, 13:41–43, 13:49, 22:10, 25:37, 46). In these cases, they refer to eschatological judgment. In one of them, however, all of these persons do not remain divided up; most end up as chosen ones (22:10). In one case, all persons are considered evil (7:11).[53] The Father in heaven is not in the business of judging one group in and another out, whether it is the present time or the future. Eschatological judgments are primarily executed by the Son of Man (13:41–43, 25:37, 46) and the angels (13:49).

The use of "Father in heaven" or "heavenly Father" in 6:1–21 can now be interpreted in light of the meaning in chapter five. The phrase occurs three times (6:1, 6:9, and 6:14). The first use follows immediately after 5:48: "be perfect, therefore, as your heavenly Father is perfect" flows directly into "beware of practicing your righteousness before others in order to be seen by them; for then you have no reward from your Father in heaven." In the first and the last use of "the Father in heaven" in this section, the phrase is associated with reward or reciprocity. Heaven is not only the dwelling place of God, it is also the locus of salvation/rewards. The Father in heaven, then, is the source of the μισθός. Reward and recompense language permeates Matthew's narrative both between humans and between God and humans. Therefore, it is not a question of whether there should be rewards or not but what is the nature of the reward.[54]

Reward in Matthew is not a calculable tit for tat.[55] Individuals are not repayed precisely in accordance with what they have paid or done, either by God or other persons. Rewards, especially from God, have a gift quality to them and often come as a surprise.[56] Even in interpersonal relationships, persons are not to repay others in measure for what they have received. Thus, the disciples are to exceed the righteousness of the scribes and Pharisees (5:20), are not to repay evil for evil (5:38–42), and are to do for others before others act toward them (an act not based on the response of mere equal payment; 7:12).

Rewards occur in the present in the narrative, as well as in the eschatological future.[57] The grammar in this section reveals two cases in the context of this first thematic unit. In 5:46, reward is expected in the present, "for if you love the ones loving you, what reward do you have." Likewise, in 6:1, "you have no reward from your Father in heaven." While strongly arguing that rewards are generally eschatological in Matthew, Morhlang comments that the reward language, particularly in chapter six, may be "indefinite" in nature.[58] Davies and Allison suggest that there is a present reward in the act of praying (6:6).[59]

This brief survey of reward in Matthew and the connection of reward language with the Father in heaven lay the groundwork for my reading of 6:1 and 6:14: the Father in heaven is indeed the source of reward. The use of the present tense in 6:1 and the nature of forgiveness in 6:14 (and elsewhere in Matthew—6:12, 9:5–6, 12:31–32, 18:21, 27, 32, 35) suggest that the reward is expected in the present time not at the end of time.

Forgiveness is a kind of reward or payment. It appears that forgiveness from the heavenly Father in 6:14 is measured out according to how much one forgives others. But this is not quite the case. On the one hand, whether forgiveness from the heavenly Father happens or not depends on whether one forgives others or not (6:12, 6:14–15, 18:35). On the other hand, the nature of forgiveness is not an even-handed trade but is excessive in its offering. Forgiveness is a generous act which extends beyond any gauged response for a particular deed (9:5–6, 12:31, 18:21–27).

The heavenly Father does appear, at this point, to treat reward (and forgiveness) more as a measured wage than a gratuitous gift.[60] But this measured, judgmental picture of the Father is tempered by two other depictions of the heavenly Father. I have discussed the first which is the heavenly Father as creator who relates to all his creatures without favor. The Father extends the benefits of nature on both the good and the evil. The second portrayal surveyed is "the Father in heaven who sees in secret will reward you."

The Father Who Sees

The Father who sees is a further clarification of the heavenly Father and includes the Father who sees all, knows all, and creates all from his throne above. This Father reaches out to those in need. He not only sees in secret but is in secret, hidden for a short time, but will become manifest as the narrative continues. The Father image in 6:1–21 is defined by the two phrases, "your Father in secret" (τῷ πατρί σου τῷ ἐν τῷ κρυπτω) and "your Father who sees in secret" (ὁ πατήρ σου ὁ βλέπων ἐν τῷ κρυπτῷ). The image of the Father who sees in secret is first introduced in 6:4.[61] The image of God who sees is found in the Hebrew Bible and Apocrypha.[62] The image of God could be noted in two separate but related images: the all-seeing sky God and the all-knowing God, both of which point out the characterization that God sees.[63] The all-seeing sky God is found primarily in the Psalms (Pss 10:14, 33:13–15, 113:5–9, 138:6) where God is depicted as enthroned on high, looking down from heaven, with all of the inhabitants of the heavens and earth in view, observing all their deeds and reaching out in particular to the poor, needy, afflicted, helpless, troubled, and grieving.[64]

The all-knowing God is delineated particularly in wisdom and apocalyptic literature, common especially in Sirach.[65] In this case, God sees into the secret or hidden places of life—the abyss, the human heart, the thick darkness. God not only searches but also has knowledge of and is present in these places, places where humankind itself cannot see or does not comprehend. Even more, God responds to the situations in these secluded places and provides deliverance.

How can God see these hidden places? God is the one who created everything and knows everything. Within the image of the Father who sees are two other images—the God who knows and the God who creates. First, God as the one who sees in hidden places is also the one who knows. The two images are intertwined. Because God "looks to the ends of the earth and sees everything under the heavens," God also "understands the way to it, and he knows its place" (Job 28:23). "God searches out the abyss and the human heart; he understands their innermost secrets. For the Most High knows all that may be known; he sees from of old the things that are to come" (Sir 42:18).

Second, the seeing and knowing God is also the God who creates. The three aspects cannot be separated. God as creator is emphasized in the texts where God can see in hidden places. God gave to the wind its weight, apportioned out the waters by measure, made a decree for the rain and a way for the thunderbolt (Job 28:23–28). God "formed my inward parts" and "knit me together in my mother's womb" (Ps 139). "The bee is small but produces the best of sweet things…the works of the Lord are wonderful, and his works are concealed from humankind" (Sir 11:2–6).

Matthew 6:1–21 reflects several of the common characteristics of the image of the Father who sees. In ch. 6, the Father sees into the secret or hidden places of life. The Father sees into the hidden room behind a closed door (6:6) and also sees those who fast in private but cannot be recognized as those who fast by others because they wash their faces and put oil on their heads like everyone else (6:17). Even more revealing, the Father sees and knows about acts and places that persons themselves do not know about themselves. When a person gives alms, her left hand does not even know what the right hand is doing yet the Father sees and knows. This leads to a second characteristic; the Father who sees also knows what people need.

At the beginning and end of Matthew 6:1–21, the primary image of God is as the Father who sees. In the middle of this section, however, the "Father who sees" becomes the "Father who knows what you need before you ask him" (6:9). This is not a change in theology but is encompassed within the image of the seeing Father. Because the Father can search the human heart, he understands its innermost secrets (Sir 42:18) and can know what a person needs before they verbalize it. Finally, the Father who sees into secluded places also responds to the situations he discovers there and delivers his people. The motif of deliverance can be found in the provision of bread (6:11), the forgiveness of debts (6:12), and rescue from the evil one (6:13).

The Father who sees in secret is also the Father who rewards. Before describing the seeing Father, the depiction of the heavenly Father in Matt 6 was responding to his children in a measured way—forgive those who forgive, reward those who practice their righteousness in certain ways. But this is not a Father whose goal is to meticulously scrutinize his children in order to know their every move so he can reward or punish them.[66] Rather, he looks in on them to know and respond to their needs (in prayer) and to recognize them for their good work in providing for those he himself has created (e.g. the good and evil, righteous and unrighteous).[67] Thus, the image of God as the one who rewards is integral to the God who sees, knows, and creates, and is influenced by its interaction with the other images (i.e. Father, Father in heaven, Father who sees). These images converge on God's work as creator, God's blessings without favor, and God's desire to deliver.[68]

Not only does the Father see in secret, but the Father *is in secret*.[69] In the Hebrew Bible God is hidden and, in fact, should not even be seen.[70] Being in secret is part of being divine. God's hiddenness is accessible only through revelation. God is able to make Godself known but does so only through revelation to those who fear God and seriously seek God. In Matthew's narrative, God and the kingdom of heaven have been intentionally covered up (10:26) and have been so since the beginning of the world (13:35). The divine has particularly been hidden from certain persons—the wise and the intelligent (11:25), the righteous and the prophets (13:17), those whose hearts are dull and eyes are shut (13:15). But the secrecy of God is not to continue. That which is hidden will be revealed (10:26), in fact has been revealed (11:25, 13:11, 13:35), should be revealed (25:14–30) and cannot but be revealed (5:14–16). Uncovering what has been in secret is a fulfillment of prophecy (13:34–35). There is no intention to keep God or the kingdom of heaven hidden.

The pattern of making known God's hiddenness unfolds through the narrative (concentrated mostly in chapters 10–13, but also chapter 25). The mandate to reveal God's hiddenness, however, is first introduced in 5:14–16 to give the audience a glimpse of what is to come. The instruction in chapter six is received with the knowledge that what is in secret will not remain hidden.

Therefore, the Father who is in secret and sees the one praying (6:6) and the one who fasts (6:18) will not remain in secret. What follows, then, is the proposal that those who also are in secret will not remain so. As the Father relates to the world, so his children will relate to the world. Those who practice righteousness in secret—give alms in secret, pray in the hidden room, and fast without others knowing—will not always be hidden but will manifest righteousness in the open. The closing verses of the section (6:19–21), as discussed earlier, point not only to the practice of giving away what was stored, but the practice of doing it in the open instead of in secret.

Summary of God as Authoritative Father

The study of characters and setting in 6:1–21 reveals an ambivalent message about the community's relationship with the world. Along those same lines, the study of theology characterizes the Father's relationship with the world wavering between a secret, rather stingy interaction and a public, generous interaction. In 4:1–11 the audience is led to believe that God is the Father of his one son Jesus, yet the explicit use of Father language for God in chapters 4–7 indicates that God is the Father of the disciples and not yet the Father of Jesus. Likewise, reward language in Matt 6 suggests that the Father rewards a few of the righteous in secret, but 5:43–48 (and later texts on reward) propose that the Father showers his beneficence on the good and evil, the righteous and unrighteous. At first glance, the "Father who sees in secret" appears to look only into private, hidden places, yet a full disclosure of the image highlights one who sees all the inhabitants of the earth. Finally, the Father's preference to remain "in secret" will change as his identity becomes manifest to many. The construction of God as authoritative Father who creates, sees into and provides for his children sets the terms of the relationship in which food is exchanged between Father and children.

Food Exchange and Social Relations

The overt message in 6:1–21 is that the exchange of food takes place within the household between Father and children. Before the community learns how to act in public and integrate into the wider world, it discovers its source of food at home. Passive children request real, material bread from an authoritative Father for their immediate, daily food source and to strengthen social bonds. As they seek out food, the children show their trust and acceptance in God as their source of food. The Father maintains his position of authority as primary food provider and his role as leader of the community to maintain the community's identity within the larger world. The covert message includes the image of God as Mother who provides food out of her body, the earth, for the community and the wider world outside the community. This image coincides with the image of God as cosmic Father who sees and knows the needs of all his creatures but demonstrates a divine portrayal that moves toward a more horizontal structure of authority in relationship to the world. To explicate these conclusions, I examine three component parts: food as a present, material need, children who request food from their Father, and food as provided from the earth.

Food as a Present, Material Need

I interpret bread in 6:11 as a present, material need. Matthew's Jesus is telling his audience to request daily bread from the heavenly Father for its needs today. This focus on the present implies that food is a material need and not an eschatological symbol. Throughout the Hebrew Bible and New Testament, bread is interpreted in a variety of ways as a material need or as a spiritual, social, and eschatological symbol.[71] Many interpreters consider the petition in 6:11 from a primarily eschatological perspective.[72]

The last three petitions (i.e. bread, forgiveness, temptation) relate to present circumstances.[73] As discussed earlier, the nature of forgiveness in Matthew suggests that it is primarily a present activity.[74] In like manner, the meaning of temptation in the prayer is de-eschatologized.[75] Most scholars claim, as they do with the interpretation of the bread petition, that the testing is eschatological.[76] That is, the testing relates to the tribulations of the end-time that precede the eschaton. As evidence, scholars point out the use of the aorist tense in the sixth petition (i.e. εἰσενέγκῃς) to suggest a one-time event, argue that the seventh petition sounds eschatological (i.e. deliver us from the evil one), and contend that the whole passage has an eschatological tenor.[77] But testing can also refer to everyday testing, the endurance of general, daily affliction, or suffering.[78] The evidence for this interpretation is convincing: (a) πειρασμόν lacks the definite article and therefore does not refer to one particular temptation or testing event, (b) the use of πειρασμόν is not eschatological in its other uses in Matthew (16:1, 19:3, 22:18, 22:35), (c) the disciples in Matthew are not delivered from (or escape) a time of trial but try to persevere through the trials,[79] (d) περιασμόν is not an apocalyptical technical term in Jewish apocalyptic texts or in other New Testament texts,[80] and (e) other Jewish parallels suggest everyday life temptations (e.g. *b. Ber. 60b*, 11QPs24).

From this perspective, the petition for bread is a request for present, material bread. To require daily bread fits in with a common theme in the Hebrew Bible of God's provision of food required for survival in the present.[81] The use of daily (ἐπιούσιον) along with today (σήμερον) puts a double emphasis on the present time: "Give us today our bread that we need today!"[82] Finally, the use of today (σήμερον) and daily (ἐπιούσιον) in the context of three uses of whenever (ὅταν) in 6:2, 5, and 16, reinforces the view that food is needed in regular, repeated intervals, that is, on a daily basis. Whenever (ὅταν) is used with the present subjunctive, as in these three verses that introduce each of the acts of righteousness, it carries the meaning of a regular, repeated action (e.g. whenever the Matthean community gives alms, prays, and fasts on a regular basis).[83] The request in 6:11 for daily bread today is set in this context. Therefore, the community is to pray on a recurring basis that it needs bread on a regular basis and, specifically, that it needs the bread daily. Food needs are, almost by definition, daily needs. Food is necessary and urgent. Food needs do not go away after a day but recur each day.[84]

Children Request Food from their Father

The exchange of food in 6:1–21 is within a kinship group between a father and his children. Those who pray ask their Father for bread. The "span of social distance between those who exchange" in 6:1–21 is close and the "interaction is intense."[85] A family shares food. The kinship relationship is confirmed by the setting, which is within the household. Prayer, one of the acts of righteousness in 6:1–21, is to take place not in public but in a private space, the home, inside a room with the door closed (6:6).

This type of exchange can be identified as generalized reciprocity and is the most common form of exchange within a close kinship distance.[86] The children request bread from the Father and the assumption is the Father will be munificent in providing food for his children. The Father knows what you need before you ask him (6:8). There is a sustained one-way flow of food from parent to child. The parent has little expectation of a return gift, certainly not one that is equal in quantity or quality. The giving of food meets social needs; it solidifies social ties and provides for the family members a sense of belonging.

The provision of food in this type of exchange is not only an act of selfless giving, though; it also preserves authority. While the Father is already in a position of authority in the family order, the request for food reinforces this status. Food has power, specifically political power.[87] A leader's authority and status is maintained by having more food, or better access to food, than any other person in the community. If a leader can give more or "better" food than others are able to reciprocate, the leader has greater authority.[88] As the one with power, then, the Father is the source of food. God as the source of food is pervasive in the Hebrew Bible.[89] Matthew's narrative emphasizes this point in 4:1–11—God, not Jesus or the devil, is the source of food. The leader who provides food is not only ascribed power and authority, he is considered generous. Generosity is expected of a community leader who is in power and may even be necessary to maintain power.[90] The Father's authority to give food to the Matthean community differentiates it from the world around it. The Father, not Satan (4:1–11) or the Gentile gods (6:7–8), provides food for the Matthean community. Thus, there is a political motivation present in 6:1–21 for the exchange of food as the community maintains its identity in relation to the larger world by expressing its power and independence.

While a clear sense of authority and power are given to the Father who is the source of food and who is Father of the household, the authority of the Father in food distribution does not require a vertical structure of authority or an "authoritarian" manner.[91] The exchange of food within the family context emphasizes the reciprocal relationship between Father and children: the responsibility of the Father to sustain his offspring and the children's acceptance of the Father's gift of food.[92] The Father is more like a parent who cares and guides than a king who rules and demands obedience.[93]

The children request the food. While the word "children" is not used in 6:1–21, the request of food is directed to "our Father" and the image and language of children permeates this first thematic unit. The request puts those praying in a passive position of receiving the bread.[94] At this point in the narrative, they are not actively producing or distributing the bread they consume. They indicate their complete dependence on the Father for the food. Those praying are not self-sufficient.[95] The children must request food; it does not appear that it is given to them without a request.

Yet, they do actively seek the bread by requesting it boldly. Ask (αἰτέω; 6:8) and pray (προσεύχομαι; 6:7, 9) are the two words used to request the bread and both refer to "requests and presumed responses" and have the sense of urgency and intensity in common.[96] The community is at the beginning stages of seeking out food. Here, they simply ask and pray, but it demonstrates a confidence and hopefulness in the quest for food.[97] Those praying do not doubt that God will provide. To trust in God's provision is to trust in God's power and authority.[98] Those who pray have taken note from the negative example of the tempter in Matt 4 who encouraged Jesus to question or test God's ability to feed him. Instead of trusting in his own powers, or those of the tempter, Jesus placed confidence in God's ability to feed. The temptation to doubt God's ability to feed would not be foreign to Matthew's audience, who would be familiar with the Israelites in the wilderness who spoke against God's faithfulness (Exod 16; 17; Ps 78:17–22; Deut 6:16).

The request for bread, in particular, also shows that those praying accept God as their Father. The request is not for food that is forbidden or food that God does not supply, but for the food God is offering. God offers bread (4:4) and this is what is requested by those praying. Again, Matthew's audience would remember stories in their Scriptures about those who sought after food that was not provided (Num 11:32–34; Ps 78:18) or food that was forbidden (Gen 3:1–7, Gen 25:29–34, Exod 32:6). Those praying accept the food that God offers and in doing so accept his authority and not the authority of other providers.[99] Alongside the metaphor of God as authoritative Father who maintains his status and the community's identity in generously providing food for his children in 6:1–21 is God as a nursing Mother who provides food out of her body, the earth, for the Matthean community and the larger world.[100]

Food is Provided from the Earth

The placement of earth next to bread in 6:10–11, the image of God in the Hebrew Bible as feeding God's creation out of the natural world, and the pattern of feeding in 6:1–21 suggest an image of God as a Mother who nurses her children, who continues to give life to her child after birth.[101] The structure of the relationship is more horizontal than that of authoritative Father and a more continuous connection is maintained between God as Mother and the Matthean community as children.

In Matt 6:11, earth (γῆς) is the word immediately preceding bread (τὸν ἄρτον), which suggests a connection between the two. Betz suggests that the connection reflects an "older 'agrarian theology' which implies that the earth provides the resources for humanity to survive. 'On earth' means not only the space where bread is made but also the resources of the earth in the sense that the earth provides the grain which feeds humanity."[102]

As the one who provides for both the human sphere and the natural world, God is the one who feeds, nourishes, and gives food to his world. The image of God as one who nourishes is not new to the Hebrew Bible tradition but is used very little in the New Testament.[103] In the Hebrew Bible tradition, the primary manner in which God feeds God's creation is through creation. God feeds out of the natural world, from "nature's storehouse."[104] God brings forth food out of the earth so all creatures can eat.[105] For example, "You cause the grass to grow for the cattle, and plants for people to use, to bring forth food from the earth" (Ps 104:14). Specifically, food comes from the mountains, the land, and the rocks.

The mountains yield food for the behemoth/wild animal, grass comes out of the earth and feeds the cattle, and plants grow for people to use (Ps 104:14). God provides pasture in the wilderness for every living thing, makes grass grow on the hills. Land produces its yield and trees produce fruit (Lev 26:4). Springs gush forth in the valleys (Ps 104), the mountains drip sweet wine, the hills shall flow with milk, and all the stream beds of Judah shall flow with water for the people of Israel (Joel 3:18). Rocks also provide a home for the eagle and a place from which it spies its food (Job 39:26–29). In addition to providing food, God also manipulates other parts of nature in order to bring forth food. God rains[106] on the earth so grass can grow, land can yield its produce, and trees their fruit. God makes it rain to cause things to grow. Not only does God distribute the food through the created order, but the food is provided at just the right time. God gives God's creatures their food in due season (Pss 104:24ff, 145:15–16; Lev 26:4–5) just when they need it (also Exod 16).

This feeding process conjures up the image of God as mother who nurses all living things from her body, the earth.[107] When a mother nurses her child a child is hungry and shows signs of hunger by crying out or "asking" for food and a mother feeds the child immediately, just when the child needs it. The mother who gave birth to the child and provides for the child knows what the child needs, understands the nuances of her own child's personality and communication style, and responds appropriately to that child. The mother feeds the child from her body; the natural milk produced in her body flows from her breasts to nourish the child.

The earth nourishes all living things as a Mother nourishes a child. Food comes out of the earth. Milk flows from the hills (Joel 3:18), sweet wine drips from the mountains (Joel 3:18), grass comes out of the earth and feeds the cattle (Ps 104:14), food comes from the land and the rocks (Ps 104:14). The food is provided when creation needs it, in due season. God, like the earth, is the ultimate image of the one who nourishes. In the Hebrew Bible, God is depicted as a mother who gives birth to her children, Israel (Deut 32:18, Num 11:12, Isa 42:14, Isa 49:15), nurses them (Isa 49:15), and demands justice for them (Hos 13:8). The creation looks to God to satisfy its hunger and thirst (e.g. Pss 104:27, 146:7, 107:9; Isa 66:11–13). Therefore, God or God's body may be imagined as the earth which nurses God's creatures.

The pattern of feeding in 6:1–21 can be imagined as God the Mother nursing the Matthean community.[108] The children request bread out of the earth, the body of God (6:10–11). Food comes forth from the Mother's body. As a mother attends to the complicated, daily, and often hidden needs of her children, so God attends to the community. In 6:1–21 God is creator, the one who gives birth to creation, who "formed my inward parts" (Ps 139). God sees all that happens, knows and attends to the innermost needs of God's creatures. God continues to give life to God's creation. To give food is to sustain the creation the Mother first brought into being and her relationship with that creation.[109] As a child cries out for food from her mother, so does the Matthean community. The children ask for food from a passive position with a sense of urgency. The emphasis is on today, "give us today our daily bread."

The image of food coming forth from the earth, however, moves beyond the feeding of the Matthean community to the feeding of the world. The earth feeds the cattle, birds of the air, Israel, humans, and all living things. The context of 6:9–13 suggests that the earth will provide bread for the Matthean community but the image of God as a Mother who provides food out of her body for all creation moves food exchange beyond the Matthean community.

Summary of Food Exchange

As with the study in 6:1–21 of characters and setting and theology, the examination of food exchange uncovers a message not always clear about the Father and community's relationship with those outside the private kinship group. At this stage in the narrative, the focus of food exchange and subsequent relationships is on those within the Matthean community, the Father and children in the household. The community is distinct from the world. The children, while in the household, request bread from their Father ("our Father"). Food comes forth from a Mother for her children. Food exchange promotes a tight social bond within the family. Yet God is also the cosmic Father who sees and knows the needs of all creation and God is nursing Mother who feeds all living creatures from the earth. This begins to point to a view of food exchange between God and all creation.

Conclusion

This subunit, 6:1–21, is the starting point for the audience's perception of food exchange in Matthew's narrative. The reader is left with a strong impression that food distribution occurs in the private household between Father and children. God as Father is one who is related to God's children as a concerned parent and provider who continues to have authority over God's dependent children, who sees them from his throne, and who feeds those who address him as heavenly Father.[110] This God has the power and authority to provide food for the Matthean community, who receive it as passive children, and to maintain its identity in the larger world. The subunit uses kinship language and the secrecy motif—for both the practice of righteousness and for the image of the Father—to make the point. The direct nature of the relationship between Father and child, regarding both reward (i.e. the Father rewards the children directly) and food exchange (i.e. the children request food directly from the Father) calls attention to the tight bond between parent and child. To drive home the point, the focus on privacy is contrasted with the example of inappropriate public practice.

The audience, however, does not leave this subunit without some other impressions. The audience does not come to see the private realm in opposition to the public realm. Certain practices are simply needed to be carried out in a private manner, but those practices themselves draw one out into interaction with the public arena. One is to be a part of the larger world, albeit in particular ways. The images of God present in this subunit corroborate this point. The Father may interact directly with his children through reward and food provision, but God is also a cosmic Father and a nursing Mother who interact with the larger world. God as nursing Mother is one who gives birth to all her children and provides food for them out of her body, the earth. This image, along with the image of God as cosmic Father, demonstrates God's emerging relationship in the narrative with the larger world outside the community. The community, too, will be drawn into a cooperative relationship with the world as the narrative continues.

This subunit, in the beginning of Matthew's narrative, is reflecting the audience's initial understandings of food exchange (and subsequent community interaction with the world and God's interaction with world) as that which occurs in the household between Father and child. As the narrative continues, the audience will be challenged to rethink that understanding to include the world beyond the private household.[111]

Chapter 4

Birds of the Air (6:25–34)

Introduction

Food exchange in 6:25–34 follows the same themes as in 6:1–21 but begins to expand the location and audience of exchange as well as the view of God and the seeking activity of the Matthean community. As in 6:1–21, God as heavenly Father feeds the Matthean community, food flows in one direction from parent to child, and the implied location of food exchange is the household. Food continues to be exchanged according to the economic form of generalized reciprocity.

These contours, however, shift in 6:25–34. God is portrayed more clearly as creator and provider who is active in the created order, interacts with the nonhuman world, and provides food out of the earth. The Matthean community continues to be dependent on God's provision but is to actively seek to be in relationship with those who will give life. The emphasis in 6:1–21 on kinship language and God's depiction as heavenly Father fade in 6:25–34, although there is still language of dependence. The setting for the community remains in the household, but God also feeds the birds of the air in the outdoors. The passage also brings out the theme of anxiety in acquiring food and food becomes a means of encouragement. God feeds creatures and provides food for humans as they seek God's providential activity.

Matthew 6:25–34 affirms the material need for food for a community that is hungry.[1] Food exchange, however, goes beyond meeting biological needs. The problem the passage addresses is the community's need to understand food as a part of a larger social, natural, and theological context. The exchange of food is connected with other life in the world and with God. One is to move out into the larger world and interact with it in particular ways in order to access food.[2] God's provision of food does not take a secondary role to God's kingdom (or righteousness or rule or law) but that provision is primarily what the kingdom is about. A repetitive-progressive pattern in the passage underscores these major points: food as connected to other parts of life; a community that recognizes and seeks those connections and relationships; and God's provision of food in due season, today.

The structure of 6:25–34 displays a repetitive pattern and, within that pattern, a progression of thought. The passage can be structured in this way:[3]

- Introduction (v. 25a—"therefore, I tell you")
  - imperative (v. 25b—do not worry about your life or body)
    - question (v. 25b—what you might eat, drink, wear)
      - clarification (v. 25c—life more than, body more than)
        - example with "look" (v. 26–27—birds of the air)
        - example with "consider" (v. 28–30c—lilies of the field)
          - concluding remark (v. 30 c–d—today, tomorrow)[4]

- Introduction (v. 31a—"therefore")
  - imperative (v. 31a—"do not worry")
    - question (v. 31b what might we eat, drink, wear)
      - clarification (v. 32 "For it is the Gentiles . . ."
        - example with "seek" (v. 33—seek first . . .)
          - concluding remark (v. 34—today, tomorrow)

The first repetition "therefore" (οὖν or διὰ τοῦτο) begins both sections (v. 25 and v. 31), as does the verb "worry" (μεριμνάω). Second, both sections begin with the questions one is not to ask (i.e. what one might eat, drink, or wear). Third, there is a clarification to these questions which includes a contrast: is not life/body more than food/clothing (v. 25) and the Gentiles strives for all these things but the heavenly Father knows you need all these things (v. 32). The repetition refers to whether or not life is connected to the heavenly Father. The first phrase implies it but the second phrase makes implicit this association—the Gentiles do not understand how the heavenly Father interacts and you should understand. The fourth repetition leads to the primary progressive element in the texture (i.e. the alignment of the examples of the birds of the air and lilies of the field and the example to seek the kingdom of God and his righteousness). "To seek..." is a repetition and reinforcement of v. 26, 28–30 (i.e. look at the birds of the air and how the heavenly Father feeds them, observe the lilies of the field and how God clothes them). Both of these examples use words for seeing/vision and give examples of how one is to proceed in life instead of asking questions. Seek in Matthew's narrative is used in different ways but the dominant use is that of looking, identifying, searching out, trying to find or locate a missing, lost, or sought after object more than striving to live a certain way.[5] The final repetition is the concluding remark which highlights the focus on today not tomorrow.

Self and Body

The passage begins with an exhortation for the audience: you are not to be anxious about your life or your body (v. 25). This is often interpreted to mean that one is not to be overly concerned with materials, with food and clothing, that one is to trust God and focus on spiritual matters and not to concentrate on earthly materials. Yet, this devalues the importance of material needs. I argue that this passage instructs the audience to seek materials within the context of relationships and not to seek isolated objects out of context.[6] One is to seek out food with an awareness that it comes from God and is acquired through the larger world, not with a focus on food as an isolated piece of nutrition.

Is Not the Body More Than Clothes

In 6:1–21, certain parts of the body were a place of secrecy, a place that was to be kept secret from the public or the world. A person was to give alms so the left hand did not know what the right hand was doing. A person was to wash her face and put oil on her head so that fasting could not be seen by others. These parts of the body were not to be recognized or emphasized; they were not to stand out to others in public or the world so that one's whole person ("you") might be recognized by God in secret. By not recognizing one's body or act, one was more aware that God was rewarding them (i.e. what God was doing) and how their act was helping others in the world. How one treats a smaller part affects the relationship to a larger entity.

In 6:25–34, there continues to be a concern that a certain part of the body is not to be overly recognized so that a larger entity can also be recognized, "(do not worry) about your body, what you might put on...(is not) the body more than clothing?" (v. 25). Clothing was considered an extension of the body. The skin was considered the boundary of the physical body and, by extension, clothing becomes that boundary.[7] Therefore, the clothing, as the "outer skin" is that part of the body that is not to be excessively emphasized in place of the larger entity, the body itself. The lilies of the field do not worry about clothing, they neither toil nor spin, yet God clothes them.[8] The lilies do not overemphasize their clothing to the exclusion of their bodies, yet their bodies are more glorious than even Solomon's clothes. The emphasis is on what God is doing. The lilies do not worry, yet they grow because God clothes them (vv. 29–30, "clothed liked one of these. But if God so clothes the grass"). The focal point is the work of God to clothe the lilies/grass—this is the larger entity that is to be pointed out instead of the smaller entity.[9] If one focuses on the clothes and the lilies, one overlooks the bigger picture that God is doing the clothing.

Is Not Life/Self More Than Food

"Do not worry about your life/self, what you might eat or what you might drink...is not life more than food" (v. 25). As the clothes are to be deemphasized in order to be aware of the larger body or what God is doing for the body, so food as an isolated object (i.e. what you might eat or what you might drink) is to be deemphasized for the purpose of focusing on the relationship of food to social and theological relations (i.e. life/self). As in 6:1–21, the references to food and life in 6:25–34 give support that food plays a role in social and theological relationships, a role that goes beyond, although still includes, understanding food as merely a nutritive substance that feeds the physical body. In addition, the passage indicates that not just any social or theological connection will do, but those which are life-giving.[10] The audience is not to focus on food as an object that is disconnected from life or God, but is to see the larger entity of life that is connected with family, others, the world, and God.

Life/self (ψυχή) refers primarily to the earthly life or soul or self, the totality of life, and is differentiated from "body," which refers to the physical, material, corporeal body.[11] Life/self is used in 6:25b in association with eating and drinking and frames two different types of lifestyles.[12] It refers to life or self in this world either in relationship and service to God or in service to other powers. In general, ψυχή refers to daily, earthly existence in relationship with the world (10:39, 16:25), with God (10:39, 16:25), with family (10:37–39). The word carries a positive sense when talking about life in relationship with God or identified with those who serve God (10:39b, 16:25b) and a negative sense when discussing life that is not in relationship with God (10:39a, 16:25a).[13] Ψυχή, then, is associated with life, with God, and with family.

Reading verse 25, then, gives an apparent double message. On the one hand, the audience is told not to be overly concerned about "what you might eat" or "what you might drink" (v. 25b), that one is not to see food as an inert object, an isolated piece of substance disconnected from any other person or plant or organism.[14] The verse (v. 25b) does not say, "do not worry about *who is feeding you* or *where food comes from*," rather it says, "do not worry about "*what* you might eat," that is, "that thing, that piece of food you might eat." The next part of the verse (v. 25c) reinforces this, "life is more than food." That is, life in the positive sense, life that is connected with God and others who participate in God's realm is of greater value than a piece of food which is divorced from other life, from the one who made it, from the earth that grew it.

On the other hand, when the reader/audience recognizes the association between "life" and "food and drink" in v. 25b, the audience might be confused at first. One is not to worry about life? Is not life worth more than food? Yet ψυχή in v. 25b is a negative use of the term, ψυχή that is disconnected from God (10:39a, 16:25a). This, again, reinforces the reader's understanding of food—food that is disconnected from other organisms is like life that is disconnected from God or those who serve God. The implied audience is to understand in 6:25–26 that the smaller part is not to be emphasized to the exclusion of the larger entity. Do not call attention to the isolated food object to the exclusion of the larger entity of a life in relationship with family, the world and God.

The proper relationship between food and life is then explained in v. 26. Food is seen in v. 26 as that which is given from the heavenly Father to the birds. Food is not isolated from other life (i.e. what piece of food might we eat?, v. 25), but is provided by the Father through nature to those eating it. As with God clothing the lilies of the field, so God feeds the birds. The focus is on what God is doing, the relationship of food with God. It is important to focus on who is providing the food and on where the food comes from; it is less important to focus on what that food scrap is.[15] Now that I have established the importance of focusing on food in relationship with a larger social and theological context, I expand on the larger context—how God interacts with those God feeds and how those fed are to respond to God.

God as One Who Provides

Matthew 6:25–34 makes explicit the image of God introduced in 6:1–21 as the one who feeds God's creation as it makes a further and stronger connection between the images of heavenly Father, nursing Mother and creator. "Your heavenly Father" is also the one who provides for the birds of the air and the lilies of the field.[16] The heavenly Father and nursing Mother is the creator who continues to provide for the creation she made. God relates to and provides for the natural world beyond the human sphere.

Birds of the Air

The setting for food distribution has expanded from the household or kinship relations to the natural world and therefore models a larger audience for food provision. The passage begins and ends with a reference to the domestic setting by asking the question, "what will you/we eat?"(vv. 25b, 31b), a question that can best be imagined in a family setting. The example to explore this question, however, is set in nature with the use of the birds of the air (v. 26–27). The expansion to include the natural world primarily looks ahead to what is to come (i.e. Matt 10, 12, 14–15) since the passage ends with a reference back to the domestic, household setting (v. 31). By framing the extended spatial setting of the created order with the kinship setting, the narrative is pointing to places the spatial setting will go, but is not quite ready to venture yet.

The birds of the air function in two ways in this passage: as wise teachers who instruct the audience and as examples of God's provision.[17] The birds of the air are wise creatures and can teach humans about God's provision and works.[18] The birds of the air, along with the animals and plants of the earth and the fish of the sea, know that the hand of the Lord holds the life of every living thing and the breath of every human being (Job 12:7–10). It seems that only God the Maker can teach humans more or make humans wiser than the animals of the earth and the birds of the air (Job 35:11).[19]

The birds of the air teach the audience about God's provision. The birds of the air are both representative of God who cares for God's creation and recipients of God's provision/care. When the audience finishes the first phrase, "look to the birds of the air," the audience may associate the birds of the air with the divine.[20] Matthew's audience has already heard about the Spirit of God which descended from heaven like a dove (3:16), the dove offering an olive branch to Noah representing deliverance and God's promise to creation, and the Spirit hovering (as a bird) over the waters at creation (Gen 1:2).[21] To look at the birds of the air is to see the One who creates and delivers. Furthermore, the audience is invited to "look at" (ἐμβλέψατε εἰς) the birds of the air, to look up into the sky. Since οὐρανός is used for both sky and heaven, the abode of God, the audience may think of the birds as associated with God. As the birds dwell in the sky/heaven, so God dwells there. The Hebrew Bible and Old Testament Pseudepigrapha include passages where persons are to look to God who provides food and creates all life.[22]

Yet, the birds of the air do not feed the creation in this passage; God does. Therefore, while the birds of the air may function to remind the audience of God and God's provision, they are primarily recipients of God's provision. In this way, they exemplify God's provision. In the Hebrew Bible and in other places in Matthew's narrative about the birds of the air, the emphasis is on a place to live, with an acknowledgement that this "home" includes food and drink.[23] The birds of the air are given a home, fed, and given drink by God to signify God's providence and generosity.[24] The birds of the air receive God's food. God feeds them. Food is not an isolated object; rather the giving of food is part of a larger relationship of provision (e.g. a home, clothes). Life is more than an isolated bit of food; life includes the giving of food, which itself is associated with a broader lifestyle that is connected to God and God's provision.

God Unveiled

In 6:25–34 God interacts openly with God's creatures. The Father in secret in 6:1–21 has now become the Father whose activity is manifest in the open sky and field, not behind a closed door.[25] Betz claims that this phenomenon is a contradiction of previous theologies: God's hiddenness (6:1–6, 16–18) and God's manifest activity in creation (5:45, 6:25–34, 7:11, 24–27).[26] Yet, as was stated regarding 6:1–21, there is a literary tradition that the hidden Father is gradually revealed. The movement from a hidden God to a God who is manifest in the world is not a distinct jump in theologies but a continuous development. The primacy of secrecy in 6:1–21 is swinging to more openness. God feeds the birds in the spatial setting of the sky (οὐρανός) and clothes the lilies in the spatial setting of the field (ἀγρός).[27] The sky and the (wild) fields[28] can be classified as inhabited areas, although this might be surprising at first. They are probably not situated in the city or marketplace, in heavily populated areas. The fields are wild and not tended. The passage does instruct the audience, however, to look and observe these places, which suggests they are within sight or within a reasonable distance. The grass in the fields is used to put in the oven. And birds can certainly fly over inhabited areas. These settings can be considered in the country or rural as opposed to in the city, but that still puts them in an inhabited area, even if it is less inhabited.[29] God does not feed the birds or clothe the lilies in secret as God interacts with humans in 6:1–21, where people are intentionally hidden behind closed doors in an inhabited area. God feeds the birds without hiding the act.

This setting suggests there is a movement at least away from the household of the Matthean community out into a space that is less inhabited and more connected to the physical features of the earth. The passage does begin and end with a setting that implies the household or family, those asking "what there might we eat or drink." Food exchange is still primarily located inside a kinship setting, but the audience is being prepared to hear later in the narrative about food exchange locations outside the family.

God Nourishes the Matthean Community

The view of God as Mother who feeds the world from her body, the earth, continues in 6:25–34. The view is expanded as God is seen as creator and deliverer, and food comes not only from the earth but possibly through other human communities. Similar to the pattern of feeding in 6:1–21,[30] the Matthean community cries out or hungers for food, "what might we eat, what might we drink" (6:25b, 31b). The community is portrayed less as children than in 6:1–21, with only one use of the heavenly Father in the passage, but they are still described with diminutive language, "you of little faith." God, as an attentive mother who knows what her children need, feeds the community and the creation.[31] God feeds the birds of the air out of the earth, out of God's body. The birds neither sow nor reap nor gather into barns, rather food is provided from nature's storehouse (6:26). God knows what you need before you even ask (6:32, cf. 6:8). The portrait of God who feeds according to this pattern in the Hebrew Bible is one who created the earth, heavens, and sea and delivered the Israelites out of distress, brought them into the Promised Land, and returned them to their land after exile.[32] Finally, the community is fed today, when food is needed. The passages emphasize the needs and worries of today not tomorrow (6:30, 34).

God feeds the Matthean community as creator, ordering creation with the community so it can be fed. The community is designated as "you of little faith," struggling to trust God and work with the created order to receive God's food provision. The community is to seek out God's righteous activity of provisioning the world and be connected to God and others who give life. The final word in 6:25–34 is one of encouragement, that God provides enough today to satisfy the community's needs.

You of Little Faith. After using the analogy of birds of the air, and clothing the lilies of the field, the narrative addresses the audience as "you of little faith," (ὑμᾶς, ὀλιγόπιστοι). This is one clue for the audience concerning how the community might receive food. The phrase is used at the end of the remarks about clothing and some consider it a conclusion to that section.[33] But it is also well placed as a transition sentence from the discussion thus far about clothing and food (vv. 25–30c) to the conclusions regarding the whole chapter (vv. 31–34).[34] Therefore, I consider it a reference to the audience, "you" (used everywhere in chs. 5–7), which addresses the deficiency (not lack) of faith that the listeners have regarding the provision of both food and clothing.

The reference to those who are ὀλιγόπιστοι appears here in the Matthean narrative for the first time but is used four other times in the narrative.[35] Three central themes emerge from surveying its other uses. First, each reference involves an encounter with uninhabited parts of nature: sea, wilderness, and mountains.[36] Second, the disciples have a fearful, anxious response to the uninhabited parts of nature instead of working and coping with the natural world.[37] Third, Jesus brings creation into order[38] for the disciples so the two are able to live together. Jesus reorders the relationship between nature and the disciples that has become unmanageable (out of order).[39]

There is also an encounter with nature in 6:30 as the question is asked, "what might we eat or drink." Food comes from the natural world and the disciples are asking how to get food from nature. The crisis is clear with the use of μεριμνάω, the repeated questions about food, drink, and clothing, the general concern about tomorrow, and the existence of trouble today (v. 30, 34). God, not Jesus, demonstrates the order that is in creation. In 6:25–34 there is order in creation where the birds of the air are fed and the lilies grow, but the disciples do not recognize this order. These elements, seen in the other passages with ὀλιγόπιστοι and in 6:25–34, match the pattern of God feeding: God is seen as creator who orders creation, the disciples are in crisis crying out for food, and the food is needed today.

The disciples are ones of little faith because they do not trust that God can work with them and nature in order to provide food. The disciples are to see the order in creation and work in relation to it to obtain food. Nature is good, a part of creation, a part of God's good creation, ordering itself to God's creative powers. It is not evil or rebellious. The natural world may be challenging and difficult, but it does not have an evil intent to harm humanity. It can work in harmony with humanity, and humanity is called to respond to it—not out of fear or anxiety but out of the desire to seek how God will order the natural world in relation to humanity so humanity can be fed.[40]

Seek Out God's Righteous Activity. Matthew's community is to seek how God will order the world in relation to itself and not to strive solely for food and water. To seek (ζητέω) the kingdom of God and his righteousness is to seek out God's provisions as they are made available through the natural and human worlds, to be connected to those worlds, and to trust that God will provide. Those who strive (ἐπιζητέω) are those who are antagonistic or anxious about the world around them, unable to trust God to provide for them, and disconnected from all that gives life. Being at odds with the world, they try to manipulate the world, control it, and maneuver around it.

How the listeners are to seek (ζητέω) in 6:33 is in contrast to how the Gentiles strive (ἐπιζητέω) in 6:32.[41] Ἐπιζητέω is used in Matthew's narrative in the context of those who strive for a sign, as an evil and adulterous generation strives for a sign (12:39, 16:4).[42] An "evil and adulterous generation" is a phrase used in the Hebrew Bible for the Israelites who grumbled against God and did not trust God's provision[43] for them while they lived and traveled in the wilderness. Those who strive do not trust in God's provision and, in addition, attempt to test and manipulate the world around them.[44] They are in an antagonistic relationship with the world.

The Gentiles ἐπιτζητέω for "all these things"(6:32), referring to the food and clothing in the first part of the passage. This striving is for isolated objects that are not connected to God or those who serve God.[45] The Gentiles do not recognize that the "Father knows that you need all these things," that it is the Father who feeds and clothes.[46] They do not cry out to God as Matthew's community does. They simply strive for food and clothes outside of life-giving relationships. They do not trust God's provision and attempt to manipulate the world around them in order to attain "all these things."

Those who seek (ζητέω), conversely, look to a heavenly Father who can be trusted because the seekers realize the Father knows what his children need. To seek the kingdom of God and his righteousness is to identify and discern God's righteous activity with the created world and to participate in that activity.[47] The kingdom of God and his righteousness refers to the concrete activity of God to provide for God's created order.

Seeking the kingdom of God and his righteousness has generally been interpreted as striving to live a moral, law-abiding life under God's political rule. The kingdom is read as God's sovereign rule or the activity of God's reign. God is the king who rules with power and judgment.[48] Righteousness in Matthew is most often interpreted as right human moral conduct which God demands or as a gift from God. Even those who interpret righteousness in 6:33 to include God's gift agree that one lives a certain law-abiding life out of that gift.

Righteousness is living according to a norm which is governed by God.[49]

By contrast, given the perspective of a reading of Matthew focused on food exchange, God is interpreted primarily as creator and provider who supplies material goods (e.g. food and clothing) for God's creatures, not a political governor who provides a system of ruling for the human community. Instead of striving to live according to a law under God's political rule, one is to seek out how God is providing for God's creation. In 6:25–34, seeking the kingdom and its righteousness in the second section is used in parallel with observing how the heavenly Father feeds the birds and clothes the lilies in the first section. The use of ζητέω in 6:33 is connected with other verbs in the passage that emphasize looking and observing. The repetitive-progressive pattern aligns the following verbs and phrases: "*look* at the birds of the air" (v. 26), "*observe* the lilies of the field" (v. 27) and *seek* for the kingdom and its righteousness.[50] To seek, in the context of looking and observing, moves beyond the urgent requests of "asking" and "praying" in 6:1–21 toward careful investigation and searching, the attempt to learn new information, and the beginning steps of processing this new information.[51] To seek in 6:25–34 is to seek "the kingdom and God's righteousness," which is to examine and learn and process how God feeds the birds of the air and how God clothes the lilies of the field, how God justly provisions the creatures of the earth.

Furthermore, the use of righteousness in 6:33 parallels its use in 5:6, and the comparison between the two passages reinforces several elements of the pattern of feeding in this section: feeding is a gift or activity of God as one who creates and delivers, those who cry out or hunger request food, and feeding is provided in due season. The two passages are shown below:

> Seek first the kingdom of God and his righteousness and
> all these things will continue to be added as well (6:33).
>
> Blessed are those who hunger and thirst for righteousness,
> for they will be satisfied (5:6).

Both 6:33 and 5:6 refer to righteousness as a gift from or activity of God.[52] In 5:6, hunger and thirst have a double meaning. They are used in the Hebrew Bible and Pseudepigrapha as metaphorically/figuratively (i.e. as longing for God, a seeking for God and God's deliverance) and literally (i.e. as hungering and thirsting for material food and water).[53] Both uses could be conceived of here as referring in general to God's activity of providing for material needs. According to the metaphorical usage, those who hunger and thirst for righteousness are yearning for God's righteousness and deliverance from anonymous enemies or some other type of deliverance. This use matches the element of crying out in the pattern of feeding in this passage: those who cry out in distress, those who ask "what might we eat." With the literal usage, blessed are those who hunger and thirst for material food and drink, for they will be satisfied with material goods. This use of hunger matches another element in the pattern as well—God feeds those who are literally hungry. Satisfied might very well have a general meaning of "fulfilled" in the first metaphorical use of hunger and thirst. But it matches well the second literal use of hunger and thirst—their real hunger and thirst pains will be satisfied with material food and drink.[54]

Finally, with the parallel uses of "will continue to be added as well" (προστεθήσεται)[55] and "will be satisfied" (χορτασθήσονται), both passages anticipate a response in the near future and, in fact, highlight the primacy of the reality of the present. As future passive indicatives, and read as typological references, they underscore the reality of the present (or near future) (i.e. today) in distinction from the possibilities of the future (i.e. tomorrow).[56] The beginning phrases, "those who hunger and thirst for righteousness" and "seek first the kingdom of kingdom of God and his righteousness" refer to the present time. The use of "first" (πρῶτον) (i.e. "but seek first the kingdom of God and his righteousness, and all these things will continue to be added as well") reinforces the emphasis on the present time. It is often interpreted as "above all else" or as a "priority."[57] I interpret it as both a priority and as what occurs early, first in a sequence. It is not first in sequence as a condition—that is, in order to be fed—but what is to be done in the present, today, an urgent need—to recognize how God is feeding and to be connected to other parts of life and God.

Encouragement for Today. The final piece of the repetitive-progressive texture (vv. 30 c–d and 34) hones in on the temporal setting, continues this emphasis on "today" that is present in 6:33, and offers a word of encouragement. The concluding remarks to both the first (vv. 30 c–d) and second (v. 34) parts contrast today and tomorrow. Both use a typological reference as they spell out "today" as a kind of time and contrast "today" with "tomorrow." Therefore, "God clothes the grass of the field, which is alive today and tomorrow is thrown into the oven" (6:30). This does not refer to a specific day but "today" in general as it is different than "tomorrow" in general. The contrast gives a sense, especially when compared to 6:34, that there is not much time in life, whether for grass or humans, and one should focus on today.[58] Today is a time of life when God provides and tomorrow is a time of death. The focus of food exchange is on today, when food is urgent and necessary and relationships are to be recognized and strengthened. Tomorrow is too late for one who is hungry.

The contrast between today and tomorrow continues in 6:34: "Therefore, do not be anxious for tomorrow, for tomorrow will be anxious for itself. Sufficient for the day is its own crisis."[59] The contrast of a kind of time is clear between today and tomorrow. Here, though, not only are there problems to be expected tomorrow, but there are also problems today. It seems natural to take this as a pessimistic sign, that there is no use planning for the future and even today is a burden.[60] Yet, some readers take this as a sign of hope,[61] especially coming on the heels of 6:25–34, that God provides sufficiently today in the midst of trouble. This latter interpretation makes sense in light of the whole passage and 6:30, that today is a time of life, but it is also a time of crisis—that is, questions about how to find food, drink, and clothing. Both the spatial setting (i.e. less inhabited, potentially a place of threat or danger but finally a place of provision) and the temporal setting in 6:25–34 suggest that the "heavenly Father" provides for God's creatures in this place and time of difficulty in order to sustain life. Time and anxiety are linked in this passage and one is given cause to be anxious about the passing of time. Today, however, is a time of life.

One further piece of evidence in the passage points to an emphasis on "today." The implied audience is instructed not to ask questions or worry about what *might* happen in the future, what you might eat or what you might drink or what you might wear. In both 6:25 and 6:31, the references to eating and clothing use the subjunctive mood, language that expresses the possibility that something might happen in the future.[62] The audience is not to wonder about future possibilities regarding food, drink, and clothes. To strengthen the emphasis even more, the aorist subjunctive of the verb μεριμνάω is used with μὴ before the question in 6:31 and before tomorrow (αὔριον) in 6:34. This is the subjunctive of prohibition and is used to prohibit the beginning of an action. One way to translate this phrase is "never be anxious" or "don't ever be anxious,"[63] a strong warning against the action. Therefore, "never be anxious about" what you might eat or drink or wear and "don't ever be (even think about being) anxious" about tomorrow.

The focus of the temporal setting in 6:25–34 is on "today" in contrast with "tomorrow." Today is the focus of attention for the listener and the heavenly Father's provisions are available to satisfy today's needs. Those smaller parts that are not to be focused on (i.e. clothing, isolated pieces of food) are aligned with the possible future while the present—and the certain continuation of the present into the future—is aligned with the act of God feeding, the relationship of God's creatures with God.[64]

Conclusion

The Father in heaven who operates in secret in 6:1–21 has becomes the Father in heaven who is more clearly creator and provider in 6:25–34. God is seen as feeding not only humans but also the birds of the air. A reinforced pattern of feeding emerges: God, as creator, provider, and deliverer, feeds today those who are hungry or cry out. Matthew's community is hungry and needs material food today.

Matthew's community is not to cry out for food as an isolated object, but to seek to be in relationship with those who give life and provide food, to continue to see the community as part of a larger world. A shift becomes apparent in this section between the type of dependence on God in 6:1–21 and a type of dependence in 6:25–34 that includes a more active seeking by Matthew's community. In the former, with more explicit kinship language, Matthew's community asked God for bread as a dependent child. In the latter, the language of dependency remains but it shifts from exclusively familial language of parent and child to other language that signifies a more mature relationship. God is characterized as Father and Mother but Matthew's community is no longer seen as a child. The community is characterized as "you of little faith," with the use of diminutive language, but they are "of more value" than the birds of the air (6:26, cf. 6:30). The community is instructed to observe God's providential activity, to be encouraged that God provides today for God's creatures through nature and the world, and to seek out connections to God and others who give life.

Chapter 5

"Ask, and it will be given you" (7:7–11)

Introduction

The first thematic unit (i.e. 6:1–21, 6:25–34, 7:7–11), which focuses on the distribution of food from the Father to his children within the domestic setting, draws to a close with 7:7–11. This passage encompasses the main features which are shared with the rest of the unit: God as Father and Mother who functions as creator and provider and feeds God's children with material food, the children as Matthew's community who passively receive the provision, and the household or family setting where the food exchange takes place. Food exchange occurs in the context of generalized reciprocity with asymmetric power relations. The 7:7–11 passage continues themes introduced in 6:25–34: being connected and seeking food through relationships, finding encouragement in the midst of crises, and expecting food provision today. As with 6:25–34 and 6:1–21, the community is motivated by a need to reinforce social bonds within the Matthean family and principally to maintain its identity over and against the surrounding world. Matthew 7:7–11 refers less prominently to two features that have begun to emerge in this unit and which will be more pronounced in subsequent units: the active participation of Matthew's community in distributing food coupled with the character of God becoming less visible and the exchange of food with those outside the community. Identified as a repetitive-progressive texture, 7:7–11 serves as a transition from the first to the second thematic unit and provides a road map for the audience to follow regarding the way in which the Matthean community exchanges food through the narrative.

Material Gifts

The terms ask, seek, and knock in 7:7–11 are primarily requests for material gifts, not prayer, between humans while also including a request from God in the final verse.[1] There is no mention of prayer, of communicating with God, until the conclusion of the passage (v. 11). The verses leading up to v. 11 discuss the general topic of asking and receiving and may refer to general life experience with other humans rather than praying to God.[2]

The focus in vv. 7–10 is on human relationships and the exchange of material gifts. The tripartite (i.e. ask, seek, knock) refers to the request of materials gifts from other persons or the search for persons who might provide these material items.[3] The life example given in vv. 9–10 illustrates this type of interchange—the giving of food, real food, bread and fish, between parent and child. The final verse, v. 11, following a discussion of an earthly father giving bread and fish to his son, then broadens this type of giving by using the phrase "good gifts," which can also refer to material gifts.[4]

The repetitive-progressive nature of this passage reinforces the reading that humans are requesting material items from other humans and from the heavenly Father. Those who ask, seek, and knock are engaged with the rhythm of the text and are moved to expect the request to be granted. The one who asks becomes more expectant and active through the passage as one who also receives and gives. The unknown item that is requested at the beginning of the passage is interpreted as food later in the passage. The heavenly Father is brought into this exchange of food at the end.

Repetitive-Progressive Texture

As with 6:1–21 and 6:25–34, then, 7:7–11 is shaped by a repetitive-progressive texture. The structure in 7:7–11 follows that of 6:25–34 in particular. The general structure of each includes: (a) a repetition of questions and/or imperatives,[5] (b) a repetition of examples from life,[6] and (c) a conclusion of how the heavenly Father provides for the audience the same that he provides for those in the examples.

In 7:7–8, the idea of requesting or seeking out what one needs is repeated three times with three different verbs within 7:7 (αἰτέω, ζητέω, κρούω) and then that tripartite itself is repeated in 7:8. The tripartite reinforces the request and emphasizes expectations. The verbs in 7:7 are in the imperative, which jump out and grab the audience and function to add a sense of urgency to the request.[7] The audience is assured three times within 7:7 that if an inquiry is made, there will be a response. A further assurance comes in 7:8. The three verbs in 7:8 switch from the imperative to the present indicative—the one (who keeps) asking receives, the one seeking finds, and to the one knocking it will be opened. In addition, two of the future passive verbs (δοθήσεται and εὑρήσετε) change to present active verbs (λαμβάνει and εὑρίσκει), which has two effects. It shifts the focus from a future possibility to a present reality and from a more passive stance (i.e. it will be given to the one who asks) to a more active stance (i.e. the asker receives). These two changes soften the command and substantiate for the audience that if it continues inquiring there will be a response. The asker becomes the receiver. The repetition, at this point, has only a hint of progression. This is enough, however, to suggest a movement, an unfolding of something new—encouragement and assurance.[8]

Matthew 7:9–10, following the close repetitions in vv. 7–8, introduces considerable variation but continues using the first verb pair—ask (αἰτέω) and give (ἐπιδίδωμι), which continues the repetitive pattern. As the audience moves on to v. 9, however, the asker/receiver becomes the giver. Those addressed as "you" in vv. 7–8 (ὑμῖν) now become the parent/father—"is there a human among you (ὑμῶν) who, if his son asks for bread, will surely not give to him a stone." The asker/receiver is now the one who gives.

Two examples are given from the human realm to specify what one might ask for and be given: the child asks for bread or a fish and the father gives it to him. The word for give, ἐπιδίδωμι, is a variation of δίδωμι in v. 7. It means to "give over" or "to hand over" and is used with food analogies.[9] The example used, then, to explain vv. 7–8 is one of food. Those who ask, seek, and knock are, at least, requesting food. The repetitive pattern has continued in vv. 9–10 (i.e. the use of αἰτέω and ἐπιδίδωμι), but it has developed into a food exchange between humans, in particular a father and son.

Finally, in v. 11, the repetitive pattern continues with the use of αἰτέω—δίδωμι, but the characters and the context change. The first change involves the giver, who now becomes the one who asks. This character began as the one who asks (7:7), then became the one who receives (7:8), then the one who gives (7:9–10), and now the one who asks (7:11). The character has come full cycle. Second, the context has shifted from an earthly father who gives bread and fish to his son to a Father in heaven who distributes good things to those who ask him.[10] The references to human parents in the bulk of the passage, with one final reference to the heavenly Father at the end of the passage, highlight the increased attention to the Matthean community regarding food exchange and the reduced focus on the visible role of God.

Having read through the basic repetitive-progressive pattern of 7:7–11, this study will now look at two issues that are part of this pattern: (1) exchange as generalized reciprocity within a family/kinship unit, and (2) the movement from generalized exchange within a family/kinship unit to generalized exchange outside the family/kinship unit.

Family Exchange

The type of exchange in 7:7–11 indicates that the focus is on the family/kinship unit. The ease at which exchange occurs, the family language, and the asymmetric power relations point to generalized reciprocity as the type of exchange of material gifts between humans and with the Father in heaven. The repetitive-progressive texture develops this notion of generalized exchange as the audience reads the passage.

The ease and quick movement of exchange in vv. 7–8 implies there are no set controls or limits on exchanging gifts between parties.[11] The repetition in vv. 7–8 sets up a momentum where exchange is encouraged and expected. The emphasis is on a generous sharing of resources based on need and not on whether the party who receives the gift is capable of reciprocating. There are no regulated expectations in the exchange on how and when the party will repay the gift. This type of exchange fits a family/kinship relationship that is primarily social and personal and less economic and balanced. Not only does the type of exchange in vv. 7–8 suggest a focus on the family/kinship unit, but the language of "family" or "insider" is apparent as well. Verse 7 refers to "you" twice, which has been interpreted in Matthew 6–7 as those within the Matthean community and, particularly, as a reference to the disciples.[12]

This type of reciprocity and the focus on the family continue in vv. 9–11. The language of family is made explicit. The setting itself is a household—a father gives bread and fish to his son. His son (ὁ ὑἱος αὐτοῦ) and your children (τοῖς τέκνοις ὑμῶν) are used. For God, parental language (i.e. your Father in heaven) continues to be used as it has been throughout this unit.

The way in which the questions are asked—about whether someone will feed their son bread instead of a stone, fish instead of a snake—assert an expectation that the parent will care for the child, a generous one-way flow of gifts with no conditions (of repayment) attached.[13] Both questions are asked in a way to expect a negative response (with the use of μη): μὴ λίθον ἐπιδώσει αὐτῷ; (7:9) and μὴ ὄφιν ἐπιδώσει αὐτῷ; (7:10). The audience is led to respond, "of course a father will feed his son good food and not bad food." In v. 11, then, the expectation of responding to a child is continued with the shift to "your Father" in heaven. If the earthly parent will respond in this way, the one in heaven will respond to an even greater degree. The Matthean text once again uses the arguments *a minori ad maius*[14] moving from the lesser to the greater.

The image of God as a nursing Mother is called to mind as daily sustenance is assumed without expecting an explicit request. The mother knows she must feed the child and expects to offer her food without an explicit request.[15] The request, as with the child's request in vv. 9–11, is simply to alert the parent that "now" is the time for feeding. It is a question of "when" not "if." Food is urgent and necessary to sustain life each day. In vv. 9–11, the focus is on the one who gives and there is no expectation of a return payment, at least not one of equal value or in the immediate future. This asymmetric power relation is in accord with generalized reciprocity.

Beyond the Family

At the same time that generalized reciprocity is evident in the passage to reinforce the focus on the family and those social bonds that tie the kinship unit together, a subtle shift is occurring in vv. 7–11 that suggests that generalized reciprocity is occurring with those outside the basic family/kinship unit. While the focus within the family is evident in v. 7, the term "everyone" (πᾶς) is used in v. 8 to open up the exchange to those outside the family.[16] Most scholars limit πᾶς to include only those who are part of the Matthean community.[17] Πᾶς is not addressed to any one group throughout the narrative and it is difficult to say that it is addressed to any one group at any one time. It is often addressed to the disciples, but other addressees include the crowds, those who have confessed Jesus or left family to follow Jesus, and whatever wider audience might be listening.[18] From a narrative critical approach, addressing the story to πᾶς opens up the story beyond the group of disciples (or whatever group it is addressed to) to that audience that is paying attention to the story.[19] While πᾶς may certainly include the disciples in 7:8—every disciple who asks receives—it also points beyond the disciples to everyone who asks.[20]

See, for example, 5:42, which asserts that one is to give to those who ask. This passage follows a series of statements telling the "you" (disciple) to refuse to oppose: "whoever" hits you (v. 39), those who wish to sue you (v. 40), "whoever" will force you to go one mile (v. 41), those who ask you (v. 42), and those who want to borrow from you (v. 42). Clearly, the groups represented by "whoever"[21] and "those who . . ." are outside the Matthean community and point to the implied audience. The use of πᾶς in v. 8 suggests that those addressed in vv. 7–11 include an audience beyond the disciples or Matthean family/community.

The use of ἄνθρωπος in the v. 9 has a similar function to that of πᾶς; it addresses those beyond the Matthean community: those in public spaces with which the community is not to be interacting (i.e. at this point in the narrative) and those to whom the disciples are to be in mission.[22] In 6:1–21, those addressed ("you") are not to practice their righteousness before ἄνθρωπος (vv. 1, 5, 16, 18) or to seek to be glorified by ἄνθρωπος (v. 2). The disciples/"you" are not to be "seen" by ἄνθρωπος (vv. 1, 5) or "appear before ἄνθρωπος" (v. 16, 18) out in public or on the streets regarding their righteous practices. In the two other uses in chapter six and in two uses in chapter five, ἄνθρωπος means those to whom the disciples are in mission and those the disciples are to forgive.[23] Those referred to as ἄνθρωπος are those outside the Matthean community.

In 7:9, the meaning of ἄνθρωπος depends, in part, on the reading of ἐξ.[24] First, it may refer to a person from among those addressed, a person who is within the group that is addressed. Hence, "what human/person from this group of disciples would...." This would read ἐξ as that which denotes separation from within a group—"out of" or "from within".[25] Another way to read ἐξ is "away from" or "apart from," in that a separation has already taken place and is to remain severed.[26] So, "what person (even) apart from you disciples would...." I read with this second meaning and therefore can be translated in this way: "is there *even a human outside of your group* who will give his son a stone if he asks for bread?"

This second reading is plausible for several reasons. First, as already stated, the previous use of ἄνθρωπος in 6:1–21 is clearly as one outside the Matthean community, one separated from that group. Second, the identification of "you" with "evil" in 7:11 eliminates any differentiation that might exist between insiders and outsiders based on being evil or good and suggests that "you disciples" are just like "those humans on the outside." As was argued in 6:1–21, the designation of evil in Matthew's narrative does not refer to either those inside or outside the Matthean community (the disciples). All humans are considered evil.[27] For example, 6:23 seems to clearly state that one within the Matthean community has the capacity to be evil,[28] whereas 12:34 portrays the Pharisees, a group outside of the Matthean community, as evil. The word, ἄνθρωπος, then, refers to one who is outside the group, outside the Matthean community.

Finally, as further evidence beyond the use of πᾶς and ἄνθρωπος that 7:7–11 is referring to those outside the Matthean community, the final phrase in 7:11b reads "the ones asking him" instead of "your children." The reader expects "your children" at the end of 7:11b to make it parallel with the end of 7:11a:

> 7:11a: If therefore you who are evil know how
> to give good gifts *to your children*
>
> 7:11b: how much more will your heavenly Father in heaven
> give good things *to those who ask him.*

"Your children" would indicate a reference to the disciples, the family, the focus of food exchange during this unit (chs. 6–7). The use of "the ones asking him," however, leaves it open to the children of the disciples ("your children"), or the children of everyone (read insiders or outsiders; v. 7), of humans (read outsiders; v. 9), or of those who are evil (read insiders or outsiders; v. 11a). Matthew 7:11, then, can be translated:

> 7:11a: If you, being evil like humans/outsiders, know how
> to give good gifts to your children,
> as humans/outsiders give good gifts to their children,

7:11b: how much more will your heavenly Father
give good things to those who ask him,
whoever they are.

This reference to outsiders has several implications. First, the reference acknowledges that families or communities outside the Matthean community feed their children just as those inside the community. Second, the nod to those outside recognizes that the heavenly Father feeds those outside the community as well as those within the Matthean community. There is no indication at this point in the narrative that food exchange is occurring between the Matthean community and the world outside the community.[29] The reference to outsiders and their food exchanges, however, suggests that the Matthean community may be able to trust outsiders and open up the possibility of exchanging food with them.[30]

How Food Is Exchanged

The character of God in 7:7–11, as is the case for this beginning thematic unit (chs. 6–7), is the primary and direct provider of food for God's children and the children passively receive the food. This relationship reflects the Matthean community's dependence on God for food in the beginning of the narrative. God feeds God's creatures directly as a parent who knows the children need good (not bad) food to survive. There is some evidence, however, that God uses intermediaries to feed God's children. The ones who need food are primarily passive receivers of the food and accept the good food that is offered, but they also become givers of food and, as parents, repay the gift of food by providing for their children.

God Feeds Directly

In a very clear way, God, as Father and Mother, feeds the Matthean community directly and therefore there are no intermediaries. Both images of Father and Mother can be teased out of the text. The heavenly Father (7:11) is provider and this shows the direct and authoritative link between the heavenly Father and the Matthean community. The Father is much more ("how much more," v. 11) capable of supplying good things to those who ask him. The way the Father in heaven provides food is as a parent. The example in vv. 9–10 shows a parent feeding a child. Explicit language for children, which is rare in this unit, is used. The ease and expectancy with which one can ask and receive food in this passage, the way the questions are framed in vv. 9–10 to expect a negative response and the family language all indicate a willing parent who feeds the children. This, then, summons the image of God as a mother who nurses the children she brought into the world. The audience is led to the realization, "of course, a parent will feed the one she brought into the world." There is a sense of intimacy and continued connection between God and "those who ask him."[31] The creator will continue to sustain the one whom she created and the parent will do the same for her child. Isaiah 49:15 is called to mind,[32] "Can a woman forget her nursing child, or show no compassion for the child of her womb? Even these may forget, yet I will not forget you." There is an understanding that the parent has a "unilateral nurturing responsibility" in relation to her child.[33] The parent will not forget, she knows her child needs fed.[34]

God as the one who "knows" is apparent in all three passages this study has covered so far (i.e. 6:1–21, 6:25–34, 7:7–11) as all three use "know" (οἶδα) in relationship to the Father in heaven.[35] The Father in heaven is an all-knowing God who sees into secret or hidden places of life, has knowledge and is present in these places. God sees and understands. As nursing Mother, she knows she must provide food out of her body, the earth, for her creatures. As this study claimed in 6:1–21, this is also the same God who creates—the three aspects of seeing, knowing, and creating are intertwined in 6:1–21 and so here.[36] The Father in heaven, the nursing Mother know that their children need food.

God provides "good things" (ἀγαθὰ), which at least includes good food, to "those who ask him."[37] God does not, then, provide bad food,[38] such as a stone or a snake.[39] Both stone and serpent are associated with the devil tempting God's creatures by feeding them that which they are not to have. The stone recalls Matthew 4 where the "the one tempting" (ὁ πειράζων) offers Jesus a stone and tempts him to make it into bread. This can be seen as an act of competition between God and the devil as to who is the provider of food—the devil offers stones, God offers bread (from heaven). In 7:9, then, even though those offering food are evil, they are not the devil and they provide food from God in heaven. The parent becomes aligned with God due to the parent's choice of offering. God provides good food, bread from heaven and not bad food (i.e. stones), which the devil supplies. Once again, the early part of the narrative is reinforcing the community's distinct identity as separate and independent from those who receive food from sources other than God.

The serpent in 7:10 is often associated with the tempting of Eve in Genesis 3. While Eve is not tempted to eat the serpent (as in 7:10), the presence of the serpent in 7:10 suggests that Genesis 3 (and Matthew 4) might be recalled. All three passages (7:10, 4:1–11, and Genesis 3) have three elements in common: the serpent/devil,[40] food, and temptation. Genesis 3 portrays a serpent that tempts Eve with fruit, the devil tempts Jesus with stones/bread in 4:1–11 and a parent is tempted to give a serpent as food to his child in 7:10. As a parent is tempted to feed a child a stone instead of bread in 7:9, in 7:10 a parent might also offer the child a serpent instead of fish, which implies that food might come from the devil instead of from God. But, as the parent chooses bread over the stone, so the parent chooses the fish over the serpent. The parent once again is aligned with God, not the devil, as the one who provides food. The association that 7:9–10 makes with Genesis 3 further sets the image of God in the context of one who creates. While not explicitly asserting that God is creator in 7:7–11, the reference to God who knows (οἶδα) in 7:11 and the association with Genesis 3 both imply God who feeds is the one who creates.[41]

God Feeds Indirectly

God feeds directly. There is also evidence, however, that there are intermediaries to God's provisions such that food is given indirectly. The life example given in the argument in 7:7–11 is of earthly parents feeding their children. Clearly in this example, children get their food through their earthly parents not straight from God. The sequence of giving in 7:7–11, moreover, is from God to human parent to children. Those who ask in vv. 7–8 become those who give in vv. 9–11a (human parent) who then become those who ask and receive in v. 11b. Therefore, following the chain of giving, God (from whom all food begins) gives food to the human parent ("those who ask" in v. 7–8 who become the human parent givers in v. 9–11a) who give food to their children (vv. 9–11a).[42]

Human participation is emphasized more in 7:7–11 than in 6:11 and 6:25–34. In the former two passages, Matthew hints at some human participation in the food exchange process as the community is involved with the process of acquiring food yet it is still primarily receiving the food. Humans seek food—look for ways God is providing food—and there is an indirect comment in 6:25–34 (when talking about what birds of the air do not do) to acknowledge the human effort to sow, reap and gather. In 7:7–11, however, humans have a more direct role in the distribution of food as they give bread to their children. Human participation is increasing through the narrative while God's role is beginning to move behind the scenes.

In the exchange of food it is necessary to explain not only how food is distributed but also how food is received. There are two groups of people who receive food in this passage: (1) "son" and "children" and (2) "those who ask." These two groups and the way they are involved in food exchange charts the course for how food is primarily received in chapters 6–7: as passive recipients who, nevertheless, are beginning to show signs of becoming more actively involved in food distribution. God is the one who gives, but the earthly parent also serves as an intermediary to receive and give to his human children. Therefore, as those who receive, there are the son and the children in one group (vv. 9–11) and "those who ask" and receive in the second group (vv. 7–8, 11b).

The reception of food in 7:7–11 follows the second and third steps in the Maussian process.[43] The first group, the "son" and "children," receive food as they are obligated to (i.e. second step) and the second group, "those who ask," offer repayment (i.e. third step). The process of food exchange within the family exemplifies the obligatory nature that Mauss outlines and reinforces the strong social ties among a kinship group.

The son and children ask for bread and fish and there is an expectation they will be given such. This first group coincides with the second step in the model for Mauss' gift exchange—the obligation to receive. The son and children do not appear to refuse the food but receive it. They are passive receivers, portrayed as completely dependent upon their parent for food. They are not producing or distributing bread. Reminiscent of 6:1–21, this group actively, urgently, and intensely asks (αἰτέω in 7:9, 10) for food, which shows a confidence in receiving it, a confidence which is depicted in vv. 7–8.

The children also ask for the food which the giver most probably is providing and do not ask for forbidden food or food that is not available. This is the flip side of the fact that the parents do not provide bad food. As with 6:11, the son and children ask for bread, which is the food God offers (4:4). They accept the authority of God and deny the authority of other providers, thus the devil. They also ask for fish.[44] In the narrative, God compassionately supplies fish to those within and outside of the Matthean community (7:10, 14:13–21, 15:29–38).[45] Fish are from the sea, an uninhabitable part of the natural world, and God as creator orders the relationship between nature and humanity to feed the world.[46] Asking for and accepting fish recognizes God as the one who brings the creation into order.

The second group, "those who ask" (vv. 7–8 and 11b) coincides with the third step—the obligation to repay. This is the first instance of this third step in the Matthean narrative. They ask and are assured that they will receive food in vv. 7–8 and 11b. At this point, they are similar to the "son" and "children" in vv. 9–11a—they are dependent, passive receivers who may ask for their food but do not in any other way participate in the food distribution process. This second group is, however, more assertive than the first group in that it asks, seeks, and knocks, demonstrating a higher level of activity of seeking. More than the seeking in 6:25–34 (i.e. careful investigation and the processing of new information), this second group is knocking on doors with the expectation of finding and obtaining food from others.[47] Even more, as mentioned before, this group then becomes the givers, the parents in vv. 9–11a. Here, they distribute food to their children. This act of distribution can be considered the third step in the Maussian process—the obligation to repay. While this second group does not repay the original giver—the Father in heaven—that direct repayment is not necessary. Because the exchange is asymmetric in power (i.e. the Father in heaven has more power than "those who ask"), the repayment does not have to be equal in kind or timely in nature. This type of generalized reciprocity may not even have a repayment. It may, however, take the form of service or loyalty.[48] One form of service to the original giver, God, is the giving to others.[49] This is what happens in vv. 9–11a where the one who asked and received (the second group) gives to the son and children (the first group).

The sequence of food exchange in 7:7–11, then, follows a similar sequence as Mauss' three obligations in exchanging gifts: to give, to receive, to repay. In the way Mauss' model has been used here, it has included an understanding of Sahlins' generalized reciprocity model, a gift-like generalized exchange which is made between partners with asymmetric power relations and the receiver thus responds with a repayment that is not necessarily equal in kind or time. In 7:7–11, the passage moves through giving, receiving and repayment. It begins with the one who asks (7:7a), who quickly becomes the one who receives (7:7–8). The one who receives then becomes the one who gives or repays (7:9–10), who finally becomes the one who asks of a gift from the ultimate giver (7:11). While the passage begins with receiving the gift, the order of events follows Mauss' model: receive (the asker receives), repay (the receiver gives back), give (the ultimate giver, the heavenly Father, gives). The power relations are asymmetric as made clear by the parent—child relationship in 7:9–10 and the divine-human relationship in 7:11. The type of exchange has a gift quality to it since there are no expectations of equal or timely repayments.

Conclusion: Matthew's Narrative and 7:7–11

The passage in 7:7–11 is paradigmatic for the way that the Matthean community exchanges food within its own borders and with the world through the Matthean narrative. As a transition passage from the first unit to the second unit, 7:7–11 charts a course for the audience to follow. Regarding the order in which the community receives or gives food, the sequence in 7:7–11, as explained above, moves from asking to receiving to giving and then cycles back to asking. In the larger Matthean narrative, the community is primarily the receiver of food at the beginning of the narrative but then becomes more and more assertive in giving food as the narrative unfolds. The community, however, also cycles back to receiving through the narrative. Specifically, the narrative begins with the community asking for food (6:11) and proceeds to the asker receiving food (6:25–34, 10:5–11:1). The asker then becomes the one who gives or repays beginning with 7:9–10 and continuing in 14:13–22. In 15:29–39, the community participates in giving but also receives, cycling back to the beginning.

Not only does this ask-receive-give-ask sequence follow the narrative, the ask-seek-knock sequence in 7:7–11 demonstrates how the Matthean community becomes more assertive in participating in food exchange through the narrative while the role of God quietly moves to the background. The community asks, as in prayer in 6:7–8, 11, then seeks more actively in looking for God's providence in 6:25–34. In 10:5–11:1, the community goes house to house, "knocking on doors", receiving food in exchange for work and participating, even if misguided, in finding food for the crowds (Matt 14:13–22, 15:29–39). God, in the meantime, is not directly mentioned in food exchange in Matt 10 or Matt 14 and 15, although his role is apparent in the context of food exchange. These shifting roles support the view of God as one who acts in the world, not on the world, and encourages responsibility among humans.

The emphasis in 7:7–11 is on the exchange of food within the family, the strengthening of social bonds, and the distinction from the world around it. Still, there are subtle references to the sharing of food with those outside the family or community as a sign that ties with the larger world are forthcoming. The beginning of Matthew's narrative focuses on the exchange of food within Matthew's community and only gradually opens up that exchange with the wider world. Later in Matthew's narrative, the community exchanges with the larger Jewish community (10:5–11:1), some Jewish leaders and the natural world (12:1–8), and the larger world Jewish and Gentile world (14:13–22, 15:29–39).

Part III

Food Exchange Outside the Community

Chapter 6

Hospitality (10:5–11:1)

Introduction

Second Thematic Unit

The second thematic unit (i.e. Matthew 10:5–11:1 and 12:1–8) emphasizes the exchange of food with those outside the Matthean community. Food continues to flow in one direction into the Matthean community, as with the first thematic unit, but does so through the larger Jewish community outside the Matthean boundaries. The lost sheep of the house of Israel feed the laborers in 10:5–11:1. In 12:1–8, the larger Jewish community through its gleaning laws and grainfields, with the inclusion of the Pharisees but a distinction from those associated with the Temple, feed the disciples.

The location of food exchange, reflecting the broader sphere of sharing, is situated in the households and grainfields of the larger Jewish community. The arena expands outside the Matthean households into the homes of extended family (10:5–11:1) and then out into less inhabited, outdoor places. The trend in the narrative is toward space more related to the physical features of the earth, which begins in this unit and continues in the third unit. As the locations and channels of food distribution expand, so does the conflict surrounding exchange. The disciples receive food amidst persecution from Jewish and Gentile authorities in 10:5–11:1 and controversy with Jewish leaders, particular those associated with the Temple, in 12:1–8.

God becomes less visible as the human community and natural world take more responsibility as intermediaries in distributing food. The explicit use of God as Father continues to fade in this second unit but the image of God as Mother who gives and defends life continues to be present while the view of God as creator, provider, and liberator gains strength. The Matthean community takes more initiative in seeking out food but is still portrayed as dependent and vulnerable as sojourners, guests, laborers, and the poor. Finally, as the Matthean community reaches out to interact with the larger Jewish community, food exchange emphasizes the social needs of belonging to this community in 10:5–11:1 and 12:1–8. The sharing of food, however, also highlights the need to differentiate and maintain independence as the Matthean community is juxtaposed with two sets of Jewish leaders in 12:1–8 allying with the Pharisees but distinguishing itself from those associated with the Temple.

Matthew 10:5–11:1

Matthew 10:5–11:1 begins the second unit of this study. The Matthean community moves out into more public and dangerous space to receive food from God indirectly through those outside its community. God's character is revealed yet emphasis is shifted to the human community in distributing food. God as Father and Mother becomes more directly linked to God as creator. Matthew's community is more active in participating in food exchange yet remains largely dependent upon others as it is depicted in vulnerable ways as laborers, guests and "little ones." The larger Jewish community, as the lost sheep of the house of Israel, becomes the main channel through which God feeds through its hospitality. Food exchange, based on need and not status, widens the sphere of kinship relations beyond the Matthean community to include the larger Jewish community and provides comfort in the context of conflict and suffering. As the Matthean community ventures out beyond its household, social needs to connect with the larger Jewish community becomes the predominate motivation for food exchange and political needs to show independence becomes less critical.

The specific subunits that will be discussed within this larger section are: 10:5–15, 10:26–31, and 10:40–42. These limits are chosen by identifying the passages on food exchange and then determining the narrative contexts from these passages. The passages on food exchange in the section are 10:10 ("the worker is worthy of his food") and 10:42 ("whoever gives one of these little ones a cup of cold water to drink").[1] Both of these passages fall within a larger narrative section, 10:5–11:1, in which Jesus gives instructions to his twelve disciples/apostles regarding a mission to the lost sheep of the house of Israel.

The first passage on food exchange, 10:10, is located within the first subunit, 10:5–15. This subunit focuses on instructions to the disciples, tasks to be accomplished and their reception. Beyond food exchange and the real need that disciples have for food, the household setting is a feature in common with other passages studied. The limit is set at v. 15 because the tone of the narrative changes significantly from vv. 5–15 to vv. 16–23[2] and the geographical and time setting broaden.[3]

The second passage on food exchange, 10:42, is located within the final subunit, 10:40–10:42. This subunit concludes the instructions Jesus gives to the disciples. Several features tie it in with 10:5–15 and previous passages of this study: the focus on reception, the use of δέχομαι (six times in 10:40–42; also in 10:5–15 in 10:14), the mention of reward with the use of μισθός (10:42, 6:1–21) or consequences for one's actions (10:15), the reference to Matthew's community as the "little ones" or "you of little faith" (10:42, 6:30) or those of lower status (10:10, laborers). A condensed chiastic structure of 10:5–10:42, argued by Davies and Allison, follows:[4]

(a) 5–15 (Instructions to missionaries and their reception)
    (b) 16–23
        (c) 24f
            (d) 26–32 (Consolation and encouragement)
        (c) 32f
    (b) 34–39
(a) 40–42 (Reception of missionaries and its reward)

I adjust this outline and include 11:1 at the end because it parallels 5a in providing a framework (10:5a and 11:1) around the discourse proper (10:5b–10:42)[5] and refers to *Jesus* (10:5a, 11:1) who gives *orders* (παραγγέλλω—10:5a, διατάσσω—11:1) to the *twelve* (10:5a, 11:1). This structure provides another rationale for including vv. 5–15 and vv. 40–42 in the units I cover. Both address the reception of those sent by Jesus. The structure also provides a reason to include vv. 26–32 because it is the center of the chiasm and, as such, can function as the "interpretive focal point of the passage."[6]

The third subunit is 10:26–32, the center of the chiasm, which can help to explain the whole passage and, in particular, 10:5–15 and

10:40–42, which serve as the contexts for the passages on food exchange. Not only the center, however, this unit refers to important features which are present in other passages studied: (a) the secrecy motif, with the use of κρυπτός (10:26; 6:4, 6, 18 in 6:1–21), (b) the concern for creation, in particular, birds (10:29, 6:26), (c) multiple references to the themes of fear and anxiety in 10:26–32 and 6:25–34 (φοβέομαι in 10:26, 28 and μεριμνάω in 6:25, 27, 28, 31, 34), and (d) references to God as Father (πατήρ), also used in 6:1–21, 6:25–34, and 7:7–11.

Bold Missionaries or Dependent Laborers? (10:5–15)

Introduction

Jesus sends out the twelve into cities and villages to proclaim and heal the lost sheep of the house of Israel. Matthew's community is represented as "the twelve" at the beginning of 10:5–15 and is portrayed as moving out and acting upon the world. While the disciples continue to be the main representatives of Matthew's community, the characterization of the community as "the twelve" who move out into the world is a significant shift from how they have been represented and how they have moved toward and interacted with the world in previous passages. To this point in the narrative, the community has been depicted as children or those of little faith who have remained within the Matthean household.[7] In 10:5–11:1, Matthew's community as "the twelve" is told to venture out from their own households, the primary setting where food exchange has occurred to this point in the narrative, to go into the house of Israel, cities and villages and specific houses of the lost sheep of the house of Israel, to move out and act upon the world.[8]

The use of "the twelve" (δώδεκα) draws a connection between the community and Israel's twelve tribes,[9] a tribally organized coalition with no central government that settled into the land of Canaan in approximately 1200 B.C.E. Occupying this land of milk and honey, promised to Abraham's descendants by Yahweh (Gen 12, 15, 17), marked a new beginning for the Israelites as they moved from slavery in Egypt to a become a new community with Yahweh as their God and the Torah as their law. The use of "the twelve" characterizes

Matthew's community as Israel and its movement to restore[10] the lost sheep as Yahweh's faithful people who follow the Torah as interpreted by Matthew's community. The depiction of movement toward and action upon the world, however, is not sustained in the narrative. Soon, the bold and independent twelve become vulnerable and needy laborers who depend on the lost sheep for their food.

Settings of 10:5–15

Matthew's community is instructed to enter three different settings: the house of Israel (10:6), cities and villages (10:11), and a specific house where they will stay (10:12, 13, 14). Each setting encompasses the next, so that the house of Israel is the setting in which the Matthean community will find cities and villages, and these cities and villages include a specific house where they will lodge.

House of Israel. As the Matthean community ventures out into the "house of Israel" (οἴκου Ἰσραήλ), the setting for food exchange expands from the Matthean family or household to its extended family or household.[11] The house in the sense of "house of Israel" refers not to a building or single family/household but a whole tribe of people, descendants, community or nation.[12] Ezekiel 34:30 explains that the house of Israel is "my people, says the Lord God." They are the people of Yahweh who were brought out of Egypt, given the Torah, brought into the promised land, sent into exile, and then brought back to their land through Cyrus. As Saldarini points out, Israel in Matthew points to both the land of Israel and the "historical, ethnic, religious group of people who lived in the land, believed in the God of Israel"[13] and practiced a way of life in accordance with this tradition and God.

The use of house continues the focus in Matthew's narrative within a household unit, a household, a family, but this metaphorical use broadens the meaning of house and includes an extended family,[14] a larger community.[15] In 10:5–11:1, the Matthean group[16] is now being sent out to interact with the larger Jewish community with which it is a part. The Matthean community, which has been described as a family and has interacted within its own house to exchange food, is now entering into the larger Jewish community, its extended family.

The setting is the house of Israel, but the specific characters to which the Matthean community is to preach and heal are the lost sheep. The lost sheep of the house of Israel are typically defined either as a group within the larger house of Israel or as all the people of Israel.[17] This study defines it as a group within the larger house but not in the sense of poor leaders who will need to be replaced by the leadership of the Matthean community. Still interpreting οἴκου Ἰσραήλ as a partitive genitive, the Matthean community as one part of Israel, one household/family within Israel, is seeking to proclaim to and heal another equally valued part of Israel which represents the extended household/family. As 10:5–15 progresses, the twelve who proclaim to and heal the lost sheep become the laborers who are guests at "the house" (οἰκία). "The house" replaces the "lost sheep" as the designator for those with whom the Matthean community interacts. The Matthean community, as one household within the house of Israel, interacts with "the house," another household of Israel, when the activity becomes food exchange and not the activity of proclaiming and healing.

Cities and Villages. The setting of cities and villages in 10:5–15 demonstrates that food exchange is beginning to take place in the narrative in more inhabited and public places, space more related to the physical features of the earth as topographical space, and space which is also more dangerous.[18] The place of food exchange is not only extended to a larger household or community with the use of "house of Israel" but it is also extended to all those cities and villages within that larger community. The terms "city" and "village" are coupled together only twice in the narrative: 9:35 and 10:11. In 9:35, Jesus goes throughout "all the cities and villages" teaching, proclaiming and healing. "Cities and villages" used together along with the modifier "all" is a way of saying that Jesus goes "everywhere" to teach, proclaim, and heal.[19] In many ways, the instructions to the mission of the disciples in Matt 10 imitates Jesus' own mission thus far in the narrative.[20] The nearly parallel instructions to the disciples to proclaim and heal and to go to city and village suggest that the disciples are also to go "everywhere." The phrasing is different—10:11 says "into *whichever city or village* you go . . ." The use of "whichever" reinforces the view that one is to go "everywhere" with the idea that the disciples are to go to many cities and villages in general not to a few specific cities and villages in particular.

While there is no consistent trend through the narrative on whether cities are places of security/promise or threat/danger, generally speaking cities are more likely to be a place of security and promise before chapter 10 and more likely to be places of threat and danger after chapter 10.[21] This makes chapter 10 a transition point for the narrative. Concerning the exchange of food, it is the point at which the community moves out of its own more private household in order to exchange food with the larger and more public world and it is in the world, then, that the exchange of food becomes more threatening.[22]

As a transition point, cities and villages in 10:11, 14, 15 are places of both security/promise and of danger/threat. The order is telling: verses 11–13a portray cities and villages as places of security while verses 13b–15 places of threat. In 10:11, the city or village is a place of promise and hospitality. The disciples are to inquire who in the city or village is worthy and remain there until they leave (v. 11). The assumption is that a hospitable place to stay will be present. In v. 13, two scenarios are given that provide instructions on whether to let one's peace come upon the house or not. The first scenario gives instructions pertaining to the house being worthy, letting one's peace come upon it, and staying there. Verses 10–13a, then, show a picture of cities and villages as welcoming and places of security. Beginning with 13b and continuing through v. 15, the picture shifts to cities and villages as places of inhospitality—instructions are given about how to treat houses or cities that are not worthy and do not receive or listen to the words of the disciples.

The setting for food exchanging is moving out into more public and inhabited places which are more connected to the earth as topographical spaces.[23] The Matthean community is getting more and more accustomed to exchanging food in public. Not only more public places, but more dangerous places as well. While public places were not depicted as decidedly more dangerous in 6:1–21, they are now becoming more threatening venues. Glimpses of this trend can be seen in 6:25–34 and 7:7–11,[24] but a clearer presence of danger has begun with chapter 10.

Specific Household. While the setting of food exchange moves out into a larger Jewish community (house of Israel) and into more public, inhabited places (cities and villages), it continues to be located within a household as it has been in previous passages. This new household, however, does not belong to Matthew's community but one which is part of the lost sheep of the house of Israel. As chapter 10 provides a transition point for how cities and villages are portrayed more dangerously in the Matthean narrative, so does it demonstrate a shift in how the activity within houses (οἶκος or οἰκία) are depicted as more inhospitable, unworthy and locations of judgment.[25]

In the Matthean narrative before chapter 10, houses are a place of worship (2:11), of gift-giving (2:11), where tax collectors and sinners recline at table (9:10) and of healing (8:6, 14, 9:6–7, 9:23, 9:28). The houses represented are often connected to Matthew's community (e.g. Jesus' house, house of Peter's Mother-in-law, 2:11, 8:14, 9:10, 9:28) but are also places where those with authority outside of the Matthean community reside (e.g. ruler in 9:23, centurion in 8:6). On the one hand, houses are often depicted in ways to symbolize proclamation, prophetic activity, and/or mission work (5:15) and faithful or unfaithful discipleship (5:15, 7:24–27). On the other hand, houses may be places of healing, worship, and gift-giving that are not associated with mission work, conversion, recruitment, membership or group building. In these depictions of houses, Jesus is usually the main character who heals, is worshiped, and reclines, although the disciples play a primary role in proclamation and discipleship.

In the Matthean narrative after chapter 10, houses are primarily places where opposing and evil presences reside and where conflict ensues. Rulers who are in conflict with the Matthean community live in houses (11:8) and extend their opposing authority to houses (17:25). The Temple, as a house of worship, has become a den of robbers (21:13) and Jerusalem, as a house, has become desolate (23:39). Houses are associated with evil[26] and are places of internal conflict.[27] There are a few examples in which houses are places associated with God and Jesus[28] but they are also places to be left (19:29, 24:17).

Within 10:5–15 itself, the view of houses, like cities and villages, marks a transition point in the Matthean narrative. In vv. 12–13a, like chapters 1–9, houses are potential places of hospitality for the Matthean community, worthy and peaceful locales. They are outside of the Matthean community but become connected to it through interaction. In vv. 13b–15, like chapters following Matthew 10, houses become potential locations of inhospitality, unworthiness, and judgment. They oppose Matthew's community, are associated with evil (i.e. Sodom and Gomorrah), and are places to be left (10:14). As this transition takes place and as the environment becomes more hostile, Matthew's community is extending outward to exchange food with those beyond its community.

Characters in 10:5–15

The Shift. In 10:5–15, 40–42 Matthew's community is first depicted as the one who is taking initiative, the one who will act upon another, the one going out into the cities and villages. The twelve are sent to proclaim and heal the lost sheep of the house of Israel. Matthew's community is bold and independent and the larger Jewish community is adrift and needy.[29] Weaver's concluding remarks of 10:5b–15 fit these observations, that the disciples are described in "strongly active terms" and "take initiative" while the lost sheep of the house of Israel "merely respond to their initiatives."[30]

This description of a community in the lead and providing for others is short-lived in 10:5–15. The Matthean community soon becomes a group that is vulnerable and dependent upon others both in 10:5–15 and in 10:40–42. The community does indeed take some initiative as it inquires into where food may be found, enters homes, and works for food but the bold and independent twelve become laborers and guests and the lost sheep become providers and hosts. The initial images and implied relationship of the twelve and lost sheep are presented in vv. 5–6 but are not repeated or reiterated later in the chapter. New images and implied relationships appear in vv. 10–15 where Matthew's community is described as a laborer (εργάτης) and the Jewish community becomes a home which provides hospitality.

The shift begins in v. 9, which has the opening phrase μὴ κτήσησθε (do not acquire) and ends with the image of the laborer. The terms in vv. 7–8 clearly stake out the previous depiction of independence and power: "going out," "heal," "raise," "cleanse," "cast out," "give," but v. 9 begins with "do not acquire." The verb κτάομαι can be translated as "take" or "acquire."[31] Various reasons are given for why the disciples should not either take or acquire these items.[32] I argue, however, that the narrative includes this instruction at the beginning of v. 9, along with a description of the disciples as laborers at the end of the verse, in order to demonstrate that the Matthean community continues to be dependent upon food from others.

The description of money, clothes, and accessories that one is to avoid taking[33] in vv. 9–10 ensures that the disciples were to look and act like guests with a concern about where to stay in order to receive food and lodging.[34] The description introduces vv. 11–15, which explains the process of entering a city or village and finding a house in which to stay. Households may resist hosting a guest who has high status and might threaten their power. A guest, in an ambivalent and liminal position between a hostile stranger and a rival with equal power, is always considered a potential threat in the house of the host and therefore a power difference must be maintained.[35] The disciples are to be inconspicuous.[36] The Matthean community is not only carrying out a mission but it is also acquiring food and establishing social relationships in order to survive. The lack of possessions is not primarily to be seen as a dependence on God[37] as dependence on other humans. This type of behavior is part of the process of the Matthean community slowly and cautiously increasing its interaction with the world around it in order to survive.[38]

While needing to be good guests and moving toward a more vulnerable position, the Matthean community continues to "seek" food in the food exchange passages.[39] The community is now doing more than asking (6:1–21), acquiring information (6:25–34), and attempting to obtain food (7:7–11). By inquiring, entering the house, and working for its food, the community has become more active and mobile in their participation of food exchange. In 10:5–11:1, the community has encompassed all the types of seeking it has done so far in the narrative and added new ones.

As the community enters a city or village and prepares to find a place to stay (for food and lodging), it is to inquire (ἐξετάζω) who is worthy, that is, who will host them (v. 11).[40] The community does not stop at inquiring, however, and enters the house and works for its food. The image of "entering a house" corresponds to that of "knocking and opening" in 7:7–8. The process of seeking in 7:7–11, which had progressed in the narrative to the concept of trying to obtain food and the strong expectation that it would be transferred, has moved further along than knocking in 10:5–11:1 to entering the house. Not only has the image shifted, but the setting has shifted as well. While a child attempts to obtain food from a parent in his own house in 7:7–11, a worker enters the house of another in 10:5–11. The community, then, understands the food exchange to involve labor in another person's home (10:10). No longer portrayed as a child, the community works for its food as sojourners and laborers.

"Laborer." The shift in the image of the community from the "twelve" to "laborers" further supports the view that the community is in a position of need and is seeking interaction. The community is still active in seeking, but is in a dependent position. The ἐργάτης (laborer) can be translated as a "worker" but a better translation for this study is a "laborer" or "day laborer."[41] The use in Matthew 20 (and perhaps the use in Matthew 9) corresponds with the way many scholars describe day laborers in the first-century: those who worked for minimal wages, did not have a permanent job, were lower in status than peasant farmers and tenants, and struggled for survival from day to day.[42]

The image of the laborer in 10:10 switches the power difference between those sent out by Jesus and those to whom they are sent. Instead of the Matthean community sent out to act upon the lost sheep (to proclaim and heal), the community is now in need of hospitality (to be acted upon) from those in the house. The laborer image is of one who does indeed work and is active, but also one who needs daily food, a dependent position. Verses 9–10 make sense, then, as introducing vv. 11–15 (on hospitality) rather than concluding vv. 5–8 (on mission).[43]

Hospitality not Conversion. As the characterization of the Matthean community changes from one who acts upon to one who is acted upon, so the lost sheep of the house of Israel shifts to one who acts. The focus of vv. 11–15 is usually upon disciples and their process of deciding which house to stay as part of their mission to proclaim and heal, but few comment on those who will be hosting the disciples. The οἰκία in 10:12 and 10:13, part of the lost sheep of the house of Israel, become the hosts and actively receive the laborers.[44] The laborers as guests now look to the host for a place to stay and food to eat. The lost sheep will distribute food to the laborers in return for their work.[45]

Matthew 10:11–13 describes the process of finding a house in which to stay. The criterion is whether a house is "worthy" (ἄξιος) or not. It is only in v. 14 that the audience is told that the criterion expands to whether or not a house "receives you" (δέξηται ὑμᾶς) and "listens to your words" (ἀκούσῃ τοὺς λόγους ὑμῶν). The use of "worthy," "receives you" and "listens to your words" all point to the theme of hospitality.

First, "worthy" can refer to repentance or hospitality. "Worthy" (ἄξιος) is used in 3:8, 10:10, 11, 13, 10:37, 38, and 22:8. In general, it is a word that refers to the relationship between two things or persons—how two items correspond or are comparable.[46] In the Matthean narrative, "worthy" has more than one meaning. In can be interpreted as repentance, the acknowledgment of a certain god and joining a particular group.[47] In its use in 10:10 ("the laborer is worthy of his food"), however, the meaning shifts to the realm of hospitality. Worthiness depends upon the rules of hospitality for both guests and hosts. The guest is worthy if he has fulfilled his part of the guest-host relationship, which in part is to work as a laborer in the household.

In vv. 10:11, 13, and perhaps 22:8, the meaning of worthy is similar to 10:10 and further emphasizes the idea of hospitality. In 22:8, there is no mention that those invited did not repent but rather they did not accept the invitation, they were not good guests.[48] In 10:11, 13, the house is worthy or not in relation to hosting the guests. The house is worthy not based on whether it will repent, follow Jesus or join the Matthean community; rather the house is worthy based on whether it will host the guests, whether it will receive and listen to their words. Receive and listen to their words refers to hospitality not to repentance.

Most scholars read the phrase δέξηται ὑμᾶς and ἀκούσῃ τοὺς λόγους ὑμῶν (10:14) to mean the house is to receive the message of the disciples, the gospel, and/or God's kingdom.[49] The implication of these readings is that the phrase is about receiving/believing/trusting a certain message, repentance and becoming part of the Matthean community. I argue that "worthy" is about hospitality, and to receive or, better, welcome the laborers and listen to their words is a phrase that relates to hospitality.[50] First, there is no mention of repentance in 10:5–15. Jesus does not tell the disciples to call for repentance even though he himself includes it in his ministry (4:17, cf. 3:2—John the Baptist).[51] Second, the use of δέχομαι in the rest of the Matthean narrative does not necessarily mean to receive and be committed to a message.[52] It is used three times in chapter 10, but is also used in 11:14 and 18:5 to mean intellectual assent and welcoming a child as an act of hospitality.[53]

Third, the use of listen (ἀκούω) in 10:14 is rather unique compared to its use in other parts of the Matthean narrative where "listen" is typically listed first and is followed by another action (e.g. listen and understand, 13:19, 15:10; listen and proclaim, 10:27; listen and do, 7:24).[54] The implication is that one is first to listen and then to commit to a particular act in response to what one heard (e.g. to listen and then understand, to listen and then follow, etc.). Even this pattern, however, is not followed by many of the uses of listen. Not all uses show characters that later follow Jesus or repent or become part of Matthew's community.[55] To listen does not necessarily mean to receive and be committed to someone's message. In 10:15, listen comes after receive not before it. One is to first receive and then to listen to words of the laborers.

Furthermore, there are no other hints in this passage that those in the house are to be converted or recruited or to be regular members within Matthew's community.[56] There is no call to repentance, no mention of faith/belief in or loyalty/obedience to Jesus, and no use of family language. Those in the house do not follow the disciples after the disciples stay with them. There is no clear socialization or integration into the community.[57]

To be worthy as a laborer or a host and to receive and listen to their words as a host belong in the category of hospitality.[58] This method of hosting and feeding, a household that provides for laborers, draws on a tradition within the Hebrew Bible where the household serves as a provider for members and marginals.[59] As part of this tradition, the household provides hospitality for sojourners traveling through who might stop for a day or several days on their journey. The sojourner, as the Matthean community is characterized in 10:9–10, travels and settles briefly in another household.[60] The sojourner is expected to support the household in exchange for his protection and provision. That support may have been in the form of a hired laborer.[61] As sojourners labor for the household so they become part of the household economy. In return for their labor, they receive wages and also share in the produce of the sabbatical year (Lev 25:6) as well as receive foodstuffs as part of the household economy.[62] The sojourner turned laborer has the right to gleanings, either those in the field or on the vine (Lev 19:10, 23:22, Deut 24:19–21).[63]

The lost sheep, as the larger Jewish community who share the history, land, and traditions of the Jewish people with Matthew's community,[64] would know this custom of providing hospitality to laborers. The placement of the phrase in 10:10, when addressing the Matthean community, reminds that community that those they are sent to (i.e. the lost sheep) are familiar with this custom and are called upon to enact it for sojourners, whether the lost sheep consider the Matthean community as fellow Israelites or sojourners from a foreign land.

Several aspects of hospitality are prevalent in Matthew 10:10–15.[65] The passage involves the traveling motif as the disciples are entering new cities or villages in Jewish territory. The roles of guest and host are present—the laborers are guests who need a place to stay and the house is the host where the guests will "remain." The stay is temporary as the travelers move through the area, the instructions are to "remain until you leave" (v. 11).[66] A protocol guides the hospitality process. The process of the guests are attended to more explicitly regarding how they will decide on where to stay and that they will bring peace upon the house in which they remain.[67] The process of the hosts is less explicit but the passage states that they will receive and listen to their words. To receive might refer to showing proper honor to the guests, not showing hostility, protecting and providing for the guest.[68] In addition, the host might test a guest as part of the process of receiving strangers. One form of test was to invite the guest to speak on his behalf.[69] The expectation that the host will "listen to your words" may be a reference to that test (as opposed to conversion) or simply to express good manners. Food and lodging were the primary needs of the guests and the proper expectations of hosts and both are mentioned.[70] With a history of the practice of hospitality in the Jewish community, it would be typical for those within the house of Israel to offer hospitality to a traveling stranger.

Finally, the reference to Sodom and Gomorrah provides further evidence that this passage refers to hospitality. The primary sin or reason for the destruction of Sodom and Gomorrah is not clear,[71] but one prominent reason is the lack of hospitality as the men of the city try to violently rape the two visiting guests at Lot's house (Gen 19:1–11).[72] The placement of the reference to Sodom and Gomorrah in Matthew 10:15 as a bookend to 10:5 where Jesus sends out the disciples to travel and immediately after 10:11–14 where the disciples are trying to find a place to stay mutually reinforces the point that the reference to Sodom and Gomorrah and vv. 11–14 are primarily about hospitality. The houses are worthy in that they receive and listen to the words of the disciples as good hosts. To be worthy in vv. 11–14 is to practice good hospitality. This fits with the use of worthy in v. 10, a laborer is worthy in that he is a good guest.

Food Exchange With Sojourners. The type of exchange regarding hospitality with sojourners and within the household economy of laborers is generalized reciprocity. This type of reciprocity can vary from a "pure" type of altruism where nothing is expected in return to a form closer to, but not the same as, balanced reciprocity where a counterobligation is expected but is still differentiated from trade.[73] The form in 10:5–11:1 lies somewhere along this continuum. On the one hand, it approaches altruism in its reflection of Yahweh's provision of the Israelites. Yahweh's abundant and selfless provision clearly cannot have an equal return nor is one expected. Likewise a host who provides for sojourners does not expect a similar return in time, quantity or quality. On the other hand, the exchange has aspects of reciprocity closer to the balanced form. The sojourner as laborer works in the household economy as part of his responsibilities as guest according to the customs of hospitality. While this is clearly not trade nor is it a balanced return in similar kind nor are the social ties in the exchange to be subordinated to economic needs,[74] there is a more timely and perhaps similar quantitive return of services for the gift of hospitality that is offered.

Generalized reciprocity is also supported by the statement in 10:8, freely you received, freely give (δωρεὰν ἐλάβετε, δωρεὰν δότε). This combination of an indicative and imperative is typically associated with the disciples charge to preach and heal in vv. 7–8. As the disciples have freely received, so they are to freely give in the form of preaching and healing. This certainly make sense in my study of 10:5–11 but it can also have an additional meaning which points to the exchange that will take place in vv. 9–15. As was argued before, v. 9 may refer primarily to vv. 5–8 or, as I contend, introduces vv. 11–15 in its concern on finding a place to stay and enabling social relations. So, this statement at the end of v. 8 may also serve not only to refer to the preaching and healing in v. 7–8 but also to the hospitality and exchange of food that takes place in vv. 10–15.

The statement in 10:8 sets up the expectation that interaction will occur according to this type of reciprocity. Not only has the Matthean community freely received and should freely give but the larger Jewish community, which shares the history and traditions of the Matthean community, has freely received and should freely give. The example of the sojourner and day laborer is one example. The Matthean community both hears this statement as an exhortation for their actions and as an expectation for the type of interactions that ought to take place for Yahweh's people, including the Jewish community. For the latter, then, the Matthean community can hope that they will continue to receive freely from those who have freely received from Yahweh. As with the phrase, "a laborer is worthy of his reward,"[75] so this phrase in 10:8 is a way of interacting that not only the Matthean community might embrace but others as well.

A Cup of Cold Water (10:40–42)

Matthew 10:40–42 is the final subunit within this passage (10:5–11:1) and outlines Jesus' final instructions to the disciples.[76] Several features link 10:40–42 with 10:5b–15, especially vv. 10–15: the use of δεχομαι, the representation of the disciples as those who are acted upon (i.e. as laborers and little ones), and rewards or consequences for those who either do or do not provide hospitality for the disciples.[77] The focus shifts to those who receive the Matthean community, which continues to be dependent upon the larger Jewish community and those beyond that community. In the midst of increased persecution and suffering, those receiving the community offer a cup of cold water to comfort the community. The distribution of drink is part of an ongoing generalized reciprocal exchange between the Matthean community and the world around it.

Between 10:15 and 10:40

While 10:40–42 is parallel to 10:5–15, it is necessary to briefly review the narrative between the two passages in order to better understand 10:40–42. The mission of the disciples becomes dangerous in 10:16–40 as they interact with Jewish authorities, Gentiles authorities and families. In vv. 16–25, the disciples are now portrayed as sheep and those they will encounter are portrayed as wolves.[78] Interaction increases between the disciples and the world around them, moving out from families to the leaders of the extended family (Jewish authorities) to Gentile kings and governors. As this interaction expands, the persecution increases from being delivered up (v. 17) to flogging (v. 17) to death (v. 21). As the Matthean community moves out into the world the conflict increases. The household, the starting point of food exchange in the Matthean narrative and generally a safe, healing, gift-giving location in the first nine chapters of the narrative, becomes a place of conflict and persecution.

The next section, vv. 26–31, offers a word of encouragement during this persecution since God, while one who can destroy both body and soul in Gehenna, is also one who cares intimately for sparrows who die and, even more, for the disciples who suffer and die. Finally, in vv. 32–39, the disciples hear strong words about loving Jesus more than family in order to find their life with God. While vv. 26–31 offered reassuring encouragement about God's relationship with them, vv. 32–39 offer exhortation to maintain "exclusive loyalty"[79] to Jesus during the persecution.

Shift to the Ones Receiving

As the audience reads vv. 40–42, the spotlight swings from the disciples (the Matthean community) to the ones receiving the disciples.[80] The shift to the ones receiving corresponds to the shift that has been made in 10:5–11:1 in general, that the Matthean community has become the outsiders as guests and the larger Jewish community the insiders as hosts.[81] Matthew 10:40 corresponds to this act of hospitality which puts the Matthean community on the outside as a stranger.

Welcoming (δέχομαι) in 10:40–42, as it did in 10:5–15, refers to hospitality not conversion. The interaction between the Matthean community and the larger Jewish community is one of exchanging gifts not confessing Jesus or converting others. A shift occurs between 10:32–39 and 10:40–42 from a focus on the disciples and confessing Jesus to a focus on those who receive the disciples and providing hospitality for them. Matthew 10:32–39 strongly exhorts the disciples to acknowledge/confess (ὁμολογήσει) Jesus before humans/public so Jesus will confess them before his Father (v. 32). The context for vv. 32–39 is the public witness of the disciples during persecution and the purpose of this type of acknowledgement and commitment is to encourage the disciples to maintain their witness in light of difficult circumstances. The use of worthy in vv. 32–39 refers to repentance, acknowledgement/conviction of a certain god, and being part of a particular community (i.e. belonging to Jesus), which is different from "worthy" in 10:11, 13 as the language of hospitality.[82] In vv. 32–39, the disciples are to acknowledge/confess Jesus, love Jesus more than family and to follow Jesus.

Matthew 10:40–42 does not use worthy and uses welcome/receive (δέχομαι) instead of acknowledge/confess (ὁμολογήσει). Those who δέχομαι the disciples are not instructed to ὁμολογήσει Jesus, to love him more than their family or to take up their cross and follow him. Ὁμολογήσει is used to declare Jesus publicly before others so all can see (ἔμπροσθεν τῶν ἀνθρώπων), whereas δέχομαι is used to receive the disciples in a more inconspicuous way (i.e. a simple gesture of giving a cup of cold water) to provide food and lodging (i.e. in private house). In addition, the chain of recognition from the one who confesses God (vv. 32–39) and the one who receives God (v. 40) is different. For those who confess Jesus before humans, Jesus himself confesses before his Father. For those who receive the disciples, however, the act of receiving itself functions also to receive Jesus and the one who sent Jesus.[83] The one who receives is not "on trial"[84] to find out whether Jesus will declare him just before God. Finally, the sequence from receiver to God is downplayed in vv. 41–42 and the use of reward is emphasized. The sequence is mentioned in v. 40, but the use of μισθὸν is then used three times in vv. 41–42 as the compensation/justification for receiving rather than whether one is connected with Jesus and God. In line with 10:11–15, then, δέχομαι in vv. 40–42 refers to hospitality: those who receive the disciples and offer a cup of cold water but do not repent, are not committed to believe in the god of the disciples or follow Jesus.[85]

Reward and Reciprocity

The pattern of the three sayings in vv. 41–42 follows a repetitive-progressive pattern that is consistent with a similar pattern at the beginning of this discourse (vv. 5–6) and with a similar contrast with the third instance of the repetition.[86] The third saying (v. 42), then, diverges and offers a new expectation in contrast from the first two sayings and proposes a different kind of reward for those who receive the little ones/disciples.[87] The reward (μισθὸς) in v. 42 is not an eschatological reward (vv. 41), but part of an ongoing temporal, reciprocal exchange between the Matthean community and those in the world around it.

The first two sayings are identical with the exception of the use of prophet/righteous person. This establishes a pattern that is expected to be followed by the third saying: "the one receiving x in the name of x will receive the reward of x." While the third saying follows the pattern in a general way, it diverges significantly to give a new meaning. Those who give a cup of cold water to the little ones, whether they are part of the Jewish community or other communities (i.e. the use of "whoever"), will be included in an ongoing reciprocal exchange that is based on need, not status, and functions to overcome conflict.

The similar pattern and its variation can be seen below:[88]

established pattern in first two sayings	pattern in third saying
the one	whoever
receiving	gives a cup of cold water to drink
x (prophet/righteous)	one of these little ones (x)
in the name	in the name
of x	of a disciple (y)
will receive the reward	truly I say to you, he will by no means lose the reward
of x	of him (z)

Two main differences are evident between the established pattern and the pattern in the third saying. First, the prophet and righteous ones[89] are used in distinction from the little ones/disciple and the main distinction is one of acceptance within Matthew's community and recognition by those in the world.[90] Both true prophets and righteous ones are regarded highly within Matthew's community and are formidable influences in relationship with the world.[91] The little ones, those with little faith, and those who are the least, however, need protection both within and outside the community and are not considered influential or faithful.[92] The disciples are depicted as those of little faith (6:30, 8:26, 14:31, 16:8, 17:20). Children and the least[93] are at risk in relationship to the community and the world and need to be protected and cared for (18:6, 10, 14; 25: 40, 45).

The twist in the third saying, then, draws attention away from those who have acceptance and influence to those who are vulnerable. This attention matches the movement of 10:5–11:1 itself, which has functioned to focus on the disciples (not the prophets and righteous ones) and to move from the disciples as those who act upon (e.g. the twelve who proclaim and heal, perhaps like prophets[94] and righteous ones) to those who are acted upon (e.g. sojourners, laborers, guests, and now little ones).[95]

The second difference between the established pattern and the pattern in the third saying involves the reward of the prophet and righteous ones as distinguished from "his reward" (v. 42). Both the prophets (5:12, 12:40)[96] and the righteous ones are rewarded/paid with an eschatological reward.[97] The reward in v. 42, however, is not as clear. For the prophet/righteous one, the reward is clearly spelled out as the reward of the prophet/righteous one. The "x" variable (see chart on previous page) is used three times through each phrase in v. 41 to reinforce which reward this is. In v. 42, however, the "x" variable is not repeated; rather a different word is used in each slot: "little ones" (x), "disciple" (y), and "of him" (z). The reward could be that of the little ones, the disciple or a completely different reward. In light of this ambiguity, it is helpful to look elsewhere for the meaning of reward. What will be found is a temporal reward of God's provision (e.g. food), given in the near future as a gift, and not an eschatological reward.[98]

The reward in v. 42 is in response to those who give a cup of cold water, a reference to food and drink. In previous passages in this study on food exchange, reward has referred to temporal rewards (in immediate future) and can be interpreted as exchanges along a line of reciprocal exchanges (reciprocal hospitality).[99] The future tense itself does not restrict the time frame to the end of time.[100] To understand the meaning of reward in v. 42, then, I turn initially to the discussion on the use of reward in 6:1–21, a previous passage on food and drink exchange. Then, I will turn to the use of reward or payment to the little ones and the disciples.

First, the language of reward in 6:1–21 (6:1, 4, 6, 18) is a reward from the Father, who sees in secret, not a reward "in heaven" (5:12). The Father who sees in secret is also the Father who knows the disciples/"you" intimately and is present with them on earth. To be rewarded on earth, then, is possible through the Father's presence and current relationship. Furthermore, prayers to the Father (6:9b–13) that request bread, forgiveness, and rescue from evil, do not necessarily fall under eschatological terms (i.e. bread is given in 7:7–11). While the verb ἀποδίδωμι is used in the future in 6:4, 16, 18, there is nothing explicit about an eschatological reward only a future reward.

Second, instead of translating ἀποδίδωμι as "reward," a better translation would be "repay," "give back," or "reciprocate."[101] God is repaying/reciprocating the disciples for actions to help out those in need (giving alms, fasting) and praise/honor to God. This exchange can be understood as reciprocating acts as part of generalized reciprocity. The relationship between the disciples and the Father (family language) is cast in this type of reciprocity where the exchange of gifts is not immediate such that time lags between exchanges. For God to "repay" in the future is one of God's generous gifts that is then responded to in the future by the disciples. God is not necessarily "responding" to an initial gift by the disciples but God's payments/gifts are part of the ongoing exchange of material goods and services between God and the disciples.[102]

The use of μισθός[103] in 10:42 follows the same type of exchange as that in 6:1–21, only here between "whoever gives a cup of cold water" and "one of these little ones." The translation of μισθός in this case can be payment or reciprocal exchange.[104] The reward is a temporal payment, that is, it is given in the near future and not at the end of time. The reward also has a gift quality to it, it is not part of a balanced exchange[105] but fits better into the genre of hospitality or generalized exchange.

The meaning of μισθός can also be clarified by considering the payments or exchanges that have been received in other parts of the Matthean narrative by the characters involved in v. 42: little ones (μικρὸς), little faith, least, and disciples. What has been or will be the μισθρός, the reward, the payment of these other characters in the narrative? "You of little faith," also referred to as the disciples, are given God's provision, including food (τροφή), in 6:25–34.[106] The "least" are given food and drink, among other services of hospitality/charitable deeds in 25:40, 45. The disciples are part of a food exchange that involves bread (ἄρτος) and fish (ἰχθύς) in 7:7–11. The repayment, then, is food. The repayment is similar to what is given. As drink is given, so drink and/or food will be received in the near future.[107] This is different than v. 41, where the eschatological reward is different from the gift of hospitality.

A question remains regarding 10:42: who receives this reward or payment, reciprocal food exchange, the "reward of him" mentioned in v. 42? There are three possible recipients. First, the character that has been and continues to receive (δέχομαι, 10:14, 10:40, 41) and provide hospitality for the disciples/twelve/laborers/little ones is the lost sheep of the house of Israel, the larger Jewish community. This community received (10:14) the laborers and, were "the one receiving you" in v. 40, the one receiving a prophet and a righteous person in v. 41, and the one who gives a cup of cold water in v. 42.[108] The Jewish community is the primary human actor in 10:5–11:1 regarding the provision of food and drink. But the Jewish community will be the future recipients of food exchange in 14:13–21 and 15:29–38 as the lost sheep of the house of Israel which is connected to "the crowds" in 9:36.[109]

Second, v. 42 introduces a new subject, ὃς ἀν (whoever). No longer used is the subject "the one receiving," which had directly connected v. 40 to v. 14 and the character of the lost sheep of the house of Israel. The subject has broadened to a larger group of characters with the use of "whoever." As stated above, this certainly applies to the Jewish community, who has been characterized in 10:5–11:1 as those who provide hospitality. Whoever can refer to others as well. First, it applies to whoever might give a cup of cold water to one of these little ones in the future of the narrative.[110] Other characters are included in the future of the narrative in 25:35 as those separated into the group of the sheep who had given a drink to the least of these my brothers. Second, even beyond other characters directly mentioned in the future of the narrative, the use of whoever leaves it open to who might give provisions. This open stance gives the implied audience hope whether there might be other characters within the narrative who might offer them a drink of water. Third, the implied audience itself is included.[111] Those addressed moves beyond the characters in the story and incorporates whoever is listening, which includes the implied audience.

A Cup of Cold Water

Matthew 10:40–42 peaks with v. 42 and refers to ongoing reciprocity between the little ones (Matthean community) and other outside communities (i.e. the Jewish community and those referred to by whoever). The exchange is based on need and not whether one is accepted or influential. In addition, the use of the phrase "a cup of cold water" suggests this exchange functions to relieve conflict and suffering. The little ones are given "to drink a cup of cold water" (ποτίσῃ ποτήριον ψυχροῦ).[112] This offer is part of an ongoing exchange of generalized reciprocity, offering a real cup of real water that is in fact cold. The use and meaning of cup (ποτήριον), give to drink (πὸ τίσῃ), and cold (water) (ψυχροῦ) all converge to symbolize the conflict and consolation that is a part of the Matthean community's increasing interaction with the world.

The use of cup in 10:42 is the first use in the Matthean narrative and anticipates both the suffering and relief that comes with the cup. In 20:22 and 26:39 the cup refers to a situation of suffering. In 20:22, Jesus asks the sons of Zebedee if they are able to drink the cup which Jesus is about to drink. Jesus concludes they will indeed drink that cup. The cup here refers to the suffering[113] that Jesus will experience during his passion and the suffering that the sons of Zebedee will also experience. Likewise, in 26:39, Jesus is in Gethsemane with Peter and, again, the two sons of Zebedee, and is "deeply grieved" in anticipation of his future suffering. Jesus asks his Father to let the cup pass from him.

Cup also refers to a cup of relief or liberation. In 26:27, the cup offered by Jesus at the Passover meal represents the blood of the covenant which is being shed (a cup of suffering for Jesus) for many for the forgiveness of sins (a cup of relief or liberation for "many").[114] The Exodus event is (perhaps) forefront here in the minds of the implied audience. As Moses sprinkled blood on the people to inaugurate a covenant with God (after the Egyptian slavery) so Jesus sheds blood for many to begin a covenant with God (in the midst of Roman power).[115]

The use of give to drink (ποτίσῃ) in 10:42 supplements the interpretation of the ποτήριος as a cup of relief and the act of giving someone a cup to drink as an act of reprieve.[116] Ποτίζω is used in 25:35, 37, 42 in reference to giving (or not giving) a drink to the least of these my brothers. It is used along with giving food, inviting a stranger in, clothing the naked, visiting the sick and those in prison, all charitable deeds (or hospitality) to those in need. These acts provide relief or encouragement in times of suffering and real need. Ποτίζω is also used in 27:48 when "one of them"[117] takes a sponge and fills it with vinegar and places it on a stick to give Jesus a drink while he is on the cross. This event can be interpreted as an act to relieve Jesus' suffering.[118]

In addition to the use of cup (ποτήριος) and give to drink (ποτίζω) is the use of cold (water) (ψυχρός) to support the view that the exchange in v. 42 is meant to offer relief and encouragement in the face of suffering. There is little textual evidence to give context to this saying, but cold is often used as an example of an extreme. It can have a negative connotation, e.g. those who are against Jesus,[119] or it might mean that which has no power over and yet opposes the community.[120] Cold water, however, functions at the other extreme. Experience suggests that water itself is a relief to those who thirst and *cold* water provides a touch of comfort and extra relief.[121] The Didache recommends being baptized in cold running water (7:2), perhaps the refreshing or even stimulating nature of cold water participates in the transformative act. Cold water has great power to revive a community that is suffering, even with only (μόνον) a cup of cold water.

The phrase "to give to drink a cup of cold water" is used to convey both the conflict and suffering that exists at this moment in the narrative[122] and the act taken to relieve that suffering. This makes sense in 10:42 from the conflict, persecution, and death which is expected from those sent out to proclaim and heal. The presence of conflict and violence has increased in the narrative and the use of this phrase relative to the disciples further highlights that presence. At the same time, to give to drink a cup of cold water is an act of relief which encourages and provides relief for those who are suffering.

Compassionate God Who Judges (10:26–31)

The two book ends of 10:5–11:1 (10:5–15 and 10:40–42) have as its center vv. 26–31.[123] Both 10:5–15 and 10:40–42 address Matthew's community as it goes out to proclaim and heal and has the need for hospitality in an increasingly conflictual and hostile environment. Matthew 10:26–31, the center of 10:5–11:1, provides encouragement for the Matthean community through the knowledge and activity of God. God further discloses God's work as creator and provider and acts indirectly with and through those outside the Matthean community in public settings.

This center passage is another repetitive-progressive texture structured by three uses of "to fear/be afraid of" (φοβέομαι) and depicts God's activity as moving from concealment to disclosure as creator and provider. Fear (φοβέομαι) orders the passage at the beginning (v. 26), middle (v. 28), and end (v. 31). This study follows the lead given by φοβέομαι and divides each unit beginning with φοβέομαι: vv. 26–27, vv. 28–30, v. 31.[124] The central role of φοβέομαι in this passage and the continuity (not difference) in the image of God in vv. 28–30 influence the choice for this division. Despite the conflict and violence with Jewish and Gentile leaders and with one's own family in 10:5–11:1, vv. 26–31 encourage the disciples not to fear because of the God who creates and sustains their lives. This extended use of φοβέομαι and the repetitive-progressive texture recall the extended use of μεριμνάω in 6:25–34, where the disciples were not to be anxious about what they might eat or drink or wear but to seek God's provision.

God Reveals Through Jesus and the Disciples (10:26–27)

In vv. 26–27, reflecting the movement of the Matthean narrative, God is becoming less visible and yet continues to act but through Jesus and the disciples. The disciples are encouraged not to fear because that which has been concealed will be revealed and that which is hidden will be made known. The idea of concealment and secrecy (κρυπτός) recalls 6:1–21 and the Father who is in secret.[125] In 10:26, the use of passives (i.e. has been veiled, will be revealed, will be made known) designates God as the one who has been concealing and who will be disclosing. God is the one who acts, the one to make public that which has been hidden.[126] The next verse, however, shifts from the use of passives and the focus on God to the focus on Jesus and the disciples. "What I say to you" refers to what Jesus is saying to the disciples (in 10:5b–10:42 as instructions for the mission). The disciples themselves, then, become the ones who are to disclose what has been hidden as the narrative uses aorist active imperatives—speak! (εἴπατε), preach! (κηρύξατε).[127] God acts but through Jesus and the disciples.

What is it that the disciples are to say and preach? Given the persecution that surrounds them, why should the disciples not fear that which will be revealed? The disciples are to preach that the kingdom of the heaven has drawn near (10:7). The kingdom of heaven is the activity of God as creator and provider who is present on earth among and working for creation.[128] To preach that the kingdom of heaven has come near is to proclaim a view of God. God is the one who acts to disclose God's very own activity as creator and provider. God is making public God's own work in creation.

The language of veiling (καλύπτω), revealing (ἀποκαλύπτω), hidden (κρυπτός), and knowing (γινώσκω), is the language of apocalyptic literature in which the secret or hidden meanings of prophecies are disclosed by God at the end time/judgment so that the faithful understand God's purposes and live by them.[129] The revelation(s) does not come, however, on the final judgment day but during the series of events that marks the coming of the end.[130] Matthew's implied audience understands that with Jesus' life and teaching (4:17), the end-time events were initiated by God and are now being disclosed by the disciples, who "speak in the light" and "proclaim on the housetops" (10:27).[131] God's initiative to disclose who God is as creator and provider continues through the narrative in contexts of food exchange.

One View of God Not Two (10:28–30)

The second subunit begins with the second use of φοβέομαι in v. 28 and gives a clearer picture of who this God is who is proclaimed in v. 27. At first glance, taking v. 28 as separate from vv. 29–30, it is a God who judges and destroys life (v. 28) only to become later to have a different characterization as a more "gentle"[132] and "loving"[133] God (vv. 29–30). On closer examination, however, it is one and the same characterization of God as one who has the power to create and take away life (i.e. taking vv. 28–30 together), who brings to life and actively defends those in relationship with God. In particular, God provides for the weak and helpless.

The disciples are not to fear those (plural) who will kill the body (σῶμα) but are not able (δύναμαι) to kill the soul, referring to those in Matt 10 who are persecuting the disciples.[134] The disciples should fear, however, the one (singular) who is able (δύναμαι) to destroy (ἀπόλλυμι) both body (σῶμα) and soul (ψυχή) in Gehenna. The "one who is able" refers to God not Satan[135] and this verse becomes problematic for some who see God as judge and destroyer in this verse and a different characterization of God who cares for and knows intimate details of the sparrows and disciples in vv. 29–30. The description of God in v. 28, however, includes the description of one who is able (i.e. has the power) to take away life and therefore has the power to give and sustain life (vv. 29–30).

It is helpful to look at the use of body (σῶμα) and soul (ψυχή) to sort this out.[136] In 10:28, one does not need to fear[137] those who kill the body because both those who kill and the body in this case are not connected with God. In one sense, the body in Matthew's narrative is simply the physical body whose parts (5:29) or the body itself (27:52) can be destroyed but the relationship with God is not lost neither is the soul, which is the totality of life in relationship with God.[138] Rather, one does need to fear[139] God who has the power to destroy both body and soul. In this clause, one's body and soul that are not in relationship with God can be destroyed but one's body and soul that are in relationship to God, that fear (i.e. give reverence to, worship) God, will not be destroyed. Those who remember who they are connected to, as disciples of Jesus giving witness to God during their mission even during persecution, will not be destroyed.

The image of God as the one who destroys is described by some scholars as a God who judges at the end time and is differentiated with the God who is characterized in the next verse, v. 29.[140] This description focuses on God acting as judge at the judgment day and is differentiated with God as a loving Father who cares daily for the disciples. Weaver describes the shift as an "abrupt switch."[141] I argue for continuity between images: the God who has the power to destroy and is working for justice is also the God who has the power to create. God is the final judge, yes, but is also judge along the way who discerns and guides. This same judge is also God who provides on a daily basis. The image of God as Mother who has the power to create and actively defends her children matches these verses well.[142]

While a subtle difference, verse 28 depicts a God who is capable of destroying, but not one who kills. The disciples are encouraged not to fear the ones killing (ἀποκτείνω) the body but not able (δύναμαι) to kill the soul; rather to fear (i.e. show reverence) the one who is able (δύναμαι) to destroy (ἀπόλλυμι) both body and soul. The use of δύναμαι and ἀππόλυμι places the focus on who has the power to do that. The human opponents of the disciples can kill the body but they are not able, they do not have the power, to kill the soul. God is able, has the power, to destroy both body and soul. 'Αποκτείνω refers to the opponents of Matthew's community who physically kill the body of those who are associated with the faithful community (i.e. Jesus, disciples, Hebrew prophets).[143] While ἀπόλλυμι can refer to the same type of violence, it also refers to dissolving the life-giving ties between God/Jesus and those who follow him and prospective followers both in the present time and after death.[144] Only God has the power to give, sustain, and take away present and future life with humans.

Verse 28 gives a "negative" example of God's power (to destroy) and then the narrative turns to verse 29 which gives a positive example of God's power to create, have knowledge of and compassion for life. Verse 29 introduces two sparrows (στρουθίον)[145] and asks, "are not two sparrows sold for a penny?" with the answer, "yet not one of them will fall to the ground apart from your Father." Interpretations center in on sparrows as cheap food and then, with v. 31, talk about how much more value humans are.[146] Sparrows have a history for the implied audience, however, as represented in two ways: (1) those who are weak and helpless and pursued by enemies and (2) those who are provided for by God. I will explore these two meanings of sparrows before returning to their economic value.

Sparrows are portrayed in the Hebrew Bible as birds that are hunted and taunted by enemies, who flee to the mountains and try to escape.[147] They are also those creatures for whom God, as creator and provider, supplies food and a home.[148] They are weak and helpless creatures for whom God provides.

This sets the context for reading the next line, v. 29b, and the use of ἄνευ τοῦ πατρὸς ὑμῶν, which has been read as meaning (1) without knowledge and consent of your Father, (2) without the presence of your Father, and (3) without the will or help of your Father.[149] The meaning in this study follows most closely to the first and second interpretations, "without knowledge and consent" and "without presence." Both are needed because the latter, "without presence" is ambiguous without the clarification of either #2 or #3.[150] That is, is the Father present and has knowledge of the act or is the Father present and wills the act? I choose the former, the Father is present and has knowledge (and consent) but does not will or help the sparrow to fall to the ground.

The immediate context in this passage and the larger context of Matthew's narrative support this interpretation. The previous discussion above concludes that sparrows were helpless creatures for which God provides. There is no discussion in the Hebrew Bible or in 6:25–34 about God willing or helping the birds to die. There is ample discussion, however, focusing in on God's knowledge of the fate of God's creatures in Matthew's narrative, which echoes the Hebrew Bible.[151] This interpretation also fits the larger context of chapter 10 where the disciples, like the sparrows, are depicted as weak, helpless creatures (e.g. laborers, sheep in the midst of wolves, little ones) that God provides for through various means.[152] God does not will or help the disciples to die, although they might die, but God does have knowledge and appears to consent to their persecution and death as inevitable outcomes to their faithful witness.

The view of God, then, in v. 29 is of God as one who provides for the weak and helpless sparrows and knows, because God has been present all along in their lives, when they die. God relates to the natural world beyond the human world.[153] God who has the power to destroy body and soul of humans is also the God who is able to give (providing for sparrows often in the context of God as creator) and sustain life and is compassionate when physical life has ended.

The narrative turns back to the human sphere in v. 30 ("and even the hairs of your (i.e. disciples) head are all numbered") but continues with the image of God as creator and provider who is present, has knowledge, and cares for the creation. Two interpretations pervade the discussion of this verse[154] but neither focus on God as creator whose intimate knowledge of humans and non-humans moves God to care and provide for the creation. The passages used in the first interpretation and the idea that God has compassion for creation in the second interpretation can be brought together for an alternative view. In the context of vv. 26–31, v. 30 emphasizes the view of God as creator[155] who can see and observe all the inhabitants of the earth (i.e. humans in v. 30 and non-humans in v. 29), who reaches out to those who are helpless and troubled (i.e. demonstrating the presence not distance of God for sparrows who need help and die and for disciples who are being persecuted and may die) and who has intimate knowledge of those parts of creation which are secluded or hidden (i.e. sparrows are known as small birds[156] and the hairs on a person's head cannot be seen by that person). The context of vv. 26–31 supports the view of God as one who destroys and also creates, who has knowledge of, is present with, and provides for sparrows and humans.

The use of different images for God in 10:26–31 is often approached by showing the discontinuities between them. Here, the two primary images are: God as the one who has the ability to destroy and God as the one who loves and cares for humans. There does not have to be an "abrupt shift" between the images as if the two cannot be considered together. The language of God is not literal and does not speak to the essence of God, rather the language is metaphorical and demonstrates an analogy that is both similar and different.[157]

Some scholars do attempt to demonstrate the continuities between the images but subsume the image of God as creator and provider under the image of God as sovereign. "Sovereignty" is a typical word used to describe the first image of God in this passage, v. 28 (the one who destroys).[158] Then, when the second image comes along of a God who is concerned about sparrows, the sovereign image is adjusted but maintained. Therefore, when discussing the image of God in v. 29, "the judge is also the loving Father whose sovereign care is known in the present,"[159] or "they (sparrows) too fall within the scope of his sovereign power and care,"[160] or "the heavenly Father…is also the sovereign Lord of the trying and mundane present."[161]

The father image also becomes a primary image to the exclusion of God as creator and provider. Father suggests a God of humanity not one who relates to the natural world. Father also becomes subsumed into the orbit of the sovereign and political world. So the father becomes sovereign father, political father, and patriarchal father who controls, rules absolutely, demands obedience, governs humans, reigns with benevolence at times but only from a distance, acts on the world not in and with the world.[162] Another option would be for the father to become creator father, provider father, and parental father who cares, is compassionate, guides, interacts with the human and the non-human world, is intimate, acts in and with the world to ensure just relationships.[163] Yet another possibility is to imagine God as a Mother who gives life to all creatures and works for justice to make sure those creatures can survive, have access to the basic necessities of life, and are able to continue life.[164]

The nature of the repetitive-progressive texture of 10:26–31 moves the implied audience to embrace the last image of God in the text and to include previous images under this climactic image instead of subsuming later images under the first image. Therefore, the God of the sparrows and the one who counts the hairs on humans is the primary image that then includes God as the one who judges.

Sparrows Are Valuable Too (10:31)

The final subunit of vv. 26–31 also begins with φοβέομαι and is a short conclusion, "therefore, do not be afraid, you are worth more than many sparrows." The μὴ οὖν forms an inclusio with μὴ οὖν in v. 26. The ὑμεῖς refers to the disciples, as the whole chapter has been addressed to, and states that they are worth more than many sparrows. For Weaver, "Jesus indicates that his primary concern is not with *insignificant* sparrows, but rather with *infinitely* more valuable disciples."[165] I read this as the disciples are more valuable (but not infinitely more valuable) than many (not all) sparrows and that sparrows are still valuable even if less valuable than the disciples. This phrase aligns with 6:25–34 where the disciples are also said to be more valuable than the birds. Yet the heavenly Father still feeds the birds in 6:26 and the Father has knowledge of and provides for the sparrows in 10:29. There is no reason to assign "infinitely" less value to the sparrows simply to assign more value to the disciples. Value may be ranked on a continuum here instead of a scale of bipolar extremes. Yes, the disciples are worth more but the sparrows also have value.

Matthew 10:31 also is parallel with 6:27–30 where the question expecting a positive response is asked, "will he not much more cloth you?" referring to how God clothes the grass of the field in a magnificent way yet will clothe the disciples even better. It is significant what happens to the grass in this verse as it parallels what happens to the sparrows. Even though God values the grass and clothes them, the grass is alive today and tomorrow is thrown into the oven, suggesting some useful function for heating or cooking.[166] Likewise, even though the sparrows are valued (v. 29b), so they are still sold for a penny in the market. Put another way, even though the sparrows are sold for a penny, they are still valued.

The fact that they are sold for a penny does not mean they have no value. In fact, one could read v. 29a with a tone of disapproval,

> I cannot believe two sparrows are actually sold in the market, and for a penny! Don't you know sparrows are good food and, as with any food, are worth more than a commodity and should be bartered and not sold at market. Yet, even though humans do not value sparrows for food, God values them for food and, even before they become food, as living creatures.

The disapproving reference in v. 29a may indeed be referring to the value of sparrows as food. In intracommunity/village economies, food has too much social value to sell as one might sell baskets, pots, or other goods.[167] Food was to be exchanged with generalized reciprocity, given away, with some expectation perhaps that food would be returned in the future, but certainly not to be sold directly for money. The use of πωλέω (sold) in Matthew's narrative suggests that the use here in 10:29 is not to be a positive assessment but a critique of the practice. Πωλέω is used in two ways in the narrative, the first use does not appear to match the use here in 10:29 but the second use, seen in 21:12 and 25:9, provides a helpful background to interpreting 10:29.[168]

In 21:12, Jesus is throwing out those who are selling and buying in the Temple, those who are turning a house of prayer into a den of robbers. In 25:9, the wise virgins do not give the foolish virgins any oil to keep their lamps burning so the latter must go to the ones who are selling oil and buy some for themselves. On the one hand, there is nothing disapproving about selling oil *per se*. On the other hand, while the foolish are out buying oil, they miss the bridegroom. The activity of buying and selling prevents the foolish from going with the bridegroom into the wedding banquet. One might also read into this that if the wise were willing "to give" (generalized reciprocity) the foolish some oil, the foolish would not have missed the bridegroom.

The use of πωλέω in 10:29 fits this second meaning in 21:12 and 25:9. The activity of selling impairs social and theological relationships. The use of money in a political economy and/or balanced reciprocity does not feed relationships of solidarity.[169] This is true in Matthew's narrative for any goods and is especially true for selling food. Sparrows, in particular, were thought to be cheap and were food for the poor.[170] Particularly for the poor, then, food should be bartered or even given as a gift and not sold in a marketplace.[171] Sparrows were to be valued as food and as living creatures. Yet, the disciples are valued more, not infinitely more, just more.

Conclusion to Matthew 10:26–31

The progressive pattern[172] in this unit, 10:26–31, yields the following reading regarding the view of God and the Matthean community and its interactions with the world. The view of God begins with God as the primary actor who will reveal that which has been hidden, yet the use of passive verbs keeps God "behind the scenes" (v. 26). The work of revealing, then, is taken up by Jesus and the disciples in v. 27 such that God is interacting with the world indirectly through them. God still acts but continues behind the scenes as God works through others. The trend through the narrative to this point continues: God's interaction with and feeding of the world moves from more direct interactions with the Matthean community in private settings to more indirect interactions with and through those outside the Matthean community in public settings.[173] In 10:5–11:1, God is interacting indirectly through Jesus and the disciples with the lost sheep of the house of Israel in cities and villages (in proclaiming and healing) but through the lost sheep of the house of Israel in cities and villages with the Matthean community (in food exchange). God is becoming less visible and humans are gaining more responsibility in exchanging food.

The view of God moves toward a God who has knowledge of both human and non-human creation and has the power to create and sustain creation. God is primarily the God who creates and provides and the role of God as "judge/ruler/monarch/sovereign," who has the power to destroy body and life, is included within and subordinate to this primary designation.[174] The link between Father/Mother and creator continues to be strengthened in the larger narrative.

The disciples, as representative of the Matthean community, began in 10:26-31 as active participants in revealing and making known who God is as they proclaim and heal. As the section continues, however, the disciples are to show reverence to the one who is able to destroy both body and life in Gehenna and to the one who is able to care and provide for those who are in need. The emphasis shifts from the disciples as active participants proclaiming God in the world to those who are dependent and in need of God. That is, in the context of a discussion on sparrows, vv. 29–31 depicts disciples as those who are being persecuted and in need of the one who sees and knows them, reaches out to them because they need help, and has intimate knowledge of them. This shift parallels 10:5–11:1 as a whole as the characterization of the disciples evolves from the twelve who proclaim and heal (i.e. independent, acting upon the world) to the laborers who work but are dependent upon others and the little ones who need a cup of cold water (i.e. dependent, being acted upon by the world). The implied audience can see the difference between the disciples' (Matthean community's) interaction with the world when proclaiming and healing and when exchanging food.

Conclusion

The disciples, as laborers (representing the Matthean community), are fed by those who host them, the lost sheep of the house of Israel (representing the larger Jewish community outside of the Matthean community). God as Mother/Father and creator gives life to the sparrows and disciples and defends that life as a just God. God becomes less visible but works through part of the human community, the lost sheep, to feed the disciples.[175]

Through food exchange, the Matthean community is connecting with and dependent upon its extended family, the larger Jewish household. As the twelve, the Matthean community is approaching this household to preach and heal, to act upon them. As those in need of food, however, the community is composed of sojourners, laborers, guests and little ones who are dependent upon the household as one with more power and resources. While dependent, the community continues to be active in inquiring after food, entering houses and working for food.

The food exchange, in the form of generalized reciprocity, connects the two households and (re)unites them in kinship relations. This type of material flow "initiates social relations."[176] The exchange of food promotes a type of relation that preaching and healing would not. The phrase at the end of 10:8 ("freely you received, freely give") echoes the type of interactions that were prevalent in 7:7–11, interactions that demonstrated the ease and freedom of exchange among family (Matthean community) and perhaps even beyond family in Matthew's narrative world.[177] The exchanges that take place in 10:40–42 also resonate with this type of reciprocity in two ways. First, both the quick repetition in 10:40–42[178] and the climactic exchange in 10:42, as one exchange within a broader framework of generalized exchanges, give the implied audience the sense that these interactions are without controls or limits and support a generous sharing of food based on need and not on whether the other party is capable of reciprocating.

Second, the use of "whoever" in 10:42 points to the exchange of food, and here the provision of food, by those beyond the family of the Matthean community and perhaps even beyond the extended family of the Jewish community. In 7:7–11, the use of ἄνθρωπος and πᾶς opened up the possibility of food exchange moving beyond the immediate family to those outside the family. In 10:5–11:1, food exchange has indeed moved out into the extended family.

The Matthean community is dependent upon food and so receives the food as those with a lower status. Yet even with a lower status, the exchange endorses kinship relations. The view of family in the

Matthean narrative has broadened from the Matthean community to include the larger Jewish community.

Food exchange not only widens the sphere of kin but it also provides comfort for those suffering. The Matthean community is depicted as those who are persecuted, as marginalized laborers, as little ones who need protection, and as guests who live in an ambivalent state of danger. But the comfort and compassion and generosity of food help to alleviate conflict. Food exchange here is based on need not status. The community receives food not because it has high status or is able to act upon others as the twelve, prophets or righteous person; rather it receives food precisely because it has little status and is acted upon.

Chapter 7

In the Grainfields (12:1–8)

Introduction

In Matthew 12:1–8, the second passage of the second thematic unit, the Matthean community continues to exchange food in public and contentious space outside its own community and to receive food from God indirectly through those outside the community. The setting moves out beyond a household or architectural space into an inhabited topographical area, the grainfields. God feeds the Matthean community through the natural world through the assistance of gleaning laws established by the larger Jewish community. God is not identified as Father but as creator, liberator and provider who establishes the sabbath for rest, liberation, and the access of food and gleaning laws to feed the marginalized out of her body, the earth. While the setting of the sabbath depicts God as the one in covenant with Israel, the setting also recalls God as creator of "heaven and earth, the sea, and all that is in them" (Exod 20.11) as well as provider for the slave and resident alien. The Matthean community continues to be active in participating in food exchange as they take the initiative to pluck grain but also remain dependent upon others as those portrayed as the poor and alien. While the larger Jewish community and its laws make possible the access to food, the Pharisees disagree with Jesus on the interpretation of those laws for the sabbath. Matthew's Jesus interprets the laws, in conversation not condemnation of the Pharisees, to argue that the distribution of food through these laws on the sabbath is a better way to provide access to food than through more centralized and institutionalized means symbolized by the house of God and the temple. The Matthean community is more allied with the Pharisees in the grainfields than with David in the house of God and the priests in the temple. As the community moves farther out into the world to establish relations, it associates with the larger Jewish community and one set of leaders to satisfy the need to make social ties and differentiates from part of the Jewish community to stake out its identity and independence.

Many commentators mark out the structure on 12:1–8 based on the argument between Jesus and the Pharisees concerning the proper interpretation of the sabbath laws. Davies and Allison, for example, argue that the passage falls into three parts: the setting (12:1), the criticism of the disciples by the Pharisees' (12:2), and Jesus response (12:3–8).[1] This structure lends itself to reading a divide between Jesus and the Pharisees. The two examples in vv. 3–5, therefore, are understood as providing support for the disciples' choice to pick and eat the grain on the sabbath over and against the Pharisees' objection. Both David and the priests, like Jesus and the disciples, set aside laws regarding sacrifices or sabbath laws in order to meet human needs.

I identify a fourfold repetitive-progressive texture that is based on the shift in characters and setting through the passage and not on the opposition between Jesus and the Pharisees. The first element is 12:1–2 with Jesus, the disciples, and the Pharisees situated in the grainfields on the sabbath. The second element is 12:3–4 with David, the ones with him, and the priests in the house of God. The third element is 12:5 with the priests in the temple and the fourth element, 12:6–8, reconnects with the first element, vv. 1–2, and concludes the section. The structure underscores the way in which food is distributed (i.e. through gleaning laws or the sanctuary and temple) and not an argument between two opposing parties regarding the interpretation of sabbath laws.[2] The two examples in vv. 3–5, therefore, are understood as foils to demonstrate that community laws that allow the poor and alien and wandering travelers access to food in the grainfields is a preferable means to acquire food in Matthew's community than centralized sanctuaries and temples that employ state officials to collect and redistribute food to settled citizens.[3]

Jesus, Disciples, and Pharisees (12:1–2)

In the first element of the pattern Jesus and the disciples are going through the grainfields on the sabbath and the disciples are hungry and begin to pick heads of wheat and to eat them. The Pharisees see this and accuse the disciples of doing what is not permitted to do on the sabbath. The temporal setting is established with "at that time" and "on the sabbath" while the spatial location is the grainfields. The characters are Jesus, the disciples, and the Pharisees.

The disciples wander through the grainfields on the sabbath to glean food together. They actively seek food yet rely upon those who own the grainfields for access to this food. The traditions of the sabbath and gleaning represent the larger Jewish community's commitment to provide for the poor and alien. These traditions were put in place as the community understood God as creator, the one who liberated the Israelites from Egypt and sustained them in the wilderness. While the Pharisees charge Jesus and the disciples with violating the sabbath, they are more aligned with Jesus and the disciples regarding the way the poor are to access food than the forthcoming priests in vv. 3–4.

"At that time"

The passage begins with the temporal setting, "at that time" (Eν ἐκείνῳ τῷ καιρῷ). Most interpreters consider this "merely a transition phrase"[4] from Matt 11. Yet the use of this phrase is ripe with meaning. The phrase "at that time" is used in three places in the narrative, 11:25, 12:1, and 14:1, all of which "occur within the context of controversy or immediately following it."[5] With 12:1 as the second occurrence a pattern is not firmly established but the audience may still expect some type of controversy, especially if the audience, understood as a second or third-time reader, has some recollection from a previous reading.[6] The disciples and Jesus are traveling together as a group and decide it is the right time to eat together in the grainfields with respect to the natural processes of life and the social situation.

"At that time" can be considered a type of procedural time. Procedural time is rooted in the biological and ecological processes of life and is focused on the completion of tasks "at the right time."[7] The audience will learn in the next sentence that the disciples are hungry and therefore it is the right time to eat. In addition, it is harvest time, which was "a threshold which marked the end of one growing and herding season and the beginning of another."[8] It is the "right time" to harvest the crops. Gundry translates the phrase "in that season"[9] which underscores the kind of time as harvest time and as procedural time. The audience will also link "at that time" with the sabbath, which further specifies what kind of time this is. The phrase "at that time" is also considered a social time where the emphasis is on the completion of social interactions instead of an adherence to schedules that put less priority on social life.[10]

Sabbath, Grainfields and Gleaning

The sabbath calls to mind God as creator of all living creatures and the one who liberates from slavery and provides daily food for the Israelite people. The sabbath is the time for the wandering disciples to have access to food.[11] Israelite laws for gleaning in the grainfields provide that access and mitigate the difficult situation which surrounds the Matthean community as those who are depicted as hungry and poor.

Sabbath. The earliest references to the sabbath in the Hebrew Bible appear in the Pentateuch in three main narratives: the creation story (Gen 1–2:4a), the exodus (Deut 5:12–15), and the daily provision of manna in the wilderness (Exod 16:16–30).[12]

The sabbath celebrates God's creation of the world and recalls God's rest on the seventh day.[13] God's day of rest gives humans the opportunity to acknowledge God as creator and to participate in the rest of other humans and creation.[14] The sabbath called for social and economic structures that provided for freedoms and food for those easily marginalized parts of creation such as the land, wild and domesticated animals, the poor, the alien, and slaves.[15] The connection with the creation story also marks the completion of creation on the seventh day and looks forward to the anticipated completion of creation.[16] The first creation story leads up to the sabbath as the completing moment of the creation but even there it may be "understood as a symbol of the world to come, which would be 'all Sabbath.'"[17] With its concern for social and economic justice, the sabbath points to a "completion of God's just purposes."[18]

The sabbath is a type of procedural time. It is rooted in the biological and ecological processes of life. The seventh day and the seventh year are times for rest and humanitarian aid. The completion of these tasks are paramount at this particular time, this is the "right time" for the disciples to find food.

The second and third narratives refer to the exodus and the provision of food in the wilderness. Sabbath observance is connected to

God's deliverance of the Israelites from slavery in Egypt (Deut 5:12–15).[19] It also recalls God's supply of daily manna in the wilderness as the Israelites left Egypt and traveled toward the promised land (Exod 16:16–30).[20] The formation of God's people through the pivotal event of the exodus and the giving of the law at Mount Sinai reminds the reader of the sabbath's association with God's covenant with Israel (Exod 31:16, Ezek 20:12).[21] The disciples clearly understand themselves in 12:1–8 as part of the Jewish community.

While mentioned throughout the history of Israel, sabbath practice was "especially prominent before, during, and after the Exile in Babylon"[22] and it is possible that a tension existed between the sabbath and the Temple. This tension will unfold in the second element of 12:1–8 as the type of food exchange in the grainfields on the sabbath is contrasted with the food exchange in the house of God and temple.

Grainfields and Gleaning. The disciples glean grain out of the grainfields which recalls Israelite history and its laws of food provision for the poor and resident alien, those both inside and outside the Israelite community. Coupled with the meaning of the sabbath, God is creator and liberator who provides for all those who reside in Israel. The disciples take initiative to access the food but remain deeply dependent on others who provide this life sustaining material resource.

The grainfields are topographical space, physical features of the earth that can be seen from an aerial photograph but have no political boundaries.[23] Grainfields are inhabited spaces but are not populated locations—humans work to maintain them but do not live there.[24] The grainfield was probably situated on the edge of an inhabited area, just outside a town.[25] The reference to grainfields in 12:1 recalls the first creation story and God as creator and provider as well as the gleaning laws in Deuteronomy and Leviticus and God's role as liberator and the source of justice, who is to be imitated. The provision of food through God's creation and gleaning laws provides the poor and alien (Matthew's community) ready access to food through the natural world and functions as generalized reciprocity for the ease of distributing food.

The use of grainfields (τῶν σπορίμων)[26] recalls the Septuagint translation in Genesis 1:29 where God gives "every tree which has in itself the fruit of seed that is *sown* (σπορίμου),[27] to you it shall be for food" (Gen 1:29). In the first creation story God gives humans food to eat, that food which is sown in the ground. The ending of this priestly story includes the sabbath as God rests from God's work of creation. God structures the created order in such a way that the earth provides food for humans and the sabbath is the celebration that recognizes God's role as creator and provider.[28]

The disciples of Jesus (i.e. "his disciples" and thus are associated with Jesus) are hungry and begin to pick the heads of wheat in the grainfields and to eat them. The plucking of grains from the grainfields in Matthew evokes the gleaning laws in Deuteronomy and Leviticus. In the narrative of the Hebrew Bible, Leviticus and Deuteronomy record the gleaning laws in the context of the Israelites traveling through the wilderness on their way to the promised land. Gleaning laws provided a basic amount of food for the poor and the resident alien.[29] The laws extended the provision of food to the Israelites as well as those outside the Israelite community.[30] Both Deuteronomy and Leviticus justified their laws, particularly those regarding food, based on the Israelites' experience as aliens (Lev 19:34) and slaves (Deut 24:22) in the land of Egypt, where Israelites did not have free access to food.[31] The reference to oppression in Egypt highlights God's role as liberator who delivered the Israelite people from slavery in Egypt. The Israelites know the experience of slavery, being aliens and slaves in a foreign land, and are to treat those among them from other lands differently, as part of the community. The social order created by the Israelites was to provide and protect those who shared in their daily lives.[32]

The implied audience in Matthew would associate the disciples with this history, either as those who are poor or as resident aliens. They are hungry, they are walking through the grainfields and plucking grain, the setting of the sabbath and the gleaning of grain recall the Israelites and their wandering through the wilderness uncertain about food supply and the gleaning laws for the poor and resident alien.

This depiction of the disciples continues the one in the previous passage, 10:5–11:1, where they are sojourners, guests, and laborers who are traveling and then working as marginal members of a household. In 10:5–11:1, the disciples, as representative of the Matthean community, show some initiative as they inquire into where they might stay, enter a house, and work for their food. Yet they continue to be dependent, as laborers, guests, and little ones on other households and subject to persecution and conflict.

In 12:1–8, the disciples also show initiative but continue, as well, to be dependent on other means for food and subject to conflict. Several active verbs are used to describe the disciples. Although not mentioned explicitly, they are mostly likely with Jesus as they go (πορεύομαι) through the grainfields—Jesus and the disciples are on the move. The disciples then begin to pick (τίλλειν) and to eat (ἐσθίειν) the grain. They go after the food by themselves. Jesus, while mentioned first, is not directing them[33] or giving them permission.[34] The disciples decide for themselves and take action to feed themselves. Jesus is, on the one hand, a main character. He is mentioned first and referred to last in the passage, and he defends the disciples.[35] The disciples, however, are the ones who take the initiative to feed themselves and are at the center of the action.

The disciples' initiative and activeness is reinforced throughout the passage. The Pharisees accuse them by commenting, "your disciples *are doing* what is not permitted *to do*." The verb "to do" (ποιέω) is used twice in reference to their action. When comparing their action in the other two elements, active verbs are used again. Jesus asks the Pharisees, "have you not read what David and the ones with him did (ἐποίησεν) when he hungered." David entered (εἰσῆλθεν) the house of God and ate (ἔφαγον) the bread of the presence. The priests desecrate (βεβηλοῦσιν), that is *they do* what violates a certain custom,[36] the sabbath. The disciples, as David and the priests, act upon the world, they go, pick, eat, and do.

Yet the disciples are dependent upon others for food. They depend on those who own the fields, grow the wheat and leave a part of it for others to glean. They rely on those who participate in making and enforcing the laws regarding gleaning. And they depend on God, the creator who orchestrated the earth such that it would have food for humans to eat and the one who provided the law as a gift to the Israelites and included laws for gleaning. This dependence means that tension and conflict surrounds them. Their spatial setting in the grainfields[37] and the temporal setting of the sabbath manifests this discord. Jesus and the disciples are depicted as hungry, wandering travelers in need of food. The setting of the sabbath reinforces this tension by recollecting the Israelite wandering in the wilderness and the need for daily sustenance. Furthermore, the disciples are about to encounter the Pharisees and their accusations and the disciples will also be compared to the priests in the temple, which will emerge as a greater source of conflict with the Matthean community later in the narrative.[38]

"And the Pharisees"

Jesus, the disciples, and the Pharisees are grouped together in the first element of the passage. The conjunction used to introduce the both the disciples and the Pharisees, δέ, may refer to a contrast but it may also be used to connect a list of similar items and be translated as an "and."[39] There is a hierarchy established with the sequence in which the characters are mentioned in vv. 1–2, Jesus, the disciples, the Pharisees, and there is clearly tension between the Pharisees and Jesus, but they remain within the same grouping and have more in common than the new characters, David and the priests, who will be introduced in vv. 3–5.

The Pharisees, as the disciples, are introduced with the same conjunction but many English translations will begin the phrase with the disciples without a conjunction (thus, "The disciples . . .") and the phrase with the Pharisees with either "when" or "but," noting a contrast.[40] Robbins, who makes a point at identifying the uses of δέ in 12:1–8 and translates them as "and" when referring to the conjunction itself, still uses "but" (i.e. "But when the Pharisees…") when translating v. 2.[41]

These English translations, which note a contrast, are supported by the charge from the Pharisees. The Pharisees accuse, instead of question,[42] the disciples of "doing what is not permitted to do on the sabbath" (12:2) and this accusation is then received by Jesus as a condemnation (12:7).[43] Jesus also reacts to the accusation with two polemical statements which begin with, "have you not read" (12:3, 5), questioning the Pharisees' familiarity with and challenging their interpretation of Scripture. The Pharisees' charge refers to the sabbath laws that require that "no work is to be done by persons or animals on the sabbath."[44] The definition of work varied, however, and caused controversy surrounding the sabbath laws throughout Israelite history.[45] In addition, many exceptions were made to allow for work on the sabbath (1 Macc 2:39–41).[46] The second verse demonstrates the continued struggle between two Jewish groups on how to define work and whether to allow non-compliance in certain circumstances.

Despite the opposition between Jesus and the Pharisees, this initial conflict moves to the background as Jesus responds to them in vv. 3–8 and the main conflict moves to the foreground between Jesus, the disciples, and the Pharisees who are situated in the grainfields and David and the priests who are situated in the sanctuary and temple. Therefore, I read v. 1–2a by translating δέ as connecting the disciples and the Pharisees instead of distinguishing them, "In that season, Jesus went through the grainfields on the sabbath. And his disciples hungered and they began to pick the heads of wheat and to eat them. And the Pharisees, seeing this, said to him...."

David and the House of God (12:3–4)

The second element of the pattern begins with a shift in setting and characters. David and the ones with him enter the house of God and eat the bread of the presence. Three items mark the transition. The spatial setting itself changes from the grainfields to the house of God. The temporal setting shifts from "at that time" to the time of David cued by the phrase "have you not read." Finally, the characters shift from Jesus, the disciples and the Pharisees to David and "those with him" (v. 4). Represented by King David and the priests, centralized sanctuaries and a redistributive economy where resources are pooled and redistributed restricts access to food and runs counter to the generalized reciprocity of gleaning practices and sabbath traditions as represented by Jesus, the disciples, and the Pharisees in the grainfields.

Matthew 12:3–4 refers to 1 Samuel 21:1–6 when David comes to the sanctuary at Nob to the priest Ahimelech. David has just been anointed king in 1 Samuel 16 but he is not functioning as a king yet, rather he is a fugitive on the run from King Saul, who plans on killing David. There are several parallels between Jesus and the disciples plucking grain in the grainfields on the sabbath and David and the ones with him eating the bread of the presence in the house of God. First, Jesus and the disciples parallel David and the ones with him.[47] Second, David and the disciples are "doing" (ποιέω), they "hunger" (πεινάω) and they "eat" (ἐσθίω). Third, both sets of characters are in the middle of conflict.[48] Fourth, both Jesus and David set aside certain laws in order to meet human needs.[49]

Alternatively, when reading with food exchange in mind, the parallels with David are overshadowed by the conflict with David, the priests, and the house of God. The second element restricts the setting of food exchange and limits those who receive the food. The house of God is a more centralized setting for food exchange than the grainfields. A shift occurs from those wandering in grainfields to priests in the "house of God."

In the first setting, wandering and traveling disciples pluck and eat food from a grainfield reflecting the wandering Israelites in the wilderness. Food is gathered from the natural world, which provides for Israelites and those outside the Israelite people who reside with them. In the system of sacrifices, highlighted in the second setting,[50] goods are pooled and centralized into a handful of locations where the sanctuaries are located. In this time period, many sanctuaries were scattered throughout the land of Israel, but the gathering and redistributing of goods from these locations is managed by the priests and their political organization. The house of God is located in a central location and is located inside.[51] The bread of the presence underscores the covenant between Yahweh and Israel, and while this covenant includes, to some degree, those outside the Israelite people, it focuses on insiders.[52] Among the Israelites, the priests, the few who administer the ritual, are those who are allowed to consume the loaves. In this second setting, food is distributed in a centralized system and the spotlight is on a limited few priests who have access to eating a special type of food in a confined spatial location. This runs counter to the movement of the Matthean narrative where food is being shared with a greater sphere of people outside the Matthean community (chs. 7 and 10) and in a widening sphere of locations outside the household.[53]

In addition, the reference to David and the priests further draws attention to the centralized and oppressive nature of this type of food exchange. David is identified as a king in the genealogy (1:6). A multitude of passages throughout the Matthean narrative indicate the oppressive and exploitive nature of kings.[54] David's kingship, while a model in many ways,[55] was also problematic. David commits adultery with Bathsheba, has her husband Uriah killed, and does not discipline Amnon's rape of Tamar. Jesus may be the Son of David and carry the line of this kingship promised by God, but there are distinctions between the two.[56] For example, Jesus cures the blind and lame in the temple (21:14) while David excludes them (2 Sam 5:6–10).[57] In

21:14–17, the priests are also associated with David and the temple and in conflict with Jesus as they become angry when the children cry "Hosanna to Son of David." Jesus as Son of David also recalls Solomon. Solomon was known for oppressive practices of forced labor and burdensome taxes for the temple construction and other building projects (1 Kings 4–12) as well as his marriages with foreign women and worship of other deities (1 Kings 11).[58] Both David and Solomon's reign are especially associated with the centralization of government, with establishing Jerusalem as the capital and building the Jerusalem Temple.

Priests and Pharisees (12:5, 6–8)

The third element in the pattern discusses the third setting, the priests in the temple desecrate the sabbath. The temporal setting returns to the sabbath (as the second setting does not refer to the sabbath). The time range in v. 5 implies the period when the Jerusalem temple (ἱερός) is in operation and is cued again by the phrase, "have you not read." The mention of the temple shifts the discussion from many sanctuaries diffused around the land of Israel to the one temple in the one location of Jerusalem.[59] The priests are the characters.

The fourth element (vv. 6–8) recalls vv. 1–2 with the current narrative time ("at that time," sabbath), space (grainfields, "here"), and characters (Jesus, the disciples, and the Pharisees indicated by the phrases "but I say to you" and "but if you had known"). Jesus then draws conclusions about the three different settings.

Priests in the Temple (12:5)

The spatial and temporal settings in v. 5, along with the activities in those settings, provides a view of food distribution that is further centralized and constrained compared to the second setting in vv. 3–4. The spatial setting of the temple imposes a greater restriction on who makes the decisions about food distribution and who has access to food. Not one "house of God" among many scattered throughout the land, but this setting focuses on one temple in Jerusalem. The place to collect and redistribute goods has become more centralized and institutionalized, concentrating the power to oversee and make decisions about resources in the hands of a few.[60] The temple space is hierarchical and exclusive, marking out space where Gentiles, Israelite women, Israelite men, priests, and the high priest were allowed to be. The grainfields, in contrast, are an inclusive, communal, diffused space that is shared by all in need. The poor and alien are provided for by its food. In the Matthean narrative, the place to encounter God and gain access to food shifts from the temple to interaction with Jesus, his community, and the world outside the community.[61] Jesus certainly interacts with the temple yet the temple is co-opted by King Herod (2:4–6) and the devil (4:5) and judged by Jesus with the overturning of tables of the moneychangers (21:12) and the tearing of the temple curtain (27:51).[62]

The sacrifices offered on the sabbath by the priests in the Jerusalem temple, a doubling of the daily sacrifices, are described in Num 28:9–10. They were burnt sacrifices and community sacrifices. The former designation refers to sacrifices that were completely burned in the fire, thus all of it was offered to God.[63] The sacrifice was probably interpreted as a gift to God, a way to give thanks and honor God.[64] Although not all agree, the offering may have been considered food for God.[65] This sabbath burnt offering, while offered by the community, is consumed only by God. No one else shares in the meal, a further restriction of food. The community sacrifices were offered by the whole Jewish community, made possible through the priests. The sacrifice was paid by the temple tax of one-half shekel, which also supported the overhead cost of the temple.[66] Money flows in from all over the "world" by adult male Jews to a centralized location and is then redistributed out of the Temple.[67]

The use of "desecrate" (βεβηλοῦσιν) in v. 5, "the priests in the temple desecrate the sabbath and are innocent," may have been a typical reference to this practice[68] or its use may be a critique of the priests' practice. On one level, this, again, supports the case against the Pharisees that it is appropriate to set aside certain divine regulations (sabbath requirements of rest) in light of greater divine demands (temple service) or human needs.[69] On another level, the priests literally violate the sabbath with their practices in the temple which do not facilitate greater access to food supply as the sabbath was intended. To desecrate, "to perform an act that violates the sanctity of a custom or place,"[70] refers back to the previous use of "to do" (ποιεῖν) in vv. 2–3 and the disciples act of picking the heads of wheat. The disciples are also desecrating the sabbath, according to the Pharisees ("are doing what is not permitted to do"), yet "desecrate" is not used in reference to the disciples only to the priests. The disciples "perform an act" that gains necessary access to food. The priests in the temple "perform an act" that hinders that access and thus desecrate the very institution established to ease that access.[71]

The temporal setting in 12:5 further highlights the problem of centralization. The temporal setting in 12:1, "at that time," coupled with the disciples plucking grain, would suggest that it is harvest time and it can be inferred in 12:5 that it is also harvest time. Harvest time is the point at which priests determine how much produce is to be collected from each household for sacrifices and redistribution and therefore a reminder of the centralized means to exchange food.[72] Verse 5 returns to the sabbath setting, which is mentioned twice for emphasis. The reference to the sabbath practice in the temple sets up a contrast with the previous sabbath practice in vv. 1–2, which, along with the setting of the grainfields, was interpreted in light of communal structures of social and economic justice to feed the marginalized and God's commitment to provide daily food. Instead of providing greater access to food, the priests and the temple further restrict access. The gap between Jesus, the disciples, and the Pharisees in the grainfields and David and the priests in the temple continues to widen in 12:1–8.

Back to the Pharisees and Grainfields (12:6–8)

The third element of the pattern flows into vv. 6–7 of the fourth element with the continued use of temple language: temple (ἱερός) in v. 6 and sacrifice (θυσίαν) in v. 7. The use of innocent (ἀναιτίος) also connects v. 5 to v. 7. The setting and characters, however, shift back to those in vv. 1–2: Jesus, the disciples, and the Pharisees on the sabbath in the grainfields. The Matthean community is more aligned with the Pharisees and access to food through the grainfields than it is with the priests and access to food through the temple.

Jesus claims in v. 6 that something greater than the temple is here. He does not identify what that something is and scholars have argued a whole list of possibilities.[73] What is greater than the temple is the type of food distribution made possible through the community laws regarding the grainfields. The reference to the spatial setting "here", the use of Hosea 6:6 for the second time in the narrative and the pattern reiterated in 12:1–8 of how to acquire food all support this claim.

The meanings of the spatial setting, "here," in Matthew's narrative are instructive in its use in 12:6. Characters situate themselves "here" or look "here" in the wrong places and assume that they or the ones they look for should be stationary and fixed.[74] Similarly characters do not recognize what they ought to recognize,[75] including the means to acquire food,[76] and characters do not approach and prepare properly for eating.[77] Finally, Jesus prophesies that the temple will no longer be "here" (24:2).

In 12:6, the temple, as stationary and centrally located, is not the spatial setting to look for and acquire food. Not only is it an unjust way to distribute food but it will no longer be "here." Matthew's community is not to look "here" in the temple for food but to look in the grainfields. The grainfields are where Jesus, the disciples, and Pharisees are already located and the literal meaning of "here" in the story refers to the grainfields themselves. While the grainfields are a fixed entity, they are diffused throughout the countryside and Jesus and the disciples are moving through (ἐπορεύθη διὰ) them. Jesus is directing the disciples, the Pharisees, and the audience to recognize what is already in front of them, the grainfields as the most just means to acquire food, and to approach and prepare for eating the food by plucking the grain.

Jesus then quotes Hosea 6:6 in v. 7. Hosea is an eighth-century prophet in Israel who is calling the Israelites back to an obedient covenant relationship with Yahweh. In 6:6, Hosea is reproving Israel not for worship of Baal but for a false worship of Yahweh in making sacrifices a priority to the exclusion of mercy and justice in accord with the covenant.[78] While Hosea employs strong words of judgment and condemnation, he is admonishing the Israelites to return to obedient and ethical lives. Hosea, like many of Israel's prophets, were covenant mediators who advocated for a restoration of the covenant between Yahweh and Israel.[79]

The use of Hosea 6:6 supports a point previously made in 12:1–8 and advances a new one. First, its use favors the priority of mercy over sacrifice, of access to food to those who hunger and are marginalized over the centralized system of sacrifices in the temple. This point confirms the split in 12:1–8 between Jesus and the disciples on the one side and the priests, the temple, and the house of God on the other. Second, its use calls for those in Israel who have veered from the covenant to return to an obedient relationship with Yahweh. Jesus quotes Hosea to the Pharisees and calls them back to the covenant, which is interpreted by Matthew's Jesus. As Hosea reproves the Israelites, so Jesus reproves the Pharisees, not to condemn them but to invite them back to covenant loyalty.[80]

In 12:7, Jesus quotes Hosea 6:6 to the Pharisees for the second time in the narrative (cf. 9:13).[81] The pattern is similar in both passages and both passages involve food: Jesus or the disciples are eating in a way that is opposed by the Pharisees, the Pharisees see (ἰδόντες; 9:11, 12:2) this and question or accuse Jesus or the disciples, then Jesus responds in an instructive (not condemning) way to the Pharisees and quotes Hosea 6:6. In 9:13, Jesus' instructive response is to "go and learn" about Hosea 6:6. In 12:7, Jesus says, "if you had known what this means...you would not have condemned the innocent."

The use in 12:1–8 of "seeing," "go and learn," "have you not read," and "if you had known...you would not have condemned," follows a pattern already established in the narrative for the disciples to seek out and participate in God's provisioning of food for the creation. In order to discover how to acquire food, to recognize how God provides foods, and to participate in the exchange of food, the disciples have or have been instructed to ask/pray (6:9), look, consider, and seek (6:25–34), ask, seek, and knock (7:7–11), inquire, knock, enter and work (10:5–15). They are to "see" how food is acquired through God's provision and act upon it, which is exactly what they do in 12:1—they are in the midst of grainfields, clearly see that there is food, and pick and eat the food. They understand what Hosea 6:6 is about, the priority of merciful and just relations, recognizing that the type of food distribution practiced through community gleaning laws (generalized reciprocity) is more just than the type of distribution practiced through the temple (pooling and redistribution).[82]

The Pharisees, however, "see" the disciples doing it but do not understand (12:7) and condemn the disciples. They were to go and learn, to read, to know and not condemn. In addition, they accuse the disciples—who are going and picking and eating, that is, participating in the exchange of food as they have been instructed through the narrative—of "doing (ποιέω) what is not permitted to do (ποιέω) on the sabbath" (12:2). Instead, the Pharisees themselves are to support the reciprocal exchange of food and not redistribution. While not catching on as the disciples are, the narrative is treating them very similarly to the disciples and still, in 12:1–8, expecting them to learn how God provides food.[83] Matthew's Jesus is calling the Pharisees back to certain types of practices (i.e. the reciprocal exchange of food) that represent God's intent for human's interaction with God and the world.

This alliance between the Matthean community and the Pharisees proves more resilient than the association with the priests and the temple. The Pharisees are not allied with the temple in Matthew's narrative—the temple is the domain of the chief priests and elders. The Pharisees and Jesus interpret differently the laws around the sabbath and gleaning but they are not divided on whether gleaning is appropriate or not. The Pharisees, as part of the larger Jewish community who established and maintained these laws, support the distribution of food to the poor and the alien.[84] In addition, food exchange is being encouraged with one set of the Jewish leaders, the Pharisees, and discouraged with another set of Jewish leaders, the priests. The Pharisees are instructed to participate in food exchange through generalized reciprocity. The line in 12:1–8 is drawn between Jesus, the disciples, Pharisees and reciprocal exchange in the grainfields on the sabbath on the one hand and David, the priests, and centralized redistribution in the sanctuaries and temples on the other hand.

Food Exchange

In 12:1–8, God, the earth, and the human community are necessary to feed the Matthean community. The Matthean community, then, takes initiative to participate in food exchange in order to meet its biological, political, and social needs. As the larger Matthean narrative has progressed, God has been increasingly less visible in passages dealing with food exchange, has worked more indirectly to feed, and has gradually shifted from the image of Father to image of creator and provider.[85] The reference to the sabbath and the practice of gleaning in 12:1–8 echoes the God who created the heavens and the earth, liberated the people of Israel from slavery in Egypt and sustained them through the wilderness. God, as creator of all creatures and liberator and provider for the Israelite people and those from other nations, commands that sabbath and gleaning laws are established through the Jewish community to provide food for the marginalized, the resident alien, the poor, the traveler. God provides generously for

Israel and all of creation in an outpouring of goods to those in need. This giving represents generalized reciprocity with a sustained one-way flow of goods and services with little if any expectation of return.

The setting of food exchange for the Matthean community in 12:1–8 is the grainfield. As the Matthean narrative unfolds, the setting of food exchange moves from inside, architectural/artificial, inhabited spaces within the Matthean community (i.e. the inner room of a household within the Matthean community in 6:1–21) to outdoor, natural, less inhabited spaces more connected to the earth that are outside the Matthean community (i.e. birds of the air in 6:25–34, household outside the community in 10:5–11:1, and the grainfields in 12:1–8). The grainfield is a setting for food exchange, then, that is broadening out beyond the household into the natural world, outside, in the open space, and presumably still within the larger Jewish community. The movement demonstrates more interaction with those outside the Matthean community, with the natural world, and in contentious spaces. God, as creator and provider of all creatures, provides food for and through the Matthean community in these spaces located farther away from its inner kinship circle and from safety and security.

The space of the grainfields, as inhabited space yet on the edge of town, is public and contentious.[86] Jesus and the disciples encounter the Pharisees but Jesus also mentions the priests in the temple. Inhabited areas are often associated with security and promise while more isolated areas are considered venues of danger and threat.[87] As a space outside of town, one might expect a place of threat, as is also indicated by the exchange with the Pharisees and the reference to the priests in the temple. The settings of food exchange in the narrative have also, however, reinforced the themes of security and reassurance in the midst of conflict. The same is true in 12:1–8. "Something greater than the temple is here" refers to more accessible distribution of food for the poor and alien through gleaning practices in the grainfields than the centralized economy of the temple. Mercy is emphasized over sacrifice to encourage acts of steadfast love. The disciples are declared innocent for their work on the sabbath to pick grain (12:7). The Son of Man is the lord of the sabbath and the sabbath tradition of rest and provision trumps any conflict over sabbath laws. Finally, the image of God as creator, liberator, and provider assures the Matthean community of security and promise.

God, the earth, and the human community all collaborate with the Matthean community to make possible the exchange of food.[88] Through the creation of an earth which produces food, the establishment of the sabbath practice (and its association with access to food),[89] and the enactment of gleaning laws, God provides food for the poor and alien, the Matthean community. As argued in 6:1–21 and 6:25–34, God nourishes humans out of God's body, the earth,[90] as a mother nursing her child. God as creator of the world (one who gives birth to the world) provides food in due season to those who cry out. As a baby or toddler child cries out to her mother and seeks God's body for nourishment, so the Matthean community is to seek God's earth and all living things for food. In 7:7–11, God's body takes the form of parents who feed their children and in 10:5–11:1 it is specific households within the larger Jewish community. In 12:1–8, the form of God's body includes feeding directly from the earth (i.e. the grainfields which are made possible by the fruitfulness of the earth) and the human community (i.e. the larger Jewish community which grows the food and makes laws such that certain parts of creation, the poor and alien, are provided food).

The Matthean community would not eat, however, if it did not take advantage of these laws of the Jewish community and participate in the food exchange. The disciples take initiative as they go through the grainfields, pick and eat the grain. They do not ask Jesus for permission nor are they directed by him. They feed themselves. Depicted primarily as travelers, poor and marginalized (sojourners or resident aliens), they rely on God's food-producing earth, the owners of the fields who raise the grain, and the larger Jewish community who establish and enforce gleaning laws. Within these constraints, however, the disciples take action to feed themselves.

The three primary motivating actions for exchanging food in the Matthean narrative (i.e. biological, political, and social) are all evident in this passage. First, the disciples are hungry (12:1), they have biological needs that must be fulfilled. The situation in the first century, reflected in the Matthean narrative, suggests a number of people in the Matthean community would have been poor and scrapped for food every day.[91] The disciples have been depicted as day laborers and sojourners in 10:5–11:1 and this portrayal continues in 12:1–8 as they are traveling and stop in the grainfields to glean wheat, a practice established for the marginalized of society.

Second, the disciples' acquisition of food from the grainfields and Jesus' defense of them expresses the community's power and independence in relation to both the Pharisees and the priests in the temple. The exchange of food differentiates and separates. While the Matthean community does not exchange food with the priests in the temple, the comparison of the type of reciprocity the two communities engage in draws an unambiguous line between the two. The Matthean community practices generalized reciprocity, food created by God is distributed through the natural world by means of economic structures within the Jewish community to provision the poor of society. Food flows primarily one way and there is little expectation of a return gift. The priests in the temple practice the redistribution of centralized resources. This may be considered negative reciprocity where the temple attempts to maximize its own profits at another's expense and where material gain takes the priority over social relations.

The differentiation with the Pharisees is more ambiguous. On the one hand, there is a distinction made concerning the interpretation of the sabbath laws. Looked at from this perspective, the Pharisees are not exchanging food with the Matthean community but arguing about how food should be distributed and, again, a comparison can be made between the two views of reciprocity. The Pharisees agree with Jesus that gleaning is an appropriate practice, but it must not be practiced on the sabbath. This would fall under generalized reciprocity but at the end of the spectrum where some type of counterobligation is expected from the recipient—in this case in the form of restricted gleaning on the sabbath. The Matthean community is differentiating itself from the Pharisees regarding interpretation of the law. This is the typical interpretation of this passage and this study recognizes that some tension exists between the two communities based on this difference.

Food exchange in this case is influenced by kinship rank.[92] A gift is given based on need but it also creates a followership when a gift cannot be returned, compelling those with lower status to demonstrate loyalty to the leader. In a situation where several leaders and their groups are in competition with other leaders and groups, the leader or Big Man who is most generous often wins the most supporters.[93] Jesus is out-giving the Pharisees and ensuring the continued support of the disciples. The reference to the Son of Man in v. 8 also reinforces Jesus' Big Man status. As Son of Man, Jesus is an itinerant who has voluntarily decided to be "in solidarity with the marginalized and broken."[94] He does not withdraw from society but interacts with the world in his earthly ministry with authority and a special intimacy with God.[95] The use of Lord reinforces the view of Jesus as having superior status, power, and authority.[96]

On the other hand, Jesus, with the use of Hosea and a reoccurring pattern in the narrative that is reiterated in 12:1–8 about how to acquire food,[97] calls the Pharisees to participate in generalized reciprocity as Jesus understands it—where no counterobligation is expected from the disciples. Jesus is attempting to call the Pharisees back to loyalty to the covenant with God, to identify with Jesus' understanding of a certain interaction with God through food exchange. This third motivating action for food exchange addresses the need for solidifying social relations. While the Matthean community may, in part, be exerting its own independence, it also understands itself as part of and participating in the larger world around it.[98] A delicate balance must be drawn here between recognizing the Pharisees as a competing Big Man contending Jesus for his followers and the Pharisees as leaders who may interact cooperatively with the Matthean community. Even competing Big Men and their factions would exchange food and interact with other Big Men and their factions, always with tension because of competition but also with the need to maintain social relationships.[99]

In addition, the community connects not only with the leaders but it continues (as it did in 10:5–11:1) to connect with the larger Jewish community in general. The disciples glean food from the grainfield of a member of the larger Jewish community. The influence of kinship wealth is apparent in this exchange. As Sahlins argues, wealth disparities may, assuming social bonds between rich and poor are to be maintained, call for the special provisioning of resources for the poor.[100] This action may be motivated by compassion based on previous experience or social forces due to the weight of tradition. The Israelites experience that they were once slaves/aliens in Egypt is one example of a previous experience of a people that might elicit compassion for those who are marginalized. The subsequent practice and laws around the sabbath and gleaning that evolved around that experience, as well as the use of Hosea 6:6 as part of the prophetic tradition of emphasizing mercy over sacrifice, are examples of social forces due to tradition.

A final example of this third motivating action is the Matthean community's direct reliance on and association with the natural world. The grainfields are the Matthean community's exchange partners. This is where the community receives its food and the "community" with which it directly interacts. The relationship between the Matthean community and the natural world has been addressed already in the narrative. The placement of earth (γῆς) next to bread (τὸν ἄρτον) in 6:10–11 implies that the earth supplies the resources for humanity to feed.[101] That God, who feeds and relates to the Matthean community, also feeds the birds of the air, cares for the sparrows, and clothes the lilies of the field reinforces God's relationship with the natural world and encourages the Matthean community to seek out the natural world for its food (6:25–34, 10:5–11:1). In 12:1–8, however, it is made explicit that the Matthean community depends directly on the earth for its food. Receiving food directly from the food-producing earth solidifies the relationship between the community and the natural world.

Part IV

Food Exchange Inside and Outside the Community

Chapter 8

In Transition (14:13–22)

Introduction

Matthew 14:13–22 and 15:29–39 comprise the third and final thematic unit of this study. A shift occurs with these two passages as the Matthean community is for the first time distributing food to those outside its community instead of only receiving food. In addition, the community is exchanging food with those beyond the larger Jewish community.

A transition is signified in 14:13–22 as the Matthean community exchanges food in a liminal and thus ambiguous and precarious setting (i.e. *by* the sea, in a deserted *place, outside* the villages, during the time *between* day and night) with characters who are also in the margins (i.e. disciples and crowds). Initiated by the disciples, redirected by Jesus and provided by God, the Matthean community feeds the crowds (made up of mostly Jews but also Gentiles). The disciples take on the greatest agency thus far in the narrative to participate in food exchange. An altruistic form of generalized reciprocity, not the market system, is the means for exchanging food. The setting and characters are situated in an in-between reality and indicate a permeable membrane between the Matthean community and the larger world around it. The crowds represent the world and they, as well as the food, move with ease both in and out of Matthew's community reminding the reader that the flow of food and the flow of social relationships go both ways. There is evidence of continuity between the community and the world. The Matthean community sees itself as part of the larger Jewish and Gentile communities and seeks to maintain social ties with these groups. The crowds themselves begin to take initiative to seek out God's provisions through social connections.

Expanding Food Exchange Practices

The settings and characters in 14:13–22 demonstrate that this is a point of transition from one state to another, a liminal situation. This transition is evident in the references to the boat and the sea, in the location of the feeding (by the sea, in a deserted place, outside villages and cities), in the temporal setting (evening, the hour has already passed), and in the portrait of the crowds and disciples. The Matthean community is beginning to expand its food exchange practices as the community itself distributes food with those outside its community. Both the spatial and temporal settings demonstrate continuity between the Matthean community and the world.

The beginning and ending limits of both passages point to this transition as Jesus or the disciples pass through the sea or to the other side or into new borders.

14:13	14:22	15:29	15:39
Jesus withdraws in a boat to a desolate place	disciples enter a boat and go to other side	Jesus passes over from there	Jesus enters into a boat and goes into the borders of Magadan

The boat (πλοῖον) appears in three of the four passages. The boat provides a passageway on the sea from land to land. For the implied audience, knowledgeable about the Hebrew tradition, the sea is a dangerous place of chaos, evil, and destruction.[1] While land is a secure, permanent dwelling location, a place of promise, production, and order, the sea is a threat, a temporary place to be and a place of disorder.[2] The boat provides a means to move across the sea as a dangerous place to the other side. The sea, then, becomes a bridge not a barrier.[3]

In the Matthean narrative, the boat is a place of transition where two disciples are called to follow Jesus (i.e. James and John leave their boat to follow Jesus in 4:21–22), where the disciples learn more about who Jesus is (i.e. Jesus calms the storm and the disciples are amazed in 8:23–24), and Peter shows initiative and tries something new (Peter attempts to walk on the water in 14:23–33). In each case, the boat is a place of change, growth, and learning. In 14:13–22 (and at the end of 15:29–39), the references to the boat and the sea signal a transition. The Matthean community is on the verge of expanding their practice of food exchange.

Settings as Transitional

Both the spatial and temporal settings give evidence to a liminal state in 14:13-22. The lack of a definite spatial location is one indication. The characters are in a desolate place (ἔρημον τόπον; 14:13, 15)—they are not in the wilderness itself but a deserted place. The location is also somewhere by the sea, Jesus withdraws to this desolate place in a boat (v. 13), but they are not on the sea. The crowds have traveled "from the cities" "by land" and the disciples suggest the crowds go "into the villages" to buy food, but they are not located on land or in any city or village. They are located in reference to, next to, or marginally to several areas (i.e. sea, wilderness, land, villages, cities) but are not located positively by any specific areas. The characters are in-between the sea and land and wilderness, the city and village.

The temporal setting in 14:13–22 also alerts the audience to an in-between state. The audience hears that it is evening ('Οψίας δὲ γενομένης, literally "now evening having come") and that "the hour has already passed (ἡ ὥρα ἤδη παρῆλθεν).[4] Evening (ὀψίας) can mean "late" or is used as a general term for the evening time. It is not clear whether it is before or after sundown.[5] Used often in Matthew (8:16, 14:15, 14:23, 20:8, 26:20, 27:57), evening is a time in 14:13–22 to mark God's generosity (cf. 20:8), to prepare for a new phase in the community's life (cf. 26:20, 27:57) as they distribute food to those in the larger world. It is an in-between time, however, and life is at a pause.[6]

Hour (ὥρα) often refers to the time of day and, in particular, the lateness of the hour.[7] Used in the phrase "the hour has already passed" and in conjunction with "evening," the narrative is emphasizing the lateness of the day. The hour, often referring to a particular moment when something is to take place,[8] is also the time for eating. The crowds have missed the time to eat, the day is ending, the evening has come, the time is moving on to an uncertain, transitional time. Both typological references to time[9] (i.e. "evening" and "hour") emphasize that the crowds need to eat now, this evening, this hour. There is urgency in this use of time.

The references to "evening" and "hour" also suggest that this time is between day and night, it is dusk. In her studies on marginal social life and transitional states,[10] Mary Douglas discusses the nature of dawn and dusk as in-between times, as moments when a break occurs in social reality and the typical structures of life (i.e. routines, chores, etc.) are suspended.[11] Dusk is neither day nor night, where the colors are neither dark nor light, but a gradual transitional state when people experience this pause in social reality with a sense of eeriness, ecstasy, danger, and sacredness.[12] During this gap in conventional social organization, distinctions between self and the world are blurred. One loses a sense of clear identity and boundaries between self and the larger environment soften. Therefore, a feeling of continuity exists between an individual or group and the world around them.[13]

Evening has come and the hour has already passed in 14:13–22. No longer day but not yet night, dusk has gradually moved in. Boundaries are softening between the Matthean community and the crowds. They have found themselves together in this transitional place at this transitional time and they will exchange food. The separate identities between the two groups are blurry—at the end of their time together, the narrative reports no distinctions between the two, "everyone ate and they were satisfied" (14:20, 15:37), "the ones eating were men about five thousands apart from women and children" (14:21, 15:38).[14] At the end of each passage, distinctions reemerge (i.e. the crowds separate from the disciples) but during the time of food exchange, the continuity between the two groups is highlighted.

Characters as Transitional

The Crowds. The crowds function as the world beyond the Matthean community including both the larger Jewish community and the Gentile world.[15] The crowds are a public group, in particular the poor masses, representing the world outside the Matthean community who exchange food with that community. Further, the crowds move in and out of the Matthean community throughout the narrative, particularly apparent in 14:13–22 and 15:29–39. They are in transition and marginally related to the Matthean community. This movement shows the permeable membrane of the Matthean community boundaries as well demonstrate that the crowds in 14:13–22 are beginning to take the initiative to seek out God's provision.

The crowds are not portrayed as clearly and completely Jewish or Gentile in the Matthean narrative. On the one hand, most scholars assume they are Jewish, often without giving much supportive evidence, and argue more substantially against a Gentile identity.[16] The evidence for interpreting the crowds as Jewish includes: the

Matthean group is intent on ministering to the lost sheep of the house of Israel (10:6b, 15:24b), the crowds are associated with the lost sheep as sheep without a shepherd (9:36), they are from areas where Jews lived,[17] the crowds refer to the Jewish scribes as "their scribes" (7:29),[18] they are associated with Israel (7:33, 15:31),[19] and the crowds glorify the God of Israel as Jews also do (15:31).[20]

On the other hand, Saldarini, Carter, Cousland, and Davies and Allison admit that there might have been a Gentile presence[21] in the crowds, although only Cousland goes into any detail. The areas where the crowds originated were also places where Gentiles lived, especially the Decapolis,[22] Gentiles also admired and worshiped the God of Israel[23] and followed around healers who claimed divine power.[24]

In addition, I contend that the crowds function like Gentile characters in the Matthean narrative. Eight similarities show a close resemblance of how the crowds and some of the Gentile characters function in the narrative (often as transitional, ambiguous characters). They are both on the periphery of the Matthean group yet are present and interact with the group.[25] Both are distinguished from the disciples (i.e. they do not continue to follow Jesus and they are not called),[26] yet crowds (14:13, 15:30) and Gentiles (8:5–6, 15:22) both seek out and approach Jesus. The crowds (7:29, 9:33, 15:31) and the Magi and centurion at the cross are commended for their recognition of Jesus' special identity and work.[27] Both receive healing (14:13–22, 15:29–39, 8:5–13, 15:21–28). Both sets of characters emerge for a brief time and then disappear.[28] The crowds and the Gentiles are differentiated from unfaithful authorities.[29] Finally, they are both portrayed as ambiguous groups with faithful and positive responses to Jesus and the Matthean community as well as unfaithful and negative responses.[30] This comparison suggests that the crowds may very well have had a Gentile presence and certainly functioned as some of the Gentile characters.

Neither the Jewish nor the Gentile characteristics, however, are emphasized in 14:13–22 or 15:29–39. They are the multitude, the masses, the people. Not just the masses of the Jewish world but of the Gentile world as well and thus the crowds function as the public or the world (as opposed to the elite, which would include the Jewish and Gentile leaders, and more than the larger Jewish community). The crowds are referred to simply as the crowds. Crowd (ὄχλος) is defined as a "crowd, throng, (multitude) of people" and "the (common) people, populace"[31] and Cousland rightly argues that these are the two definitions that best fit Matthew's portrait of the crowds.[32] Given that there was a mix of Jews and Gentiles in the general population in Israel in the first century,[33] there may have been a mix in the crowds as well.

Meyer brings to light a tradition since Aristotle in which the crowds are considered a public group distinct from a private person or a small closed circle.[34] Speaking in private is differentiated from the public assembly; the larger public is contrasted with a particular intellectual or political group or leadership. The ὄχλος is a mass of people or a mob with no leader or political and cultural association.[35]

Simply referred to in Matthew as "the crowds" (οἱ ὄχλοι), "the crowd," "a great crowd," (πολὺν ὄχλον) or "great crowds" (ὄχλοι πολλοὶ), this character has no name and therefore is anonymous, no ethnic designation, no leadership, and no structure.[36] It lacks a concrete identity and organization and appears to be in a permanent liminal state. In relationship to the Matthean community, the crowds are neither inside nor outside the community yet freely move in and out. They are not associated with the disciples but also are not primarily aligned with the Jewish leaders,[37] therefore fitting the designation as a public group contrasted with a smaller circle or political leadership.[38] The use of "impersonal, indefinite or inclusive pronouns and expressions"[39] such as "everyone" (14:20, 15:37) highlights this portrayal as the broad public and also connects the vision of exchanging food with those beyond the Matthean and larger Jewish communities with 7:7–11 (πᾶς, 7:8; ἄνθρωπος, 7:9) and 10:42 ("whoever").

The large size of the crowds is also emphasized in the Matthean narrative, underscoring the contrast between the crowds as a public group (i.e. the world outside the Matthean community) and a smaller group or leadership (i.e.Jewish leaders, disciples, or even the larger Jewish community). First, Matthew uses the plural for this character (i.e. "crowds") 31 times compared to Mark's one time. This is seen in both 14:13–22 (vv. 13, 15, 19) and 15:29–39 (vv. 30, 36, 39).[40] The use of the plural and the phrase "a great crowd" makes an impact on the audience in Matt 14. The audience is inundated with references to this great mass of people as they hear about the "crowds" in v. 13, a "great crowd" in v. 14, the "crowds" in v. 15, and then two references to "crowds" in v. 19. The effect is to enlarge the view of the crowd for the audience (i.e. there are crowds not just one crowd, a great crowd in fact), to emphasize the large, public nature of this group with which the Matthean community is exchanging food and to symbolize the larger world outside the Matthean community.[41]

The second way the crowds are highlighted as a large body is that Matthew tends to place the crowds in locations without specific geographical references, giving the audience the impression that they are everywhere. Where in Mark crowds have some associations with cities, regions and bodies of water (e.g. Mark 5:21, 7:31–33, 8:34–37), Matthew disconnects the crowds from particular locations.[42] This placement of the crowds in limbo fits well with 14:13–22 which places all the characters *by* many different locations but not *in* any one location. The crowds are pervasive, located no place in particular but everywhere in general.

Third, 14:13-22 and 15:29-39 include the phrase "apart from women and children" as it identifies the number of people who are fed at the end of the two feeding stories. Not only are 5,000 and 4,000 men fed, but women and children are also fed. The inclusion of women and children increases the number who are fed and the anonymous reference to the number of women and children leaves the final tally open-ended which gives the impression that there were well beyond 5,000 and 4,000 people who were fed.

Fourth, the crowds as a large body are thrown together, in great need, and open to following those who will help. They reflect 90% of the population, the "poor" in the first-century Mediterranean world. Society was structured in antiquity with the elite comprising the upper 10% of the population (e.g. ruling classes, the military, priesthood, retainers) and the nonelite the lower 90% (e.g. peasants, artisans, laborers, slaves).[43] The crowds represent Jews and Gentiles of lower status who are scarcely able to survive with little hope for upward mobility or access to power.[44]

The crowds, as the larger public/world, move in and out of the Matthean community throughout the narrative. They emerge briefly for an interaction with Jesus or the disciples and then they disappear. At times they seem to be waiting in the background, floating in and out of the presence of Jesus and the disciples (e.g. 8:18, 9:33, 11:7). At other times they have a more definite entry point and exit point (e.g. 13:2–36, 14:13–22, 15:29–39). This is the case in the two feeding passages as the crowds follow or approach Jesus and then are sent away by him after the feeding. See the chart on the top of the next page.

14:13	14:22	15:30	15:39
the crowds followed him by land from the cities	he (Jesus) might send away the crowds	great crowds approached him	Having sent away the crowds

Even a reference within 14:13–22 suggests the crowds are a fleeting presence. Jesus orders them to recline on the grass (χόρτος), a word that recalls the use of grass in the food exchange passage in 6:25–34 where God clothes the grass of the field, which is alive today and tomorrow is thrown into the oven (6:30). So the crowds, too, will be here in this moment but gone in the next.

The crowds are in transition, marginally related to the Matthean community, drifting in and out of the community. In most instances, the crowds have relatively easy access to the Matthean community, moving in and out, with little resistance to being present with the community for short periods of time. In those interactions with the crowds where Jesus heals or feeds them (e.g. 4:23–25, 8:1–4, 12:15–16, 14:13–22, 15:29–39, 19:1–2), there is even greater ease in the interaction with the Matthean community. Jesus does not rebuke the crowds for misunderstanding, for example, but is readily available to heal and feed the crowds. Compassion (σπλαγχνίζομαι) is associated with Jesus' healing and feeding (i.e. 9:36, 14:14, 15:32).

The interactions with the crowds are short-term. Jesus is not calling the crowds to be disciples but is feeding them. This is particularly clear in 15:29–39 where Jesus differentiates between the disciples and crowds. Jesus calls (προσκαλεσάμενος)[45] the disciples but wants to feed the crowds so they do not become weary "on the way" (ἐν τῇ ὁδῷ), on their journey separate from the Matthean community. The Matthean community engages with those outside its community in ways other than as a conversionist sect.[46] As the community exchanged food with, but did not convert, those in the larger Jewish community in 10:5–11:1 as they stayed in their homes so it exchanges food with the crowds here. There are no signs of an attempt to call or convert: there is no call for repentance, the crowds do not join the community or express faith or loyalty in or obedience to Jesus, and there is no use of family language for the crowds. Part of Jesus' ministry/mission involves compassion, healing, and feeding (10:7–8) which do not necessarily include conversion.[47]

This short-term interaction between Jewish and Gentile groups in the first century is typical. Assuming the crowds are representative of the "world" (the mix of Jewish and Gentile groups), it is appropriate to discuss the variety of ways in which Jews and Gentiles related to each other in the first century as a way to demonstrate how the Matthean community related to those outside its community and the larger Jewish community. Gentiles interacted with Jewish communities in a variety of ways, some of which suggested they remained a Gentile and some in which they "became a Jew."[48] In the former scenario Gentiles admired some aspect of Judaism (e.g. endurance under persecution, Moses as a legislator), acknowledged the power of the god of the Jews, and were friendly or benefited the Jews without themselves becoming a Jew.[49] The crowds in Matt 14 and 15 appear to admire (and seek out) Jesus' healing powers and glorify the God of Israel (15:31). This does not necessarily mean they are becoming Jewish, or becoming Matthew's type of Jew, but it could fit under the characteristic behavior of some Gentiles.

Jews could also interact with Gentiles in a variety of ways. Scott McKnight suggests there were several ways in which a Jew in the Second Temple Period might integrate into or have a favorable attitude toward Gentile society and still maintain his or her identity as a Jew.[50] The Jews recognized God as creator of all humanity and Gentiles were clearly within God's providential concern.[51] The Jews also expressed a friendly disposition toward Gentiles, worked beside their Gentile neighbors, and served on the city council with them.[52] The interactions of Jews toward Gentiles, depending on the particular Jewish group, were diverse and did not necessarily include an aspect of conversion. The actions of Jesus and the disciples toward the crowds in Matt 14 and 15 would fit under these types of interactions, particularly identifying the crowds, both Jewish and Gentile, as under the care of God's compassion.

This ease in the crowds relating to the Matthean community regarding healing and feeding, the crowds' quick movement in and out of the community, and the repetition of this movement through the narrative suggests an ease in the relationship between the Matthean community and the crowds (as the world) around the topic of healing and feeding. The same pattern is seen in 7:7–11 with the ease at which food is requested and given and implies few if any controls or limits on the exchange of food. The Matthean community has an openness to the world when it comes to food exchange, a permeable membrane that is easily crossed as the world, and food, moves in and out of the community.[53]

Not only is the relationship between the crowds and the Matthean community in flux as the crowds cross over the permeable boundary of the Matthean community to receive food, the nature of the crowd itself is in transition from 14:13–22 to 15:29–39 as they begin to seek out God's provision.[54] In a similar process to how the Matthean community learned to seek out God's provision in 6:1–21 and 6:25–34, so the crowds seek out food. Both the crowds, as the world, and the Matthean community seek out interaction with each other to eat and make social contacts (survive biologically and socially) in order to survive as marginalized communities (i.e. under the Roman imperial order and some of the Jewish leaders).

In 14:13–22, the crowds "hear" about and "follow" Jesus in a way that closely resembles how the Matthean community "asks" and "prays" for food in 6:1–21. The Matthean community asks (αἰτέω, 6:8) and prays (προσεύξομαι, 6:7, 6:9) for food; both requests are located in a sub domain (L, M, N) of the Louw-Nida communication domain (no. 33) that focuses in on requests and presumed responses which take on a sense of urgency and intensity.[55] In 14:13–22, the crowds "hear" (ἀκούω, 14:13), they receive the news that is communicated to them that Jesus has withdrawn in a boat and moved to a desolate place (14:13). To hear is not only a sensory event (i.e. to be able to hear; domain 24) but a way to be informed of particular news.[56] 'Ακούω fits into the communication domain as well and is immediately next to the sub domain of ask and pray, suggesting a similar sense of urgency and intensity that is conveyed by ask and pray.[57] The crowds are not asking or praying for food but they are making an attempt to seek out food, they receive news about Jesus' movement and respond to it, knowing that Jesus provides for the needs of others.

This sense of immediacy can also be seen with the phrase that comes after ἀκούω in 14:13, "having heard (ἀκούω) this the crowds followed (ἀκολουθέω) him by land from the cities." To follow is probably best interpreted here as Carter does, to physically follow Jesus and not to respond to Jesus' call to become a disciple, adhere to his teachings, and/or promote his cause.[58] Yet, the placement of "follow" immediately after "having heard this," suggests that the crowds are in a hurry to follow Jesus and to follow him with some intent—to have their physical needs met and possibly to make social contact. The crowds have already experienced Jesus' healing in the narrative (4:23–25, 8:1–4, 12:15–16) and now they will experience his feeding.

While their activity may appear base and self-serving, they are, as the poor masses, taking initiative to seek out provisions to survive.

The Disciples. Like the crowds, the disciples are marginal figures in 14:13–22, situated in-between Jesus and the crowds, not identified with either character but connected to both as they receive food from Jesus and distribute it to the crowds. The disciples repeatedly move between the crowds and Jesus which represents their shifting between the world and the Matthean community. Not only do the disciples themselves shift but their control of food shifts as well between the disciples and Jesus.

The disciples have no identified location at the beginning of the passage.[59] Jesus withdraws by himself and the crowds follow him from the cities but the disciples are not mentioned until v. 15 when they appear out of nowhere. Gundry suggests they come "out of the crowds" when they approach Jesus.[60] Although the disciples and the crowds are not the same character, as Gundry suggests, the boundary between the crowds and the disciples is permeable as both move in and out of each other's territory. The disciples themselves oscillate back and forth in reference to the crowds and Jesus.

The disciples do appear to come out of the crowds in v. 15 and then approach Jesus. They immediately suggest the crowds go to the villages for food and therefore separate from the crowds (v. 15). After a discussion with Jesus, the disciples receive food from Jesus, then move away from him and back toward the crowds as they give them food (v. 19). The three characters (i.e. Jesus, the disciples, and the crowds) then merge in v. 20a, "and everyone (πάντες) ate and they were satisfied," as the boundaries momentarily disappear between the world and the Matthean community. When the eating is finished, however, the disciples carry away[61] the leftovers, again separating and moving away from the crowds (v. 20b). Jesus amplifies the separation "immediately" and urges the disciples to enter the boat and go before him to the other side while he sends away the crowds. The disciples are now completely separated from the crowds and Jesus with the sea as a barrier between the two.

Not only do the disciples move back and forth between two characters but their control of food shifts between themselves and Jesus in 14:13–22. The disciples initially take charge of ensuring the crowds are fed. They notice that the spatial (i.e. a desolate place) and temporal (i.e. the hour has already passed) settings are not conducive for the crowds to obtain food and are first to boldly recommend a solution. The disciples throw an imperative toward Jesus, "dismiss (ἀπόλυσον) the crowds," so they may go to the villages and buy food for themselves. Jesus changes the plan, briefly taking control away from the disciples, but then he puts the power back in their hands, "you yourselves give them something to eat" with an unnecessary second person pronoun for emphasis.[62]

The disciples, however, continue to hold to their plan and argue that they "have nothing here but five loaves and two fish." They lay claim to their own food, which is in and (they hope) will stay in their control. They also use the adverb "here" when referring to the loaves and fish. As discussed earlier, "here" is used in Matthew's narrative with characters that situate themselves "here" or look "here" in the wrong places and assume they or the ones they look for should be stationary and fixed. The disciples maintain that the five loaves and two fish should remain "here" with them and the crowds should go to the villages (i.e. "there") to get food, food which is controlled by the village markets. They do not recognize that the food they have "here" should go "there" to the crowds. As they themselves move back and forth between the world and their community, so should the food.[63]

Jesus takes back control of the food and asks that they bring the loaves and fish "here to me." The food will not remain "here" in a fixed position but is now moved to Jesus, who then continues to move the loaves and fish about. He takes them, blesses them, breaks them, and gives the loaves to the disciples who give them to the crowds. Having taken the loaves, Jesus looks up to heaven and then blesses them. Jesus looks to God in heaven for provision not the village markets. Looking up (ἀναβλέπω) evokes his own instructions to the disciples to look (ἐμβλέπω) to the birds of the air who themselves depend on God to feed them (6:26).

While the food is moved around—back to the disciples then to the crowds then to the disciples who carry away the leftovers—the disciples continue to have primary control. As the food moves from Jesus to the crowds, it goes through the disciples hands. The disciples are mentioned twice in its handling, once in receiving the food from Jesus and once in giving the food to the crowds (v. 19). After the eating, then, the disciples[64] carry away twelve baskets full of leftovers. In charge of clearing up or disposal of the food,[65] the disciples continue to be in control of the food. The reference to *twelve* baskets recalls the use of "the twelve" in 10:5 where the disciples, like the twelve tribes of Israel, are depicted as bold and independent as they act upon the larger Jewish community.[66] The control of food begins and ends with the disciples but shifts back and forth in the process. Food, like characters, is to move between the Matthean community and the world. The disciples are primarily seen as bold and in control in the passage, although their interpretation of food exchange is challenged by Jesus. Food is left in their hands to determine how to use next, leaving open in the narrative what the Matthean community will do with the food.

Food Exchange and Motivation

For the first time in the narrative, the Matthean community is no longer the primary recipient of the food and participates in distributing the food to those outside the community. In both passages, loaves and fish, initially belonging to the disciples, are taken, blessed, and broken by Jesus, then given to the disciples who give them to the crowds. In 14:13–22 the disciples take control of the food and feed the crowds; the emphasis is on generalized reciprocity and the Matthean community's sharing of food with those beyond its borders.

The question raised regarding food exchange in this first feeding passage is "where must one go to get food?" or "where must the crowds go to get food?" The disciples suggest going to the villages to buy (ἀγοράζω) food for them. Buying and selling carry negative connotations in the Matthean narrative. As mentioned in the analysis of 10:29–31, selling (πωλέω) impairs social and theological relationships. Buying and selling are referred to in 13:44, 46, 21:12, 25:9–10, buying is also referred to in 27:7 and selling in 10:29. All but 13:44, 46 refer to these concepts in a way that blocks non-hierarchical, non-exploitive relationships among those within the Matthean community and with the world. Along the same lines, marketplaces also do not fare well in the narrative; they are places where workers are exploited and leaders exploit.[67] The type of centralization of goods and power that occurs in the temple institution as mentioned in the analysis of Matthew 12:1–8 is also present in the market system. To send the crowds to the villages to buy food is to separate the world from the Matthean community and to encourage the use of the market system run by the imperial economy.[68] Buying and selling segregates instead of unites as evidenced by the references to hierarchy and exploitation in the Matthean passages as well as the two references to reflexive pronouns in 25:9 (i.e. "go rather to the dealers and buy *for yourselves*") and 14:15 (i.e. "and buy food *for themselves*").

As an alternative of sending the crowds to the villages to buy food for themselves, food is made available as a gift through sharing and reciprocity. The Matthean community's sharing of food with the crowds in 14:13–22 can be understood in two interrelated ways: as reciprocating to the larger Jewish community the food it received in 10:42 and as those with resources sharing with the desperate poor who have little access to resources. First, the Matthean community had expected to receive hospitality from the larger Jewish community according to Jesus instructions in 10:5–11:1, a place to stay (10:11), food provision (10:10), and a cup of cold water (10:42). In response, those who offered this provision were to receive a reward in return (10:42). The reward (μισθός) in v. 42 was not an eschatological reward but part of an ongoing temporal, reciprocal exchange between the Matthean community and those in the world around it. This reward is now being made in 14:13–22 in which the Matthean community is responding by feeding the crowds. As the larger Jewish community was feeding the Matthean community in 10:5–11:1, now the Matthean community is feeding the larger Jewish community. While the crowds in Matt 14 and 15 are not to be identified solely with the lost sheep of the house of Israel in Matt 10, the crowds would include some of the larger Jewish community and this sharing of food would be one way in which the Matthean community is giving back to the larger Jewish community.[69] In addition, the giving of food to the crowds who also represent the Gentile world suggests that this world has or will be involved in providing food for the Matthean community as well.[70]

The second way this sharing of food can be understood is that wealth differences, as Sahlins argues, might motivate giving. Even if there is not a consistent difference in wealth between two parties, in a community where everyone might be in a situation of need from time to time generous sharing is more prevalent. The recognition of need, and the experience of need, engenders compassion from the one who has for the one who does not.[71] The Matthean community has not always been the wealthy party in relationship with the larger Jewish community, as argued in Matt 10:5–11:1. The community in Matt 14 and 15 now has access, however, to resources and because it has been in a situation of need before and because it has a history as part of the

Jewish people to give to those in need, it is showing compassion to the crowds. The crowds have been described as the masses that live in desperate poverty and are clearly in need at this moment in the narrative. This way to understand sharing is also related to the first view in that there is an ongoing exchange of food among those who, from time to time, have a situation of need.

By sharing food with these two understandings, the Matthean community sees itself as part of the larger Jewish and Gentile communities and seeks to maintain social ties with these groups. A stronger bond has been established with the larger Jewish community because of its shared history and previous exchanges in the narrative. A bond appears to exist, however, with the Gentile community, in particular the poor masses, because of its shared situation of need but also because of the Matthean community's understanding of God as the creator of all life and the Jewish community's understanding of the gathering of the Gentiles according to the Zion traditions, which are invoked in 15:29–39.

Conclusion

In 14:13–22, the disciples take greater responsibility and distribute food to those outside its community. While most of the narrative to this point has focused on the Matthean community receiving food, it is now exchanging food with the larger Jewish community and the Gentile world. Food travels both ways through the porous borders between the Matthean community and the world outside the community and those involved in the food exchange passages in this study have depended on others for food but also have been active participants. No human party has claimed sole power to the control of food.

Chapter 9

Food from God's Earth (15:29–39)

Introduction

Matthew 15:29-39 concludes the final unit of this study. In this passage, Jesus takes control of the feeding, the disciples become less active in handling the food and more dependent upon others, and the crowds take on a greater agency in seeking out God's provision as those who "approach" Jesus, "see" the work of God, and are considered the righteous who suffer. The setting shifts from the marginal locations in Matt 14 to the mountain and wilderness, the most uninhabited and isolated places in the narrative but also places of new community and provision. The setting of food exchange has shifted to space intimately connected to the physical features of the earth. The new setting on top of the mountain (recalling the Zion traditions and mountains as places of fertility) and the references to the earth (v. 35) change the emphasis of food exchange to God feeding the Matthean community and the world through the earth. Whereas in 14:13–22 the flow of food moves from God to the Matthean community to the crowds, in 15:29–39 the food flows from God through the earth to both community and world. The earth is God's body as God nurses God's creation and the Matthean community gives thanks to this God.

Both 14:13–22 and 15:29–39 echo the view of food exchange in 6:1–21 and 6:25–34. The recipients of food are portrayed as those who are crying out in need for food, food is quickly delivered from God, as creator and deliverer, an allusion to God as nursing the community is apparent, and the receiving community are those who are to look for God's provisions. As the Matthean community received food from God's body in Matt 6 and then was encouraged to seek and participate in God's provision, so now the crowds in Matt 14 and 15 follow the same pattern. God is intimately related to the world, working in the world not acting on it, and encourages the world to participate as responsible agents. The flow of food between the Matthean community and the world in 14:13–22 and between God's earth and the community and world in 15:29–39 intimates that the implied audience is to reach out and be open to the larger world (i.e. the Jewish community, the Gentile world, and the natural world) and to see God as the one who provides for those in the larger world outside the Matthean community.

Disciples and Crowds

Disciples

As with 14:13-22, the disciples and crowds are two primary characters in 15:29-39. The disciples are much less active in this passage than in 14:13–22, both in moving between Jesus and the crowds and regarding food exchange. The crowds, on the other hand, approach Jesus, see the work of the God of Israel, and are considered righteous. The move to 15:29–39 shifts the focus from the Matthean community (i.e. the disciples) feeding the world to the earth feeding the Matthean community and the world.

Jesus, not the disciples, handles the food situation in 15:29–39. While the disciples initiate the question of food for the crowds in 14:13–22, Jesus does so in 15:29–39. Jesus must call the disciples over to him to tell them he wants to feed the crowds. The disciples offer no plan, as in 14:15, but only ask in bewilderment, "where will we get that much food in the wilderness?" The disciples do not bring the food to Jesus as in 14:18, Jesus must get the food himself (15:36). The disciples do offer the food to the crowds after receiving it from Jesus but this is the only action they take in the whole passage to contribute to the feeding. They do not even collect the leftovers after everyone eats (15:37) as they did in 14:20.

This shift in the disciples' control of the food from 14:13–22 to 15:29–39 reflects the shift in the disciples' activity in 10:5–15.[1] From Matthew 14 to Matthew 15, the disciples change from those who are acting upon the world, in control of food, to those who are more dependent upon others to receive food. This pattern highlights the dual needs of the Matthean community, as those who both actively participate in food exchange and distributing food and those who are dependent upon those outside its community (i.e. God, the larger Jewish community, the larger world) for food.

Crowds

In 14:13–22, the crowds are crossing over the permeable boundary of the Matthean community and taking initial steps to seek out food. In 15:29–39, the crowds take a greater initiative to seek out God's provision than in 14:13–22 and as compared to the efforts of the disciples in 15:29–39. As the Matthean community has been gradually increasing its efforts to seek out God's provision throughout the narrative, the crowds, as representative of the world, now begin to do the same. The contrast of the crowds' increased activity and the disciples decline highlights that the world outside the community also seeks out God's provision. This juxtaposition also brings to light a specific dynamic of food exchange. While in 14:13–22 the Matthean community feeds the world, in 15:29–39 the earth feeds both the Matthean community and the world.

In 15:29–39, the crowds "approach" (προσέρχομαι) Jesus, "see" (βλέπω) his works, and are portrayed as righteous in a similar way to how the Matthean community was engaged in looking, considering, and seeking in 6:25–34. The crowds have moved on from "hearing" and "following" in 14:13–22 and, in 15:29–39, are learning more about and making connections with those who can provide food. The crowds "approach" Jesus in 15:30. "Approach" is used extensively in the Matthean narrative and highlights Jesus' authority and majesty.[2] The crowds do not simply move physically closer to Jesus, they come before him with some sense of awe and deference. This is confirmed by two subsequent actions of the crowd. The crowds put the lame, blind, crippled, and mute *at Jesus' feet* (15:30), which suggests the recognition of Jesus as one with authority,[3] and they *glorify* the God of Israel (15:31) as an act of reverence.[4]

Furthermore, the crowds "see" (βλέπω) the work of Jesus and the God of Israel. There is an emphasis on seeing in 15:31 with three references: "so that the crowd was amazed *seeing* the mutes speaking, the cripples healthy, the lame walking around and the blind *seeing*; and they glorified the God of *Israel*."[5] The crowds see the work of Jesus as he heals. That the blind see, mentioned last in the list in 15:31 as a bookend with the crowds seeing (βλέποντας), highlights the crowds' process of now being able to see. The third reference to seeing is the mention of Israel. Israel was used in the first and second century to mean "one who sees God."[6] The crowds glorify the God of Israel, praising the God of the people who see. They are now also people who see.

But more than simply being able to see, the crowds recognize and consider what this means.[7] They have approached (προσῆλθον) Jesus with more knowledge of and reverence for his work and they see it for themselves and are learning more about God's work in Jesus. They no longer hear about and follow Jesus as some distant, unknown charismatic figure, but they approach reverently and see more clearly the one who is doing the work of the God of Israel. Seeing in this context for the crowds means to notice Jesus' healing, to learn about and process what is happening in front of them, and to begin to understand Jesus' work.[8]

How the crowds see (βλέπω) in 15:29–39 reflects how the Matthean community looks (ἐμβλέπω), considers (καταμανθάνω), and seeks (ζητέω) in 6:25–34. Both communities are seeking, looking, observing, being aware of how God provisions creation. Both are processing information and learning about how God provides for the creation so they may seek out God's provisions, even through one another, to survive as dispossessed groups. The Matthean narrative has focused on how the Matthean community is to interact within its own community and with the world around it (i.e. the larger Jewish community, the natural world, some of the Jewish leaders, and the Gentile world) to make connections and find food and now the narrative is shifting to how the world around the Matthean community is to do the same.[9]

The crowds are portrayed in 15:29–39 not only as approaching Jesus with respect and seeing how God provides, but also as righteous. Jesus summons the disciples and tells them he has compassion for the crowd, "for already they remain with me three days" (15:32). The reference to three days may refer to the frequent motif in the Hebrew Bible that God does not allow the righteous to suffer more than three days and will rescue them.[10] Those who suffer for three days include both Jews and Gentiles,[11] which would fit the crowds' ethnic composition. That the crowds are considered righteous in Matthew's narrative seems unlikely if the definition of "righteous" is God's demand for right human moral conduct.[12] Yet, the Matthean community has been portrayed in this study as seeking righteousness in that they seek out and participate in God's righteous relationship with the created world in providing food.[13] The crowds in 15:29–39 are also seeking God's righteous activity.

In addition, there is a convergence of the themes of seeking, righteousness, and satisfaction in three passages in the Matthean narrative: 5:6, 6:33, and 15:37.[14]

> Blessed are those who *hunger and thirst* for *righteousness*,
> for they will be *satisfied* (5:6).
>
> *Seek* first the kingdom of God and his *righteousness*
> and all these things will continue *to be added* as well (6:33).
>
> And everyone ate and they were *satisfied* (15:37)

In all three passages, those who seek righteousness (hunger and thirst in 5:6, Matthean community seeks in 6:33, crowds "approach" and "see" and "suffer three days" in 15:37) are satisfied (χορτάζω; 5:6, 15:37) or continue to be provided for (6:33). Both the Matthean community and some of the world around it seek God's righteous activity of provisioning the world, participate in it, and are satisfied.

In addition, the crowds are linked to those who are righteous through a connection among sheep, Israel, the crowds, and righteousness that runs through 9:36, 10:6, 15:29–39 and 25:31–46. The crowds are referred to as "sheep without a shepherd" in 9:36, a common representation of Israel in the Hebrew Bible.[15] The characterization of Israel as "the lost sheep of the house of Israel" in 10:6, and their contiguity,[16] links the two and suggests that the crowds are the lost sheep of the house of Israel. In both passages, the sheep/Israel are portrayed as suffering and afflicted, yet in 10:5–15 the lost sheep shift to a position of power as they offer hospitality to the Matthean community. They participate in God's righteous activity as a vehicle of God's feeding. In 15:29–39, the crowds are not the same group as the one depicted in 9:36 and 10:6 as they include Jews and Gentiles yet they share some similarities. Both groups are suffering (9:36, "weary," ῥίπτω; 15:32, "faint," ἐκλύομαι) and portrayed as righteous (i.e. the lost sheep feed the Matthean community in 10:5–15; the crowds with Jesus "three days" in 15:32) as they participate in God's activity of feeding. The crowds in 15:29–39 are not referred to as sheep explicitly but the connotation remains. In 25:31–46, then, sheep reappear as they participate in God's righteous activity of feeding. They feed those who are hungry (25:35) and are deemed righteous (25:37). While the composition of the group has changed from Israel

(9:36, 10:5) to a mix of Jews and Gentiles (15:29–39, 25:31–46), the references to the crowds and sheep continue the idea that these groups are righteous and participate in food exchange.

That the crowds "glorify" (δοξάζω) the God of Israel or are considered righteous does not indicate that they have faith in Jesus or are showing exclusive loyalty to the God of Israel. As Cousland and others have argued,[17] the crowds do not glorify or praise or worship Jesus, they glorify God. While there is a hint of reverence (or perhaps respect) for Jesus with the use of "approach" (προσέρχομαι), this may indicate more a recognition of his authority than that he is God.[18] The crowds are not ready to join Matthew's group of Jesus' believers.

The crowds' praise of the God of Israel does not necessarily indicate exclusive loyalty to that god. If one considers the crowd's composition as including Jews and Gentiles, the Jewish parts of the crowd would be devoted only to the God of Israel but the Gentile parts of the crowd would not. Many Gentiles acknowledged and admired the power of the Jewish god but would not offer exclusive loyalty to that god, much like other pagans of antiquity who might offer sacrifices to the God of Israel along with their pagan gods.[19] The reference to the crowds as righteous also does not mean they are only composed of Jews loyal to God. Those who suffered for three days, and were considered righteous, in the Hebrew Bible also included Gentiles who were not part of the covenant community.[20]

As a corporate character representing the masses, the world, "the crowds" who "approach" Jesus and "glorify" the God of Israel are showing respect and reverence for the Matthean community, its leaders and god, they are seeking after God's provision, but they are not joining the community or demonstrating sole allegiance to the community's divinity.

Mountain and Wilderness

Mountain

Both the mountain and the wilderness, the two main settings in this passage, are desolate locations yet places of God's provision where God, as creator, feeds from the earth. The mountain is often interpreted in the Hebrew Bible and New Testament as an isolated and uninhabited location, especially in the context of the exodus and Matt 15:29–39 (i.e. the mountain in the desert), yet it is also a place of provision and promise.[21] While located in the desert as the Israelites wandered after the exile, for example, Mount Sinai was also a place for divine rescue and the establishment of community.[22] The mountain, along with other features of 15:29–39 (i.e. gathering of crowds, healings of the lame, maimed, blind, and dumb, feedings, pastoral imagery), also conveys the symbolism of a Zion theology.[23] In this theology in the first testament and the Second Temple Period, one portrait of Yahweh is as a sovereign king over all the political nations but there are also traditions that focus on Zion and God in relation to the whole cosmos.[24] In the latter image, Zion is the center of and linked to all creation, is the new Eden and source of the river of life which produces food, and, like other mountains, is a place of fertility which brings forth water to give drink and grow food for animals.[25] Yahweh is the creator who feeds the whole creation.[26] The mountains shall drip sweet wine and the hills shall flow with milk and wine (Joel 3:18, Amos 9:13). A river will flow from Zion (and specifically the Temple) that is full of fish to eat and which will water trees that bear fruit and fields which will grow grain (Joel 3:18, Ezek 47, Pss 46:4, 65:9).[27] Furthermore, the city Zion, Jerusalem, pairs up with God to give birth, feed, and raise their children Israel and all the nations (Isa 66:7–13).[28] The earth, the Temple, and Jerusalem feed God's creation.

These are illustrations of the abundance of food that will be provided by God in the future restoration of Israel, and all the nations, following the exile and a time of judgment.[29] The images also exemplify how God feeds through the earth and natural world (i.e. the grapevines, the cows, and the mountains and hills) and how the previous images of Jerusalem and the Temple as centralized, oppressive institutions are transformed into images of God's maternal care and life-giving resources.[30]

These "Zion complex of ideas"[31] in 15:29–39 suggest that the Zion traditions are invoked and therefore the passage anticipates the new age, the time and place in which God's people gather as a new community (scattered Jews and Gentiles), healing and feeding take place, and Yahweh is worshiped.[32] God feeds through the earth and the oppressive Jerusalem Temple mentioned in Matt 12 is transformed into mountains and rivers which feed God's people. The anticipation, however, does not mean completion and while the crowds are fed they do not feast with plenty left over. While some claim seven full baskets is a sign of abundance, it seems more like a very narrow margin when feeding 4,000 men apart from women and children.[33] This appears to be closer to the exodus traditions when God feeds the Israelites just enough for each day. Furthermore, though the crowds worship, they do not join the community. A glimpse of the new age is noticed, perhaps, but fulfillment is not reached. Yet this glimpse demonstrates that in isolated, uninhabited locations, God provides from the earth enough food for all creation.

Wilderness

To the audience of the Matthean story, who would be familiar with the Hebrew Bible, the wilderness is a place of danger and providence.[34] Locating this feeding in 15:29–39 on a mountain and in the wilderness, as well as by a body of water,[35] emphasizes this place as the most isolated and uninhabited location in the Matthean narrative for food exchange. The immediate danger in 15:29–39 is a lack of food for the crowds and the concern that they might become weary on their way (15:32). The feeding in 15:29–39 recalls the exodus of the Israelites from Egypt and their travels in the wilderness.[36] The characteristics of the story in Matthew 15 match those in Exodus: in the wilderness, a large group on a journey/"on the way" (15:32), the need for safe passage, the divine provision of bread, the scene on a mountain. In addition, the sequence of events is also similar, although reversed in 15:29–39: the movement across a body of water (15:39; Exod 14 and the parting of the waters), the feeding (15:32–38; Exod 16), and the mountain (15:29; Exod 18).[37] Like the Israelites, the Matthean community and the crowds are endangered in the desert yet provided food and a safe passage by God. Even in the most remote setting of the narrative, God provides.

The wilderness setting also functions as the location of a new creation which anticipates a new beginning. Both the exodus motif and creation themes are prevalent, for example, in Second Isaiah as the Israelites returned through the wilderness to the promised land after the exile. Here, God promised food, water, safe passage, and new inhabitants.[38] Echoes of the second creation story (Gen 2:4b–25), however, permeate these passages: water coming out of the dry land, Eden, a garden, rivers in the wilderness. The exodus images are mixed in with creation images.[39] Not only is God liberator who brings God's people out of slavery but God is creator of all things.

In Matthew 15:29–39, the wilderness functions as a place of new creation, a new beginning. The combination of wilderness and food in 15:29–39 echoes similar features in Matt 4:1–11, where Jesus is fed in the wilderness by the angels. Once this connection with 4:1–11 is made, further links can be seen with 4:1–11, 7:7–11, and the creation story in Gen 3 which allude to temptation, food, and the devil. Thus, food and the wilderness in Matt 15:29–39 find an indirect path to the creation story in Gen 3. Furthermore, food from heaven is apparent here in Matt 15 (i.e. giving thanks to God in 15:36), and especially in 14:19 (i.e. "having looked up to heaven") as it is in 4:11, 7:11, and *The Life of Adam and Eve*, which records that Adam and Eve ate the "food of angels" (2–4).[40] Having food in the wilderness brings to mind the creation story and a new beginning for the Matthean community.

The use of wilderness, as the use of mountains, recalls the creation motifs within the Zion traditions. Isaiah 51:3 reports that Yahweh provides comfort in the waste places, making the wilderness like Eden (e.g. with the abundance of food) and thanksgiving will be heard. In Matt 15 God through Jesus shows compassion and gives food to the Matthean community and the crowds in the wilderness and thanksgiving is expressed (14:19, 15:36). Fountains and pools will also arise in the midst of valleys and wilderness so "that all may see and know, all may consider and understand, that the hand of the LORD has done this, the Holy One of Israel has created it" (Isa 41:18–19). In 15:29-39, the mountains are signs of fertility and the crowds "approach" and "see" the creative and healing work of the "God of Israel" in the wilderness. As God feeds the Matthean community and the crowds in the wilderness in 15:29–39, a new start is anticipated.

Food Exchange and Motivation

In 14:13–22 the question raised regarding food exchange is "where must one *go* to get food?" In 15:29–39, the disciples ask where the food will *come from*, that is "from where (is there to come) to us in the wilderness so many loaves so as to satisfy such a great crowd?" (15:33). There is no mention of going to the village to buy food and, as previously stated, the disciples lose control of handling the food. Furthermore, the similarity of the story in 15:29–39 to 2 Kgs 4:42–44, the references to the earth (v. 35) and the mountain (v. 29) shift the emphasis of food exchange. While in 14:13-22, the flow of food moves from God through the Matthean community to the crowds, in 15:29–39 the flow of food moves from God through the earth to both the Matthean community and the crowds. The world is God's body as God nurses God's creation.

The feeding stories in Matt 14 and 15 are compared to several stories in the Hebrew Bible (e.g. Exod 16, Num 11, Isa 25) but 15:29–39 also has some particularly similar features to 2 Kgs 4:42–44. In 2 Kgs 4 and Matt 15, the leading character (Elisha and Jesus) takes control of the feeding and the secondary character (the servant and the disciples) resists the suggestions of the leading character and ask questions. Both use loaves of bread (ἄρτος) and both can be interpreted to suggest there was just enough food for all and not an abundance. In 2 Kgs 4, the LXX reads "they shall eat and leave" (φάγονται καὶ κατᾶ λείψουσιν). The Hebrew and most English translations read, "they shall eat and have some left." In the LXX, which was probably the version the author of Matthew used, there is no emphasis on how much is left over rather it is translated as the people leaving after they eat. Even the Hebrew can be translated as "some left" or "some remaining."[41] Likewise, having seven baskets full of leftovers does not necessarily suggest abundance, just that there was enough.[42]

Finally, both can be interpreted to refer to bread from the earth and the act of sharing food with those in need as tied to sacrifice and thanksgiving to God. The man from Baalshalishah was bringing bread of the first fruits, bread from the harvest, from the earth, that was to be offered as a sacrifice. In Matt 15:35, the narrative uses the word earth (γῆν) when referring to the crowd reclining on the earth. This is a change from 14:13–22 where the crowds recline on the grass (χόρτος) (14:19). Immediately following the reference to the earth, Jesus takes the seven loaves, gives thanks, breaks them, and gives them to the disciples who then give them to the crowds. Four words after earth comes the word "loaves." The proximity of these two words brings to mind to the implied audience a similar passage in 6:10–11 where "earth" and "loaves" are situated next to each other. In 6:10–11, Betz argues that the placement of these two words implies that the earth provides the resources for humanity to survive.[43] While the connection is not as immediate in Matt 15, the similar proximity and order of "earth" and "loaves" lead the implied audience to get the same message. The use of these two words for the first and last food exchange passages in this study also suggests intentionality in the narrative. The disciples ask where in the wilderness will we get loaves and, after a reference to the earth, Jesus takes the loaves they have and enough loaves are then produced. The earth has provided the bread. The reference to the crowds reclining on the ground may also feed this interpretation. To recline (ἀναπίπτω) is to sit at table to eat.[44] The crowds sit around the earth to eat of its produce. The crowds sit on the grass in 14:19 to emphasize the temporary nature of this transitional passage (cf. 6:30), but the crowds are now in a more permanent location, on top of the mountain, in the desert, and on the earth, and are to partake of the produce of the earth, the enduring place of God's provision.

Both 2 Kgs 4 and Matt 15 refer to bread from the earth, share food with those in need, and connect these elements to sacrifice and thanksgiving to God. The sharing of food from God's earth is associated with giving thanks to God and underscores the theological and social motivation for sharing food in 15:29–39. Betz argues that in agrarian theology "the gift of thanks given to God was always bound up with the provision of social help to those who are in need and destitute."[45] This pattern is present in Matt 14 and 15 as Jesus gives thanks to God and immediately shares the loaves and fish with the crowds.[46] The Matthean community shares gifts with God's people as a response to having received gifts from God. This motivation follows the first two motivations attributed to 14:13–22 in how to understand the sharing of food with the crowds: the Matthean community once had need and received food from God through the larger Jewish community (10:5-11:1) and is responding by providing for that larger Jewish community (Matt 14 and 15). Jesus instructions in Matt 10:8, "freely you received, freely give," reinforce this process of reciprocal gift-giving. The first two motivations in 14:13–22, however, focus on a social motivation for maintaining a relationship with those in the larger community while this motivation in 15:29–39 emphasizes a theological motivation for maintaining a relationship with God who provides for all creation. All three motivations, however, include a social and theological dimension.

God Nurses the Matthean Community and the Crowds

Several clues are apparent in 15:29–39 to send a message to the implied audience that God provides through the earth. As discussed in the analysis of Matt 6:1–21, the Hebrew Bible suggests food and drink come forth from the earth, God's body: the mountains drip with sweet wine and flow with milk, the wilderness and rocks bring forth rivers and water to drink, and the earth produces grain. God's feeding through the earth conjures up the image of God as a mother who nurses her creation. The earth nourishes all living things as a Mother nourishes a child. God participates intimately with the world instead of ruling it from a distance.

The method in which the crowds and the Matthean community are fed in Matt 14 and 15 is similar to the way the Matthean community was fed in 6:1–21 and 6:25–34 as well as how the Israelites were fed in the wilderness in Exod 16:13–35 and Num 11:7–15, 31–32.[47] It is illustrated with the image of God as a mother nursing her child. The characteristics of this pattern include: (a) those fed are hungry and/or crying out, (b) food is provided when needed (i.e. regularly, daily, and/or immediately) (c) God is portrayed as creator and deliverer who births and nurses her children, (d) the nature of the feeding is miraculous yet unobtrusive[48] and (e) no cultivation or preparation of the food is necessary except gathering or distributing.

In nursing, an infant or young child cries out for food when she is hungry and the mother, as the one who gave birth to her and provides for her, responds immediately to nurse the child. The feeding is quite remarkable, perhaps even miraculous or mysterious that a mother's body provides for a child, yet there is no elaborate technique or manipulation in the feeding and no preparation of the natural milk that flows from the breast.

In Exod 16, the Israelites complained and cried out for food in the desolate wilderness (Exod 16:2–3) and food was provided each day "as each of them needed" (Exod 16:16, 18, 21). God is portrayed primarily as one who delivers God's people from slavery in Egypt and brings them through the wilderness. Additionally, in Num 11, God is depicted as the one who conceives, gives birth and nurses the Israelite people (Num 11:12). God feeds the Israelites in the wilderness by raining bread from heaven and bringing down quails to cover the camp but with no sophisticated performance or manipulation.

The Israelites only must gather the food, there is no harvesting or processing.

The feedings in Matt 14 and 15 follow this pattern. First, the crowds do not cry out or make an explicit request for food but the reader presupposes, and is given clues, that the crowds are in distress and need.[49] The crowds do hear about and follow Jesus (14:13) for some reason, presumably healing and feeding. Even more explicit in 15:30 the crowds approach Jesus with their lame, blind, crippled, and mute for healing and Jesus makes evident that the crowds must be hungry (15:32). Second, food is given to the crowds when it becomes clear to the Matthean community that there is a need. In Matt 14, the hour has passed and the crowds must eat. "They have no need (χρείαν) to go out" (14:16) to the villages for food but they do have need for the disciples to give them something to eat (14:16). In Matt 15, the crowds have remained with Jesus for three days and require food. Food is given to the crowds as it is assessed they need food, without prolonging the wait.

Third, God in 14:13–22 and 15:29–39 is the God of deliverance and creation, the God who the people "look to" for food and provision. With loaves in hand in 14:13–22, Jesus looks to (ἀναβλέπω) heaven (14:19). This gesture indicates that Jesus is looking to heaven, the abode of God,[50] to give God thanks for the food.[51] To "look to" God, "to lift up your eyes" or "your face" to God as the one who creates all of life and provides food for the creation is part of the Jewish tradition.[52] God is described as one who opens God's hand and satisfies the desire of every living thing, hears the cry of the people, and saves them (Ps 145:15–19), the one who creates all living creatures and feeds them (Ps 104; *Pss. Sol.* 5:10). The view of God here is not a distant patriarch who dominates and provides infrequent benevolence but one who is concerned, reaches out to those who fall, creates and continues to provide for the creation.[53] Jesus seeks out God as the one who provides food not the village market system which is controlled by and disproportionately benefits political leaders.[54]

In 15:29–39, the view of God is shaped by the settings in the wilderness and on the mountain coupled with the crowds glorifying the God of Israel. As God observed the misery and heard the cries of the Israelites in Egypt (Exod 3:7), liberated them from slavery, and gave them food and water in the wilderness, so God recognizes the situation of the crowds and provide them with food in the wilderness. The wilderness is a place where God delivers and creates anew. But lest the crowds be identified only with the Jewish people, there is support that there were Gentiles present and the setting of the mountain invokes Zion traditions and anticipates that this is a place in which scattered Jews and Gentiles gather (Isa 2:2–4, 35:8–10; Mic 4:1–4; Jer 31:10–12, Ezek 34:16) and feasting takes place (Isa 25:6–10, Jer 31:12–14, Ezek 34:25–31) at the beginning of the new age.[55] What better way to anticipate this eschatological gathering than to have all the players present. Finally, the crowds glorify the God of Israel. The phrase, God of Israel, was used in the Jewish tradition quite extensively and in a variety of ways.[56] One grouping of its uses includes God's care of the sick, provision of the needy, and deliverance of the persecuted, which fits its use in 15:31 where the sick are healed. God reaches out to and delivers the marginalized. The phrase "God of Israel" also underscores those who "see," who look to God for provision, as in 14:13–22. Israel came to mean "one who sees God."[57] Both the Matthean community and the crowds see God. In 15:29–39, God is deliverer and creator, healer and provider of the Jewish and Gentile worlds and particularly the marginalized. God is like a mother who gives birth and nurses her children, who look to her for food and guidance.

Fourth, the feeding is miraculous but unremarkable in its execution. No detailed description of the miracle of multiplication itself, no magical words or special handling are performed. The miracle "simply" happens and everyone is fed. Finally, and related to the fourth item, no cultivation is needed to prepare the food for eating. While there was initial harvesting to obtain the original loaves and fish, no further preparation or processing was necessary to feed the crowds. Earlier in the narrative Jesus instructed the disciples to look (ἐμβλέπω) to the birds of heaven (οὐρανός) for they do not sow or reap or gather into barns and yet the heavenly Father feeds them (6:26). Jesus looks (ἀναβλέπω) to heaven (οὐρανός) himself in 14:19 and, once again, no cultivation is needed. Food is "naturally" given to the crowds as birds receive food from nature and an infant receives food naturally from her mother.

Conclusion

The larger world outside the Jewish community has been the last participant to join the exchange but it has begun its activity through the crowds in 15:29–39. While the Matthean community was initiated into food provision as an "infant" nursed by God and then was encouraged to be more active in God's provision, so the crowds are being nursed by God's body through the earth and then are becoming more involved in food exchange as those who are righteous and "approach" and "see." A new cycle is beginning to encourage the world to participate in God's activity of providing food. Through both Matt 14 and 15, God has been explicitly less visible in food exchange and the human and natural worlds have gained greater responsibility. God is active with the world as the world works to find food.

The place of food exchange and the parties involved have moved to the farthest spatial and kinship distance from the "inner room" in which the Matthean family first received food in the narrative: from an inhabited, safe, enclosed house which fed only the Matthean community to an uninhabited, dangerous, outdoor mountain and wilderness where the Matthean community, larger Jewish community, and Gentile world are receiving food. While the Matthean community has, at times, exchanged food in order to express its independence, it has predominately albeit cautiously exchanged food in order to envision itself as part of the larger social and natural world and to see God as creator, provider, and liberator of all of God's creation.

Chapter 10

Conclusion

A Synopsis

It is time to give an overview of several key ideas that are interspersed throughout the study that include how God relates to and feeds the world and how the Matthean community relates to and exchanges food with the world. The location of and characters involved in food exchange move farther away from the Matthean community, its kinship relations, and its location within a household as the narrative progresses. The location shifts to spaces that are more public, have greater conflict, are more uninhabited, and are more related to the physical features of the earth. That is, the locations shift from the Matthean household (6:1–21, 6:25–34, 7:7–11) to the households of the larger Jewish community (10:5–11:1) to the grainfields (12:1–8) to deserted places (14:13–22) to the mountain and wilderness (15:29–39). Even as the locations shift in this way, the food provision provides comfort, compassion, and solidarity in the dangerous and isolated spaces. This movement takes food exchange into areas that include characters at greater and greater kinship distance from the Matthean community: anonymous characters outside the Matthean community (7:7–11), the larger Jewish community (10:5–11:1), some Jewish leaders (12:1–8), the natural world (6:1–21, 6:25–34, 12:1–8, 15:29–39), and the larger Jewish and Gentile worlds (14:13–22, 15:29–39).

God provides food through these characters, then, to feed both the Matthean community and the world. At the beginning of the narrative, God feeds the Matthean community directly and in secret, but then uses other communities.[1] God feeds the Matthean community through the earth in 6:1–21 and 6:25–34, through the Matthean family in 7:7–11, through the larger Jewish community in 10:5–11:1, and through the natural world, larger Jewish community, and some Jewish leaders in 12:1–8. God feeds the Matthean community and those outside the community through the Matthean family in 7:7–11, through Jesus and the disciples in 14:13–22, and again through the earth in 15:29–39. Food provision takes places through relationships at a greater and greater kinship distance from the Matthean community.

As God provides food through human communities, God becomes less and less visible as a character in the food exchange passages and humans take on a greater role in participating in food exchange. God's portrayal as heavenly Father who is also cosmic creator, not monarchical ruler, fits this shift in activity from God to humans. God can be imaged as creator, provider, and deliverer in the Matthean narrative who does not act on the world from a distance demanding passive obedience from human subjects but acts in the world, encourages activity, and shares responsibility with humanity and the natural world.[2]

The natural and human activity is evident in how the earth and human characters participate and seek out food provision. The earth shares in food provision in 6:1–21 (i.e. 6:11), 12:1–8 (i.e. grainfields), and 15:29–39 (i.e. 15:35). Humanity becomes more and more active in seeking out food provision through the narrative. The Matthean community asks and prays in 6:1–21, looks, considers, and seeks in 6:25–34, asks, seeks, and knocks in 7:7–11, inquires, enters a house, and works for its food in 10:5–11:1, goes through, picks, and eats the grain in 12:1–8, and takes initiative to feed the crowds in 14:13–22. Toward the end of the food passages, the world outside the Matthean community begins this same process of seeking out food as the crowds approach Jesus and see the works of God of Israel (15:29-39).

Even though the Matthean community becomes more active in participating in food exchange through the narrative, they continue to be dependent upon others. In 10:5–11:1, the community works for their food but depends upon the households of the larger Jewish community to feed them. In 14:13–22 and 15:29–39, the community even provides food for others but is still dependent upon God, Jesus, and the earth for food provision. Communities in the Matthean narrative depend upon each other, across community borders, to exchange food. Food flows both ways across the boundaries, coming into and going out of the Matthean community. Both sides participate and both sides have needs.

Why is the Matthean community exchanging food with the world outside its community? Biological, political and social needs are the three motivating factors that underscore food exchange in the narrative. Food is clearly exchanged in order to feed biological urges, the Matthean community and the world are hungry and need material food to survive. The Matthean community also has some need to maintain its identity and express its independence in relation to other communities. While this does not predominate in food exchange, it is present. The greatest need, however, is for the Matthean community to establish and solidify social relations within and outside the community, to see itself as part of and participating in a larger world, of which its God is the creator and provider.

The mode of food exchange operative in the food passages is generalized reciprocity; the mode which best fosters strong social relationships within kinship groups. Food is give from one of greater means to one of lesser means through a sustained one-way flow with little or no expectation of return. The giving of food is primarily a gift and people receive what they need not what they pay for (i.e. balanced reciprocity or the market system) or what centralized leaders allow (i.e. centralized redistribution).[3]

Taking a Stand

From my perspective, the model I have proposed for the Matthean community's relationship with the world and with God is more relevant and compelling in today's world. Today's world experiences a tremendous amount of global, social, and economic stratification. Recent events have made this quite apparent: responses to the tragic events of September 11, 2001, immigration debates, the presidential primary race, and the recent dramatic increases in food and fuel prices. The role of the market and competition continues to be more valued than human relationships and quality of life. The effort to understand religious and cultural differences takes a back seat to political and economic values. The attempts to preserve the environment and to value the earth as an entity in and of itself are becoming more and more difficult.

The three general community-models I reviewed in Chapter 1 are problematic when confronted with today's world context. First, while these three interpretations clearly rely on legitimate textual evidence, they do not admit that they have made textual choices nor have they given contextual or theological reasons why they made the choices they did. Second, the interpretations do not consider the social, political, ecological, theological, and ethical implications for living out the readings they have selected. God is viewed as exclusively involved with the Matthean community but distant from the world outside the community. God as a ruler demands obedience from the passive community but does not encourage human responsibility in interacting with the world. The community interacts with the world through competition and conflict. It understands itself as dominant in relationship with the world, either expecting the world to convert and become a part of the community or withdrawing from the world all together. These implications only feed the current problems in our society.

My interpretation reads God as related to all creation, within and outside the Matthean community. God is not "my group's God" or the "male God" or the "human God" who is justified in oppressing one group of the human or natural world; rather God is the God of all creation. God participates in the world and encourages humans to take responsibility in interacting with the various parts of the human and natural world. The community envisions itself as integrated into the world. My interpretation recognizes the complex and positive interactions between the community and the world and attempts to avoid portraying frozen relationships of domination, subordination and exploitation; rather the interpretation encourages the depiction of relationships of cooperation and mutual support.[4] The community continues to be seen as distinct from the world, having its own identity and allowing other communities to have their own identities, but is also sees itself as part of the larger world.

This interpretation, it seems to me, makes more sense in today's complex and pluralistic world.

Notes

Chapter 1: The Problem

1. Crosby uses Gibson Winter's notion of root metaphor. Michael Crosby, *House of Disciples: Church, Economics, and Justice in Matthew* (New York: Orbis, 1988), 11. Crosby draws on narrative and reader response criticism in the literary paradigm as well as social criticism to explore the Matthean narrative.
2. Ibid., 105, 106.
3. Ibid., 30–31, 104–10.
4. Ibid., 109.
5. Ibid., 262.
6. Ibid., 221.
7. God's reign has a particular and limited territory. See Ibid., 219–21, 62ff.
8. Ibid., 107.
9. J. Andrew Overman, *Matthew's Gospel and Formative Judaism* (Minneapolis: Fortress Press, 1990), chapter 3. While Matthean Judaism shared a common social system with several other groups, it developed distinctly as it responded to its main competitor, Formative Judaism. Overman draws from the sect theory of Blinkensopp and Wilson.
10. Matthean Judaism still sees itself as replacing Formative Judaism as the true righteous group.
11. Overman, *Matthew's Gospel and Formative Judaism*, 153. They are the "heirs of God's kingdom."
12. George E. Mendenhall and Gary A Herion, "Covenant," in *The Anchor Bible Dictionary*, ed. David Noel Freedman (New York: Doubleday, 1992), 1181–83.
13. Overman, *Matthew's Gospel and Formative Judaism*, 32, 151.
14. Ibid., 151–53.
15. Ibid., 153.
16. Graham N. Stanton, *A Gospel for a New People: Studies in Matthew* (Louisville: Westminster/John Knox, 1992). See also D. Garland, *Reading Matthew: A Literary and Theological Commentary on the First Gospel* (New York: Crossroad, 1995); R. Gundry, *Matthew*, 2nd ed. (Grand Rapids: Eerdmans, 1994); D. Hagner, *Matthew 1–13, 14–28*, 2 vols., *Word Biblical Commentary* (Dallas: Word, 1993, 1995); D. R. A. Hare, *Matthew, Interpretation* (Louisville, KY: Westminster John Knox, 1993); Jack Dean Kingsbury, *Matthew as Story*, 2nd ed. (Philadelphia: Fortress Press, 1988); U. Luz, *Matthew 1–7: A Commentary* (Minneapolis: Fortress, 1989); John P. Meier, *The Vision of Matthew: Christ, Church, and Morality in the First Gospel* (New York:

Paulist Press, 1979); George Strecker, *Der Weg Der Gerechtigkeit: Untersuchung Zur Theologie Des Matthaus*, 3rd ed. (Göttingen: Vandenhoeck & Ruprecht, 1971); Wolfgang Trilling, *The Gospel According to St. Matthew*, trans. Kevin Smyth, vol. 1, 2 (London: Burns & Oates, 1969). Stanton says Meeks and Przybylski also share this approach. See W. A. Meeks, *The First Urban Christians: The Social World of the Apostle Paul* (New Haven, CT: Yale University Press, 1983); B. Przybylski, *Righteousness in Matthew and His World of Thought* (Cambridge: Cambridge University Press, 1980); Graham N. Stanton, "Revisiting Matthew's Communities," *SBLSP* 33 (1994): 126. Stanton draws on sectarian and legitimation models along with conflict theory.

17. Stanton, *A Gospel for a New People: Studies in Matthew*, 94.
18. Stanton, "Revisiting Matthew's Communities," 13–14. Stanton refers to the "world" as the "Gentile world," among other options which might be the "Greco-Roman world" or "pagan world" or "Roman empire" or "God's world" or "natural world."
19. Stanton, *A Gospel for a New People: Studies in Matthew*, 161–65. The apocalyptic theme is heightened because Matthew 24 and 25 expand on Mark's treatment of this theme according to Stanton.
20. See Hare's comment in Ibid., 134.
21. Hagner, *Matthew 1–13, 14–28*, lxx, lxxi. Hagner uses the language of "new people" and "transfer to church." He also discusses the fulfilling of God's promises to the true Israel and Matthew's community as a perfected or fulfilled Judaism.
22. Hare, *Matthew*, 249.
23. See also Stanton, *A Gospel for a New People: Studies in Matthew*, 190. Stanton discusses Matthew's Christology: a humble and meek king as the Son of David and one who sits on the throne and judges the nations as the Son of Man.
24. Garland, *Reading Matthew: A Literary and Theological Commentary on the First Gospel*, 2; Stanton, "Revisiting Matthew's Communities," 18. On the Matthean community as a third race, see Hare, *Matthew*, 249.
25. Stanton, *A Gospel for a New People: Studies in Matthew*, 163, also chapter 9.
26. For the view of God or leader as a monarch who rules and controls through both domination and benevolence, see Sallie McFague, *Models of God: Theology for an Ecological, Nuclear Age* (Philadelphia, Pennsylvania: Fortress Press, 1987), 68–79. See also Martin's description of Benevolent patriarchal ideology in the Greco-Roman world, Dale B. Martin, *The Corinthian Body* (New Haven: Yale University Press, 1995), 42–47.
27. Marshall Sahlins, *Stone Age Economics* (Chicago; New York: Aldine-Atherton, Inc., 1972), 215.

Chapter 2: Methodology

1. I draw my methodology primarily from Cristina Grenholm and Daniel Patte, eds., *Reading Israel in Romans: Legitimacy and Plausibility of Divergent Interpretations* (Harrisburg, Pennsylvania: Trinity Press International, 2000), 1–54.

2. For a discussion of the postmodernism paradigm, see C. Jencks, *What Is Post-Modernism?*, 3rd ed. (New York: St. Martin's, 1989); Kathleen M. O'Connor, "Crossing Borders: Biblical Studies in a Trans-Cultural World," in *Teaching the Bible: The Discourses and Politics of Biblical Pedagogy*, ed. Fernando Segovia and Mary Ann Tolbert (Maryknoll, NY: Orbis Books, 1998); Fernando F. Segovia, ""and They Began to Speak in Other Tongues": Competing Modes of Discourse in Contemporary Biblical Criticism," in *Reading from This Place: Social Location and Biblical Interpretation in the United States*, ed. Fernando F. Segovia and Mary Ann Tolbert (Minneapolis: Fortress Press, 1995); Fernando F. Segovia, "Cultural Studies and Contemporary Biblical Criticism: Ideological Criticism as Mode of Discourse," in *Reading from This Place: Social Location and Biblical Interpretation in Global Perspective*, ed. Fernando F. Segovia and Mary Ann Tolbert (Minneapolis: Fortress Press, 1995).
3. Grenholm and Patte, eds., *Reading Israel in Romans: Legitimacy and Plausibility of Divergent Interpretations*, 29–30.
4. Daniel Patte, *Ethics of Biblical Interpretation* (Louisville, Kentucky: Westminster John Knox Press, 1995), chapters 1 and 2; Mary Ann Tolbert, "A New Teaching with Authority: A Re-Evaluation of the Authority of the Bible," in *Teaching the Bible: The Discourses and Politics of Biblical Pedagogy*, ed. Fernando Segovia and Mary Ann Tolbert (Maryknoll, New York: Orbis Books, 1998), 170–75.
5. Grenholm and Patte, eds., *Reading Israel in Romans: Legitimacy and Plausibility of Divergent Interpretations*, 30.
6. Ibid., 1–54. These poles are also referred to in terms of frames as: contextual frame (life-context), hermeneutical frame (hermeneutical/theological perceptions), and analytical frame (textual features). See also O'Connor, "Crossing Borders: Biblical Studies in a Trans-Cultural World"; Segovia, "Cultural Studies and Contemporary Biblical Criticism: Ideological Criticism as Mode of Discourse."
7. Grenholm and Patte, eds., *Reading Israel in Romans: Legitimacy and Plausibility of Divergent Interpretations*, 20–21; Tolbert, "A New Teaching with Authority: A Re-Evaluation of the Authority of the Bible," 170–75.
8. Grenholm and Patte, eds., *Reading Israel in Romans: Legitimacy and Plausibility of Divergent Interpretations*, 16–17, 21–27.
9. Ibid., 21–27. That is, bipolar interpretations with the analytical and contextual have often been couched in terms of "what the text meant" and "what the text means." Biblical critics insist that the former is the standard while systematic theologians insist the latter must be served. By introducing the third pole, a more fluid and reciprocal relationship between the other two poles is encouraged as well as an interrelationship with all three poles.
10. Ibid., 17–18, 35.
11. Harriet Friedman, "The International Political Economy of Food: A Global Crisis," in *Food in the USA: A Reader*, ed. Carole M. Counihan (New York: Routledge, 2002), 325–326.
12. Scott Wallace, "Last of the Amazon," *National Geographic*, January 2007, 40, 59–61.
13. See, for example, Bill McKibben, *Deep Economy: The Wealth of Communities and the Durable Future* (New York: Times Books, 2007).

14. Sallie McFague, *The Body of God: An Ecological Theology* (Minneapolis, Minnesota: Fortress Press, 1993), 15–16.
15. The interpretations I critique are legitimate, i.e. based on valid textual evidence and clearly reasoned. I contend in this study that the relative values of the interpretations are less persuasive in today's world and therefore I offer an alternative interpretative that I argue is more compelling. Less attention has been given to alternative interpretations and I seek to redress this scholarship debt.
16. Heifer International, "Cornerstones Make Heifer Unique,"Heifer International, http://www.heifer.org/Our_Work/Our_Approach/Cornerstones.shtml (accessed May 22, 2008).
17. Philip A. Harland, *Associations, Synagogues, and Congregations: Claiming a Place in Ancient Mediterranean Society* (Minneapolis, Minnesota: Fortress Press, 2003); L. Michael White, ed., *Social Networks in the Early Christian Environment: Issues and Methods for Social History, Semeia 56* (Atlanta, GA: Scholars Press, 1992).
18. McFague, *The Body of God: An Ecological Theology*, 138. See also the last chapter of Claude Y. Stewart, Jr., *Nature in Grace: A Study of the Theology of Nature* (Macon, GA: Mercer University Press, 1983). See also Ian G. Barbour, *Myths, Models and Paradigms: A Comparative Study in Science and Religion* (New York: Harper and Row, 1974), ch. 8.
19. The Image of God as Father is a common interpersonal image in the Bible. See Barbour, *Myths, Models and Paradigms: A Comparative Study in Science and Religion*, 157.
20. McFague, *Models of God: Theology for an Ecological, Nuclear Age*, 63–69.
21. McFague, *The Body of God: An Ecological Theology*, 151–52. See also Deut 32:18, Num 11:12, Isa 42:14.
22. Ibid., 152–53. See also Gen 1:2, 2:7; Ps 104:30; Prov 8:30 as examples of the emanation model, creation as "empowered by the life-giving energy of the divine spirit and word." McFague, *The Body of God: An Ecological Theology*, 255 n. 28.
23. Sandra M. Schneiders, *The Revelatory Text: Interpreting the New Testament as Sacred Scripture* (San Francisco, California: HarperSanFranciso, 1991), 172–76.
24. Jack Goody, *Cooking, Cuisine and Class: A Study in Comparative Sociology* (Cambridge; NY: Cambridge University Press, 1982), 37–38. He lists five phases (each with a primary process) of commensality: production (growing), distribution (allocating/storing), preparation (cooking), consumption (eating), and disposal (clearing up).
25. This does not imply that this is the only value food has, i.e. biological value, but that it is real, material, substantive food that is being spoken about in the passage.
26. Vernon K. Robbins, *The Tapestry of Early Christian Discourse: Rhetoric, Society and Ideology* (London and New York: Routledge, 1996), 144. Powell argues that narrative criticism itself assumes the identification of social and cultural contexts and hyphenated labels for methodologies that include narrative and social approaches, such as socio-literary or socio-narratological, are unnecessary. I use one of these labels, however, to be clear that I use both narrative and social approaches in the study. See Mark Allan Powell, *What Is Narrative Criticism?* (Minneapolis: Fortress Press, 1990), 74–75.

27. Powell, *What Is Narrative Criticism?*, 74–75; David Rhoads, "Narrative Criticism and the Gospel of Mark," *Journal of American Academy of Religion* (1982): 63-72. Abrams includes the social setting as one part of the setting, which includes spatial and temporal settings as well. See M. H. Abrams, ed., *A Glossary of Literary Terms*, 7th ed. (Orlando: Harcourt Brace College Publishers, 1999), 284–85. I divide the social approach into its own section because of the greater extent to which I use the social context in the study.
28. See Annette Weiner, "Reciprocity," in *Encyclopedia of Cultural Anthropology*, ed. David Levinson and Melvin Ember (New York, New York: Henry Holt and Company, 1996), 365–71.
29. Goody, *Cooking, Cuisine and Class: A Study in Comparative Sociology*, 37–38.
30. For brief summaries of the theories of exchange, see Caroline S. Tauxe, "Exchange," in *Encyclopedia of Cultural Anthropology*, ed. David Levinson and Melvin Ember (New York: Henry Hold and Company, 1996); Weiner, "Reciprocity"; James G. Carrier, "Exchange," in *Encyclopedia of Social and Cultural Anthropology*, ed. Alan Bernard and Jonathan Spencer (London & New York: Routledge, 1996); Stephen Gudeman, *The Anthropology of Economy: Community, Market, and Culture* (Frome, Somerset: Blackwell Publishers Inc., 2001), 80–93.
31. For cultural anthropological studies on kinship, see Philip F. Esler, ed., *Modelling Early Christianity: Social-Scientific Studies of the New Testament in Its Context* (London and New York: Routledge, 1995); David B. Gowler, *Host, Guest, Enemy and Friend: Portraits of the Pharisees in Luke and Acts*, ed. Vernon K. Robbins, vol. 2, *Emory Studies in Early Christianity* (New York: Peter Lang, 1991); K. C. and Douglas E. Oakman Hanson, *Palestine in the Time of Jesus: Social Structures and Social Conflicts* (Minneapolis: Fortress Press, 1998); Malina, *The New Testament World: Insights from Cultural Anthropology*; Bruce J. Malina and Richard L. Rohrbaugh, *Social Science Commentary on the Synoptic Gospels* (Minneapolis: Fortress Press, 1992); Jerome H. Neyrey, ed., *The Social World of Luke-Acts: Models for Interpretation* (Peabody, Massachusetts: Hendrickson Publishers, 1991); Carolyn Osiek and David L. Balch, *Families in the New Testament World: Households and House Churches,* (Louisville, Kentucky: Westminster John Knox Press, 1997).
32. Hanson, *Palestine in the Time of Jesus: Social Structures and Social Conflicts*, 19–61; Osiek and Balch, *Families in the New Testament World: Households and House Churches*, 41–43.
33. Hanson, *Palestine in the Time of Jesus: Social Structures and Social Conflicts*, 20–21.
34. Leo G. Perdue, Joseph Blenkinsopp, John J. Collins, Carol Meyers, *Families in Ancient Israel*, ed. Don S. Browning, Ian S. Evison, First ed., *The Family, Religion, and Culture* (Louisville, Kentucky: Westminster John Knox Press, 1997), 192–203.
35. Osiek and Balch, *Families in the New Testament World: Households and House Churches*, 40–45; Perdue, *Families in Ancient Israel*, 180. See also Hanson, *Palestine in the Time of Jesus: Social Structures and Social Conflicts*, 23–26.
36. Hanson, *Palestine in the Time of Jesus: Social Structures and Social Conflicts*, 26; Osiek and Balch, *Families in the New Testament World: Households and House Churches*, 42–43.
37. Gowler, *Host, Guest, Enemy and Friend: Portraits of the Pharisees in Luke and Acts*, 24–26; Julian Alfred Pitt-Rivers, *The Fate of Shechem or the Politics of Sex: Essays in the Anthropology of the Mediterranean* (Cambridge, London, New York, Mel-

bourne: Cambridge University Press, 1977), 117. See also Sahlins, *Stone Age Economics*, 196–204.

38. Gowler, *Host, Guest, Enemy and Friend: Portraits of the Pharisees in Luke and Acts*, 25. Gowler, for example, refers to the "conflict between the concerns of citizenship and kinship ties" in Sophocles' *Antigone.*
39. Sahlins, *Stone Age Economics*, 204–211.
40. Philip J. King and Lawrence E. Stager, *Life in Biblical Israel*, ed. Douglas A. Knight, *Library of Ancient Israel* (Louisville: Westminster John Knox Press, 2001), 61.
41. For a discussion of these models, see Hanson, *Palestine in the Time of Jesus: Social Structures and Social Conflicts*; B. J. Malina, *The New Testament World: Insights from Cultural Anthropology*, rev. ed. (Louisville, KY: Westminster/ John Knox Press, 1993); Neyrey, ed., *The Social World of Luke-Acts: Models for Interpretation.*
42. Gowler, *Host, Guest, Enemy and Friend: Portraits of the Pharisees in Luke and Acts*, 224.
43. Osiek and Balch, *Families in the New Testament World: Households and House Churches*, 38–40.
44. Ibid., 39.
45. Victor H. Matthews and Don C. Benjamin, *Social World of Ancient Israel 1250–587 B.C.E.* (Peabody, Massachusetts: Hendrickson Publishers, Inc., 1993), 82.
46. Gowler, *Host, Guest, Enemy and Friend: Portraits of the Pharisees in Luke and Acts*, 223–24; Matthews and Benjamin, *Social World of Ancient Israel 1250–587 B.C.E.*, 82–87; Pitt-Rivers, *The Fate of Shechem or the Politics of Sex: Essays in the Anthropology of the Mediterranean*, 109–10.
47. Gudeman, *The Anthropology of Economy: Community, Market, and Culture*, 92.
48. For a discussion about Matthew's urban setting, see Carter, *Matthew and the Margins: A Sociopolitical and Religious Reading* (Maryknoll, NY: Orbis Books, 2000), 15, 17–24.
49. Ibid., 25–27. Lori Stanley, anthropologist at Luther College in Decorah, Iowa, points out that even within a wealthy society, driven by the market, some communities experience poverty and rely on generalized reciprocity for food (e.g. American Indians). Lori Stanley, Interview by Jim Grimshaw, July 14, 2003.
50. Walter Goldschmidt, "Functionalism," in *Encyclopedia of Cultural Anthropology*, ed. David Levinson and Melvin Ember (New York: Henry Holt and Company, 1996), 510.
51. Turner and Maryanski contend that many people misinterpret Malinowski to suggest he was primarily interested with meeting individual and psychological needs. See Jonathan H. Turner and Alexandra Maryanski, *Functionalism* (Menlo Park, California; Reading, Massachusetts; London; Amsterdam; Don Mills, Ontario; Sydney: The Benjamin/Cummings Publishing Company, 1979), 48–54. Rather, he addressed a variety of needs of persons and social structures within the social system. His student, Audrey Richards, focused her work on nutrition but also insisted that food exchange was an indicator of social relations, that there was a "sociological significance of food," that "man's food-seeking activities not only necessitate co-operation, but definitely foster it," and that "the giving and receiving of cooked food has become symbolic of the legal or economic relationship which entails it." See Audrey I. Richards, *Hunger and Work in a Sa-*

vage Tribe: A Functional Study of Nutrition among the Southern Bantu (Cleveland and New York: The World Publishing Company, 1932), 214, 2; Audrey I. Richards, *Land, Labour and Diet in Northern Rhodesia: An Economic Study of the Bemba Tribe* (London: Oxford University Press, 1939; reprint, 1952, 1961), 127. See also Goody on Richards in Goody, *Cooking, Cuisine and Class: A Study in Comparative Sociology*, 13–16.

52. Sahlins, *Stone Age Economics*, 205–206.
53. E.E. Evans-Pritchard, *The Nuer: A Description of the Modes of Livelihood and Political Institutions of a Nilotic People* (Oxford: Oxford University Press, 1940), 85; Sahlins, *Stone Age Economics*, 210–215.
54. Sahlins, *Stone Age Economics*, 215.
55. Ibid.
56. Anne Murcott, "Sociological and Social Anthropological Approaches to Food and Eating." *World Review of Nutrition and Dietetics*, 55 (1988): 15–34.
57. Sahlins, *Stone Age Economics*, 208. Carrier, "Exchange," 219. The further success of a group also depends upon the group's success in exchanging with other such factions.
58. This will be seen in Matthew 10 as laborers exchange food with householders.
59. Sahlins, *Stone Age Economics*, 210–215.
60. Mauss, *The Gift*, 8–12.
61. Gudeman, *The Anthropology of Economy: Community, Market, and Culture*, 80.
62. Ibid., 92.
63. Ibid., 88.
64. In general, social needs might include: family, marriage, sex, education, peace and order, religious and moral needs, cohesion, cooperation, affection, education, health care, work, political rights, freedom from crime, a place to live, emotional needs, care, inner needs, a sense of belonging.
65. Bronislaw Malinowski, *Argonauts of the Western Pacific: An Account of Native Enterprise and Adventure in the Archipelagoes of Melanesian New Guinea* (New York: Dutton & Co., Inc., 1961), 167, 175. See also Gudeman, *The Anthropology of Economy: Community, Market, and Culture*, 83–84.
66. Sahlins, *Stone Age Economics*, 196–199.
67. Ibid., 193–195.
68. Ibid., 211.
69. Marcel Henaff, *Claude Lévi-Strauss and the Making of Structural Anthropology*, Translated by Mary Baker (Minneapolis: University of Minnesota Press, 1998), 45. Claude Lévi-Strauss, *The Elementary Structures of Kinship* (Boston: Beacon, 1969), 479. See Lévi-Strauss and Henaff on the idea of exchange as "receiving from another, more precisely from another group, that which nature would allow one to give to oneself. Henaff, *Claude Lévi-Strauss and the Making of Structural Anthropology*, 45–46. Lévi-Strauss, *The Elementary Structures of Kinship*, 489.
70. Tauxe, "Exchange," 470.
71. See especially Durrenberger and Weiner on the differences between substantivists and formalists. E. Paul Durrenberger, "Economic Anthropology," in *Encyclopedia of Cultural Anthropology*, ed. David Levinson and Melvin Ember (New York: Henry Holt and Company, 1996), 365-67. Weiner, "Reciprocity," 1064. For substantivists, individuals make choices and are motivated in response to collective

forces that impinge upon them. This can be seen in particular in small-scale societies where reciprocal exchanges are influenced by and defined within the larger social system. For formalists, individuals make rational choices based on their values and self-interest. Individuals are able to negotiate the consequences of a choice and to make decisions in which they will achieve the greatest gain. Individuals are not primarily defined by their social systems, they do not need to enact what culture says they should do; rather they have the freedom to make choices that suit their interests.

72. S. B. Ortner, "Theory in Anthropology since the Sixties," *Comparative Studies in Society and History* 26 (1984): 146. Ortner suggests that the practice theorists in the 1980s and beyond recognized that the system indeed is very powerful in shaping human behavior but that there is room for some choice and freedom and calculation within the context of social forces in making decisions as well. Gudeman contends that formal and substantive meanings of economy might be cast too rigidly. Referring to Granovetter's critique of Polanyi's oppositional categories, Gudeman summarizes Granovetter's as arguing that "anthropologists utilize an oversocialized conception of human action (embedded economies), whereas economists employ an undersocialized one (disembedded markets)…in non-market economies there is more instrumental action than anthropologists recognize, whereas in market economies there is more embedded material action than economists concede," Gudeman, *The Anthropology of Economy: Community, Market, and Culture*, 19. Berger and Luckmann's dialectical process of three moments (i.e. externalization, objectivation, and internalization) captures these dynamics in that humans produce society and then objectified society turns and shapes humans. Peter L. Berger and Thomas Luckmann, *The Social Construction of Reality* (Garden City, NY: Doubleday & Company, 1966).
73. Mauss, *The Gift*, 8–12. Raymond Firth, *Symbols: Public and Private* (Ithaca: Cornell University Press, 1973), 385.
74. Henaff, *Claude Lévi-Strauss and the Making of Structural Anthropology*, 48.
75. Claude Lévi-Strauss, *The Elementary Structures of Kinship* (Boston: Beacon, 1969), 479.
76. Ortner, "Theory in Anthropology since the Sixties," 150–52. The approach regarding motivation used here is in response to interest theory. Interest theory argues that the motivation comes from an "individualistic, and somewhat aggressive, actor, self-interested, rational, pragmatic, and perhaps with a maximizing orientation as well" (151). A person is motivated to participate in a certain practice in order to actively gain, in the short-term, that which is materially or politically useful that feeds his or her self-interest. The approach of this study suggests that the Matthean community is motivated to seek out longer-term transformations of relationships, of "becoming" not "getting," of seeking that which is good in relationships and not just solving a short-term problem or seeking a short-term gain. This part of the approach emphasizes the externalization moment, that "society is a human product," in Berger and Luckmann's dialectical process. Everyday activities, routines, and daily practices influence, shape and produce larger constructions of society. Berger and Luckmann, *The Social Construction of Reality;* Ortner, "Theory in Anthropology since the Sixties," 155–58; Overman, *Matthew's Gospel and Formative Judaism*, 6–7; Robert Wuthnow, et al.,

Cultural Analysis: The Work of Peter Berger, Mary Douglas, Michel Foucault, and Jürgen Habermas (London and New York: Rutledge & Kegan Paul, 1984).

77. Ortner, "Theory in Anthropology since the Sixties," 151.
78. Ibid. Cf. Anthony Saldarini, *Matthew's Christian-Jewish Community* (Chicago: University of Chicago Press, 1994), 88–89.
79. Gudeman, *The Anthropology of Economy: Community, Market, and Culture*, 80.
80. Ortner, "Theory in Anthropology since the Sixties," 144–57.
81. Gudeman, *The Anthropology of Economy: Community, Market, and Culture*, 89–90.
82. Stephen C. Barton, "Can We Identify the Gospel Audiences?" in *The Gospels for All Christians: Rethinking the Gospel Audiences*, ed. Richard Bauckham (Grand Rapids, Michigan: William B. Eerdmans Publishing Company, 1998); Robbins, *The Tapestry of Early Christian Discourse: Rhetoric, Society and Ideology*, 144. Robbins calls this the social and cultural texture which uses "anthropological and sociological theory to explore the social and cultural nature of the voices in the text under investigation."
83. David L. Balch, ed., *Social History of the Matthean Community: Cross Disciplinary Approaches* (Minneapolis: Fortress Press, 1991); Barton, "Can We Identify the Gospel Audiences?."; Stephen C. Barton, *Discipleship and Family Ties* (Cambridge: Cambridge University Press, 1994); Esler, ed., *Modelling Early Christianity: Social-Scientific Studies of the New Testament in Its Context;* J. Neyrey, "Ceremonies in Luke-Acts: The Case of Meals and Table Fellowship," in *The Social World of Luke-Acts*, edited by Jerome H. Neyrey (Peabody, MA: Hendrickson, 1991); Robbins, *The Tapestry of Early Christian Discourse: Rhetoric, Society and Ideology;* Saldarini, *Matthew's Christian-Jewish Community.*
84. Robbins, *The Tapestry of Early Christian Discourse: Rhetoric, Society and Ideology*, 14.
85. Ibid., 3.
86. Powell, *What Is Narrative Criticism?*, 6–10; Fernando Segovia, "Introduction," in *Reading from This Place: Social Location and Biblical Interpretation in the United States*, ed. Fernando Segovia and Mary Ann Tolbert (Minneapolis, Minnesota: Fortress Press, 1995), 15–16.
87. There are many different expressions of literary criticism (e.g. narrative, structuralism, rhetorical, reader-response). See Patte for a chart that clarifies the relationships among some of these methods. Daniel Patte et al., *The Gospel of Matthew: A Contextual Introduction for Group Study* (Nashville: Abingdon Press, 2003), 54–57.
88. Robbins identifies five types of inner texture in texts: repetitive-progressive, opening-middle-closing, narrational, argumentative, and aesthetic. He also elaborates on social and cultural texture which, among other things, examines the social and cultural nature of inner texture. See Robbins, *The Tapestry of Early Christian Discourse: Rhetoric, Society and Ideology*, 46–65, 144–91.
89. Petri Merenlahti and Raimo Hakola, "Reconceiving Narrative Criticism," in *Characterization in the Gospels: Reconceiving Narrative Criticism*, ed. David Rhoads and Kari Syreeni (Sheffield, England: Sheffield Academic Press Ltd, 1999), 34–35, 40–44.
90. Mark Allan Powell, "Expected and Unexpected Readings of Matthew: What the Reader Knows," *The Asbury Theological Journal* 48, no. 2 (1993): 35–41; Powell,

What Is Narrative Criticism?, 74; Rhoads, "Narrative Criticism and the Gospel of Mark," 413.

91. Powell, "Expected and Unexpected Readings of Matthew: What the Reader Knows," 41–44.
92. Stephen D. Moore, *Literary Criticism and the Gospels: The Theoretical Challenge* (New Haven and London: Yale University Press, 1989), 20–21.
93. The term "audience" is being used more often in recent times to replace the "reader." A collection of Malbon's own work over time shows the change in the use of these terms from "reader" to "audience." Elizabeth Struthers Malbon, *In the Company of Jesus: Characters in Mark's Gospel* (Louisville, Kentucky: Westminster John Knox Press, 2000). See also Carter's use of this term in Carter, *Matthew and the Margins: A Sociopolitical and Religious Reading*, 1–7.
94. For explanations of reader-response criticism, see Robert M. Fowler, "Reader-Response Criticism," in *Mark and Method: New Approaches in Biblical Studies*, ed. Janice Capel Anderson and Stephen D. Moore (Minneapolis: Fortress Press, 1992); Moore, *Literary Criticism and the Gospels: The Theoretical Challenge;* Powell, *What Is Narrative Criticism;* Jane P. Tompkins, ed., *Reader-Response Criticism: From Formalism to Post-Structuralism* (Baltimore: The Johns Hopkins University Press, 1994).
95. S. Chatman, *Story and Discourse* (Ithaca, NY: Cornell University Press, 1978), 149–51; Powell, *What Is Narrative Criticism?*, 19–21.
96. Moore, *Literary Criticism and the Gospels: The Theoretical Challenge*, 46.
97. Powell, *What Is Narrative Criticism?*, 16–18. James Resseguie, "Reader-Response and the Synoptic Gospels," *JAAR* (1982). Susan Suleimann, "Varieties of Audience-Oriented Criticism," in *The Reader in the Text: Essays on Audience and Interpretation*, ed. S. Suleimann and I. Crossman (Princeton: Princeton University Press, 1980). Powell provides a chart drawn from Resseguie and Suleimann which organizes reader-response theories into three categories: (1) reader *over* the text (e.g. deconstruction—Derrida, transactive criticism—Holland, interpretive communities—late Fish), (2) reader *with* the text (e.g. affective stylistics—early Fish, phenomenological criticism—Iser), and reader ***in*** the text (e.g. structuralism, narrative criticism).
98. Wolfgang Iser, *The Implied Reader; Patterns of Communication in Prose Fiction from Bunyan to Beckett* (Baltimore: Johns Hopkins University Press, 1974); Moore, *Literary Criticism and the Gospels: The Theoretical Challenge;* Powell, *What Is Narrative Criticism?* For the identification of the implied reader as both ideal and real, see also Moore, *Literary Criticism and the Gospels: The Theoretical Challenge*, 102, n. 43. Moore refers also to Terrence Keegan, *Interpreting the Bible: A Popular Introduction to Biblical Hermeneutics* (Mahwah, N.J.: Paulist Press), 1985, 110; Petersen, "The Reader in the Gospel," in De Villiers, Pieter G.R., ed. "Reading a Text: Source, Reception, Setting," *Neotestamentica* 18 (1984), 44ff; Jeffrey Lloyd Staley, *The Print's First Kiss: A Rhetorical Investigation of the Implied Reader in the Fourth Gospel* (Atlanta: Scholars Press, 1988), 32–37.
99. On the view of the reader as reading with the text, in dialogue with the text, see also Grenholm and Patte, eds., *Reading Israel in Romans: Legitimacy and Plausibility of Divergent Interpretations*, 34–42; Schneiders, *The Revelatory Text: Interpreting the New Testament as Sacred Scripture*, 157–79.

100. Kelber and Edwards assume a first-time reader. Tannehill writes his commentary representing what "might be said after reading a second, third, or fourth time. It is not confined to what is happening when reading for the first time, with much of the text still unknown," Robert C. Tannehill, *The Narrative Unity of Luke-Acts: A Literary Interpretation*, vol. 1: The Gospel according to Luke (Philadelphia: Fortress Press, 1991), 6. See Richard A. Edwards, *Matthew's Story of Jesus* (Philadelphia: Fortress Press, 1985), 9–10; Werner H. Kelber, *Mark's Story of Jesus* (Philadelphia: Fortress Press, 1979), 11; Moore, *Literary Criticism and the Gospels: The Theoretical Challenge*, 21–22.
101. This method is similar to the one used by Kingsbury and Tannehill who focus on relations between Jesus and other groups and follow those relations through the Gospel story. Tannehill claims that "isolating and following the developing relations ...helps me to clarify some continuities and progressions that would be less clear if I simply followed the order of the material." He describes the text as "a rope with multiple strands. The continuity of each strand is not easily seen since it winds around other strands." Untangling the strands and following one of them, although this cannot be done without certain consequences since different themes interact, can provide new insights to how this particular theme constructs relationships between the Matthean community and the world around it. Tannehill, *The Narrative Unity of Luke-Acts: A Literary Interpretation*, 5.
102. Characterization is "a process through which the implied author provides the implied reader or audience with what is necessary to reconstruct a character from the narrative," Powell, *What Is Narrative Criticism?*, 52. Characterization goes beyond the identification of a character by furthering "the process by investing an identified character with an attribute—a trait or quality belonging to that character—or set of attributes which adds descriptive material to that character," Gowler, *Host, Guest, Enemy and Friend: Portraits of the Pharisees in Luke and Acts*, 30. See also David and Donald Michie Rhoads, *Mark as Story: An Introduction to the Narrative of a Gospel* (Philadelphia: Fortress Press, 1982), 101.
103. For a discussion of character traits and characters as ambiguous, changing, and unresolved entities, see Chatman, *Story and Discourse*, 107–10; Powell, *What Is Narrative Criticism?*, 54; McCracken, "Character in the Boundary: Bakhtin's Interdividuality in Biblical Narratives," *Semeia* (1993): 36; Elizabeth Struthers Malbon, "Narrative Criticism: How Does the Story Mean?" in *Mark and Method: New Approaches in Biblical Studies*, ed. Janice Capel Anderson and Stephen D. Moore (Minneapolis: Fortress Press, 1992), 28–29; Elizabeth Struthers Malbon and Janice Capel Anderson, "Literary-Critical Methods," in *Searching the Scriptures*, ed. Elisabeth Schüssler Fiorenza (New York: Crossroad, 1993), 247; Moore, *Literary Criticism and the Gospels: The Theoretical Challenge*, 15; Powell, *What Is Narrative Criticism?*, 54–58. See also Colleen Conway, "Speaking through Ambiguity: Minor Characters in the Fourth Gospel" (paper presented at the SBL Annual Meeting, Nashville, Tenn., November 21, 2000), 1–18.
104. Characters can include individuals, groups, animals, other non-human entities, and divine figures. Powell, *What Is Narrative Criticism?*, 51.
105. Character analysis is not, by definition, subordinate to the study of the plot. It is a legitimate study in and of itself. See Gowler, *Host, Guest, Enemy and Friend: Portraits of the Pharisees in Luke and Acts*, 48–49.

106. Chatman, *Story and Discourse*, 138–45; Powell, *What Is Narrative Criticism?*, 70; Rhoads, *Mark as Story: An Introduction to the Narrative of a Gospel*, 63.
107. Malbon offers several reasons scholars have studied biblical space, most of which focus on historical concerns: interest in historical geography, theological meaning of locations, focus on a particular place (e.g. wilderness) or set of places (e.g. Galilee and Jerusalem). Malbon is interested in narrative concerns and studies the interrelationship of spatial locations. See Elizabeth Struthers Malbon, *Narrative Space and Mythic Meaning in Mark* (San Francisco: Harper & Row, Publishers, 1986), 1–2.
108. See examples of this in Counihan and Sahlins. Carole Counihan, "Bread as World: Food Habits and Social Relations in Modernizing Sardinia," in *Food and Culture*, ed. Carole Counihan and Penny Van Esterik (New York: Routledge, 1997), 287–90; Sahlins, *Stone Age Economics*, 196–219.
109. Abrams, ed., *A Glossary of Literary Terms*, 284; Powell, *What Is Narrative Criticism?*, 69–75. Abrams offers three types of settings: spatial, temporal, and social. I have already discussed the social setting as I surveyed anthropological studies of food exchange and cultural scripts of kinship.
110. Mieke Bal, *Narratology: Introduction to the Theory of Narrative*, trans. Christine Van Boheemen, Second ed. (Toronto, Buffalo, London: University of Toronto Press Incorporated, 1997), 215.
111. Malbon, *Narrative Space and Mythic Meaning in Mark*, 15, 50–51, 106; Powell, *What Is Narrative Criticism?*, 69–83. Private is often associated with the household, family, women, childbearing, education, hospitality, food, and certain characteristics such as personal, individual, psychological, quiet, and submissive. Public is often associated with the political arena, men, city, public banquets, law courts, marketplace, and certain characteristics like collective, community, aggression. See Corley, *Private Women, Public Meals* (Peabody, MA: Hendrickson Publishers, 1993), 15–17; Firth, *Symbols: Public and Private;* Karen Jo Torjesen, "Reconstruction of Women's Early Christian History," in *Searching the Scriptures*, ed. Elisabeth Schüssler Fiorenza (New York: Crossroad, 1993), 290–312.
112. Bal, *Narratology: Introduction to the Theory of Narrative*, 216. This is one of Bal's categories.
113. Powell, *What Is Narrative Criticism?*, 72–73.
114. Ibid., 73.
115. Ibid.
116. Ibid.
117. Exodus 16:16–30. Carter, *Matthew and the Margins: A Sociopolitical and Religious Reading*, 263–64.
118. Bruce J. Malina, "Christ and Time: Swiss or Mediterranean?" *The Catholic Biblical Quarterly* (1989): 4–5.
119. Ibid., 5.
120. R. H. Lauer, *Temporal Man: The Meaning and Uses of Social Time* (New York: Praeger, 1981), 21; Malina, "Christ and Time: Swiss or Mediterranean?" 19.
121. Malina, "Christ and Time: Swiss or Mediterranean?" 22–23.
122. Ibid., 22.
123. For much of my theology, I follow Elizabeth Johnson, *She Who Is: The Mystery of God in Feminist Theological Discourse* (New York, New York: The Crossroad Pub-

lishing Company, 1992); McFague, *The Body of God: An Ecological Theology;* McFague, *Models of God: Theology for an Ecological, Nuclear Age;* Brian Wren, *What Language Shall I Borrow? God-Talk in Worship: A Male Response to Feminist Theology* (New York: The Crossroad Publishing Company, 1989).

124. For example, see H. D. Betz, *The Sermon on the Mount: A Commentary on the Sermon on the Mount, Including the Sermon on the Plain (Matthew 5:3–7:27 and Luke 6:20–49)* (Minneapolis: Augsburg Fortress, 1995), 396–97; Carter, *Matthew and the Margins: A Sociopolitical and Religious Reading,* 262–67; Amy-Jill Levine, *The Social and Ethnic Dimensions of Matthean Social History,* vol. 14, *Studies in the Bible and Early Christianity* (Lewiston, NY; Queenston, Ont.; Lampeter, Wales: Edwin Mellen Press, 1988); Patte, *The Challenge of Discipleship: A Critical Study of the Sermon on the Mount as Scripture* (Harrisburg, Pennsylvania: Trinity Press International, 1999), 203–08; Saldarini, *Matthew's Christian-Jewish Community,* ch. 5.

Chapter 3: The Family (6:1–21)

1. God, as the spirit, is never identified as a Father. Jesus, however, is identified as the Son of God, therefore it is appropriate to call the spirit the "anonymous Father."
2. Saldarini, *Matthew's Christian-Jewish Community,* 90–94.
3. W. D. Davies and D. C. Allison, *The Gospel According to Saint Matthew,* 3 vols., vol. 1, *I. C. C.* (Edenburgh: T & T Clark, 1988), 1:364. Although much of the passage might be explained as a visionary experience, food here is represented as a physical, material item and not as a metaphor or spiritual symbol. Jesus is hungry and is later fed. Jesus needs food. The temptations themselves come in between the hunger and the serving.
4. Carter, *Matthew and the Margins: A Sociopolitical and Religious Reading,* 109.
5. Davies and Allison, *The Gospel According to Saint Matthew,* 1:355.
6. The primary and secondary images of God are reversed in 6:1–21 compared to 4:1–11. God is primarily creator, deliverer, provider in 4:1–11, while the image of God as Father is hidden. In 6:1–21, however, the Father image is prevalent but the creator and provider images are hidden. Yet, the creator and provider images emerge gradually through the narrative after 6:1–21 as the Father image subsides. God is the creator who is also Father, not a Father who is also creator.
7. Carter, *Matthew and the Margins: A Sociopolitical and Religious Reading,* 109–10.
8. See Anna Meigs, "Food as a Cultural Construction," in *Food and Culture: A Reader,* ed. Carole Counihan and Penny Van Esterik (New York: Routledge, 1997), 104.
9. See Edward Adams' study of Paul's different language for world in 1 Corinthians and Romans. He examines a negative view in 1 Corinthians of "'this world,' alienated from God and doomed to perish" (242) and a good world in Romans created by God and soon to be transformed (242). Edward Adams, *Constructing the World: A Study of Paul's Cosmological Language* (Edinburgh: T&T Clark, 2000).
10. Matthew 6:1–21 is the starting point for the audience's perception of food distribution in Matthew's narrative. Matthew 4:1–11 is, on the one hand, a beginning

point for the first unit because it generally describes the distribution of food from the spirit, as anonymous Father, to Jesus the Son. There are three discrepancies in 4:1–11, however, that make 6:1–21 a stronger candidate for a more coherent introduction to the topics in the first thematic unit. First, the Father image is not explicitly named in 4:1–11 but is clearly stated in 6:1–21. Second, the recipient of food in 4:1–11 is Jesus and in 6:1–21 is the broader listening audience. Third, the setting in 4:1–11 is the wilderness while it is the household in 6:1–21. Therefore, the distribution of food in 6:1–21 from the Father to his children in the household fits the main topics that will be seen in 6:25–34 and 7:7–11. Matthew 4:1–11, then, functions primarily as an introduction to all five thematic units while, at the same time, providing a subtle transition into the first thematic unit.

11. Robbins, *The Tapestry of Early Christian Discourse: Rhetoric, Society and Ideology*, 46–50; Robert C. Tannehill, *The Sword of His Mouth: Forceful and Imaginative Language in Synoptic Sayings* (Philadelphia, Pennsylvania: Fortress Press, 1975), 43–49.
12. See also Hagner, *Matthew 1–13, 14–28*, 1:138. who explores a similar structure but does not include vv. 19–21 nor does he include the phrase "in the," which highlights the setting and therefore is central to my study.
13. I divide 6:1–21 in 6:1–4, 6:5–6, 6:7–15, 6:16–18, and 6:19–21.
14. Throughout this section (6:1–21), the audience is instructed in the proper practice of justice (δικαιοσύνη) by providing a negative example of those who do it improperly in improper places (e.g. synagogues, streets) or improper ways (e.g. disfiguring face). The use of negative characterizations is often acknowledged as a common way of identifying and strengthening a community by using an invective against opponents. Carter, *Matthew and the Margins: A Sociopolitical and Religious Reading*, 10. It is used here to demonstrate some independence of the Matthean community but it is also employed to begin to prepare and instruct Matthew's audience not on how to strengthen its own group and withdraw from the world, but on how to act in and relate to the world.
15. See Malbon, *Narrative Space and Mythic Meaning in Mark*, 106.
16. Carter, *Matthew and the Margins: A Sociopolitical and Religious Reading*, 123. See also the synagogue's designation as a separate community.
17. Malbon, *Narrative Space and Mythic Meaning in Mark*, 50–53. The "streets" would be characterized as a topographical space that is an outdoor space with no political boundaries. This is a movement away from artificial space (the synagogue) and toward more natural space (the earth in 6:19–21), although streets still have some boundaries, some artificial human-made quality to them.
18. Note how the world is divided into Jews and non-Jews; see Saldarini, *Matthew's Christian-Jewish Community*, 60, 68–75.
19. H. Kramer, *Exegetical Dictionary of the New Testament*, ed. Horst Robert Balz, vol. 1 (Grand Rapids, MI: Eerdmans, 1990), 267. Think of looking at the corner of the street from a building on the corner (thus a more concealed place) or of looking at the corner from the middle of the intersection out in the street (thus a more open area).
20. Actually a person is visible in every direction, as the saying "four corners of the earth" (Rev. 7:1, 20:8) implies.
21. The "earth" might be considered "the most public of places" also in terms of the open space, the number of people involved, and the spatial distance from the

individual household. Public places as "open places", out of doors, "those reserved for men", "where men moved freely about in the marketplace, law courts, and openly attended public banquets, theatres, and lectures." Corley, *Private Women, Public Meals*, 16.

22. The earth would be characterized as topographical space, more public and open and natural than the streets. The earth is not "human-made" and not of human origin yet, here, it has the quality of humanness as opposed to the divinity of heaven.
23. Many Matthean scholars identify the hypocrites with the Jewish leaders who are adversaries of Jesus, the "Pharisees" or the "scribes and Pharisees," for example Saldarini, *Matthew's Christian-Jewish Community*, 49–52, 65, 92–93. Matthew's narrative does indeed closely link the hypocrites with Jesus' opposing leaders in later passages (15:7; 22:18; 23:13, 14, 15, 28; 24:51). But in this earlier passage of Matthew's narrative, there is no mention of or connection with any opposing religious leaders, Pharisees or scribes. Likewise, the only other use of "hypocrites" in the SM and in this first thematic unit (7:5) does not identify the hypocrites with the Pharisees or scribes or any of the Jewish leaders, Betz, *The Sermon on the Mount: A Commentary on the Sermon on the Mount, Including the Sermon on the Plain (Matthew 5:3–7:27 and Luke 6:20–49)*, 347. In its use in 6:2 and 6:5, hypocrisy, then, is not connected with the Jewish leaders and its use with the synagogue does not link this institution with "otherness." The Jewish leaders are not singled out and the synagogue as a whole is not necessarily being attacked as an opposing institution (e.g. the use of the synagogue in 6:2 and 6:5 is not prefaced by the pronoun "their"). In fact, pointing out this abuse suggests that the synagogue and its leaders otherwise function appropriately, see Betz on 6:2 and 6:5, *The Sermon on the Mount: A Commentary on the Sermon on the Mount, Including the Sermon on the Plain (Matthew 5:3–7:27 and Luke 6:20–49)*.
24. The narrative uses a different word for "streets" in 6:5 (πλατεῖα) than is used in 6:2 (ῥύμη). In 12:19, the πλατεῖα are the places where no one hears or, better, responds to the voice of Jesus proclaiming. The implied audience will soon find out that the streets are not particularly hospitable places for those who follow Jesus.
25. The right hand/left hand image may characterize a superior/inferior comparison (so 25:31–46; right hand of God) with the right hand as a sign of power or authority. The left hand was also thought to symbolize various persons: a close friend, an unbeliever, an enemy, or even one's own wife. Davies and Allison, *The Gospel According to Saint Matthew*, 1:582.
26. See Ibid. on 6:3. This is similar to 25:31–46 (which also uses the right hand/left hand symbolism) where a person does not even know he/she is giving food.
27. We will see on 6:25 as well the emphasis about not worrying about one's own body.
28. Malbon, *Narrative Space and Mythic Meaning in Mark*, 106–07. Malbon considers the home architectural space, an artificially enclosed area. The home is not natural, outdoor space (i.e. topographical) neither is it space defined by human made boundaries of government units (i.e. geopolitical).
29. The use of inner room (ταμεῖον) in other contexts, i.e. a room within the house that is invisible from the outside and the most secret or closed off of rooms, con-

firms this sense of enclosure. *Exegetical Dictionary of the New Testament*, ed. Horst Robert Balz, vol. 3 (Grand Rapids, MI: Eerdmans, 1990), 3:332. See Gen 43:30, Isa 26:20, Sir 29:12, Exod 7:28 (LXX), Song 1:4, Matt 24:26, Luke 12:3. The latter "both emphasize the element of concealment, contrasting inner rooms and desert and private rooms (where one exchanges secrets) and housetops (public places)" (332). See BAGD, s.v. "ταμεῖον." In addition, the term for room can also mean treasury—see 6:19–21, Sir 29:11–12.

30. Bal, *Narratology: Introduction to the Theory of Narrative*, 45. A doorway can be a passage between one area to another or it can operate as a boundary between two spaces. Here, as a "closed door," the door functions as a boundary between the rest of the home and the room.
31. See Ibid., 44–45; Malbon, *Narrative Space and Mythic Meaning in Mark*, 101–03.
32. In Matthew's narrative, "Jerusalem" becomes a place of threat and danger beginning in chapter 15 to the end of the narrative. The beginning of the narrative presents "Jerusalem" as a place that is troubled, perhaps (2:1–3), but also a place that is interested in John the Baptist's ministry (3:5), Jesus' ministry and healing (4:25), and the city of the Great King (5:35).
33. One of the main points of this study is that the implied audience is being drawn out into the world to interact with it. The starting point in the narrative is inside a room behind a closed door. This is where the audience is right now, but it will be drawn out as the narrative unfolds (e.g. into other households, 10:10 and the wilderness, 15:29–39).
34. The use of the verb, Θησαυρίζω, and the noun, θησαυρός, refers the reader back to the hidden room in 6:6 and to the rewards (from the Father who sees in secret) in 6:1, 4, 6, 18. Θησαυρίζω refers to storing up, gathering, saving, reserving in plenty, BAGD, s.v. "Θησαυρίζω." The action of storing up reflects the setting of the τᾶ μεῖον, the hidden room (but also a storehouse) where one is to go and pray in secret. Θησαυρός, treasures, also would redirect the reader back to the ταμεῖον, which is where one is to "store up almsgiving in your treasury" (Sir 29:12). To pray in the hidden room is to store up treasures in heaven.
35. Carter, *Matthew and the Margins: A Sociopolitical and Religious Reading*, 172–73; Malina, *The New Testament World: Insights from Cultural Anthropology*, ch. 4.
36. "Do not gather/store up for yourselves treasures on earth," then, is parallel to "practicing your righteousness before others." Earth is in contrast to heaven as "before others" is in contrast to being seen by your Father.
37. Carter, *Matthew and the Margins: A Sociopolitical and Religious Reading*, 173. See Carter on 6:20 where he says that the treasures are "indiscriminate acts of mercy done in secret to sustain the life of all." See Sir 29:8–13. Storing up treasure (29:11) refers to almsgiving. The theme in 6:19–21 coincides with almsgiving in 6:2–4.
38. The juxtaposition of treasure and heart in 6:21 provides an appropriate closing. On the one hand, treasures (associated with God's kingdom, the word of God, commandments) are, at least initially, stored up in the heart (Ps 118:11, Prov 2:1, Job 23:12). See Hauck, "θησαυρός," *TDNT* 3:136–138. The righteous hold on and store this treasure in themselves as a way to value it (13:44). But ultimately, in Matthew's narrative, treasures are to be given away (2:11, 12:34–35, 13:52, 19:21)

and the heart is a place out of (not into) which things come (12:40, 13:19, 15:19, 18:35).

39. To put it in reader-response language, how is the audience persuaded to relate to the world around it?
40. The typical interpretations of this passage highlight the secrecy of the practices and generally make two arguments. First, explicitly religious practice is to be private to keep it pure in intent and to guard it from undue influences resulting from the praise of others. Second, modesty not boastfulness is valued. See Carter, *Matthew and the Margins: A Sociopolitical and Religious Reading*, 158–59; Davies and Allison, *The Gospel According to Saint Matthew*, 1:576, 621; Hagner, *Matthew 1–13, 14–28*, 1:140–41.
41. Malina, *The New Testament World: Insights from Cultural Anthropology*, ch. 3.
42. See Carter, *Matthew and the Margins: A Sociopolitical and Religious Reading*, 160; Davies and Allison, *The Gospel According to Saint Matthew*, 1:581.
43. Hans Mol, *Identity and the Sacred: A Sketch for a New Social-Scientific Theory of Religion* (New York: Macmillan, Free Press, 1977), 216–17.
44. The word "Father" (πατήρ) in reference to God appears in 6:11, 6:26, 6:32, and 7:11. In other passages within this thematic unit, it appears in 5:16. 5:45, 5:48, 6:1, 4, 6, 8, 9, 14, 15, 18. "Son" (υἱός) appears in 4:3, 6, 5:9, 45, 7:9. "Children" (τέκνον) appears in 7:11. "Childlike" language appears with "our Father" in 6:9 and as "little faith" in 6:30. "Your Father" (singular)" is in 6:4, 6, 18 and nowhere else in Matthew or Mark or Luke.
45. See Robert L. Mowery, "God, Lord and Father: The Theology of the Gospel of Matthew," *Biblical Research* XXXIII (1988): 28–29.
46. For many, the Father image of God suggests repressive, domineering or negative authority and is not redeemable. Carter admits that "Father" may not be a positive image (like Empire) if seen in political context or androcentric household, but that it can be positive if seen in light of one who resists oppressive power structures. Carter, *Matthew and the Margins: A Sociopolitical and Religious Reading*, 139. Sheffield sees the nature of God as a Father who cares for his children as a maternal expression. Julian Sheffield, "The Father in the Gospel of Matthew," in *A Feminist Companion to Matthew*, ed. Amy-Jill Levine (Sheffield: Sheffield Academic Press, 2001), 64. See also O'Day who, in her study of the Gospel of John, argues that the Father language is relational and therefore not primarily about patriarchy but about intimacy and family. Gail R. O'Day, "John," in *The Women's Bible Commentary*, ed. Carol A. Newsom and Sharon H. Ringe (Louisville, Kentucky: Westminster/John Knox Press, 1992), 304.
47. See especially Carter, *Matthew and the Margins: A Sociopolitical and Religious Reading*, 149, 55; Malbon, *Narrative Space and Mythic Meaning in Mark*, 56–57.
48. There is a connection between Yahweh and the sun in the HB (Deut 33:2, Isa 6:1–3, Pss 84:11, 89:15, 104:2). The sun belongs to God. God created the sun and has command over it (Ps 19:4–6, Gen 1:14–19). Betz, *The Sermon on the Mount: A Commentary on the Sermon on the Mount, Including the Sermon on the Plain (Matthew 5:3–7:27 and Luke 6:20–49)*, 316.
49. Notice the use of anthropomorphism, i.e. assigning human characteristics to that which is not human. Therefore, "God rains on" instead of "God sends his rain." Ibid., 317.

50. See Gen 2:5, Job 28:24–26, 38:12–41, Ps 104, Isa 5:6, Amos 4:7, Ezra 22:24 and later in Matt 6:26, 30; 10:29.
51. Betz, *The Sermon on the Mount: A Commentary on the Sermon on the Mount, Including the Sermon on the Plain (Matthew 5:3–7:27 and Luke 6:20–49)*, 317–18.
52. The adjective evil (πονηρός, 5:11, 5:37, 5:39, 6:13, 6:23, 7:11, 7:17, 7:18, 12:34, 12:35, 13:19, 13:38, 13:49, 15:19, 20:15, 22:10) refers to a variety of situations. It refers to the evil one (5:37, 6:13, 13:19, 13:38), those falsely accused of being evil (5:11), an evildoer (5:39), those separated in the eschatological judgment (13:49), persons with evil intentions/opinions/judgment (15:19), persons with an evil eye (6:23, 20:15). With δίκαιος and ἄδικος, the former is used to refer to righteous persons but not contrasted with the unrighteous (10:41, 23:35, 25:37, 46), a right/just wage (20:4), those who are considered righteous by some (13:17, 23:28; again not contrasted with unrighteous or evil).
53. Davies and Allison comment on 5:45 that the Father's providence/justice may be distributed to those outside the covenant during the present time but not at the end time. Davies and Allison, *The Gospel According to Saint Matthew*, 1:555. Yet, there is not a preponderance of evidence that the good/righteous and bad/unrighteous refer to those inside or outside any group, whether those part of the covenant or Matthew's community.
54. Ibid., 634.
55. My description of rewards in 6:1–21 is partially in response to Betz. Betz argues that, in order to satisfy the system of justice, only one reward is to be given out from God and, therefore, if it happens on earth, it cannot happen in heaven. Two implications follow from Betz's thought: rewards are given for individual deeds based on a strict formula/repayment plan and rewards in Matthew are meant to be eschatological. See Betz, *The Sermon on the Mount: A Commentary on the Sermon on the Mount, Including the Sermon on the Plain (Matthew 5:3–7:27 and Luke 6:20–49)*, 346–47.
56. See, for example, 20:1–16, 25:31–46, 10:42, 5:43–48.
57. Contra Betz, *The Sermon on the Mount: A Commentary on the Sermon on the Mount, Including the Sermon on the Plain (Matthew 5:3–7:27 and Luke 6:20–49)*, 346–47; Davies and Allison, *The Gospel According to Saint Matthew*, 1:634; Roger Mohrlang, *Matthew and Paul: A Comparison of Ethical Perspectives* (Cambridge, London, New York, New Rochelle, Melbourne, Sydney: Cambridge University Press, 1984), 53.
58. Mohrlang, *Matthew and Paul: A Comparison of Ethical Perspectives*, 51, n. 20.
59. On 6:6, see Davies and Allison, *The Gospel According to Saint Matthew*.
60. Reward is not so much a gift or surprise as it is the response to the right action/righteousness. One is forgiven, then, in the same manner that one forgives (6:14). Patte suggests that reward here is "wages" and not "unexpected gift" (85) because God's kingdom is the goal of disciples activities. Patte, *The Gospel According to Matthew: A Structural Commentary on Matthew's Faith*, 94.
61. The use of βλέπω with Father is only used here in chapter 6 in Matthew. It brings up an a unique image of God in Matthew's narrative, the one who sees in secret. While the image might be new to the narrative, it would be familiar to the implied audience of Matthew's narrative.
62. The main passages come from Genesis, Job, Psalms, and Sirach. How does one explain the Matthean audience's knowledge of Genesis, Job, Psalms, Sirach? For

example, how does Matthew's audience know Job? See, for example, the similarities between Job 1:6–12 and Matt 4:1–11; Job 12:10, 38:41 and Matt 6:25–34; Job 38:17 and Matt 16:18. See Margaret Davies, *Matthew* (Sheffield: JSOT Press, 1993), 28, 62, 120. See also Powell, "Expected and Unexpected Readings of Matthew: What the Reader Knows."

63. Betz, *The Sermon on the Mount: A Commentary on the Sermon on the Mount, Including the Sermon on the Plain (Matthew 5:3–7:27 and Luke 6:20–49)*, 339–43. See Betz on suggesting the image is divided up into the two related images.
64. See also Ps 90:8, Prov 35, 2 Bar 83.3. Davies and Allison, *The Gospel According to Saint Matthew*, 584.
65. See Betz, *The Sermon on the Mount: A Commentary on the Sermon on the Mount, Including the Sermon on the Plain (Matthew 5:3–7:27 and Luke 6:20–49)*, 339.
66. For a description of this Father image, see Patte, *The Challenge of Discipleship: A Critical Study of the Sermon on the Mount as Scripture*, 204.
67. For a description of this Father image, see Ibid., 206–07.
68. The image of God as Father in 6:1–21 will be rounded out while discussing the Father's role in food exchange.
69. See the text above from Sir 11:2–6, which uncovers yet another aspect of this "secret God."
70. See R. Meyer, "κρύπτω," *TDNT* 3:967–973.
71. See these references for passages and examples of how food is interpreted, Betz, *The Sermon on the Mount: A Commentary on the Sermon on the Mount, Including the Sermon on the Plain (Matthew 5:3–7:27 and Luke 6:20–49)*, 397; Carter, *Matthew and the Margins: A Sociopolitical and Religious Reading*, 166–67; Davies and Allison, *The Gospel According to Saint Matthew*, 1:607–10; Hagner, *Matthew 1–13, 14–28*, 1:149–50. Matthew 6:11 reads, τὸν ἄρτον ἡμῶν τὸν ἐπιούσιον δὸς ἡμῖν σήμερον, give us this day our daily bread. I argue that bread in this passage refers to a real, material foodstuff and is not interpreted as a metaphor or symbol for all human needs, righteousness or the end-time banquet. Therefore, 6:11 is the second mention in Matthew's narrative of a material food item to be exchanged (the first is in 4:1–11).
72. Hagner translates it this way: "Give us today the eschatological bread that will be ours in the future." Hagner argues that while there may be a "present realization" of this petition, the focus is on the "blessing of the eschaton," the "anticipation of the eschatological banquet", "the eschatological fulfillment of needs." Hagner, *Matthew 1–13, 14–28*, 1:149. Davies and Allison and others use eschatological language as well: the "final feast," "salvation meal", "bread of life", "great tomorrow", "heavenly manna". Davies and Allison acknowledge that the passage refers to bread for "today" but they quickly move on to explain that this does not exclude the primary eschatological interpretation which must be a part of the understanding of this phrase Davies and Allison, *The Gospel According to Saint Matthew*, 1:609–10.
73. See Davies, *Matthew*.
74. See its use in 6:12, 9:5–6, 12:31–32, 18:21, 27, 32, 35. Also in 5:7, 5:23–26. Davies and Allison suggest forgiveness in 6:12 has an eschatological orientation but 6:14–15 has a present orientation. Davies and Allison, *The Gospel According to Saint Matthew*, 611–12.

75. Amy-Jill Levine (classroom lecture, Apocalyptic Literature, Vanderbilt University, Nashville, TN, fall 1994).
76. Davies and Allison, *The Gospel According to Saint Matthew*, 1:612–15; Hagner, *Matthew 1–13, 14–28*, 1:151–52; D. J. Harrington, *The Gospel of Matthew*, vol. 1, *Sacra Pagina* (Collegeville, MN: Liturgical Press, 1991), 95–98.
77. Hagner, *Matthew 1–13, 14–28*, 1:151–52.
78. Carter, *Matthew and the Margins: A Sociopolitical and Religious Reading*, 168–69; Luz, *Matthew 1–7: A Commentary*, 384–85.
79. Carter, *Matthew and the Margins: A Sociopolitical and Religious Reading*, 168.
80. See, for example, Rev 3:10.
81. See Prov 30:8, Ps 146:7, Exod 16, 2 Kgs 25:29–30, Ezra 6:9, Jer 27:21. Carter, *Matthew and the Margins: A Sociopolitical and Religious Reading*, 166–67.
82. One of the problems for interpreting the meaning of bread is the difficulty in translating ἐπιούσιον. Four main proposals of its derivation and meaning have been argued by scholars: (1) ἐπὶ τὴν οὖσαν, "for the present day," (2) ἐπί plus οὐ σία, "necessary for existence", (3) ἡ ἐπιουσα, for "the following day" or "the coming day" (as in tomorrow, not the far-off future), and (4) from ἐπιέναι, "to come", "the coming day" bread for "the future." For a discussion of this issue, see these commentaries on 6:11: Betz, *The Sermon on the Mount: A Commentary on the Sermon on the Mount, Including the Sermon on the Plain (Matthew 5:3–7:27 and Luke 6:20–49)*; Carter, *Matthew and the Margins: A Sociopolitical and Religious Reading*; Davies and Allison, *The Gospel According to Saint Matthew*; Hagner, *Matthew 1–13, 14–28*; Luz, *Matthew 1–7: A Commentary*. For what seem to be both theological and grammatical reasons, most scholars choose the final option with an emphasis on the end-time banquet where there will be plenty of food. The use of σημε̃ ρον in the same phrase, Hagner argues, makes it unlikely that the author would be redundant in using a meaning for ἐπιούσιον that would mean "daily" or "today." Carter, however, points out that the other three proposals all converge on the meaning of "today." The meaning of "today" as opposed to "the future" fits, however, not only with the majority of proposals offered, but, most importantly, with the sense of the prayer and the larger context of food supply.
83. BAGD, s.v. "ὅταν."
84. Betz, *The Sermon on the Mount: A Commentary on the Sermon on the Mount, Including the Sermon on the Plain (Matthew 5:3–7:27 and Luke 6:20–49)*, 379; Carter, *Matthew and the Margins: A Sociopolitical and Religious Reading*, 166–67; Luz, *Matthew 1–7: A Commentary*, 382–83; Sahlins, *Stone Age Economics*, 215.
85. This social span refers to Sahlins' kinship distance. Sahlins, *Stone Age Economics*, 196–98.
86. Ibid., 193–94.
87. Gillian Feeley-Harnik, *The Lord's Table: The Meaning of Food in Early Judaism and Christianity* (Washington; London: Smithsonian Institution Press, 1981), 72–82; Peter Garnsey, *Food and Society in Classical Antiquity*, ed. P. A. Cartledge and P. D. A. Garnsey, *Key Themes in Ancient History* (Cambridge: Cambridge University Press, 1999), 6–7, 108–12, ch. 8; Mauss, *The Gift*, ch. 2. Feeley-Harnik claims that nourishment is used as a metaphor of political leaders and prophets to symbolize their power and authority over people: Elisha (2 Kgs 4:42–44), Saul (2 Sam 5:2), David (Ezek 34:23–24, Ps 78).

88. Mauss, *The Gift*, 39–40; Sahlins, *Stone Age Economics*, 208–09.
89. For God as source of food, see Pss 104:24, 27–30; 107:9; 146:7; Prov 30:8–9; Exod 16:32; Exod 17; Isa 66:11–13.
90. See Mauss, *The Gift*, ch. 3; Sahlins, *Stone Age Economics*, 207–09.
91. See Patte, *The Challenge of Discipleship: A Critical Study of the Sermon on the Mount as Scripture*, 203ff.
92. Ibid., 206–07.
93. McFague, *Models of God: Theology for an Ecological, Nuclear Age*, 66.
94. This seems to stand out in contrast to the more "active" role of those practicing righteousness. Yet, they do request it—an active part of the exchange.
95. Garnsey, *Food and Society in Classical Antiquity*, 23–24. See Garnsey for a discussion of food and self-sufficiency.
96. According to Louw and Nida, "ask" (αἰτέω) and pray (προσεύχομαι) fit in the communication domain. Their two subdomains (L—Ask for, Request and M—Pray) are next to each other and can be grouped with a third subdomain (Question, Answer). Johannes P. Louw and Eugene A. Nida, eds., *Greek-English Lexicon of the New Testament Based on Semantic Documents* (New York: United Bible Societies, 1989), 388–89, 407–09.
97. This seeking is different than the faithless and anxious striving in 6:25–34 by the Gentiles.
98. Feeley-Harnik, *The Lord's Table: The Meaning of Food in Early Judaism and Christianity*, 79–81.
99. Ibid. See also Ps 16:5–6 and Hab 3:12–18. Depending on the circumstances, the parent may have no expectation of a return gift (e.g. nursing) or they may be some anticipation of a counterobligation. The amount and expense of return gift is expected to be less than the original gift and the repayment may be in terms of service or loyalty. A gift creates followership and therefore develops a type of continuity between the two parties "at least until the obligation to reciprocate is discharged." Sahlins, *Stone Age Economics*, 208.
100. The use of God as Mother and God as Father in the same passage or in analyzing a view of God may be troubling to some. God as Father, however, is not to be taken literally. The mystery of God is beyond human comprehension and human language and metaphors are human attempts to describe this mystery. Take, for example, the speech of Julian Norwich and the juxtaposition of male and female metaphors:

> The mother can give her child to suck of her milk, but our precious Mother Jesus can feed us with himself, and does, most courteously and most tenderly with the blessed sacrament, which is the precious food of true life.

The language of "mother" and "her" are used with "Jesus" and "himself" but why should this be any different than the use of father with king, two very different roles? See Johnson, *She Who Is: The Mystery of God in Feminist Theological Discourse*, 34. The obvious use of God as Father and the hidden use of God as mother may support Levine's study that men co-opted food production in first-century Israel by giving a negative valuation to women's production and by taking it over themselves. The loss of control of food preparation signified a loss of honor for women. Amy-Jill Levine, "Second Temple Judaism, Jesus, and Women: Yeast of Eden," *Biblical Interpretation* 2, no. 1 (1994): 23–26.

101. See the description of McFague's model in chapter 2 of this study which incorporates the procreationist and emanationist models.
102. Betz, *The Sermon on the Mount: A Commentary on the Sermon on the Mount, Including the Sermon on the Plain (Matthew 5:3–7:27 and Luke 6:20–49)*, 397.
103. Ibid., 475, n. 03. For the Hebrew Bible, see Jer 5:24; Isa 1:19; Lev 26:4; Deut 22:6; Job 38:41; 39:26–29; Pss 104:10–17; 145:15–16; 147:8–9;14; 81:7–16; 23:5; 107:9; Exod 16–17; Lev 11; Deut 14 ; Ezek 34:23–24; Gen 1:30; 2; 9:3–5; *Pss. Sol.* 5:9–10; Job 12:10; Ruth 1:16. For the New Testament, see Acts 14:17, 17:24–25. See also L. Juliana M. Claassens, *The God Who Provides: Biblical Images of Divine Nourishment* (Nashville: Abingdon Press, 2004), especially chs. 1 and 2.
104. Betz, *The Sermon on the Mount: A Commentary on the Sermon on the Mount, Including the Sermon on the Plain (Matthew 5:3–7:27 and Luke 6:20–49)*, 475.
105. In general, God provides for the animals, the birds of the air, the plants of the earth, and the fish of the sea (Job 12:10).
106. The phrase "God rains" is used to highlight the use of anthropomorphic language for God. God is the rain, God does not just make it rain. See below, also, the idea that God is a part of the world, the earth is the body of God. Therefore, as part of the earth, God is the rain that comes down. See Betz, *The Sermon on the Mount: A Commentary on the Sermon on the Mount, Including the Sermon on the Plain (Matthew 5:3–7:27 and Luke 6:20–49)*, 317.
107. I draw the metaphor of the world or earth as the body of God from Sallie McFague, McFague, *The Body of God: An Ecological Theology*, 131–96.
108. See also Claassens, especially ch. 1, for images of God nursing in the Hebrew Bible and Rabbinic Works. Claassens, *The God Who Provides: Biblical Images of Divine Nourishment.*
109. Betz refers to the *creatio continua*, i.e. the doctrine in which God's act in relation to the world is a present, ongoing activity and not simply an action in the past, in describing the "Fatherhood of God," but here I apply it to God as mother. H. D. Betz, *Essays on the Sermon on the Mount*, Translated by L. L. Welborn (Philadelphia: Fortress Press, 1985), 120–21. See also the discussion of McFague's procreative-emanationist model in chapter 2 of this study and in McFague, *The Body of God: An Ecological Theology*, 151–53.
110. The view of God in the Matthean narrative begins as a more authoritarian and transcendent God in which the structure of authority is more vertical, although one who cares and provides for God's children. As the narrative progresses, the view changes to a God whose structure of authority is more horizontal, who is more present with God's people and who empowers them to participate in acting in the world. For a description of different views of God in Matthew 5–7, see Patte, *The Challenge of Discipleship: A Critical Study of the Sermon on the Mount as Scripture*, 204–08.
111. Notice that there is little conflict or opposition between community and world at this point. As the interaction increases in the later narrative, so will the conflict. But even as the conflict increases, reciprocal food exchange increases as well.

Chapter 4: Birds of the Air (6:25–34)

1. In reading this section, many scholars deemphasize food as a material good. They generally agree that this passage focuses on God's sphere and not the human sphere, on heaven and not earth. The audience is instructed not to worry about materialism, earthly cares, or accumulating excessive possessions—that is, do not let the attempt to secure these earthly treasures monopolize your identity and life. Rather, seek God's kingdom and righteousness, God's sovereign rule, God's demands and law, and the basic necessities of life will be provided. This type of interpretation deemphasizes the material goods of life and highlights more abstract and spiritual qualities, not unlike what feminist criticism has worked against for years to challenge the earth/material/women and heaven/spiritual/men duality of interpretation. The interpretation also generally assumes that the audience is one of means that has the time and possessions to get caught up into being materialistic. For example, see Davies and Allison, *The Gospel According to Saint Matthew*, 1:663–65; Garland, *Reading Matthew: A Literary and Theological Commentary on the First Gospel*, 82–85; Gundry, *Matthew*, 115–19; Hagner, *Matthew 1–13, 14–28*, 166–67; J. Andrew Overman, *Church and Community in Crisis: The Gospel According to Matthew* (Valley Forge, PA: Trinity Press International, 1996), 91–92. See Luz and Carter, however, who tend to follow this de-emphasis of food but also raise similar questions regarding my concerns, Carter, *Matthew and the Margins: A Sociopolitical and Religious Reading*, 176–79; Luz, *Matthew 1–7: A Commentary*, 403.
2. See the discussion in chapter 2 of this study on how Malinowski, Lévi-Strauss, and Sahlin's work support the view of food exchange as a means of meeting a community's social needs.
3. See an alternative structure in Betz, *Essays on the Sermon on the Mount*, 95–103.
4. I would argue that v. 30c might be part of both the example and the concluding remark, since clothing the lilies falls under the example but "today and tomorrow" falls under the concluding remark and is parallel with the use of "tomorrow" and "day" in v. 34.
5. Seek (ζητέω) does not have the meaning of striving or working hard to live a certain ethical life; rather it refers to identifying or locating that which is valuable. Herod and others seek (try to find) Jesus as a child; seek is used along with ask and knock in chapter 7; the unclean spirit seeks (tries to locate) a resting place; the mother and brothers of Jesus are trying to seek (find an opportunity) to speak with him (12:46, 47). Other examples include the parable of a man trying to find fine pearls (13:45), a shepherd trying to locate a lost sheep (18:12), chief priests and Pharisees seeking (trying to find Jesus) to arrest Jesus, the women trying to locate Jesus after his crucifixion (28:5). In some examples, "seek" is used to find a worthy object.
6. In 6:1–21, the emphasis was to practice righteousness in secret so that no one would notice them and therefore they would be rewarded by God. Yet those practicing the giving of alms, prayer, and fasting were also to be a part of the larger world (i.e. giving of alms to others, fasting and social justice, forgiving debts), albeit in an anonymous way that integrated into the world. In practicing the giving of alms and fasting and prayer in secret, the audience was to do so in

a way that did not focus on their own bodies/act/selves (self-forgetfulness) so as to lose their focus on (1) what God does and (2) on the larger world. This same pattern can be seen with the body and self in 6:25–34.

7. Jerome H. Neyrey, "The Symbolic Universe of Luke-Acts," in *The Social World of Luke-Acts: Models for Interpretation*, ed. Jerome H. Neyrey (Peabody, Massachusetts: Hendrickson Publishers, 1991), 283. On bodily surfaces, see also Jerome H. Neyrey, "Body Language in 1 Corinthians: The Use of Anthropological Models for Understanding Paul and His Opponents," in *Social-Scientific Criticism of the New Testament and Its Social World*, ed. John H. Elliot (Decatur, GA: Scholars Press, 1986).
8. This is not a direct analogy. For a direct analogy, the lilies (as clothes) would be less emphasized in order for the field (as body) to be more recognized.
9. It is less clear here about the "relationship to the larger world" but more clear about "the relationship with God." This assertion, that the body is more than clothing, and my explanation that the smaller part is to be less emphasized in light of the larger entity, follows from other references to parts of the body in the narrative so far. The right eye and right hand (smaller parts of the body) are to be thrown away (5:29–30; thus treated a certain way, less valued) if they cause a person to sin in order to save the body (larger entity) from going to Gehenna. Similarly, if the eye is not treated a certain way, the whole body is affected. If the eye is to be healthy (treated a certain way), then the whole body is to be healthy (full of light) (6:22–23).
10. In 6:1–21, disciples ask for bread, which is connected with the earth. God arranges for bread to be made out of the earth. Food is not merely a nutritive substance that one receives directly, disconnected from other parts of life or from God.
11. Ψυχή does not refer to σῶμα, the physical body. Ψυχή is differentiated from σῶμα both here and in 10:28. Σῶμα in Matthew's narrative is more closely aligned with the physical body; it refers to the parts of the body (5:29, 6:22; "eye" and "hand"), the body which is clothed (6:25), the body that is covered with ointment (26:12), and the dead body (27:52, 58). This use highlights the physical, material, corporeal body. Body (σῶμα) in Matthew—5:29, 6:22, 6:25, 10:28, 26:26, 27:58, 26:12, 27:52. Life (ψυχή) in Matthew: 2:20, 6:25, 10:28, 10:39, 11:29, 12:18, 16:25, 20:28, 22:37, 26:38. Life/soul does not mean, as with Greek philosophy, a disembodied soul nor should it be translated as eternal life. Ζωή is Matthew's term for "eternal life" (7:14; 18:8, 9; 19:16, 17; 19:29, 25:46). See Betz, *Essays on the Sermon on the Mount*, 104–07.
12. Dennis E. Smith, "Table Fellowship as a Literary Motif in the Gospel of Luke," *JBL* 106, no. 4 (1987): esp. 623–29, 26 n. 41. Eating and drinking is often used to describe a particular lifestyle. The phrase is a symbol of luxury in Greco-Roman and Jewish literature, with both negative and positive connotations. Negatively, in Matthew's narrative, "eating and drinking" suggests a dissolute earthly lifestyle that is to be condemned (11:19, 24:38,49). Positively, it suggests the joys of the new age/future, a joyous feast with others before Yahweh (8:11, 9:11, 22:1–14). Eating and drinking represent not simply what one needs to keep the physical body alive but the life one has that includes relationships with family and God.

13. That is, those who find a life in the world without God will lose their life in the world and have neither a life in the world or God. Those who lose their life in this world for the sake of God, will find it—both a life in this world and a life with God. See Carter, *Matthew and the Margins: A Sociopolitical and Religious Reading*, 176.
14. Meigs, "Food as a Cultural Construction," 104.
15. This interpretation values the material food, but only as it is connected with other life forms that provide it for others—food that is given and received, not just food as a separate entity. Food is not devalued as a material object completely in favor of spiritual matters.
16. The reference to God as "your heavenly Father" is continued from chapters five and six. The use of the pronoun "your" highlights the social and relational link between the Father and the disciples. The preference for the "heavenly" modifier picks up on (and is reinforced here with) the, now cumulative, meaning of the heavenly Father as one who is creator and who deals without favor with his creatures—the Father in heaven shines the sun on the bad and good and rains on the righteous and unrighteous (5:45).
17. Luz, *Matthew 1–7: A Commentary*, 401 n. 10. The phrase, birds of the air, is used 34 times in the LXX and its general meaning can be divided into three categories: (1) it is associated with God's providence and generosity, (2) birds of the air are one integral part of the whole creation, and (3) the phrase is related to God's judgment. The first two categories fit with Matthew's use.
18. Wisdom literature, with its emphasis on revelation through the surrounding world/environment, especially underscores the value of learning from animals and plants. Other animals that do work and collect food: ants (Prov 6:6, 30:25), bees (Prov 6:6, 8; Sir 11:3), oxen (Deut 25:4, 1 Cor 9:9, 1 Tim 5:18). See Prov 6:6–11 (go to the ant), Job 12:7–10, Job 40:15–24.
19. While the birds of the air are portrayed as wise teachers, this passage portrays them as inferior to human beings. A definite hierarchy of living creatures is established in the passage. The narrative flow moves from humans to animals (birds of the air) to plants (lilies of the field). This order follows the hierarchical order of living creatures in other biblical literature. Several statements within the passage demonstrate the inferiority of the birds: "are you not of more value" (6:26), "will he not much more cloth you" (6:30). Nevertheless, while the humans may be portrayed in this passage as having more value than animals and plants, the birds of the air have great value themselves to human beings. The disciples and audience are encouraged to watch them to see what they have to teach. Betz recognizes this tension as well, that there is a hierarchy but humans can also learn from birds. Betz, *The Sermon on the Mount: A Commentary on the Sermon on the Mount, Including the Sermon on the Plain (Matthew 5:3–7:27 and Luke 6:20–49)*, 473.
20. The reader or audience may be reading this the first, second, third, or fourth time. See my description of the implied audience in chapter 2 of this study.
21. Birds are awe-inspiring as they move over the earth, e.g. Prov 30:18–19. Early church Fathers thought of Gen 1 with the baptism of Jesus. See Davies and Allison, *The Gospel According to Saint Matthew*, 1:331, 34.

22. The audience will see this again in 14:19 when Jesus looks up to heaven before dispersing the bread and fish: "The eyes of all look to you, and you give them their food in due season" (Ps 145:15), "These all look to you to give them their food in due season." (Ps 104:27), "Lift up your eyes on high and see: Who created these?" (Isa 40:26), "And if they (every living thing) are hungry, they will lift up their face to you" (*Pss. Sol.* 5:10). By contrast, see the Gospel of Thomas 3 which identifies the kingdom as "inside of you" and "outside of you" but objects to the view that the kingdom is "in the sky."
23. In Ps 104:12, the psalmist provides a list of all that the Lord creates and provides for the creation and includes the birds of the air who have their habitation by the streams. The verse immediately preceding this inclusion states that the Lord gives drink to every wild animal, which would include the birds of the air. Likewise, in Dan 4:12 and 4:21, a great and strong tree provides for all and, in particular, the birds of the air nest in its branches. Before and after this description, the tree is said to provide food for "all," which includes the animals of the field, the birds of the air and all living beings. In Matthew, the birds of the air have nests just as foxes have holes (8:20). And the kingdom of heaven is like a mustard seed which grows to become a tree where birds of the air makes nests in its branches (13:32). A home and nourishment for the birds of the air are signs of God's provisions. In these accounts, the birds of the air get "everything they need," not just food but also a place to live. See also Ezek 31:6, as well as Ps 147:9 and Job 38:41 where God feeds the ravens.
24. This is made clear by the second part of 6:26, "they do not sow or reap or gather into barns, and your heavenly Father feeds them." See also Ps 104:12; Dan 4:12, 21; Ezek 31:6, 13; Hos 4:3; Jer 4:25, 9:10.
25. In 6:1–21, God's interaction with the world is ambivalent. God sees in secret yet can see all inhabitants of the earth. God is in secret yet will be revealed. God rewards a few righteous ones in secret yet in the previous chapter showers the good and bad with generosity. The primary interaction, however, is in secrecy with only a hint toward a more open relationship with the wider world.
26. Betz, *The Sermon on the Mount: A Commentary on the Sermon on the Mount, Including the Sermon on the Plain (Matthew 5:3–7:27 and Luke 6:20–49)*, 343.
27. Οὐρανός can mean "air" as in the sky or "heaven" as in the abode of God. Malbon, *Narrative Space and Mythic Meaning in Mark*, 56. BAGD, s.v. "Οὐρανός." Here, it primarily refers to air or sky, the birds in the sky, that part of the atmosphere where clouds hover (24:30b). Ἀγρός refers to a field, a piece of ground that grows plants. BAGD, s.v. "Ἀγρός." Ἀγρός is used with the same theme of provision, although it is referring to clothing and not food. The sky and the field are both topographical spaces, physical features of the earth which can be observed from an aerial photograph. Malbon, *Narrative Space and Mythic Meaning in Mark*, 53. As outdoor, isolated and uninhabited spaces, these might be considered dangerous or unsafe. Bal, *Narratology: Introduction to the Theory of Narrative*, 134. But in this passage, as it was in 4:1–11, the outdoor, uninhabited space is also a place of God's provision.
28. Wild not tended fields as opposed to the vineyards, for example, which are tended and inhabited.

29. Malbon, *Narrative Space and Mythic Meaning in Mark*, 51. In Mark, Malbon argues that "'the country' (ἀγρός) is not a wild or unpopulated area but a rural, not urban, region where people live and work."
30. The characteristics of this pattern include: (a) identifying those who are fed as "hungry" or who have "hunger" or cry out, (b) an image of God as one who created the earth, heavens, and sea and/or delivered the Israelites out of distress and brought (or returned after the exile) them into the promised land, (c) food coming out of the earth or other human communities to feed the Matthean community, and (d) providing food "in due season" (Ps 104:27), immediately.
31. See also Sheffield's argument that the heavenly Father is characterized as one who nurtures, not dominates, in Matthew. "The heavenly Father's care and nurturing of little ones is of a maternal nature." Sheffield, "The Father in the Gospel of Matthew." 64.
32. See Pss 146:7, 107:9, 36; Neh 9:15; Isa 49:8.
33. See for example Davies and Allison, *The Gospel According to Saint Matthew*, 1:625; Hagner, *Matthew 1–13, 14–28*, 1:164–65.
34. Betz, *The Sermon on the Mount: A Commentary on the Sermon on the Mount, Including the Sermon on the Plain (Matthew 5:3–7:27 and Luke 6:20–49)*, 101.
35. See Matthew 8:23–27, 14:22–23, 16:5–12, 17:20.
36. The disciples in 8:23–27 and 14:22–23 come up against strong winds at sea. In 16:5–12, the disciples are concerned about the lack of food on the sea (doesn't say on the sea or in the boat, but "reached the other side") and, according to Jesus, do not remember the provision of food in the wilderness. In chapter 17, the disciples encounter a man with a demon and Jesus' instructions include the ability to move mountains.
37. The disciples are "fearful" (8:23–37), they are terrified and cry out in fear (14:22–23). Peter is frightened (14:22–23). In 16:5–12, the disciples do not perceive what Jesus is talking about and they are instructed to beware of the teaching of the Pharisees and Sadducees. One might think that, as fisherman, those in the boat would respond without fear. The crisis does not come from creation itself, as if creation has fortified its troops and marched against the disciples. Rather, the crisis exists in how the disciples encounter creation and are coping with it.
38. Ἐπιτιμάω can be translated as to rebuke, but also to command or to order. To order can mean to regulate, to bring to a certain order. See especially 8:26 and 17:18. It is used also in 12:16, 16:20, 17:18, 19:13, 20:31.
39. In 8:23–27, Jesus orders the winds and the lake, and they obey him. These elements of nature are anthropomorphized and treated as conscious beings but they are not identified as good or evil, W. D. Davies and D. C. Allison, *The Gospel According to Saint Matthew*, 3 vols., vol. 2, *I. C. C.* (Edinburgh: T & T Clark, 1991), 74. In 14:22–33, Jesus acts as Yahweh who is creator of the sea and brings order to it. Jesus makes a safe way for the disciples (as Yahweh prepares the Sea of Reeds for the Israelites). Jesus does not dominate the sea or rebuke a rebellious and evil creation Davies and Allison, *The Gospel According to Saint Matthew*, 2:84.
40. Later in Matt 12, the earth provides heads of grain and in Matt 14 and 15, water provides fish and the wilderness provides bread.
41. Betz, *The Sermon on the Mount: A Commentary on the Sermon on the Mount, Including the Sermon on the Plain (Matthew 5:3–7:27 and Luke 6:20–49)*, 480–84.

42. The scribes and Pharisees ask Jesus for a sign (12:39) and the Pharisees and Sadducees test Jesus by asking for a sign (16:4). Both passages can be considered testing or conflict stories Davies and Allison, *The Gospel According to Saint Matthew*, 2:351. Both times, Jesus rebukes his opponents for striving for proof by miracles. As Jesus was tempted by the devil in the wilderness in 4:1–11, so Jesus is tempted by the scribes and Pharisees, who are then called an evil and adulterous generation (for evil and adulterous generation in the wilderness, see Deut 1:35, 32:5, cf. Jub 23:14, 1QSb 3:7, Isa 57:3, Isa 52:3, Jer 3;10, Ezek 23, Hos 1–3, 5:3–4). Davies and Allison, *The Gospel According to Saint Matthew*, 2:354–55.
43. That is, the provision of protection (Deut 1:26–35) and food (Deut 32:13–15).
44. While the Pharisees and Sadducees understand some signs in the sky (16:3), they cannot understand the signs of the times and they are unable to work with the world around them.
45. In 6:7–8, where the Gentiles are depicted as heaping up empty phrases to get attention of their uncaring, deaf, angry gods, they are at odds with their gods. They strive to be in relationship with their gods. Carter, *Matthew and the Margins: A Sociopolitical and Religious Reading*, 162–63.
46. As in 6:7–8, the Gentiles in 6:32 are used as an example that is associated with God as the Father who knows what you need: "your Father knows what you need before you ask him" (6:7–8) and "your heavenly Father knows that you need all these things" (6:32).
47. See also Daniel Patte, *Discipleship According to the Sermon on the Mount* (Valley Forge, PA: Trinity Press International, 1996), 381–84.
48. Seeking the kingdom of God and his righteousness has generally referred to the act of becoming a part of this kingdom, living in a way that recognizes the existence of the kingdom. Davies and Allison argue that the phrase means to come into the sphere of the working of God's kingdom, Davies and Allison, *The Gospel According to Saint Matthew*, 1:660. The kingdom itself is typically referred to as God's sovereign rule, the activity of God's reign. The clear majority of the language describing the kingdom is that of God as king, as monarchical ruler who rules, reigns, who has power and judgment. See, for example, Carter, *Matthew and the Margins: A Sociopolitical and Religious Reading*, 119–20; Davies and Allison, *The Gospel According to Saint Matthew*, 1:389–92; Hagner, *Matthew 1–13, 14–28*, 1:148; Harrington, *The Gospel of Matthew*, 18–19, 72. Carter also uses this type of language but includes other language such that the kingdom liberates, protects, has a saving presence.
49. Righteousness is most often interpreted as right human moral conduct or as a gift from God. Righteousness is used in Matthew 1:19, 3:15, 5:6, 5:10, 5:20, 6:1, 6:33, 21:32. Przybylski, in his study on righteousness in Matthew, acknowledges these two main interpretations of righteousness in the scholarship—as God's gifts to humans or as God's demand upon humans but finally interprets its meaning as the moral human conduct which God requires. Przybylski, *Righteousness in Matthew and His World of Thought.*, 1, Przybylski, who interprets righteousness here as a norm for a person's conduct, argues that humans are to live, behave, conduct themselves according to a norm which is governed by God. He comes to this conclusion by focusing on how Matthew redacts the phrase καὶ τὴν δικαιοσύνην αὐτοῦ, and then how it fits into a continuous argument from 5:20–

6:33. His interpretation of righteousness in 5:20 and 6:1 as a demand upon human conduct and his use of redaction criticism determine/influence his final interpretation of righteousness in 6:33. I look at 6:33 in light of the particular literary structure in 6:25–34 (and also within the larger unit of chapters 4–7 with a focus on the exchange of food) without a focus on how Matthew might have edited his work and come to a different conclusion than other authors. With the kingdom interpreted as God's political rule and righteousness as certain moral conduct, then seeking the kingdom and righteousness is interpreted as striving (NRSV), working hard, putting forth great effort to live a moral life under God as a political monarch. Alternatively, there is also the emphasis on spiritual life, heart language, and the abstract. Hagner, for example, interprets the phrase as making "the kingdom the center of one's existence and thus experience the rule of God full in one's heart." Hagner, *Matthew 1–13, 14–28,* 1:165–66.

50. See the repetitive-progressive pattern at the beginning of this chapter. Tannehill has used a similar type of literary approach and has, in fact, analyzed this passage, Tannehill, *The Sword of His Mouth: Forceful and Imaginative Language in Synoptic Sayings,* 66. He notes the repetitive use of look/observe but does not include "seek." He argues that 6:33 is described as a new possibility of life, seeking the Kingdom, to see world and self in a new way.

51. In 6:25–34, three verbs are used in parallel to indicate how the community is to seek food. The community is instructed to look (ἐμβλέπω) at the birds of the air to see how they are feed by the heavenly Father, to consider (καταμανθάνω) how God clothes the lilies of the field, and then to seek (ζητέω) the kingdom of God and his righteousness. All three verbs have in common the idea of thinking and learning, of acquiring, processing, manipulating information. Both ἐμβλέπω and καταμαῦ θάνω have in common the semantic domain of thinking (30) which involves the idea of processing and manipulating information, which may lead to the making of a decision. Louw and Nida, eds., *Greek-English Lexicon of the New Testament Based on Semantic Documents,* 30.1, 30.30. Ζητέω is in the semantic domain of learning (27) and primarily refers to the acquisition of information, probably referring to the step before processing and manipulating information (before domain 30). Ibid., 27.41. In particular, ζητέω in this domain refers to the attempt to try to learn, to carefully investigate or search, to learn the location of something, to try and find out by looking for something. This search may involve movement as a person looks around to gather information. The use of ἐμβλέπω and καταμανθάνω in parallel with ζητέω, however, may suggest the meaning of ζητέω here leans more toward the beginning steps of processing information. The community in 6:25–34 has moved beyond asking and praying for food toward trying to learn about out where one might find food.

52. The meaning of righteousness does not have to remain constant through the narrative, contra Davies and Allison, *The Gospel According to Saint Matthew,* 1:661; Przybylski, *Righteousness in Matthew and His World of Thought,* 1–12. Both 5:6 and 6:33, the book ends of the use of righteousness in the SM and in this first unit, use righteousness as a gift from or activity of God while the other three uses, 5:10, 5:20, and 6:1 can be interpreted as required human moral conduct. Furthermore, righteousness is modified in 6:33 with the possessive "his", thus "his righteousness," which is found nowhere else in Matthew. This use of the posses-

sive, which is in contrast with "your righteousness" in both 5:20 and 6:1, refers to the heavenly Father's righteous activity. (Przybylski argues, however, that "his righteousness" "does not deal with God's righteousness *per se*. Rather it deals with God's righteousness insofar as it is the norm governing man's conduct.") See Przybylski, *Righteousness in Matthew and His World of Thought*, 89.

53. Literal usage: Ps 107:5, Isa 49:10, 55:1–2, 65:13. Some references might be used metaphorically (i.e. for God's restoration to the promised land), but they are also based on experiences of real hunger and thirst. Metaphorical usage ("longing"): Ps 42:2, 63:1, 143:6; Amos 8:11. Davies and Allison, *The Gospel According to Saint Matthew*, 1:451. even suggest it is active seeking not passive longing.
54. This use matches other uses within the beatitudes: those who are merciful will be shown mercy, those who mourn will be comforted. While these are often interpreted as eschatological blessings—to be received at the end time—they can also be interpreted as blessings to be given in the near future before the end time. Other beatitudes, for example, imply that material blessings are forthcoming in future time, but not eschatological future (to be comforted, 2:18, 8:5, 26:53, or shown mercy, 6:2,3,4; 18:33, 9:27, 15:22, 17:15, 20:30, 31; 9:13, 12:7, 23:3). Not all the beatitudes show a direct link between the characteristics and the reward, but some do and hunger and thirst fit in with those. In addition, the use of χορτάζω in 5:6 matches that used in 15:33 and 15:37, "from where in the wilderness will come to us so many loaves so as to satisfy (χορτάσαι) such a great crowd?" Jesus and the disciples eventually give material food to the crowd and "everyone ate and they were satisfied (ἐχορτάσθησαν)" (15:37). This also fits the use of righteousness in 6:33, as God's provision of the material goods of food and clothing.
55. Προστεθήσεται is interpreted as a logical extension of seeking/looking for God's provision of material goods (see BAGD, s.v. "προστίθημι") as opposed to a separate, additional item. It proceeds, continues from. The use of the progressive future supports this, as the emphasis is put on the progress of the action. See James A. and Carlton L. Winbery Brooks, *Syntax of New Testament Greek* (Washington, D. C.: University Press of America, 1979), 96–97.
56. Read in a typological way, today does not necessarily mean the current 24 hour period but it does mean in the present time, urgent, now as opposed to tomorrow. Tomorrow would mean less urgent.
57. Betz, *The Sermon on the Mount: A Commentary on the Sermon on the Mount, Including the Sermon on the Plain (Matthew 5:3–7:27 and Luke 6:20–49)*, 482; Davies and Allison, *The Gospel According to Saint Matthew*, 1:659–60; Hagner, *Matthew 1–13, 14–28*, 1:166.
58. In Matthew's narrative, the "day" is the longest measurement of time. There is no reference to a "week" (only the "first day of the week," 28:1) or "month" or "year" in the story. Events are measured by days. The frequent use of "evening, "day", and "night" reinforce the "day" as the most significant unit of time. Powell, *What Is Narrative Criticism?*, 79–80.
59. Κακία can be translated as evil, moral turpitude or as trouble, misery, crisis (BAGD, s.v. "κακία"). I interpret it here as the latter.
60. Luz, *Matthew 1–7: A Commentary*, 409.
61. Davies and Allison, *The Gospel According to Saint Matthew*, 1:662–63.

62. The subjunctive communicates ideas that deal with the future, are objectively possible, but are not factual or certain. Brooks, *Syntax of New Testament Greek*, 119.
63. Ibid.
64. The present tense is used in v. 26 (i.e. the Father feeds) and v. 30 (i.e. God clothes) and the progressive future is used in v. 33.

Chapter 5: "Ask and it will be given" (7:7–11)

1. Many scholars argue that vv. 7–11 refer to prayer, communicating with the Father in heaven. See Hagner, *Matthew 1–13, 14–28*; Hare, *Matthew*; Harrington, *The Gospel of Matthew*; D. Senior, "Matthew," in *Abingdon New Testament Commentaries* (Nashville: Abingdon, 1998). David R. Bauer and Mark Allan Powell, eds., *Treasures New and Old: Recent Contributions to Matthean Studies* (Atlanta, Georgia: Scholars Press, 1996); Carter, *Matthew and the Margins: A Sociopolitical and Religious Reading*; Davies and Allison, *The Gospel According to Saint Matthew*; Luz, *Matthew 1–7: A Commentary*; Patte, *The Gospel According to Matthew: A Structural Commentary on Matthew's Faith*. For this interpretation in general, the three imperatives—ask, seek, knock—are interpreted as words signifying a religious longing or quest for the divine. The future passives (e.g. δοθήσεται in 7:7) are interpreted as divine passives (as in 7:1–2)—therefore God will give to those who ask and seek and God will open the door to those who knock. The final saying about the Father in heaven in v. 11 is determinative for this interpretation—those who ask (through prayer) their Father in heaven will be given good things. Therefore, the opening (vv. 7–8) and the closing (v. 11) specify God's faithfulness to answer prayer and the middle (vv. 9–10) uses a human example to illustrate the larger point of God's faithfulness, see especially Hagner, *Matthew 1–13, 14–28*, 1:173–75.
2. A few scholars recognize that there may be other interpretations of this passage besides prayer. Betz, *The Sermon on the Mount: A Commentary on the Sermon on the Mount, Including the Sermon on the Plain (Matthew 5:3–7:27 and Luke 6:20–49)*, 506; Carter, *Matthew and the Margins: A Sociopolitical and Religious Reading*, 183; Dale Goldsmith, "'Ask, and It Will Be Given.' Toward Writing the History of a Logion," *New Testament Studies* 35 (1989): 262–64. The object of the asking, seeking, and knocking may refer to gifts, to questions and answers, or to seeking wisdom, truth or God. Goldsmith contends that 7:7–11 is set in an ethical context in chapter seven and not in a context of cultic or payer material, which Matthew focuses on in chapter six (258–59). Goldsmith approaches this passage from a form critical approach, tracing the history of its formation, but some of his insights can be applied to a narrative critical approach (especially since both types of criticisms have a literary element to them). The tripartite, then, emphasizes how humans are to relate to one another.
3. See especially αἰτέω—5:42; ζητέω—23:45, 18:12; κρούω—Rev 3:20. The tripartite (αἰτέω, ζητέω, κρούω) may refer to the religious dimension but in Matthew's narrative they refer to other human relationships more often than to a relationship with the divine. Αἰτέω is certainly used in the context of prayer in Matthew (6:8,

18:19, 21:22), but it is also used in the context of asking questions of political leaders (14:7, 27:20), asking for material goods (5:42) and asking about end-time arrangements with Jesus (20:22). In Matthew, ζητέω is used in a variety of ways: to seek another person in order to hurt him (2:13, 2:20, 21:46), to seek the person of Jesus (12:46, 28:5), to symbolize the Kingdom of heaven (13:45), for an unclean spirit seeking a resting place (12:43), and for God who seeks the little ones who are lost (18:12). In Matthew's narrative, seek is used to seek the kingdom but never to seek or ask or pray to God. Finally, κρούω is only used in this passage in Matthew's narrative and can be thought of as a metaphor for entering. In other Hebrew Bible and New Testament literature, knock refers to striking a door, either in the situation of a master knocking at a door where a servant is or a servant trying to get into the master's house (usually symbolizing God). Patte, *The Gospel According to Matthew: A Structural Commentary on Matthew's Faith*, 97. See also Acts 12:13, Luke 12:36, Luke 13:25, Rev 3:20.

4. Gift(s) (δῶρον) is used in Matthew's narrative most often to refer to a gift or sacrifice to God (5:23,24; 8:4, 15:5, 23:18,19) but is also used for the gold, frankincense and myrrh the wise men give to the child Jesus. In these cases, it is a material gift, not an eschatological benefit or spiritual blessing.
5. So, the imperative "do not worry" and the questions "what you might eat" in 6:25–34 and the imperatives ask–given/seek-find/knock-open in 7:7–11.
6. The life examples are from nature in 6:25–34 and from a human household in 7:7–11.
7. Luz, *Matthew 1–7: A Commentary*, 421.
8. There may be a critique here that with only these two changes, there is no significant progression and repetition without change is "boring," Tannehill, *The Sword of His Mouth: Forceful and Imaginative Language in Synoptic Sayings*, 51. I show, however, that there is a rhythm which is important and more significant change comes in vv. 9–11. The rhythm that is set up with this repetition is significant. Tannehill notes that there are two feet or small units in each line—(1) ask (2) and it will be given, (1) seek (2) and you will find, (1) knock (2) and it will be opened—making three lines in each of v. 7 and v. 8. The use of several consecutive sets of small units that balance each other sets up a rhythm. This use of rhythm has a similar effect on the audience as music does—it draws in mind and body of the hearer and involves the hearer in a more complete way than with nonrhythmic prose (Tannehill, 49). The repetition, therefore, not only reinforces the message through reiteration but there is also a rhythm in the expression of these ideas that engages and moves the reader.
9. For example Luke 24:30, 24:42. BAGD, s.v. "ἐπιδίδωμι." Louw and Nida, eds., *Greek-English Lexicon of the New Testament Based on Semantic Documents*, 57.75.
10. Many scholars claim that this final illustration is determinative for the whole passage, therefore those who ask in 7:7 were asking the Father in prayer for "good things," interpreted primarily as eschatological benefits or spiritual blessings. In my interpretation, v. 11 is a further development of a linear progression that does not define the exchange in the earlier part of the passage. In this reading, vv. 7–10 are determinative for v. 11 instead of v. 11 determining the meaning of vv. 7–10. Verses 7–10 were speaking primarily of humans exchanging material gifts, particularly food, and now in v. 11, the Father in heaven is exchanging

"good things" with those who ask him. "Good things" is a phrase that has developed from "bread" and "fish" in vv. 9–10 and "good gifts" in v. 11a and now can continue to be seen as material gifts, inclusive but not limited to food.

11. Goldsmith, "'Ask, and It Will Be Given.' Toward Writing the History of a Logion," 263.
12. See David B. Howell, *Matthew's Inclusive Story: A Study in the Narrative Rhetoric of the First Gospel* (Sheffield, England: JSOT Press, 1990), 222–24; Patte, *The Gospel According to Matthew: A Structural Commentary on Matthew's Faith*, 153–54.
13. Goldsmith, "'Ask, and It Will Be Given.' Toward Writing the History of a Logion," 263. Goldsmith discusses unilateral nurturing.
14. See for example 6:25, 6:26, 6:30, Davies and Allison, *The Gospel According to Saint Matthew*, 1:626.
15. Sahlins, *Stone Age Economics*, 194.
16. In v. 7, those who are to receive that which is requested are referred to as "you" explicitly two times (i.e. ὑμῖν) and implicitly once (εὑρήσετε). The "you" is a reference to the disciples, those within the Matthean community. The reference to those within the community, while being sustained throughout the passage with family language, is not exclusively maintained as the use of πᾶς in v. 8 demonstrates.
17. For other readings, πᾶς refers to everyone who is a child of the Father in heaven, the sons of the kingdom, the community of the disciples, all those already participating in or receiving the kingdom reality brought by Jesus. See these commentaries on 7:8, Carter, *Matthew and the Margins: A Sociopolitical and Religious Reading*; Davies and Allison, *The Gospel According to Saint Matthew*; Hagner, *Matthew 1–13, 14–28*; Strecker, *Der Weg Der Gerechtigkeit: Untersuchung Zur Theologie Des Matthaus*. Davies and Allison claim that hypocrites and Gentiles do not have their prayers answered by God (6:5, 7) so, since 7:7–11 is about prayer, πᾶς must refer to the disciples. Yet, I do not interpret this passage as referring to prayer. It refers to human (and divine) relationships and the exchange of material goods.
18. It is addressed primarily to the disciples in 5:22, 28, 32, but the crowds may be overhearing. In 7:21, 7:24, and 7:26 the impersonal style of the address may suggest the audience addressed is no longer the disciples (i.e. "you") but the crowds, those outside the community or whatever wider audience might be listening to the story. On these matters and on the use of πᾶς in Matthew see Howell, *Matthew's Inclusive Story: A Study in the Narrative Rhetoric of the First Gospel*, 216–25; Malbon, *In the Company of Jesus: Characters in Mark's Gospel*, 95–99; Patte, *The Gospel According to Matthew: A Structural Commentary on Matthew's Faith*, 153–54. The use of πᾶς in 10:32 and 19:29 targets either the disciples or anyone who has confessed Jesus or left houses or brothers or sisters or Father or mother or children or fields.
19. Howell, *Matthew's Inclusive Story: A Study in the Narrative Rhetoric of the First Gospel*, 222–24; Luz, *Matthew 1–7: A Commentary*, 421. Betz acknowledges that it may include more than the disciples. Betz, *The Sermon on the Mount: A Commentary on the Sermon on the Mount, Including the Sermon on the Plain (Matthew 5:3–7:27 and Luke 6:20–49)*, 504–05; Malbon, *In the Company of Jesus: Characters in Mark's Gospel*, 95–99.

20. Patte, *The Gospel According to Matthew: A Structural Commentary on Matthew's Faith*, 153–54. Patte says 5:3–10 and 7:21–27 convince the readers that they are to identify with "you" throughout the sermon. This is also the case, according to Patte, for 10:32–42, which I discuss in Chapter 6 in this study.
21. "Whoever" has a similar meaning to πᾶς. See Howell, *Matthew's Inclusive Story: A Study in the Narrative Rhetoric of the First Gospel*, 221.
22. Ἄνθρωπος is used several times throughout chs. 6–7, especially in 6:1–21, a previous passage of this study: 5:13, 16, 19; 6:1, 2, 5, 14, 15, 16, 18; 7:12. Betz, *The Sermon on the Mount: A Commentary on the Sermon on the Mount, Including the Sermon on the Plain (Matthew 5:3–7:27 and Luke 6:20–49)*, 505. Betz highlights its importance as well.
23. Carter, *Matthew and the Margins: A Sociopolitical and Religious Reading*, 170.
24. The verse begins, η' τίς ἐστιν ἐξ ὑμῶν ἄνθρωπος—lit. "or what is among you a human . . ." That is, "what human is among you . . ." The phrase uses ὑμῶν first—and therefore the disciples, addressed as "you" throughout chs. 6–7, are addressed. Yet, immediately following "ὑμῶν " is ἄνθρωπος, which refers to humans.
25. BAGD, "ἐκ," 1b. See also Herbert Weir Smyth, "Greek Grammar," (Cambridge: Harvard University Press, 1956), 377–78. Evidence for this reading lies in the continued use of "you" throughout vv. 9–11 to align with the disciples—"you, being evil" and "your Father."
26. BAGD, "ἐκ," 1d—especially 1 Cor 9:19, which Paul separates himself from "all people." cf. John 17:15, Acts 15:29.
27. Betz, *The Sermon on the Mount: A Commentary on the Sermon on the Mount, Including the Sermon on the Plain (Matthew 5:3–7:27 and Luke 6:20–49)*, 505–06; Hagner, *Matthew 1–13, 14–28*, 1:174–75.
28. Matthew 6:13 may be interpreted "from evil" not "from the evil one," such that one prays to be rescued from evil, a presence, a capacity, the propensity to be evil.
29. This will happen in Matt 10, 14, and 15.
30. If you do exchange food and you are evil, perhaps the world, who is "evil", will exchange food as well and do it with you. Humans outside the community, as evil as they are, also feed their children food and maybe would exchange food with those within the community.
31. *Creatio continua* is the act of creation which also involves the continuing preservation of that creation, the continuation of the creative act. See Betz, *Essays on the Sermon on the Mount*, 120; McFague, *The Body of God: An Ecological Theology*, 151–53.
32. See Powell, "Expected and Unexpected Readings of Matthew: What the Reader Knows," 41–42. Matthew often quotes Isaiah, see 3:3, 4:14, 8:17, 12:17, 13:14, 15:7 in Matthew's narrative.
33. Goldsmith, "'Ask, and It Will Be Given.' Toward Writing the History of a Logion," 263.
34. While there is an acknowledgement that the child must ask, seek, and knock, this request is not a requirement in order to receive food. A sign of obedience is not necessary in order for blessing to take place. Against Feeley-Harnik who states that feeding good food is a sign of blessing, of favor, of life from God while feeding bad food is a sign of judgment or punishment or death. Feeley-Harnik, *The*

Lord's Table: The Meaning of Food in Early Judaism and Christianity, 72–79. There is no discussion of faithfulness or obedience as a prerequisite for receiving food. Children are to ask for food from their parents, not as a precondition to receiving but as a indication that they need it now, they are hungry now (6:11, 6:25–34, 7:7–11). For humans, the Father in heaven does not initiate the feeding, as with creatures where nature's storehouse is stocked with food ready to eat (for the birds of the air 6:25–34). Yet, by asking, food is given (6:11, 6:25–34, 7:7–11).

35. "Your Father *knows* what you need before you ask him," yet pray anyway (6:8). "Your heavenly Father *knows* that you need all these things" (6:32) and "If you...*know* to give good gifts to your children, how much more will your Father in heaven give good things . . ." (7:11).
36. This is God as creator not the monarchical God who relates exclusively to one community. McFague, *Models of God: Theology for an Ecological, Nuclear Age,* 65–66.
37. The food in 7:7–11 is not symbolic for other kinds of gifts but is material food. Scholars question whether the heavenly Father gives food or whether good things (ἀγαθὰ) refers to other blessings or gifts. Hare claims that ἀγαθὰ is to be interpreted as "Christian graces" not "material treasures." Hare, *Matthew,* 79. His example of Christian graces is the "love of enemies." Davies and Allison suggest "all that is required to live the life of faithful discipleship," Davies and Allison, *The Gospel According to Saint Matthew,* 685. Hagner claims it might mean both present material blessings and transcendent blessings, Hagner, *Matthew 1–13, 14–28,* 1:175. I argue that ἀγαθὰ refers to material goods, with a special emphasis on food. As argued above, "ask," "seek," and "knock" can certainly refer to material goods and that is the focus of this passage, the exchange of material goods in human (and divine) relationships. It would make sense that the conclusion of the passage would also refer to material goods. 'Αγαθα in 11b most clearly refers to δόματα ἀγαθὰ in v. 11a, which refers back to bread and fish in vv. 9–10. While each step in the process—bread and fish, good gifts, good things—may be widening the sphere of meaning, it certainly includes the original reference—bread and fish. A comparison between 6:25–34 and 7:7–11 also substantiates ἀγαθὰ as a material element. Matthew 6:25–34 which also uses the example of food (and material goods—clothing) and refers to πάντα ταῦτα (all these things—6:32a, 32b, 33) at the end of the passage. Most scholars, as I do, interpret πάντα ταῦτα in 6:32–33 as referring to the food and clothing, the material goods, that were mentioned earlier in the passage. They also both use an adjective as a substantive—ταῦτα and ἀγαθὰ. The text in 7:7–11 can be read in the same way as 6:25–34—"good things" refers to bread and fish stated earlier in 7:7–11 as "all these things" refers to food and clothing. 'Αγαθα in 7:11 refers to material goods, particularly food.
38. As Patte says, "a point is being stressed by the opposition between people "who *know* how to give good gifts to [their] children" (7:11) *and* hypothetical, nonexistent, people who would *not know* how to do it and thus would give bad things ("stone," "serpent") to their children (7:9–10). We have here a foil, an artificial contrast. Patte, *The Gospel According to Matthew: A Structural Commentary on Matthew's Faith,* 97.
39. There are several theories as to why stone and serpent are used. They might look like their counterparts (a stone looks like a loaf of bread, a serpent like fish), they

are associated together in previous literature (stone and bread in Proverbs 20:17), they are harmful or dangerous. See also Hanson and Oakman who interpret the stone and snake as money and suggest Matthew is critiquing the use of money and promoting reciprocal exchanges with God. Hanson, *Palestine in the Time of Jesus: Social Structures and Social Conflicts*, 127–28.

40. This association was made well after Gen 3 but was well in place by the first century (e.g. 2 Cor 11:3; Rev 12:9, 20:2). The Greek word for serpent is the same in Gen 3 (LXX) and in 7:10: ὄφις.
41. With the connection of serpent/devil, food, temptation between 7:10, 4:1–11 and Gen 3, one can also see a link between bread in 7:9, 4:1–11 and the Gen 3 story. If bread is from heaven (the Father, the one in heaven), then one thinks of food from the angels (in 4:11), which fed Jesus, who was tempted by the devil. *The Life of Adam and Eve* records that Adam and Eve ate the "food of angels" (2–4). Thus you have a link between the bread in 7:9, which is from heaven, to the food from the angels in 4:11, to the "food of the angels" that Adam and Eve ate. Bread, which is the first food mentioned in 7:9–10, and serpent, which is the last "food", both have links to the creation story in Gen 2–3. This connects the Father, the one in the heaven, with creator image—the same connection first made in 6:25–34. Father as creator and provider, not monarch and ruler, supplies food for creation.
42. This sequence or chain of giving, however, is masked in the narrative such that the direct route of God providing food is emphasized and the indirect route of giving through earthly parents is understated. The indirect path through the earthly parents is not in any literary order, requiring the audience to piece the path together. Furthermore, the human parent is never named. The only support for defining the parent as a Father instead of a generic parent or a mother is the phrase, ὁ υἱὸς αὐτοὺ (his son), and the parallel, "Father, the one in heaven".
43. See chapter 2 in this study on a brief discussion of Mauss and his cycle of giving, receiving, and repaying.
44. Fish is paired with bread in the feeding stories in Matt 14 and 15 and is used often in the narrative (along with the occupation of fishing) to refer to actual fish or fishing or is used as a metaphor (4:18, 4:19, 7:10, 13:47, 14:17, 14:19, 15:34, 15:36). Fish is a staple food, like bread, in Matthew's narrative. Fish and bread are the two specific foods most often mentioned in the Matthean narrative, a sign of their commonplace use in the Matthean narrative world. On the Matthean imagery of the farm and animals, see M. D. Goulder, *Midrash and Lection in Matthew* (London: SPCK, 1974), 100–02.
45. Carter, *Matthew and the Margins: A Sociopolitical and Religious Reading*, 359–60.
46. Ibid. Carter suggests that God is demonstrating sovereignty as God supplies the fish and controls the sea. I interpret God's characteristics in the context of God as creator who orders (i.e. brings into order) creation.
47. In 7:7–11, ζητέω is used but its literary placement in vvs. 7–8 distinguishes its use in 7:7–11 from that in 6:25–34. First, ζητέω is used along with εὑρίσκω, which is also in domain 27 and means "to learn the location of something."Louw and Nida, eds., *Greek-English Lexicon of the New Testament Based on Semantic Documents*, 27.27. While ζητεω in 6:25–34 referred primarily to searching for the location, in 7:7–8 the search leads to finding it. Second, ζητέω is sandwiched between

αἰτέω and κρούω. This suggests a meaning between the meanings of these two words. Ζητέω is more active in its search than asking, as can be seen already as the community seeks for God's provision in 6:25–34 in a more mobile and active way than in 6:1–21. But the use of κρούω pulls the meaning of ζητέω farther away from that of αἰτέω and the use of ζητέω in 6:25–34 and closer toward that of κρούω. Ζητέω here, then, means more than asking and expecting a response and more than searching and trying to learn about the location of where God might provide food. Ζητέω is learning about the location and searching for it almost to the point of knocking on doors to find it, with the extra confidence and expectation that it will be found (i.e. εὑρίσκω). The meaning might be closest to ζητέω in domain 57, which refers to meanings involving ownership or possession of objects. Ζητέω falls under the subdomain G (i.e. "take, obtain, gain, lose") and can be defined as the attempt to obtain or get something from someone. Louw and Nida, 57.59. This follows from its literary placement, that there is a high expectation of finding food and having it for consumption. The meaning of ζητέω in this subdomain focuses on the transfer of objects (i.e. food) but not necessarily on the exchange of objects. This accords with the life example given in vv. 9–10, that a child is seeking food to be transferred from parent to child but without the expectation of exchange in terms of balanced reciprocity. In 7:7–11 the community is just beginning to consider exchange and will see more of an exchange in 10:5–11:1 and most completely in passages in Matt 14 and 15.

48. John E. Stambaugh and David L. Balch, *The New Testament in Its Social Environment* (Philadelphia: The Westminster Press, 1986).
49. See especially Matthew 10:8, "freely you have received, so freely give." This can be seen in the concept of sacrifice and offerings in the Hebrew Bible. God gives food to humans. Humans offer an offering/sacrifice to God, but they may also offer a gift to the poor as part of that offering (Leviticus 23:9–22) so that thanks given to God is bound up with provision of social help. See H. D. Betz, *2 Corinthians 8 and 9*, ed. George W. MacRae (Philadelphia: Fortress Press, 1985), 100; Sahlins, *Stone Age Economics*, 218. See also Sir 35:10, Tob 4:7–11, Exod 23:10ff, Lev 23:9, Deut 26:1ff. We will see this again in Matt 15:29–39.

Chapter 6: Hospitality (10:5–11:1)

1. The food they are fed is material food and drink, τροφή (food) and ψυχρός (cold water), not to be understood as a symbol for or in a broader sense as "resources" or "subsistence" or "basic necessities of life." See for example Carter, *Matthew and the Margins: A Sociopolitical and Religious Reading*, 235; Hagner, *Matthew 1–13, 14–28*, 1:272; Herman C. Waetjen, *The Origin and Destiny of Humanness: An Interpretation of the Gospel According to Matthew*, 2nd ed. (San Rafael, CA: Crystal Press for Omega Books, 1978), 133. While the food and drink itself can have broader meanings in its material exchange, the substance that is exchanged is material food and drink. The Matthean narrative uses τροφη four times and each time material food can be argued (i.e. 3:4, 6:25, 10:10, 24:45)
2. The tone becomes one of danger and persecution in vv. 16–23 whereas in 5–15 the tone is more positive without fear of persecution. I will refer to the persecu-

tion, however, in my overall interpretation of the larger section, 10:5–11:1. See Dorothy Jean Weaver, *Matthew's Missionary Discourse: A Literary Critical Analysis* (Sheffield: Sheffield Academic Press, 1990), 89–92.

3. The geographical setting moves into governors and kings (from a Jewish setting to a Gentile setting) and the time setting moves from the mission in the present to an eschatological setting, the end of the age. Ibid., 15–16.
4. Davies and Allison, *The Gospel According to Saint Matthew*, 2:162.
5. Weaver, *Matthew's Missionary Discourse: A Literary Critical Analysis*, 83–84.
6. James L. Bailey and Lyle D. Vander Broek, *Literary Forms in the New Testament: A Handbook*, 1st ed. (Louisville, Kentucky: Westminster/John Knox Press, 1992), 53.
7. In 6:1–21, the community is referred to with the personal "you" who prays to "our Father." While no family language is used for the disciples themselves in vv. 1–21, the use of children in 5:9 and 5:45 spills over and the extensive use of "Father" in 6:1–21 influences the characterization of the disciples in 6:1–21 as children. Although they are called upon to give alms and to be in public in inconspicuous ways, they practice righteousness in private not in public and withdraw to an inner room to pray for bread. In 6:25–34, the disciples continue to be referred to in the second person plural, the family language diminishes but is still present (no use of children and "Father" is used only twice while θεος is used twice), and the disciples are referred to as "you of little faith." The community, however, is not asked to withdraw to an inner room but to look for and seek out God's provision of food. In 7:7–11, there continues to be the use of the second person plural and there is a resurgence of family language but the community is also identified, perhaps along with those outside the community, as "those who ask him." This latter representation, along with the call to the community to "ask," "seek," and "knock" demonstrates a community with a greater initiative (resourcefulness) to acquire food, although the location of food remains within the household/family. To this point in the narrative, then, the disciples are mostly characterized as children and those of little faith who are dependent on their Father. They primarily remain within the Matthean household and move out into the world only with caution.
8. This is the primary reason that 10:5–11:1 begins the second main unit of this study. Notice the use of active verbs that suggest movement (e.g. being sent out, to go, make a careful search)
9. Carter, *Matthew and the Margins: A Sociopolitical and Religious Reading*, 233; Davies and Allison, *The Gospel According to Saint Matthew*, 2:151; Norman K. Gottwald, *The Tribes of Yahweh: A Sociology of the Religion of Liberated Israel, 1250–1050 B.C.E.* (Maryknoll, NY: Orbis Books, 1979), 284.
10. Or one might say "renew" or "reform."
11. Luz, *Matthew 1–7: A Commentary*, 73. House of Israel is used widely in the Hebrew Bible and appears more frequently in the LXX.
12. Levine, *The Social and Ethnic Dimensions of Matthean Social History*, 55 n. 60. BAGD, s.v. "οἶκος," 2. The passages studied so far in the Matthean narrative have focused explicitly (6:1–21) or implicitly (6:25–34, 7:7–11) upon the house and the family unit that exchanges food within the house. The house of Israel is a metaphorical use of this category of space.
13. Saldarini, *Matthew's Christian-Jewish Community*, 28.

14. Levine, *The Social and Ethnic Dimensions of Matthean Social History*, 55 n. 60; Perdue, *Families in Ancient Israel*, 178.
15. Saldarini, *Matthew's Christian-Jewish Community*, 85–87. Regarding the use of the term, community, and the relationship between the Matthean community and the larger Jewish community, Saldarini describes those believers-in-Jesus to whom the Matthean narrative addresses the "Matthean group," which is a subgroup of the larger gathering of Jewish people he refers to as the "Jewish community."
16. I have referred to this "group" as the Matthean community.
17. The difference in interpretations is usually based on the use of the genitive, οἴκου Ἰσραήλ. If this genitive is defined as a partitive genitive where the genitive is the whole and the noun it modifies is a part (or genitive of a divided whole) then the lost sheep are one part or a group within the larger house of Israel. As a partitive genitive, then, the Matthean community is called to proclaim to and heal the sheep (i.e. Jewish people, those marginalized) who have been led astray by their shepherds (i.e. the Jewish leaders or elites). The Matthean community, then, will replace the Jewish leadership. See especially Saldarini's interpretation of 21:33–46, Saldarini, *Matthew's Christian-Jewish Community*, 58–63. Some scholars call it genitive of apposition but claim it is all Israelites except the elite leaders while others consider this interpretation a genitive of divided whole. If the genitive is defined as a genitive of apposition (or explanation or epexegetical)] where "the word in the genitive is identical with the word it modifies," then the lost sheep are identified with the house of Israel. Brooks, *Syntax of New Testament Greek*, 16–17. For a discussion of this issue, see Brooks, *Syntax of New Testament Greek*, 16–17; Hagner, *Matthew 1–13, 14–28*, 1:270–71; Levine, *The Social and Ethnic Dimensions of Matthean Social History*, 55–56; Smyth, "Greek Grammar"; Weaver, *Matthew's Missionary Discourse: A Literary Critical Analysis*, 155 n. 6.
18. Malbon, *Narrative Space and Mythic Meaning in Mark*, 89–93. While specific cities and/or villages would fall under the category of geopolitical space, general cities and villages are considered topographical space. They are the type of space one can see from an aerial photograph, are human-made, but are not considered "political" when referred to as general places. A general place would be a "city" or "village" as opposed to a particular city like "Capernaum." The locations of food exchange began in architectural space (i.e. a household in 6:1–21, 6:25–34, 7:7–11) but are now moving out into topographical space. Matthew 10 is located in an inhabited topographical space but the location of food exchange will soon shift to uninhabited topographical space (Matt 12, 14, and 15). Topographical space includes inhabited and isolated places. Cities and villages are clearly inhabited and "public" places (i.e. places more open to public gatherings as opposed to private dwellings).
19. cf. Struthers Malbon on the use of "cities and villages" in Mark, Ibid., 91, 101.
20. Weaver, *Matthew's Missionary Discourse: A Literary Critical Analysis*, 84–85.
21. City (πόλις) is used in the following passages and I have indicated whether the city is a place of security/promise or threat/danger or neither or both: 2:23 (security), 4:5 (both), 5:14 (neither), 35 (security), 8:33 (threat), 34 (threat), 9:1 (both), 9:35 (promise), 10:5 (threat), 11 (both), 14 (threat), 15 (threat), 23 (threat), 11:1 (promise), 20 (threat), 12:25 (both), 14:13 (neither), 21:10 (threat), 17 (security), 18

(threat), 22:7 (threat/danger), 23:34 (threat), 26:18 (security/promise), 27:53 (promise), 28:11 (threat).

22. Kingsbury, *Matthew as Story*, 72–74. Kingsbury claims that from 11:1 to 16:20 conflict increases between Jesus and Israel and Israel repudiates Jesus' ministry. I agree that conflict increases after 11:1, but by looking at food exchange, the relationship between the Matthean community and the larger Jewish community experiences moments of solidarity in ch. 10, 12, 14 and 15.
23. In 6:1–21, the proper practice of righteousness was to be done in more and more private places while the improper practice was occurring in more and more public places. Public places were not, however clearly dangerous or off limits. The Matthean community was to participate in public (i.e. alms, after fasting) but to do so in inconspicuous ways. The community was to be cautious about its interaction in public spaces but not to see public space as dangerous or off limits. In 6:25–34, the heavenly Father feeds the birds of the air and clothes the lilies of the field in a topographical space that is specified as outdoor, rural, and a minimally inhabited place. The passage refers to a space more public than 6:1–21, although it is not in a heavily populated area, and a place more connected with the physical features of the earth as a topographical space. While this new setting for food exchange is introduced, food continues to be distributed to the disciples in the household. In 7:7–11, food exchange also occurred within the family in a more private space, a household, but there are nuanced references to food exchange with those outside the family.
24. In 6:25–34, anxiety is present about where to get food and drink. In 7:7–11, a question is raised, almost a temptation about whether a parent will feed his child or not.
25. I agree with Crosby that οἶκος and οἰκία are used interchangeably in Matthew, see Crosby, *House of Disciples: Church, Economics, and Justice in Matthew*, 1–11.
26. Houses are associated with evil in these examples: Beelzebul (10:25), the strong man (12:29), unclean evil spirits (12:44), an enemy sowing weeds (13:27), the wicked slave (24:45).
27. Examples of conflict include: there are foes within one's own household (10:36), a house divided against itself (12:25), and a place where its own prophet is not honored (13:57)
28. Houses that are associated with God and Jesus include: the house of God (12:4), where Jesus lives and teaches (13:1, 36), the faithful (24:45).
29. For an opposing interpretation of Jews in the Matthean narrative who are faithful and active, see Levine, *The Social and Ethnic Dimensions of Matthean Social History*, 7–8, passim.
30. Weaver, *Matthew's Missionary Discourse: A Literary Critical Analysis*, 89.
31. The verse might read then, "do not take gold or silver . . .," that is, do not take these items to travel with, or "do not acquire gold or silver . . .," that is, do not accept money or the other items in exchange for one's work. It might refer to both Carter, *Matthew and the Margins: A Sociopolitical and Religious Reading*, 235.
32. The disciples should unloose ties to the present age, not do it for sake of money (false prophet), trust in providential care instead, distinguish themselves from the Cynics, not be anxious, be totally committed, rely exclusively on God, be oriented toward the kingdom. See Davies and Allison, *The Gospel According to*

Saint Matthew, 2:171–74; Hagner, *Matthew 1–13, 14–28*, 1:272; Patte, *The Gospel According to Matthew: A Structural Commentary on Matthew's Faith*, 146–47.

33. I choose "taking" to show that from the start they were intentional about being inconspicuous.
34. The description in vv. 9–10 is usually explained with a primary focus on the mission described in vv. 5–8. Therefore, one is not to take these items so one can be seen as a true prophet/follower/missionary sent by God (9:38) and instructed and sent by Jesus (10:5). The verse can be interpreted differently, however, by paying attention to how it might introduce vv. 11–15.
35. Pitt-Rivers, *The Fate of Shechem or the Politics of Sex: Essays in the Anthropology of the Mediterranean*, 107–12. A host and guest cannot have equal power since that would promote conflict and conflict must be avoided in this particular relationship. While the guest is given precedence and afforded honor, he continues to have standing only in relation to the host, who has greater standing. The guest is dependent upon the host for food.
36. Carter, *Matthew and the Margins: A Sociopolitical and Religious Reading*, 235. Carter uses the term "inconspicuous" to mean that the disciple is not to take/acquire these items in order the minimize opposition and increase safety. I argue that it is done to increase interaction with the world/Jewish community/those in public in order to make social ties in part to survive physically and in part to see itself as part of the larger community.
37. For commentary on how lack of possessions is dependence on or trust in God, see Ibid; Davies and Allison, *The Gospel According to Saint Matthew*, 2:171.
38. See my interpretation of 6:1–21 and 7:7–11 especially. See also Harland who argues that Jewish, Christian, and Greco-Roman communities in the first century interacted in complex and sustained ways with each other. Harland, *Associations, Synagogues, and Congregations: Claiming a Place in Ancient Mediterranean Society*.
39. The community's seeking began with requests for food in prayer (6:1–21). These requests progressed to thinking and learning about how to find food (6:25–34) to the more active attempt to obtain food (7:7–11).
40. Ἐξετάζω falls under two semantic domains: communication (33) and learn (27). Louw and Nida, eds., *Greek-English Lexicon of the New Testament Based on Semantic Documents*, 27.37, 33.182. On one level, according to the communication domain, to inquire is to ask a question, to examine carefully. This meaning fits with the subdomain grouping that prayer and asking (αἰτέω) fall under and therefore is closely aligned with the type of seeking done in 6:1–21, to ask, to pray for bread. On another level, according to the learn domain, to inquire is to learn, to search carefully in order to acquire information. This meaning is parallel to that of 6:25–34 and part of 7:7–11 in which the community is seeking to gather information, beginning to process it, and moving toward obtaining the needed object of food.
41. Ἐργάτης is used in Matthew 9:37 and 38 to refer to those who harvest the crops (and metaphorically for the disciples to do mission work) and it is used in 20:1, 2, 8 to refer to those who wait in the marketplace each day in order to be hired out temporarily for menial work (i.e. in this case working one day in a vineyard).
42. See Carter, *Matthew and the Margins: A Sociopolitical and Religious Reading*, 598; D. Duling, "Matthew and Marginality," in *Society of Biblical Literature 1993 Seminar Papers*, ed. E. H. Lovering Jr. (Atlanta: Scholars Press, 1993), 652–56; Schottroff,

"Human Solidarity and the Goodness of God: The Parable of the Workers in the Vineyard," in *God of the Lowly*, ed. W. Schottroff and W. Stegemann (Maryknoll, N.Y.: Orbis Books, 1984), 132–35.

43. The "laborer" image certainly picks up on 9:37–38, which is about mission/harvesting, but the end of v. 9 depicts the laborer not as one who will be working by harvesting but as one who needs to receive food to eat, "the laborer deserves his food."
44. The οἰκία (vv. 12, 13) refers to the οἶκος earlier in the section (10:6) which refers to the lost sheep of the house of Israel. While the first use (v. 6) refers to the larger Jewish community, the extended household of the Matthean community, the second and third uses refer to particular houses, buildings, single households where the laborers of Matthew's community will stay. To reiterate, this is the third setting of the three settings in 10:5–15 (i.e. house of Israel, cities and villages, house) and is included within the previous settings (i.e. this single household is within a city or villages that is within the larger house of Israel). The connection between οἰκία and οἴκου Ἰσραήλ can be made since both refer to a household, the single household is set within the larger setting of the house of Israel, and since the development of the plot logically follows that if the Matthean community set out to visit those in the house of Israel it would come upon a house in which to lodge.
45. See also 25:31–46 where the sheep feed the hungry.
46. BAGD, s.v. "ἄξιος." Ἄξιος can relate to the moral, economic, social, or religious spheres.
47. Matthew 3:8, 10:37 and perhaps 22:8 carry the meaning of repentance, the acknowledgment of a certain god and joining a particular group. See Nicholas H. Taylor, "The Social Nature of Conversion in the Early Christian World," in *Modelling Early Christianity: Social-Scientific Studies of the New Testament in Its Context*, ed. Philip Francis Esler (London; New York: Routledge, 1995), 129. The Pharisees are to be worthy of repentance as they come for baptism from John the Baptist (3:8), the disciples are to be worthy of being a follower of Jesus (10:37), and those invited to the wedding banquet are not worthy to be present, perhaps referring to those worthy of being a part of the Matthean community or the kingdom of heaven.
48. One could interpret worthy in 22:8 as belonging to a group or as poor guests.
49. Therefore, for Carter the phrase means "listening to words about God's empire," "those who are not worthy are those who do not "believe and follow," Carter, *Matthew and the Margins: A Sociopolitical and Religious Reading*, 235. For Hagner, the phrase reads "rejection of the gospel," Hagner, *Matthew 1–13, 14–28*, 1:272–73. For Davies and Allison, the phrase means "the message of the kingdom is rejected," Davies and Allison, *The Gospel According to Saint Matthew*, 2:177–78. For Patte, the phrase is interpreted as receiving "the message of the kingdom," Patte, *The Gospel According to Matthew: A Structural Commentary on Matthew's Faith*, 147. For Garland, the phrase means "the message and messenger," "the message has to do with the coming kingdom of heaven," Garland, *Reading Matthew: A Literary and Theological Commentary on the First Gospel*, 114.

50. For a discussion of hospitality, see Gowler, *Host, Guest, Enemy and Friend: Portraits of the Pharisees in Luke and Acts*; Pitt-Rivers, *The Fate of Shechem or the Politics of Sex: Essays in the Anthropology of the Mediterranean*.
51. Weaver, *Matthew's Missionary Discourse: A Literary Critical Analysis*, 84 n. 68. Weaver claims that the reader assumes that since Jesus called for repentance so will the disciples.
52. Δέχομαι is used in 10:14, 10:40, 41, 42, 11:14, 18:5. Δέχομαι might mean to receive someone (literarily, hospitality, to receive as guest), to take something in the hand, or to approve, accept, which could mean a teaching. BAGD, s.v. "δέχομαι ."
53. In 11:14, the implied audience is asked whether they are willing to "accept it" that is, to accept whether John is the forerunner as Elijah was. The use of δέχομαι is "probably not an appeal to faith," but an understanding that is called for. See Carter, *Matthew and the Margins: A Sociopolitical and Religious Reading*, 253; Davies and Allison, *The Gospel According to Saint Matthew*, 2:258. In 18:5, δέχομαι is used in terms of receiving a child in Jesus' name. Children may be a metaphor for the disciples. Carter acknowledges that the reference to a child may mean a literal child but thinks it probably refers to the disciples, Carter, *Matthew and the Margins: A Sociopolitical and Religious Reading*, 363. Levine describes children as "ideal members of the new movement,"Amy-Jill Levine, "Matthew," in *The Women's Bible Commentary*, ed. Carol A. Newsom and Sharon H. Ringe (Louisville, Kentucky: Westminster/John Knox Press, 1992), 259. She also points to 11:25, 19:13–15, 21:16. But it also might mean welcoming a real/literal/flesh and blood child as an act of hospitality. Jesus does set a child (παιδίον) in the midst of those gathered in 18:1–5 and he places his hands on παιδία in order to pray for them in 19:13–15. In this case, δέχομαι refers to welcoming a child, receiving children, hosting them, praying for them. Δέχομαι in chapter 10, then, may refer to welcoming and hosting the disciples not necessarily receiving and being committed to their message.
54. See also 7:26, 13:20, 13.22, 13.23, 11:4, 13:17, 13:13, 17:6, 19:25, 20:24, 20:30, 21:45, 22:22, 22:33, 22:34, 27:47.
55. The crowds have either no subsequent response (15:10–20) or are simply amazed at Jesus' teaching (22:33). The chief priests and Pharisees listen and understand but do not follow (21:45) and the Pharisees listen and assemble and test (22:34–35) or listen and are amazed and go away (22:22).
56. Taylor outlines three aspects of conversion: (1) conviction/acknowledgment of divinity, perhaps worship; (2) conformity/observance, involving practice of Law, (3) socialization, affiliation and integration into the community. Taylor, "The Social Nature of Conversion in the Early Christian World," 129.
57. This is similar to 25:31–46 where there is an expectation of doing good works (i.e. hospitality), the threat of judgment if that is not pursued (i.e. more tolerable for Sodom and Gomorrah), but no emphasis on becoming part of the Matthean group. See Levine, *The Social and Ethnic Dimensions of Matthean Social History*, 226–27; Saldarini, *Matthew's Christian-Jewish Community*, 252 n. 47.
58. Hospitality is the "practice of receiving a guest or stranger," John Koenig, "Hospitality," in *The Anchor Bible Dictionary*, ed. David Noel Freedman (New York: Doubleday, 1992), 299. See also the discussion of hospitality in chapter 2 of this study as well as Gowler, *Host, Guest, Enemy and Friend: Portraits of the Pharisees in*

Luke and Acts, 24; Pitt-Rivers, *The Fate of Shechem or the Politics of Sex: Essays in the Anthropology of the Mediterranean*, 117. And in other more contemporary (tribal) communities, Sahlins, *Stone Age Economics*, 216–17.

59. Perdue, *Families in Ancient Israel*, 192–203.
60. A sojourner could be from a foreign land or a fellow Israelite. The Matthean community is depicted more as a fellow Israelite, but one who is traveling and needs temporary hospitality. The community is also similar to a resident alien in many ways (except they do not seem to be foreign immigrants) in that the community does not seem to own land and they depend upon others for food, shelter, and protection. As I discuss the Matthean community in Matthew 10, I use the language of sojourner but include references in the Hebrew Bible to resident aliens as well. Both were given similar protections by Israelite households. Ibid., 198–199.
61. The designation of laborer in 10:10 makes sense, then, as the Matthean community turns sojourner turns laborer, The phrase recalls the laws in the Torah for the Israelites to provide for day laborers and sojourners whether they were native Israelites or foreigners. Matthew uses "laborer" as his term here, which might have recalled for the larger Jewish community a closer connection to and emphasis on the household. Sojourners tended to be less connected and more temporary while laborers could have been a more permanent part of the household. See Perdue, *Families in Ancient Israel*, 198–99. See also Deut 24:14–15.
62. Ibid., 199; Sahlins, *Stone Age Economics*, 210. A laborer has a claim on the fruits of his productive efforts. See also Deut 10:18.
63. Perdue, *Families in Ancient Israel*, 199.
64. Saldarini, *Matthew's Christian-Jewish Community*, 28.
65. For some aspects of hospitality, see Koenig, "Hospitality"; Bruce J. Malina, "Hospitality," in *Harper's Bible Dictionary*, ed. Paul J. Achtemeier (San Francisco: Harper & Row, 1985), 408–09; Robbins, *The Tapestry of Early Christian Discourse: Rhetoric, Society and Ideology*, 162–64.
66. Some suggest those in the house are part of the Matthean church, residents, who are hosting, but this temporary role would suggest they are not part of the church but part of the lost sheep of the house of Israel who provide this temporary service. See Carter on 10:41–42 for a similar conclusion, Carter, *Matthew and the Margins: A Sociopolitical and Religious Reading*, 245.
67. See Malina, "Hospitality," 408–09; Robbins, *The Tapestry of Early Christian Discourse: Rhetoric, Society and Ideology*, 164–65.
68. See Malina, "Hospitality," 408–09.
69. Ibid., 408. See also Acts 13:14–15.
70. Ibid., 408–09; D. Smith, "Greco-Roman Meal Customs," *ABD* 4 (1992).
71. Carter mentions "covenant unfaithfulness, especially idolatry (Deut 29:15–29); social injustice (Isa 1:9–10, 17; Amos 4:1, 11); immorality (Jer 23:14; *T. Levi* 14:6; *T. Benj.* 9:1); not recognizing the Lord's angels (*T.Ash.* 7:1)." Carter, *Matthew and the Margins: A Sociopolitical and Religious Reading*, 236.
72. Gen 19:1–11. On the sin of Sodom and Gomorrah as inhospitality in Gen 18–19, Walter Brueggemann, *Genesis*, ed. James Luther Mays, *Interpretation* (Atlanta: John Knox Press, 1982), 164. On the meaning of Sodom and Gomorrah in Matthew 10:15 as a reference to inhospitality, see Alfred Plummer, *An Exegetical*

Commentary on the Gospel According to St. Matthew (Grand Rapids, Michigan: Baker Book House, 1982), 151.

73. Sahlins, *Stone Age Economics*, 233, 40, 45.
74. For some differences between generalized reciprocity and balanced reciprocity and differences within generalized reciprocity, see Polanyi, *The Great Transformation*, 47–55, 269–79; Sahlins, *Stone Age Economics*, 194, 219–21, 31, 33, 45.
75. The phrase, "for a laborer is worthy of his food" (10:10) is a clue that God is behind the feeding. The phrase is used in a way to signal a reflection of a previous principle or guideline to follow. In a sea of imperatives in 10:5–15 addressed to a group referred to as the "twelve," this generic phrase pops up with the assumption of a present indicative "is" and the use of the singular "worker." The phrase is used as if scripture is being quoted, in the singular, as a past law. The phrase harkens back to Lev 19:13, Deut 24:14, Lev 25:6, Mal 3:5, Perdue, *Families in Ancient Israel*, 198–99. The worker is "worthy" of his food because he is worthy of God's compassion, deliverance and provision as the Israelites were also worthy while slaves in Egypt and God's people in the wilderness. The laws concerning sojourners/laborers were established to support three perspectives of God's character and activity: (1) Israelites were once sojourners and God saw and heard, delivered, and gave them a new land, (2) God as protector of poor and weak, and (3) the covenant depends upon participation of all community. See T. M. Mauch, "Sojourner," in *The Interpreter's Dictionary of the Bible*, edited by George Arthur Buttrick (Nashville: Abingdon Press, 1962), 398.
76. Matthew 11:1 concludes 10:5–11:1 where 10:5a and 11:1 are the bookends of the discourse proper (10:5b–10:42).
77. Davies and Allison, *The Gospel According to Saint Matthew*, 2:162. Davies and Allison suggest that 10:40–42 and 10:5–15 form the same parts of a chiasm with their focus on the reception of missionaries.
78. Carter, *Matthew and the Margins: A Sociopolitical and Religious Reading*, 236; Weaver, *Matthew's Missionary Discourse: A Literary Critical Analysis*, 90–91. Weaver now says the disciples become passive and acted upon by the lost sheep. So Weaver recognizes the lost sheep as persecuting but not as hosting.
79. Carter, *Matthew and the Margins: A Sociopolitical and Religious Reading*, 240–42.
80. The opening sentence uses the word δέχομαι four times and states that those who receive "you" (i.e. the Matthean community) receive Jesus, and the ones who receive Jesus receive the one having sent Jesus (i.e. God).
81. In 10:5–15, the change in characterization of the Matthean community from the twelve to laborers and guests marked this movement from insider (i.e. in 6:1–21, 6:25–34, and 7:7–11) to outsider (i.e. as marginalized members of the household).
82. As was argued before, worthy has more than one meaning in the Matthean narrative. In 10:37 (see also 3:8, 22:8) ἄξιος refers to repentance, acknowledgement/conviction of a certain god, and being part of a particular community (i.e. belonging to Jesus). The use of ὁμολογήσει along with τοῦ πατρός and the injunctions to love Jesus more than family and to "follow" Jesus all point to this meaning of ἄξιος.
83. cf. 25:31–46. Pitt-Rivers, *The Fate of Shechem or the Politics of Sex: Essays in the Anthropology of the Mediterranean*, 100–01. See Pitt-Rivers on the functional use of

a disguised God as a stranger to encourage and support undifferentiated exchange.

84. This is the judicial or even public use of ὁμολογέω. BAGD, s.v. "ὁμολογέω ."

85. Carter, *Matthew and the Margins: A Sociopolitical and Religious Reading*, 245–46; Davies and Allison, *The Gospel According to Saint Matthew*, 2:225–30. Both Carter and Davies and Allison suggest that reception here involves both hospitality and a commitment/faith.

86. Many scholars read the three sayings in verses 41–42 in continuity with each other. An attempt is made to reconcile the use of the prophet and righteous ones along with the little ones/disciples and the meaning of the rewards of the prophets and those of the righteous person in relationship to the reward in v. 42. The repetitive pattern in 10:5b–6, at the very beginning of this discourse 10:5b–42, has three sayings: do not go in the way of the Gentiles/ do not enter into a city of the Samaritans/ but go instead to the lost sheep of the house of Israel. The first two commands are negative and the third is positive, offering a different message than the first two. The first two sayings establish a pattern and draw in the implied audience to set up an expectation and suspense for the third saying. The implied audience anticipates the third saying wondering if it will be similar or different. There is a difference in the third saying (10:6), which functions as a contrast and not a climax. It is made clear what the implied audience is to understand, "go to the lost sheep of the house of Israel." Tannehill argues that if the third instance is simply a "forceful example of this same pattern," then "it becomes the climax, for we approach it with the feelings and meanings gathered from the two previous instances." If, however, the third instance contains "an important difference," then "the first two instances serve as a foil for the third," and it serves as a contrast, Tannehill, *The Sword of His Mouth: Forceful and Imaginative Language in Synoptic Sayings*, 43–44. See also Weaver, "This shifting of a fixed pattern draws the attention of the implied reader to those features which distinguish the third element in the series from the first two and thus establishes the third element as the crucial one." Weaver, *Matthew's Missionary Discourse: A Literary Critical Analysis*, 84 n. 64.

87. Weaver, *Matthew's Missionary Discourse: A Literary Critical Analysis*, 120–22, n. 227.

88. As with 10:5b–6, the repetition catches the attention of the implied audience and creates anticipation as the third saying is approached. And as with 10:5b–6, the variations in the third saying create enough differences to mark it as a contrast, not a climax, to the first two sayings. While some of the meanings gathered from the first two sayings are carried through (i.e. the concept of receiving another and of receiving a reward), the differences are such that the implied audience comes to a new understanding of the three sayings, Tannehill, *The Sword of His Mouth: Forceful and Imaginative Language in Synoptic Sayings*, 43–44.

89. Prophets and the righteous ones are present in Matthew's narrative and community and the two are often coupled together, but they are not a main feature of 10:5–11:1. Prophets are generally supported in the Matthean narrative but false prophets are harshly critiqued so there is an ambivalent interpretation of prophets in the narrative. See Saldarini, *Matthew's Christian-Jewish Community*, 104–05.

The righteous ones are generally portrayed in a good light but not always (e.g. 13:17, 23:28 are negative portrayals and 5:45 is a neutral portrayal).

90. Weaver, *Matthew's Missionary Discourse: A Literary Critical Analysis*, 121. Weaver refers to the difference as "outward honor" but never defines what she means by honor.
91. True prophets bear good fruit (7:15–20) and are involved in mission work (10:41, 23:34). Prophecy itself is valued in the narrative and is used to legitimate much of the activity in the narrative. See Saldarini, *Matthew's Christian-Jewish Community*, 104–05. Prophets are often victims of violence in the world but are often so because of the influence they have (i.e. influence with crowds, 11:9; 14:5; 21:26, 46. The righteous ones are honored for their mercy and for following the law (1:19) and for their charitable deeds (25:37, 46). They have also suffered by those outside the community as a result of their faithfulness (23: 35, 27:4, 19, 24).
92. Μικρὸς and ἐλάχιστος share the meaning of little status or being unimportant. Ὀλιγόπιστος, related to ὀλίγος, can mean slight, to a small degree and can be interpreted as being of a lesser status. Louw and Nida, eds., *Greek-English Lexicon of the New Testament Based on Semantic Documents*, 87.58, 87.66, 78.8. See μικρῶν (little ones)—10:42, 11:11, 13:32, 18:6, 10, 14; ὀλιγόπιστος (little faith)—6:30, 8:26, 14:31, 16:8, 17:20; ἐλάχιστος (least): 2:6, 5:19, 25:40, 25:45.
93. Both the "children" and the "least" may refer to the disciples.
94. See Weaver, *Matthew's Missionary Discourse: A Literary Critical Analysis*, 120.
95. The focus of food exchange, then, is on those who have need, not those who are already accepted or recognized by the world. Food exchange is based on need not status. See Goldsmith, "'Ask, and It Will Be Given.' Toward Writing the History of a Logion," 264.
96. Eschatological rewards often came to those who died faithfully (i.e. Daniel, 2 Maccabees). The prophets receive different rewards as well as they are mostly recipients of violence: many are killed or victims of violence (23:31, 34, 37) or potential victims of violence (14:5, 21:46) or dishonored (13:57).
97. For the "righteous ones," see 1:19, 5:45, 9:13, 10:41, 13:17, 43, 49; 20:4, 23:28, 29, 35; 25:37, 46; 27:4, 19, 24. In 13:43, 49 and 25:37, 46, the righteous ones "will shine as the sun in the kingdom of their Father," and "inherit the kingdom prepared for (them) from the foundation of the world," respectively, and Jesus is raised from the dead (27:19, 24; 28:6). The righteous ones also receive different rewards (i.e. 5:45, 9:13, 27:19, 24).
98. The meaning of reward in vv. 41–42 is typically defined in one way for all three rewards as an eschatological reward to be received in heaven. Weaver, *Matthew's Missionary Discourse: A Literary Critical Analysis*, 122. Weaver says it is not an immediate reward nor for physical remuneration. See also Carter, *Matthew and the Margins: A Sociopolitical and Religious Reading*, 246; Davies and Allison, *The Gospel According to Saint Matthew*, 2:227; Luz, *Matthew 1–7: A Commentary*, 120–22. Scholars point to the use of the future tense ("will receive") and previous uses of reward in the narrative (6:1, 4, 6, 18). While the meaning of reward in v. 41 appears to follow this interpretation, it does not necessarily follow for v. 42.
99. The reward in v. 41 is in response to those who δέχομαι, which I have argued refers to hospitality in general. The reward in v. 42 is in response to food and drink, a particular reference to a subset of hospitality. This moves the investiga-

tion initially to previous passages on food and drink. Then, I will look at reward in v. 42 in light of what is received by (a) little ones, (b) disciples, and (c) lost sheep/chs. 14–15. The specific references in v. 41 to prophet and righteous ones located the primary investigation of reward in narrative references to prophet and righteous ones.

100. As I argued before, some of the beatitudes imply that material blessings are forthcoming in future, but not eschatological, time. Furthermore, I have suggested before that not all rewards are eschatological in Matthew's narrative with 5:46, 6:1, and 6:6 as examples.
101. BAGD, s.v. "ἀποδίδωμι," 2.
102. Carter, *Matthew and the Margins: A Sociopolitical and Religious Reading*. See Carter on 5:12, 46; 6:1, 2, 4.
103. Μισθός and ἀποδίδωμι refer to the same kind of reward. Ἀποδίδωμι is a payment in response to an obligation. Μισθός is an amount offered for services or work done. They are both in the same semantic domain, Louw and Nida, eds., *Greek-English Lexicon of the New Testament Based on Semantic Documents*, 38.14, 38.16.
104. See the previous discussion of rewards in 6:1–21 in this study.
105. Balanced reciprocity assumes the same amount is expected in return in the immediate future without delay. Sahlins, *Stone Age Economics*, 194–95.
106. "All these things (including food) will continue to be given to you." As I noted in 6:25–34, "all these things" are given to those seeking the kingdom of God and his righteousness not as separate, additional items but as logical extensions that are naturally associated with the seeking of God's provision and being in relationship to God and the world. This can be understood as the long-term sequence of exchange in generalized reciprocity where relationships (with God and world) are maintained and food is shared.
107. The form of this saying also supports the idea that the reward will be in the near future before the end time. The use of οὐ μὴ (he will *by no means* lose his reward) in the Matthean narrative refers predominately to the near future. At times it refers to what will happen between the present and the end of time but it never refers to the end of time. See 5:18, 5:26, 10:23, 13:14, 15:6, 16:22, 16:28, 23:39, 24:34, 24:35, 25:9, 26:29, 26:35 (5:20, 18:3, 24:2, 24:21). All are in near future, not at the end of time. Many are in context about the end, but what will happen between now and the end and not *at* the end.
108. This aspect can be seen in continuity from 10:40 through 10:42. The one who gives a cup of cold water is providing hospitality just as the one receiving provides hospitality.
109. Edwards suggests the addressee has shifted in v. 42 to the "crowd," Edwards, *Matthew's Story of Jesus*, 36. Cf. Howell who disagrees with Edwards, Howell, *Matthew's Inclusive Story: A Study in the Narrative Rhetoric of the First Gospel*, 224. I am not proposing this shift, the lost sheep of the house of Israel is a different character than the crowd and the crowd is not addressed in 10:42. Yet the crowd and the lost sheep are connected and the lost sheep might be part of the crowd (although the crowd does not encompass the lost sheep). The feeding of the crowd in Matt 14 and 15, therefore, is one way that food is given back to the lost sheep who fed the disciples/little ones in 10:42. This character has shifted from the one who is on the receiving end of proclamation and healing in the begin-

ning of the passage (i.e. characterized as the lost sheep of the house of Israel, vv. 5–8) to the one who is on the giving end of hospitality (and therefore the one who receives the community) during the rest of the passage (i.e. characterized as a host in vv. 9–15 and 40–42).

110. See Malbon, *In the Company of Jesus: Characters in Mark's Gospel*, 98. The phrase, ὃς ἂν ποτίσῃ, uses the aorist subjunctive and can be translated "whoever might give to drink," a reference to the future and what might happen in the future.
111. Howell, *Matthew's Inclusive Story: A Study in the Narrative Rhetoric of the First Gospel*, 221–25; Malbon, *In the Company of Jesus: Characters in Mark's Gospel*, 98.
112. Ψυχρός means cold and is a substantive for cold water, BAGD, s.v. "ψυχρός."
113. The cup is interpreted as suffering as part of God's wrath or judgment upon wickedness in the world, W. D. Davies and D. C. Allison, *The Gospel According to Saint Matthew*, 3 vols., vol. 3, *I.C.C.* (Edinburgh: T & T Clark: 1997), 3:89. For the cup as suffering, see Pss 11:6, 75:7–9; Isa 51:17, 22; Jer 25:15, 17, 27–28; 49:12; Lam 4:21; Ezek 23:31–2; Hab 2:16, *Pss. Sol.* 8:14–15; 1 QpHab. 11:14; 4QpNah 4:6, Rev 14:10, 16:19, 18:6. The cup may also refer to God's salvation through Jesus' suffering, Carter, *Matthew and the Margins: A Sociopolitical and Religious Reading*, 401–02. See also Koester who says drinking the cup symbolizes martyrdom, Helmut Koester, *Ancient Christian Gospels: Their History and Development* (Philadelphia and London: Trinity Press and SCN Press, 1990), 278. See also BAGD, s.v. "ποτήριον," 2.
114. See Carter, *Matthew and the Margins: A Sociopolitical and Religious Reading*, 506–07. The cup signifies liberation, the release from Egypt and from Babylonian captivity. See also Exod 24 and Davies and Allison, *The Gospel According to Saint Matthew*, 3:467.
115. See Carter, *Matthew and the Margins: A Sociopolitical and Religious Reading*, 506–07. The implied audience would also remember Jeremiah who, in the midst of the Babylonian crisis in which the Jewish people are being enslaved by another imperial power, refuses to let his people partake of the customary cup of consolation for the death of their Fathers or mothers (16:7).
116. Ποτιζω (10:42, 25:35, 37, 42; 27:48) can be translated as making it possible for someone or something to drink or to give to drink. It is used with those passages where food/drink is exchanged or given. BAGD, s.v. "Ποτίζω." Πίνω (6:25, 31, 11:18, 19; 20:22, 23; 24:38, 49; 26:27, 29, 42; 27:34) can be translated as to drink or eat or to drink what someone sets before you, BAGD, s.v. "Πίνω."
117. This person might have been a Jewish bystander instead of a Roman soldier. See Davies and Allison, *The Gospel According to Saint Matthew*, 3:626; Hagner, *Matthew 1–13, 14–28*, 2:845.
118. The event has also been interpreted as way to further torment or mock Jesus' suffering. As an act to torment or insult or mock Jesus' suffering, the interpretation comes from the possible allusion to Psalm 69:22 (LXX) and the hostile context of the passage. The allusion to the Psalm is the use of ὄξος (vinegar or sour wine): "They gave me poison for food and for my thirst they gave me vinegar (ὄξος) to drink." The drink may have been given to prolong Jesus' suffering. The context itself, from 27:27–27:54 is one of hostility to Jesus and this incident would fit in as a hostile act. Davies and Allison, *The Gospel According to Saint Matthew*, 3:626. Regarding the interpretation as an act to relieve Jesus' suffering, ὄξος was

considered a wine that was good for satisfying thirst. Plutarch, *Cato Min.* 2.14. See Davies and Allison, *The Gospel According to Saint Matthew*, 3:626–27; Hagner, *Matthew 1–13, 14–28*, 2:845. BAGD, s.v. "ὄξος." The use of εὐθέως after Jesus cries out might be an immediate humanitarian response to someone who is hurting. cf. Hagner, *Matthew 1–13, 14–28*, 2:845. Furthermore, it is not clear that v. 48 is in the middle of a "hostile context." Certainly 27:27–46 introduces a hostile prelude to this act and v. 49 could be read as more mockery. After v. 49, however, the plot moves on with apocalyptic signs of hope (vv. 51–53), a nod of reverence from a centurion and those with him (v. 54), the acknowledgment of faithful followers (vv. 55–56), and a respectful burial (vv. 57–61). Offering wine to Jesus on the cross in v. 48 could well have been the first of many generous acts surrounding his death. Davies and Allison argue that the δέ in v. 49 has "continuative force" and so should be read "and the others," which would suggest that there was mockery in v. 48 and it continues here. Davies and Allison, *The Gospel According to Saint Matthew*, 3:627. Δέ, however, could be and indeed often is read as a word that contrasts (i.e."but" as it is in the NRSV), which would show the difference between a kind act in v. 38 and more mockery in v. 49. Hagner and Patte conclude it was a compassionate act, Hagner, *Matthew 1–13, 14–28*, 2:845; Patte, *The Gospel According to Matthew: A Structural Commentary on Matthew's Faith*, 386. It is unclear whether the passage is to be thought of as an act to relieve suffering or one that is to cause suffering. Whichever the case, the idea of giving someone a drink while suffering clearly expresses the notion that suffering is to be relieved. To do it in order to torment or mock someone is to distort the primary meaning of the act, especially since the use of ποτίζω in the rest of the narrative is used to relieve suffering.

119. Those in the church in Laodicia are lukewarm, neither hot nor cold (Rev 3:15–16). Cold is an extreme, probably meaning those who are against Jesus.

120. The torture of seven faithful brothers inflicts no pain and has no power on the martyrs, the fire of torture is "cold to us" (4 Macc 11:26). In Greek literature, "cold" refers to that which is dead and cold-hearted. Cold is that which has no power over and opposes the community.

121. Cold water was a basic need in the dry climate of Palestine, Hagner, *Matthew 1–13, 14–28*, 1:296.

122. Contra Plummer, "the idea of persecution passes out of sight in the three sayings (40–42),"Plummer, *An Exegetical Commentary on the Gospel According to St. Matthew*, 157.

123. Dale C. Allison, Jr., "Matthew 10:26–31 and the Problem of Evil," *St. Vladimir's Theological Quarterly* 32, no. 4 (1988).

124. Many scholars break the passage into three units, the first two starting with φοβέομαι (vv. 26–27 and v. 28) and the third beginning with v. 29 and ending with φοβέομαι. See Carter, *Matthew and the Margins: A Sociopolitical and Religious Reading*, 239; Davies and Allison, *The Gospel According to Saint Matthew*, 2:202–03; Weaver, *Matthew's Missionary Discourse: A Literary Critical Analysis*, 107. This divides the image of God into two images: v. 28 as one and vv. 29–30 as another.

125. In 6:1–21, the first of the passages in the Matthean narrative on food exchange, the Father works in secret and exchanges food behind a closed door (6:6). The Father moves out, however, into more public spaces in 6:25–34 to provide for the

birds of the air and in 7:7–11 to provide for those beyond the Matthean community.

126. Weaver, *Matthew's Missionary Discourse: A Literary Critical Analysis*, 107–08.
127. Ibid., 108.
128. See my previous discussion of the kingdom in 6:25–34.
129. Carter, *Matthew and the Margins: A Sociopolitical and Religious Reading*, 240; John J. Collins, *The Apocalyptic Imagination: An Introduction to the Jewish Matrix of Christianity* (New York: Crossroad Publishing Company, 1992), ch. 1; D. S. Russell, *The Method and Message of Jewish Apocalyptic, 200 BC–AD 100* (Philadelphia: Westminster Press, 1964), 178–87.
130. Not all apocalyptic literature, however, is eschatological and deals with the end time. In Matthew, the audience probably understood that with Jesus' death, the end time events were initiated, but the end has been "delayed" (compared to Mark) and the community is to be faithful while waiting for the second coming/judgment day (i.e. Matt 24). It is during this waiting time that Matthew's community is living and exchanging food. In the narrative world, the kingdom has come near, initiated by God and proclaimed by Jesus in 4:17. This kingdom, which includes the view of God as creator and provider is being disclosed more and more through the narrative. Matt 10:26–31 is one of those points.
131. Carter, *Matthew and the Margins: A Sociopolitical and Religious Reading*, 240.
132. Carter uses "gentle," Ibid., 241.
133. Hagner and Davies and Allison use "caring," Davies and Allison, *The Gospel According to Saint Matthew*, 2:209; Hagner, *Matthew 1–13, 14–28*, 1:286.
134. See Carter, *Matthew and the Margins: A Sociopolitical and Religious Reading*, 240–41; Davies and Allison, *The Gospel According to Saint Matthew*, 2:205–06; Weaver, *Matthew's Missionary Discourse: A Literary Critical Analysis*, 109.
135. See Carter, *Matthew and the Margins: A Sociopolitical and Religious Reading*, 240; Davies and Allison, *The Gospel According to Saint Matthew*, 206–07; Weaver, *Matthew's Missionary Discourse: A Literary Critical Analysis*, 109.
136. The combination of body and soul and the use of φοβέομαι (and its association with μεριμνάω, right next to φοβέομαι in Louw/Nida) calls to mind for the implied audience its use in 6:25–34. In 6:25–34, the body, which is closely associated with the physical body in Matthew's narrative, is not to be focused on to the exclusion of who it is that is in relationship with the body. Therefore, do not worry about what you will wear, the clothes, how the lilies are adorned; rather focus on who clothes the lilies, who makes the body (i.e. God makes the body and clothes the lilies). Similarly, the soul carries a negative connotation in 6:25–34 and in the narrative when discussing life that is disconnected with a relationship with God and those who serve God but a positive connotation when discussed in terms of those relationships.
137. Fear can be read in parallel with worry in 6:25–34.
138. Carter, *Matthew and the Margins: A Sociopolitical and Religious Reading*, 240–41.
139. A different use of fear is used here, to mean respect, awe, worship. BAGD, s.v. "φοβέομαι."
140. Thus, scholars divide the passage between v. 28 and v. 29. Carter, *Matthew and the Margins: A Sociopolitical and Religious Reading*, 240–41; Davies and Allison, *The*

Gospel According to Saint Matthew, 2:207; Hagner, *Matthew 1–13, 14–28*, 1:284–86; Weaver, *Matthew's Missionary Discourse: A Literary Critical Analysis*, 109.

141. Weaver, *Matthew's Missionary Discourse: A Literary Critical Analysis*, 109.
142. Johnson, *She Who Is: The Mystery of God in Feminist Theological Discourse*, 181–85; McFague, *Models of God: Theology for an Ecological, Nuclear Age*, 109–23.
143. 'Αποκτείνω is used in Matthew 14:5; 16:21; 17:23; 21:35, 38, 39; 22:6; 23:34, 37; 24:9; 26:4.
144. 'Απόλλυμι in the sense of killing a body/member is used in Matthew 5:29, 30, 10:28a, 8:25, 2:13, 12:14, 21:41, 22:7, 26:52, 27:20; in the sense of losing life-giving ties, it is used in Matthew 10:6, 15:24, 10:39, 10:28b, 16:25, 18:14
145. References to sparrows (στρουθίος) are found in Pss 11:1, 84:3, 102:7, 104:17, 124:7; Jer 8:7; Job 41:5; Lam 3:52, 4:3; Ecc 12:4.
146. Carter, *Matthew and the Margins: A Sociopolitical and Religious Reading*, 241; Davies and Allison, *The Gospel According to Saint Matthew*, 2:207–10; Hagner, *Matthew 1–13, 14–28*, 1:286; Harrington, *The Gospel of Matthew*, 150.
147. Pss 11:1, 84:3, 102:7, 124:7, Job 41:5. See also Bauernfeind for a discussion of the "sacrificial motherly love of weak and helpless sparrows," O. Bauernfeind, "στρουθίον," *TDNT* 7:730.
148. See Pss 104:17, 84:3; see also my section on 6:25–34 which discusses birds in general as those who receive God's provision.
149. John G. Cook, "The Sparrow's Fall in Mt 10 29b," *ZNW* 79 (1988): 138–44. cf. BAGD, s.v. "στρουθίος ."
150. Cook, "The Sparrow's Fall," 139.
151. God, in 6:1–21, is depicted as an all-seeing and all-knowing God who sees all creatures and knows and understands even their innermost secrets. Continuing in 6:25–34, the Father knows what the disciples need and will provide for them (6:32–33). Finally, in 7:7–11, just as parents know how to give good gifts to their children, so the Father in heaven does as well.
152. See Matthew 10:19–20, 10:22.
153. The narrative continues to show that God's activity as provider is opening up to those beyond the human sphere. In 6:1–21, God as Father was the Father of the disciples with only a hint of God as creator and provider (feed through the earth, 6:11). In 6:25–34, God as Father was also God as creator and provider who relates to the birds of the air. In 7:7–11, the use of serpent, food and temptation set God in the context of Gen 1–3 as creator of all things. In 10:26–31, God as the one who destroys becomes God as Father and provider again in v. 29 with the use of Father and the reference to the sparrows in the same verse.
154. The first argues that v. 30 is making the claim about God's knowledge over human ignorance such that God knows what the disciples will be going through even if they do not understand. This reading focuses on those passages where God is able to number various parts of creation (e.g. sand, stars, streams, clouds), although the passages do not include hairs on the head. The emphasis of this interpretation of v. 30 is on the difference between the knowledge of God and the ignorance of humans, the distance between them, and the vast dependence of humanity on God. This supports the view of God as sovereign and ruler of humanity who is independent from humanity. See Carter, *Matthew and the Margins: A Sociopolitical and Religious Reading*, 241; Davies and Allison, *The Gospel According-*

ing to Saint Matthew, 2:209; Patte, *The Gospel According to Matthew: A Structural Commentary on Matthew's Faith*, 152–53. See also Job 38:37–38, Sir 1:2, *1 En* 93:14, *4 Ezra* 4:7–12. The second interpretation claims the verse is about God's care and protection of the disciples in the face of enemies such that they will not perish. The focus is on the phrase, "not one hair of your head will fall." This reading relies on passages with the phrase, "not one hair of your head will fall." This interpretation is suitably critiqued for focusing on "one hair" not "the hairs" and on situations where humans' physical lives are being rescued from enemies. In Matt 10, disciples may die and that is accepted as part of a faithful witness. There is little attempt to save their lives. See Davies and Allison, *The Gospel According to Saint Matthew*, 2:209; Hagner, *Matthew 1–13, 14–28*, 1:286. See also 1 Sam 14:45, 2 Sam 14:11, 1 Kgs 1:52, Luke 21:18, Acts 27:34.

155. The passages used to support the claim that God has knowledge to human's ignorance also talk about God as creator who can number clouds, streams, stars, sand because God created them.
156. O. Bauernfeind, "στρουθίον," *TDNT* 7:730.
157. Johnson, *She Who Is: The Mystery of God in Feminist Theological Discourse*, 33–34; Sallie McFague, *Metaphorical Theology: Models of God in Religion Language* (Philadelphia, Pennsylvania: Fortress Press, 1982), chs. 1–2.
158. Sovereignty refers to the ideas of absolute and supreme power, independence, and political rule. The use of these ideas to describe God, even when caring for sparrows and having intimate knowledge of humans, underwrites a view of God as absolute, distant, and separate.
159. Carter, *Matthew and the Margins: A Sociopolitical and Religious Reading*, 241.
160. Hagner, *Matthew 1–13, 14–28*, 1:286.
161. Davies and Allison, *The Gospel According to Saint Matthew*, 2:207.
162. McFague, *Models of God: Theology for an Ecological, Nuclear Age*, 65–69.
163. Ibid.
164. McFague discusses the metaphor of God as mother-creator and suggests that God as mother is not "built upon stereotypes of maternal tenderness, softness, pity, and sentimentality, but upon the female experience of gestation, birth and lactation. This experience....engenders not attributes of weakness and passivity but qualities contributing to the active defense of the young so that they may not only exist but be nourished and grow." Johnson, *She Who Is: The Mystery of God in Feminist Theological Discourse*, 181–85; McFague, *Models of God: Theology for an Ecological, Nuclear Age*, 113. It is probably difficult for many readers to move between God as Father and Mother, to cross the gender line rather than moving from God as king to creator to father but, again, these are metaphors not literal descriptions. Johnson, *She Who Is: The Mystery of God in Feminist Theological Discourse*, 33–34. While many readers are more at ease with accepting the idea that God typically functions as a sovereign, powerful judge who might every once in a while act as benevolent Father, it is more difficult for many readers to grasp the idea that a compassionate, guiding, providing creator may also work for justice.
165. Weaver, *Matthew's Missionary Discourse: A Literary Critical Analysis*, 110.
166. Davies and Allison, *The Gospel According to Saint Matthew*, 1:655.
167. Hanson, *Palestine in the Time of Jesus: Social Structures and Social Conflicts*, 124–25; Sahlins, *Stone Age Economics*, 218.

168. The first use involves situations where one is to sell all that one has. In 13:44 and 19:21, one is to sell all that one has to buy the field where a treasure is hidden (13:44) and one is instructed to sell all his possessions and give to the poor and follow Jesus (19:21).
169. Sahlins, *Stone Age Economics*, 218.
170. Carter, *Matthew and the Margins: A Sociopolitical and Religious Reading*, 241; Hagner, *Matthew 1–13, 14–28*, 1:286; Harrington, *The Gospel of Matthew*, 150. See also O. Bauernfeind, "στρουθίον," *TDNT* 7:730.
171. See Sahlins on reciprocity and wealth, Sahlins, *Stone Age Economics*, 211. The greater the wealth gap, the greater the need toward generalized exchange, especially food-sharing between the haves and have-nots.
172. Contra Weaver who sees contrasts (i.e. extremes) in each segment (10:26–27, 28, 29–31): concealment/disclosure (vv. 26–27), limited power of humans/ultimate power of God (v. 28) and insignificant sparrows/infinitely more valuable human beings (vv. 29–31). Weaver, *Matthew's Missionary Discourse: A Literary Critical Analysis*, 110. I see a more continuous evolution of thought.
173. In the 6:1–21, God interacted directly and in private with the Matthean community. In 6:25–34, God continued to interact directly with the community but was also interacting with the larger natural world in more public areas. In 7:7–11, God interacted more indirectly (through parents) mostly with the Matthean community but also with those outside that community.
174. See also Thomas R. W. Longstaff, "God," in *Harper's Bible Dictionary*, ed. Paul J. Achtemeier (San Francisco: Harper & Row, 1985); Ronald Simkins, *Creator and Creation: Nature in the Worldview of Ancient Israel* (Peabody, MS: Hendrickson Publishers, 1994), ch. 3. In the canonical story of the Bible, God is first creator and sustainer and then God of history, king, and ruler.
175. Note the pattern here through the Matthean narrative: bread is requested from God in 6:1–21, God provides food through nursing as an infant in 6:25–34, then through parents feeding children in 7:7–11, then by working in Matt 10, then on their own initiative in Matt 12, then given to others in Matt 13 and 14. The Matthean community develops through the narrative as a child develops into an adult.
176. Sahlins, *Stone Age Economics*, 186.
177. See Goldsmith, "'Ask, and It Will Be Given.' Toward Writing the History of a Logion," 262–63.
178. See Goldsmith as he describes quick repetition as ricocheting, Ibid., 263.

Chapter 7: In the Grainfields (12:1–8)

1. Davies and Allison, *The Gospel According to Saint Matthew*, 2:304. Hagner and Luz read a similar structure. See Hagner, *Matthew 1–13, 14–28*, 1:327–28; Ulrich Luz, *Matthew 8–20: A Commentary*, ed. Helmut Koester, trans. James E. Crouch, *Hermeneia – a Critical and Historical Commentary on the Bible* (Minneapolis: Fortress Press, 2001), 179–80. Patte divides the passage into two narrative oppositions, both of which contrast the Pharisees (12:2) with Jesus' response (12:3–8). See Patte, *The Gospel According to Matthew: A Structural Commentary on Matthew's*

Faith, 167. Robbins notes the use of the conjunction δε in v. 1 to introduce the action of the disciples, v. 2 to note the speech of the Pharisees, v. 3 to mark the opening response of Jesus and then vv. 6 and 7 to introduce the final arguments. See Vernon K. Robbins, "Plucking Grain on the Sabbath," in *Patterns of Persuasion in the Gospels*, ed. Burton L. Mack and Vernon K. Robbins (Sonoma, California: Polebridge Press, 1989), 133.

2. This highlights my main methodological focus in this study, to pay attention to food exchange instead of the divergent interpretation of the laws between groups.
3. On mobility vs. stasis in Matthew, see Levine, *The Social and Ethnic Dimensions of Matthean Social History*, 7–8.
4. Carter, *Matthew and the Margins: A Sociopolitical and Religious Reading*, 263; Davies and Allison, *The Gospel According to Saint Matthew*, 2:305; Hagner, *Matthew 1–13, 14–28*, 1:328.
5. John Mark Hicks, "The Sabbath Controversy in Matthew: An Exegesis of Matthew 12:1–14," *Restoration Quarterly* 27 (1984): 80.
6. See chapter 2 in this study for the view of the reader.
7. Malina, "Christ and Time: Swiss or Mediterranean?" 22–23.
8. Matthews and Benjamin, *Social World of Ancient Israel 1250–587 B.C.E.*, 187.
9. Gundry, *Matthew*, 221. See also BAGD, s.v. "καιρός."
10. Malina, "Christ and Time: Swiss or Mediterranean?" 19.
11. Carter, *Matthew and the Margins: A Sociopolitical and Religious Reading*, 263–64.
12. Ibid., 263; Gerhard F. Hasel, "Sabbath," in *The Anchor Bible Dictionary*, ed. David Noel Freedman (New York: Doubleday, 1992).
13. God's creative work and the rest to remember this work is reiterated in others parts of the Pentateuch and in the prophets (e.g. Exod 20:8–11, Deut 5:12–15, Isa 58:13–14).
14. Carter, *Matthew and the Margins: A Sociopolitical and Religious Reading*, 263; Hasel, "Sabbath."
15. Daily rest takes on a humanitarian gesture as ox and donkey, homeborn slave and resident alien may be refreshed (Exod 23:12). See Harrington, *The Gospel of Matthew*, 175. This daily rest was extended to a sabbath year rest that included rest for the land, vineyard and olive orchard so the poor, male and female slaves, wild animals, and livestock could eat, freedom for the male Hebrew slave, and remission of debts. See also Carter, *Matthew and the Margins: A Sociopolitical and Religious Reading.*, 263. See Exod 21:2–6, 23:10–11; Lev 25:1–7; Deut 15:1–18.
16. Carter, *Matthew and the Margins: A Sociopolitical and Religious Reading*, 263; Saldarini, *Matthew's Christian-Jewish Community*, 127.
17. Eduard Schweizer, *The Good News According to Matthew*, trans. David E. Green (Atlanta: John Knox Press, 1975), 277.
18. Carter, *Matthew and the Margins: A Sociopolitical and Religious Reading*, 263. The mention of the sabbath in 12:1, along with the transition "at that time," may indeed refer back to 11:29 where Jesus says, "I will give you rest" and "you will find rest for your souls."Carter, *Matthew and the Margins: A Sociopolitical and Religious Reading*, 263; Schweizer, *The Good News According to Matthew*, 277. The sabbath time, then, clarifies what "at that time" references.

19. Carter, *Matthew and the Margins: A Sociopolitical and Religious Reading,* 263; Harrington, *The Gospel of Matthew,* 175–77.
20. Carter, *Matthew and the Margins: A Sociopolitical and Religious Reading,* 263. God supplied twice as much food on the sixth day so the people would have adequate food on the sabbath when they rested on the seventh day.
21. Ibid; Garland, *Reading Matthew: A Literary and Theological Commentary on the First Gospel,* 135; Saldarini, *Matthew's Christian-Jewish Community,* 127. The sabbath was a distinctive practice of Israel which set them apart from other nations and peoples (Jubilees 2:31).
22. Harrington, *The Gospel of Matthew,* 175–76. "Deprived of its temple, capital city, and homeland, the Jewish exiles emphasized the sabbath as a very important religious obligation (see Isa 56:2; 58:13–14; Jer 17:21–27; Ezek 20:11–21). Observance of the Sabbath was not dependent on the existence of the Temple." Harrington continues to say that the sabbath was not necessarily a rival to the temple but provided an important religious practice that would, along with food laws and circumcision, maintain the Jewish identity. He does raise the question, though, of a possible tension between the sabbath and worship in the Jerusalem Temple.
23. The spaces where food has been exchanged in the Matthean narrative have been architectural (i.e. in a household or with a family as in 6:1–21, perhaps 6:25–34 and 7:7–11, and 10:5–11:1) and topographical (i.e. in the grainfields in 12:1–8 and deserted places and mountain in 14:13–22 and 15:29–39). None of the spaces have been geopolitical which suggests the downplaying of the political element present in the exchange of food.
24. Topographical spaces on land can be considered inhabited or uninhabited. See Malbon, *Narrative Space and Mythic Meaning in Mark,* 101–02. Grainfields are not uninhabited—such as mountains and the wilderness—and therefore fit with inhabited areas such as villages, city, country, and region.
25. Saldarini suggests the location is in a field outside a town and that is why "previously prepared Sabbath food was not available to them." See Saldarini, *Matthew's Christian-Jewish Community,* 131. For a picture reconstructing a village and the surrounding countryside with a grainfield, see King and Stager, *Life in Biblical Israel.*
26. The form here (τῶν σπορίμων) is from the substantive, τὰ σπόριμα, and is in the genitive neuter plural form. The lexical form is σπόριμος. It can be translated as standing grain or grain fields BAGD, s.v. "σπόριμος."
27. The form here (σπορίμου) is from σπόριμος and is in the genitive neuter singular form. It means "sown."
28. Carter, *Matthew and the Margins: A Sociopolitical and Religious Reading,* 264.
29. Patrick D. Miller, *Deuteronomy,* ed. James L. Mays, *Interpretation: A Bible Commentary for Teaching and Preaching* (Louisville: John Knox Press, 1990), 174. Gleaning laws served two functions: they protected the owners of fields and vineyards from those who would exploit their fields by taking an excess of crops and they provided a basic amount of food for the poor, traveler, and resident alien.
30. Leviticus 19:9–10 and 23:22 require that owners of the field leave gleanings of the harvest when they reap it and grapes on the vines when they gather them. "You shall leave them for the poor and the alien: I am the Lord your God" (Lev 19:10,

23:22). The holiness code in Leviticus 17–26 extends holiness to the entire land and the people who reside in it. Yahweh is holy, the source of holiness, and Yahweh's people must strive to imitate this holiness. The repetition of "I am the Lord your God" throughout the holiness code reinforces Yahweh as the source of holiness. Jacob Milgrom, "Leviticus," in *The HarperCollins Study Bible*, ed. Wayne Meeks (New York: HarperCollins, 1993), 152. Kin who fall into difficulty are also to be provided food, not through gleaning, but as a gift. "You shall not...provide them food at a profit" (Lev 25:35–37). See Carter, *Matthew and the Margins: A Sociopolitical and Religious Reading*, 264. In Deuteronomy 23:25, 24:19–21 gleaning laws also required owners to leave gleanings of grain, olives, and grapes for the alien, orphan, and the widow. A tension is prevalent in Deuteronomy 23–25 regarding holiness on the one hand and relationships with other nations on the other hand. Holiness and purity are emphasized to set Israel apart from other nations, especially in relation to those who are to be admitted to the assembly of the Lord (23:1). The Ammonites or Moabites were not allowed admission to the assembly, even to the tenth generation (23:3). Yet some nations, the Edomites and Egyptians, were allowed to be admitted. The Edomites were considered kin and the Israelites had been aliens residing in the land of Egypt and received hospitality at some points in their shared history (e.g. Abraham and Sarah in Gen 12, 20; the Joseph story in Gen 39–50). The degree of conflict in the shared political history between the Israelites and other nations may have indicated whether the nations would be included in the assembly or not. Similarly, aliens from other nations were to be protected by gleaning laws. See Miller, *Deuteronomy*, 175–76.

See also Perdue, *Families in Ancient Israel*, 192–203. Laws in Leviticus and Deuteronomy offered provision and protection to those who were outside the Israelite community. Holiness and subsequent justice were to be extended (ideally) to all who resided in the land. Laws, for example, offered protection to the resident alien as a marginalized member of the household. The resident alien was a "foreign immigrant who did not own land." The resident alien was not to be oppressed, was to be considered a fellow citizen, and was to be loved as the Israelite himself (Lev 19:33–34). Ruth is a resident alien, a Moabite, who is allowed to glean in the fields of Boaz (Ruth 2). The resident alien was to participate in sabbath rest (Deut 5:13–14) and worship (Lev 16:29, 17:8, Deut 16:11, 14; 26:11), and receive a fair hearing (Deut 1:16). The laws included the distribution of food to resident aliens, who were to receive gleanings from the harvest of grain, olives and grapes (Lev 19:9–10, 23:22; Deut 23:25, 24:19–21).

31. Miller, *Deuteronomy*, 174.
32. Miller refers to McBride, see S. Dean McBride, "Polity of the Covenant People: The Book of Deuteronomy," *Interpretation: A Journal of Bible and Theology* 41 (1987): 242–43; Miller, *Deuteronomy*, 174–75.
33. The disciples have more initiative here to feed themselves than in Matt 10. In Matt 14 and 15, the disciples, while still requiring assistance and guidance from Jesus, feed not only themselves but also feed others.
34. Luz, *Matthew 8–20: A Commentary*, 180–81.
35. Robbins, "Plucking Grain on the Sabbath," 133–39.
36. Ibid., 135.

37. The inhabited area of the grainfields is, at one glance, a place of controversy as Jesus and the disciples argue with the Pharisees. It is also set within a larger framework where Jesus and the disciples are expecting (10:5–11:1) and encountering (Matt 11) conflict with those they interact with as they travel into cities (11:1), grainfields (12:1–8), synagogues (12:9–14) and interact with the crowds (12:15–50). See the use of "their synagogue(s)," which becomes contentious in 10:17 and 12:9. See 6:1–21 when "their synagogue" is not used yet in the narrative as a place of conflict.
38. The conflict with the temple foreshadows the increased conflict surrounding the temple that is yet to come in the narrative.
39. BAGD , s.v. "δέ."
40. NAB, RSV, NRSV, NIV, REB. The use of the aorist active participle, ιδόντες, helps explain the use of "when" but the effect is still to note a difference.
41. Robbins, "Plucking Grain on the Sabbath," 132–33.
42. See Mark 2:24 and Luke 6:2 where the Pharisees pose a question.
43. A question can be raised about the notion that the Pharisees were following Jesus and his disciples around the countryside. Yet, the narrative tells a story and the Pharisees and their interactions with other characters are integral to that story. The Pharisees are present, they see that the disciples are picking grain and address their concern directly to Jesus.
44. Saldarini, *Matthew's Christian-Jewish Community*, 127. Food was not to be prepared on the sabbath (Exod 16:22–30) nor was firewood to be gathered (Num 15:32–36), goods were not to be transported (Jer 17:21–22; Neh 13:15–22), buying and selling goods were not allowed (Neh 11:31), war was forbidden as was sexual intercourse (Jubilees 50:8, 13).
45. Ibid., 127–28.
46. Davies and Allison, *The Gospel According to Saint Matthew*, 2:307.
47. David is king as Jesus is called king and Jesus is referred to as the Son of David. As the disciples accompany Jesus so "those with him" accompany David. It is not an exact parallel, but there are many similarities. See Carter, *Matthew and the Margins: A Sociopolitical and Religious Reading*, 265 n. 10.
48. David and those with him are fleeing Saul, running for their lives. They stop at the sanctuary at Nob to get food (1 Sam 21:3) and a sword (1 Sam 21:8–9), items necessary for their survival. Jesus and the disciples are usually not interpreted as running for their lives or in dire need of food to survive. Yet they are on the move and facing increasing hostility in Matt 12. Jesus and the disciples expect hostility as the disciples receives instructions in Matt 10, Jesus encounters conflict in Matt 11, and Jesus and the disciples face accusations from the Pharisees concerning work on the sabbath in 12:1–8.
49. David sets aside the laws regarding the eating of the Bread of the Presence by the priests and Jesus sets aside laws about work on the sabbath.
50. In the first setting, while its historical context shares a similar sacrificial system as the other settings, the setting highlights that part of the system that provides food for the poor through gleaning. The setting also highlights the laws prevalent in Lev and Deut, where the story is about wandering and traveling (in the same way Matthew's community is depicted in chs. 10, 12, 14, 15). The other two

settings in 12:1–8 highlight what's going on in the sanctuaries and Temple and are from narratives that are moving or have moved toward kingship.

51. See King and Stager, *Life in Biblical Israel*, 320–38. See also Matthews and Benjamin, *Social World of Ancient Israel 1250–587 B.C.E.*, 191–93. The "house of God" refers to one of the many sanctuaries or shrines that were situated throughout Israel (and later Israel and Judah) before Josiah's reform in 622/621 B.C.E. when worship was centralized in Jerusalem. The time period, with David on his way to being a king, is the tenth century B.C.E and therefore occurs during the united monarchy and before the divided kingdom. With the kingship of Saul, Israel is now considered a state and priests serve as state officials who collect produce from fields and animals as sacrifices. One of the ways that sacrifices function is as a tax. Sacrifices are used as a means for collecting, storing and redistributing goods through a centralized system. Priests determine the amount of goods to collect from each household, store them, and then redistribute them to state officials, soldiers, in the form of loans to households, to pay for state building projects, or for use in emergencies.

52. In the context of this system of sacrifices and rituals, one of the rituals each sabbath involved placing unleavened bread in the presence of God. In the tabernacle, the bread of the presence was placed on a table outside the curtain separating the table from the holy of holies. In Solomon's Temple, bread of the presence was displayed in the sanctuary just outside the holy of holies. With Solomon's temple, the sanctuary refers to the first chamber of the central building which was divided into two chambers: the "sanctuary" and the Holy of Holies. The sanctuary was the nearest chamber to the Holy of Holies. Paul V. M. Flesher, "Bread of the Presence," in *The Anchor Bible Dictionary*, ed. David Noel Freedman (New York: Doubleday, 1992); E. P. Sanders, *Judaism: Practice & Belief: 63 B.C.E.–66 C.E.* (Philadelphia: Trinity Press International, 1992), 55, 310–14. The high priest would place twelve loaves of unleavened bread, in the presence of Yahweh, on a golden table every sabbath and leave it there for the week. The bread would be rendered holy by its proximity to the holy of holies, its nearness to Yahweh. The old bread would be removed and eaten by priests in a holy place, that is within the temple complex. The bread symbolized the covenant between Israel and Yahweh and its regular placement in the sanctuary represented Israel's commitment to that covenant. See Lev 24:5–9, Exod 25:23–30.

53. On the political economy of the first century and centralized redistribution, see John H. Elliot, "Temple Versus Household in Luke-Acts: A Contrast in Social Institutions," in *The Social World of Luke-Acts: Models for Interpretation*, ed. Jerome H. Neyrey (Peabody, Massachusetts: Hendrickson Publishers, 1991); Hanson, *Palestine in the Time of Jesus: Social Structures and Social Conflicts*, ch. 4.

54. King Herod seeks to kill Jesus and murders young children (ch. 2), the disciples are warned that they will be delivered up to kings to be judged (10:18), kings wear soft robes in palaces and are not prophets in the wilderness like John the Baptist (11:7–15), Herod the Tetrarch beheads John the Baptist (14:10), kings of the earth burden the people by collecting excessive taxes and tolls (17:25), and kings are angry and violent, murder prospective guests and burn cities (22:7). Jesus is called a king but usually by Roman soldiers, Jewish leaders, and bandits who accuse, strip, torture, and/or mock him as king (27:11–14, 27–31, 37, 41–44).

There are also positive connotations associated with kingship (e.g. 21:5, 25:34), but they are outnumbered by negative references.

55. Solomon, David's Son, is associated with healing. There is certainly a theme running through Matthew that the Son of David is associated with Jesus' acts of healing. See 9:27, 12:23, 15:22, 20:30–1. Carter, *Matthew and the Margins: A Sociopolitical and Religious Reading,* 227–28; Davies and Allison, *The Gospel According to Saint Matthew,* 2:136.
56. See also Carter, *Matthew and the Margins: A Sociopolitical and Religious Reading,* 228. David is not able to raise a dead child (2 Sam 12:13–23) while Jesus can.
57. For a discussion of this tradition of David's exclusion of the blind and lame as problematic, see Walter Brueggemann, *First and Second Samuel,* ed. James Luther and Patrick D. Miller Mays, *Interpretation: A Bible Commentary for Teaching and Preaching* (Louisville: John Knox Press, 1990), 239–42.
58. See also Carter's interpretation of 6:29, Carter, *Matthew and the Margins: A Sociopolitical and Religious Reading,* 178.
59. While this could refer to the time period before Josiah's reform when other sanctuaries existed throughout the land in addition to the Jerusalem Temple, Matthew's mention of the Temple might lead the reader to think of this as the only place where sacrifices were being practiced.
60. Elliot, "Temple Versus Household in Luke-Acts: A Contrast in Social Institutions," 230–35.
61. Carter, *Matthew and the Margins: A Sociopolitical and Religious Reading,* 418.
62. Jesus teaches and heals in the temple (26:55, 21:14) and tells a leper who has been cleansed to show himself to a priest for the proper sacrifice in the temple (8:1–4). Ibid.
63. See Gary A. Anderson, "Sacrifice and Sacrificial Offerings (OT)," in *The Anchor Bible Dictionary,* ed. David Noel Freedman (New York: Doubleday, 1992); Sanders, *Judaism: Practice & Belief: 63 B.C.E.–66 C.E.,* 104–07.
64. It was probably not an atoning sacrifice. See Anderson, "Sacrifice and Sacrificial Offerings (OT)"; Sanders, *Judaism: Practice & Belief: 63 B.C.E.–66 C.E.,* 106.
65. Sanders argues it was not food for God. But see Anderson, "Sacrifice and Sacrificial Offerings (OT)." Anderson claims "the consumable gift was thought to be in many respects the food of the deity." See also King and Stager, *Life in Biblical Israel,* 358. King and Stager argue the burnt offering "nourished the deity." See also Num 28:3, 2: "a pleasing odor to the Lord."
66. Sanders, *Judaism: Practice & Belief: 63 B.C.E.–66 C.E.,* 105. cf. Neh 10:32–33.
67. Elliot, "Temple Versus Household in Luke-Acts: A Contrast in Social Institutions"; Sanders, *Judaism: Practice & Belief: 63 B.C.E.–66 C.E.,* 105.
68. "Desecrate" may have been a typical way to phrase this practice but it also has negative connotations. See Davies and Allison, *The Gospel According to Saint Matthew,* 2:314. See also Robbins, "Plucking Grain on the Sabbath," 135.
69. Carter, *Matthew and the Margins: A Sociopolitical and Religious Reading,* 265.
70. Robbins, "Plucking Grain on the Sabbath," 135.
71. As Harrington has suggested, this may represent a tension between the temple and the sabbath that emerged during the Babylonian exile and would have been understandable in the late first century after the destruction of the Jerusalem temple. See Harrington, *The Gospel of Matthew,* 175–76.

72. Matthews and Benjamin, *Social World of Ancient Israel 1250–587 B.C.E.*, 187.
73. These possibilities include Jesus, the kingdom, love, Jesus' interpretation of the law, the community of disciples, the ministry of Jesus and the disciples, and mercy. See Carter, *Matthew and the Margins: A Sociopolitical and Religious Reading*, 266; Davies and Allison, *The Gospel According to Saint Matthew*, 2:314; Hagner, *Matthew 1–13, 14–28*, 1:329–30; Luz, *Matthew 8–20: A Commentary*, 182; Patte, *The Gospel According to Matthew: A Structural Commentary on Matthew's Faith*, 168. "Jesus" appears to be the most common reading. The use of the comparative μεῖζόν is "unexpected" according to some interpreters because it is the neuter form of μέγας. The masculine or feminine form, μείζων, would have been easier to identify with Jesus or the kingdom. As Luz argues, this makes it an open question on who or what is greater than the temple. Luz claims that mercy is greater than the temple. Luz is not suggesting that the disciples', Jesus', or God's mercy is greater than the temple but that mercy is the center of God's will and the Pharisees ought to be practicing it. They should have fed the disciples. He claims that the disciples' hunger and hungering ones should become the standard of mercy and the standard for the "correct fulfillment of the Sabbath." Luz, *Matthew 8–20: A Commentary*, 182.
74. Peter tries to set up tents on the mountain after the transfiguration instead of getting up and moving down the mountain (17:4–9), the day laborers are standing idle in the marketplace instead of going into the vineyard to work (20:1–7), people identify false Christs "here" instead of recognizing the "coming of the Son of Man" as the lightning comes (24:23), the women look for Jesus in the empty tomb instead of knowing he has been raised (28:6). On mobility vs. stasis in Matthew's narrative, see also Levine, *The Social and Ethnic Dimensions of Matthean Social History*, 7–8.
75. Something greater than Jonah (12:41) and Solomon (12:42) are here.
76. The disciples do not recognize that they have the means for themselves and the crowds to acquire food with the five loaves and two fish (14:17–18).
77. The head of John the Baptist is requested and placed on a platter at Herod's birthday party (14:8) and the guests do not wear a wedding garment to the banquet (22:12).
78. Francis I. Andersen and David Noel Freedman, *Hosea: A New Translation with Introduction and Commentary by Francis I. Andersen and David Noel Freedman*, ed. William Foxwell Albright and David Noel Freedman, *The Anchor Bible* (New York, New York: Doubleday, 1980), 429–31. Mercy (*hesed*) can be translated as steadfast loyalty, loving kindness, or faithfulness and refers to Yahweh's love toward Israel, Yahweh's expectation of Israel, and has an affectionate, emotional sense to it. See Francis; Edward Robinson; S R Driver; Charles A Briggs; Francis Brown, *The New Brown-Driver-Briggs-Gesenius Hebrew and English Lexicon: With an Appendix Containing the Biblical Aramaic* (Peabody, MS: Hendrickson Publishers, 1979), 338–39; Christian E. Hauer and William A. Young, *An Introduction to the Bible: A Journey into Three Worlds*, 5th ed. (Upper Saddle River, NJ: Prentice Hall, 1886), 143–44.
79. Hauer, *An Introduction to the Bible: A Journey into Three Worlds*, 143–44.
80. Patte, *The Gospel According to Matthew: A Structural Commentary on Matthew's Faith*, 167–69, 203 n. 54. Patte also claims, in 12:1–8, that the Pharisees are not

judged/condemned by Jesus: "While he does reprove the Pharisees, he gives them the possibility of changing attitude by offering them a teaching about Scripture and its interpretation."

81. I do not include 9:13 in this study because it is not concerned with how to acquire food, but it does deal with food issues.
82. See Carter, *Matthew and the Margins: A Sociopolitical and Religious Reading*, 266.
83. For the view that the Pharisees learn nothing from Jesus and cannot be disciples, see Ibid., 221.
84. The Matthean community is connected to the Pharisees as part of the larger Jewish community, which is argued in Matt 10.
85. While "in secret" in 6:1–21, the heavenly Father was also one who sees all inhabitants of the earth and is one who "knows all that may be known" (Sir 42:18). God feeds the Matthean community directly with no intermediaries. In 6:25–34, God's feeding of the birds of the air show that God's activity is made manifest in the open spaces, the sky and fields. God continues to be referred to as heavenly Father but is more clearly linked with God as creator and feeds those in the Matthean community directly as a mother nursing a child. In 7:7–11, God as heavenly Father, mentioned at the end of the passage, feeds those who ask him but begins to work through intermediaries to feed God's children. Here, God works through the family, and specifically the parents. There continues to be a link between Father and creator. In Matt 10:5–11:1, God is both heavenly Father and creator and is even more distant from the feeding process as God feeds the Matthean community through the larger Jewish community.
86. The settings of food exchange have increased in levels of conflict through the narrative.
87. Malbon, *Narrative Space and Mythic Meaning in Mark*, 102.
88. See also Betz on 6:11, Betz, *The Sermon on the Mount: A Commentary on the Sermon on the Mount, Including the Sermon on the Plain (Matthew 5:3–7:27 and Luke 6:20–49)*.
89. Carter, *Matthew and the Margins: A Sociopolitical and Religious Reading*, 263.
90. See McFague, *Models of God: Theology for an Ecological, Nuclear Age*. See also Clark M. and Ronald J. Allen Williamson, *A Credible and Timely Word: Process Theology and Preaching* (St. Louis, Missouri: Chalice Press, 1991), 28–30.
91. Carter argues Matthew's audience would have been a cross-section of society, Carter, *Matthew and the Margins: A Sociopolitical and Religious Reading*, 25–38.
92. See my discussion of kinship rank in chapter 2 of this study. See also Carrier, "Exchange," 219. The distance from kinship relations has increased in food exchange as the reader has moved through the Matthean narrative. Food exchange occurred in the household, within the Matthean community, in 6:1–21 and 6:25–34. In 7:7–11, subtle references were made to those outside the Matthean community ("everyone," "human," "those who ask him") suggesting a greater kinship distance. In 10:5–11:1, food exchange occurs with the larger Jewish community. In 12:1–8, kinship distance does not increase but rank and wealth become significant factors in food exchange.
93. Ibid. On the Pharisees as competing leaders with the Matthean community, see Overman, *Matthew's Gospel and Formative Judaism*; Saldarini, *Matthew's Christian-Jewish Community*, ch. 3. Even though God is the one who feeds, Jesus also func-

tions here as an agent of God and as the "Big Man" who competes against the Pharisees.

94. Carter, *Matthew and the Margins: A Sociopolitical and Religious Reading*, 208. In Matthew, the Son of Man is used to refer to the future coming of a cosmic figure, Jesus' death and resurrection, and his earthly activity, see Davies and Allison, *The Gospel According to Saint Matthew*, 2:43–53. In 12:1–8, the Son of Man refers to his earthly activity and functions as a self-designation by Jesus.
95. Carter, *Matthew and the Margins: A Sociopolitical and Religious Reading*, 266–67; Kingsbury, *Matthew as Story*, 95; Saldarini, *Matthew's Christian-Jewish Community*, 167–69, 88–91. Kingsbury makes the point that the "Son of Man" is used "with a view to the 'public' or 'world.'" Similarly, Carter emphasizes Jesus' interaction with and participation in the world as Son of Man.
96. Saldarini, *Matthew's Christian-Jewish Community*, 186–88.
97. See the section in this chapter on Matthew 12:6–8.
98. As with the other spatial settings for food exchange in the Matthean narrative, this setting of grainfields is not a geopolitical space (i.e. one based on political boundaries) and therefore the political element tends to be de-emphasized in food exchanges in Matthew.
99. See my discussion of Gudeman in chapter 2 of this study. See also Gudeman, *The Anthropology of Economy: Community, Market, and Culture*, 86–89. Luz argues that the Pharisees should have been merciful toward the disciples, perhaps implying that they show greater generosity and acknowledge Jesus' brand of generalized reciprocity. Luz, *Matthew 8–20: A Commentary*, 182.
100. Sahlins, *Stone Age Economics*, 210–12.
101. See Betz on 6:10–11, Betz, *The Sermon on the Mount: A Commentary on the Sermon on the Mount, Including the Sermon on the Plain (Matthew 5:3–7:27 and Luke 6:20–49)*.

Chapter 8: In Transition (14:13–22)

1. Malbon, *Narrative Space and Mythic Meaning in Mark*, 100.
2. Ibid.
3. Ibid., 101.
4. Both of these temporal settings are typological settings that emphasize the "kind of time" as opposed to a particular point in time (locative reference) or an interval of time (durative reference). See Powell, *What Is Narrative Criticism?*, 72–73.
5. BAGD, c.v. "ὀψίας."
6. In Matthew, evening is a time for Jesus to cast spirits out of demon-possessed people (8:16), pray on a mountain (14:23), and recline at table for a Passover meal (26:20), for workers to stop work and receive wages from a landowner (20:8), and for Joseph of Arimathea to retrieve Jesus' dead body from the cross and place it in a tomb (27:57). Evening is a time to deal with issues of life and death, to communicate with God (14:23) and recognize that God overcomes evil and brings generosity (8:16, 20:8), to prepare for a new phase in life and recognize a new beginning (26:20, 27:57).
7. BAGD, s.v. "ὥρα."

8. BAGD, s.v. "ὥρα." In Matthew, Jesus heals a servant in that hour (8:13), the disciples are given what to say (10:19), the hour marks a moment when the disciples approach Jesus (18:1), the Son of Man comes (24:44, 50) or is betrayed (26:45, 55). It marks a significant moment in time and is also a time of God's provision (8:13, 10:19).
9. Typological references often are use to contrast one kind of time with another (e.g. today not tomorrow, evening not morning, winter not summer). Powell, *What Is Narrative Criticism?*, 73. See also the discussion of "today" v. "tomorrow" on 6:25–34 in chapter 4 of this study.
10. Douglas, *Purity and Danger*; Wuthnow, *Cultural Analysis: The Work of Peter Berger, Mary Douglas, Michel Foucault, and Jürgen Habermas*, 97–102.
11. Wuthnow, *Cultural Analysis: The Work of Peter Berger, Mary Douglas, Michel Foucault, and Jürgen Habermas*, 100. Dusk, for example, is a time when people pause and watch the sun set and experience a kind of break in reality, a reverence for life, a glimpse of a "larger cosmic force," a suspension in life as usual.
12. Douglas, *Purity and Danger*, 96; Wuthnow, *Cultural Analysis: The Work of Peter Berger, Mary Douglas, Michel Foucault, and Jürgen Habermas*, 99–100.
13. Wuthnow, *Cultural Analysis: The Work of Peter Berger, Mary Douglas, Michel Foucault, and Jürgen Habermas*, 101, 02. Douglas also uses the analogy of "stickiness" to express this idea. A sticky substance is neither solid nor liquid. "When sticky things get on our hands they create a visceral reaction which seems very threatening because it blurs the boundary between self and its larger environment. Stickiness provides a continuous link between the individual and the larger world, and as such threatens the separate identity of the self."
14. Notice there are distinctions between men and women and adults and children, but no distinctions between the disciples and the crowds.
15. J.R.C. Cousland, *The Crowds in the Gospel of Matthew* (Leiden/Boston/Cologne: Brill, 2002), 3–20. See Cousland who provides a summary of scholarship on the crowds in Matthew. Some scholars define the crowds in 14:13–22 as Jewish and those in 15:29–39 as Gentile. I claim that the crowds in both passages are a mix of Jews and Gentiles and better categorized as the masses, a public group, or the world.
16. Ibid., 53–73. See this reference where Cousland gives more evidence for why he thinks the crowds are Jewish.
17. Ibid; Saldarini, *Matthew's Christian-Jewish Community*, 76. The crowds are from Galilee, the Decapolis, from Jerusalem and Judea, and from beyond the Jordan (Perea).
18. Cousland, *The Crowds in the Gospel of Matthew*, 68.
19. Ibid., 70–72.
20. For a list of passages in the Hebrew Bible and other Jewish literature where the phrase "God of Israel" is used by Jews, see Davies and Allison, *The Gospel According to Saint Matthew*, 2:569.
21. Warren Carter, "The Crowds in Matthew's Gospel," *CBQ* 55 (1993): 65; Cousland, *The Crowds in the Gospel of Matthew*, 60–61; Davies and Allison, *The Gospel According to Saint Matthew*, 2:419; Saldarini, *Matthew's Christian-Jewish Community*, 76. Davies and Allison suggest that Matthew may presuppose a Gentile presence in the crowds although they do not emphasize it. Saldarini mentions that

Gentiles would not necessarily be excluded from the crowds and Carter identifies the crowds' origin, from Galilee of the Gentiles and from Judea and Jerusalem, and contends the mission was carried out to both Jews and Gentiles (4:15, 25). Cousland suggests the reference to the Decapolis might indicate the crowds are partly Gentile.

22. Cousland, *The Crowds in the Gospel of Matthew*, 58–61.
23. Shaye J. D. Cohen, "Crossing the Boundary and Becoming a Jew," *Harvard Theological Review* 82, no. 1 (1989): 15–17, 21–24.
24. David R. Cartlidge and David L. Dungan, *Documents for the Study of the Gospels* (Philadelphia: Fortress Press, 1980), 151-165, 205-242.
25. Saldarini, *Matthew's Christian-Jewish Community*, 83, 39. See p. 83 for a reference to the Gentiles and p. 39 for a reference to the crowds.
26. Carter, "The Crowds in Matthew's Gospel," 57–58.
27. On the Gentiles, see Saldarini, *Matthew's Christian-Jewish Community*, 82.
28. On the Gentiles, see Ibid., 68. Regarding the crowds, see the beginning and ending verses on 14:13–22 and 15:29–39.
29. On the Gentiles see Ibid., 70. On the crowds, see Meyers, "οχλος," TDNT 5:587.
30. On the Gentiles, see Ibid. On the crowds, see Carter, "The Crowds in Matthew's Gospel," 57–64; Saldarini, *Matthew's Christian-Jewish Community*, 37–40.
31. BAGD, s.v. "ὄχλος."
32. Cousland, *The Crowds in the Gospel of Matthew*, 35.
33. Scot McKnight, *A Light among the Gentiles: Jewish Missionary Activity in the Second Temple Period* (Minneapolis: Fortress Press, 1991), 11–19.
34. Meyer, "ὄχλος," TDNT 5:582–83. See also Carter, "The Crowds in Matthew's Gospel," 58.
35. Meyer, "ὄχλος," TDNT 5:582–83. Waetjen refers to the crowds as the "masses" and the "multitudes" but does not elaborate on this description. See Waetjen, *The Origin and Destiny of Humanness: An Interpretation of the Gospel According to Matthew*, 161–62.
36. Saldarini refers to them as anonymous, shifting, and unstructured, Saldarini, *Matthew's Christian-Jewish Community*, 37–40.
37. Carter, "The Crowds in Matthew's Gospel," 61–62.
38. Ibid., 58–62. See Carter's discussion on differentiating the crowds from the disciples (especially in chs. 5–7) and the crowds from the Jewish leaders.
39. Howell, *Matthew's Inclusive Story: A Study in the Narrative Rhetoric of the First Gospel*, 221.
40. Cousland, *The Crowds in the Gospel of Matthew*, 37. Matthew changes Mark's "crowd" (6:45) to "crowds" (14:22) and Mark's "them" (8:10) to "crowds" (15:39). Matthew added a plural to Mark's singular 22 times.
41. Corley, *Private Women, Public Meals*, 161; Cousland, *The Crowds in the Gospel of Matthew*, 37–39; Gundry, *Matthew*, 291, 96. Gundry and Corley suggest the use of the plural "crowds" represents the largeness of the church and the future influx of large numbers of Gentiles. Cousland finally concludes it is simply one of Matthew's idiosyncrasies and has no greater significance.
42. Cousland, *The Crowds in the Gospel of Matthew*, 43.

43. Saldarini, *Matthew's Christian-Jewish Community*, 38–39. See Saldarini in his comparison of the crowds to the *Jewish* peasants. I consider the crowds the Jewish and Gentile peasants. See also Carter, "The Crowds in Matthew's Gospel," 18-21.
44. Carter, "The Crowds in Matthew's Gospel," 25–27; Saldarini, *Matthew's Christian-Jewish Community*, 38–39.
45. Call (καλέω) is used in 4:21 to call James and John to be disciples.
46. Saldarini, *Matthew's Christian-Jewish Community*, 112–16. Saldarini uses Bryan Wilson's sect typologies to describe the Jesus movement in Matthew.
47. See my discussion of hospitality and conversion in chapter 6 of this study.
48. Cohen, "Crossing the Boundary and Becoming a Jew," 14–15.
49. Ibid., 14–17.
50. McKnight, *A Light among the Gentiles: Jewish Missionary Activity in the Second Temple Period.*
51. Ibid., 13–14.
52. Ibid., 14–15.
53. Meeks, *The First Urban Christians: The Social World of the Apostle Paul*, 100, 105–107. See Meeks for a similar discussion of ambiguous boundaries and "gates in the boundaries" in the Pauline communities.
54. Gerd Theissen, *The Miracle Stories of the Early Christian Tradition* (Philadelphia: Fortress Press, 1983), 103–06. Theissen classifies these two stories as "gift miracles" (103–106) in which one of the key components is that the miracles are never initiated by requests (103–104). While no formal request is made by the crowds, they do "hear" and "follow" Jesus (14:13–22) as well as "approach" Jesus and "see" God's work and provision (15:29-39).
55. Louw and Nida, eds., *Greek-English Lexicon of the New Testament Based on Semantic Documents*, 388–411.
56. To hear can also be interpreted as understanding (domain 32) or obeying (domain 36) but the emphasis in Matt 14 is not on the crowds as understanding (cf. Matt 13) or obeying Jesus' teaching.
57. The sub domains are arranged in a particular order in each domain to suggest some interrelationships between meanings of sets of words. See Louw and Nida, eds., *Greek-English Lexicon of the New Testament Based on Semantic Documents*, 388.
58. Carter, "The Crowds in Matthew's Gospel," 58. In Louw and Nida, follow, in Carter's sense, is defined as "to go behind or after someone" (domain 15). Louw and Nida also recognize follow as becoming a disciple in domain 36. See also Louw and Nida, eds., *Greek-English Lexicon of the New Testament Based on Semantic Documents*. See also Jack Dean Kingsbury, "The Verb Akolouthein ('to Follow') as an Index of Matthew's View of His Community," *JBL* 97 (1978).
59. See the earlier section on the setting of 14:13–22 for a discussion of the whole setting as marginally located.
60. Gundry, *Matthew*, 66, 290. Gundry equates the disciples and the crowds, "since in Matthew the crowds represent professing disciples" because the crowds also followed Jesus. I do not equate the two, they are two separate characters, but suggest that there is a blurring of boundaries between the two characters as they both move in and out of each other's space. A similar phenomenon is apparent earlier in the narrative in 5:1 when Jesus sees the crowds, goes up the mountain, and his disciples come to him as if they come out of the crowds. Davies and Alli-

son and Luz both suggest there were two circles around Jesus, an inner circle of disciples and an outer circle of the crowds. Davies and Allison, *The Gospel According to Saint Matthew*, 1:422; Luz, *Matthew 1–7: A Commentary*, 224. The crowds also appear to stealthily move in and out of the space around the (presence of) Jesus in the narrative (e.g. 8:18, 9:33, 11:7).

61. See BAGD, s.v. "αἴρω," 3. The word ἦραν, from αἴρω, can be translated, "to lift up and carry away, to remove."
62. Hagner, *Matthew 1–13, 14–28*, 1:418.
63. See Patte, *The Gospel According to Matthew: A Structural Commentary on Matthew's Faith*, 210. Patte also recognizes the use of "here" in 14:17 and 14:18, although his interpretation focuses on how Jesus' presence with the disciples allows them to now play the role of society and provide food.
64. Davies and Allison, *The Gospel According to Saint Matthew*, 2:492. Davies and Allison also suggest the disciples not the crowds carry away the leftovers. A parallel in 14:1–12 might suggest this reading as well. The disciples of John the Baptist also carry away (ἦραν; same verb) the leftovers (i.e. the corpse) after the main course (i.e. the head) has been served.
65. Disposal or clearing up is the fifth phase of commensality according to Goody. *Goody, Cooking, Cuisine and Class: A Study in Comparative Sociology*, 37.
66. The use of "twelve" has been interpreted as the twelve apostles or the twelve tribes of Israel. See Davies and Allison, *The Gospel According to Saint Matthew*, 2:492, 563. The "twelve" has been further read to identify the crowds in 14:13–22 as Jewish. I argue here that it is used to identify the disciples as bold and acting upon the world as the twelve. See my discussion on Matt 10:5–15 in chapter 6 of this study for a description of how the twelve is interpreted.
67. Marketplaces are places in which day laborers are looking for work and their desperate situation is made manifest (20:3,6), this generation of Jewish leaders is acting like children and misjudge Jesus and John (11:16), and the scribes and Pharisees like to be greeted with respect in order to enhance their own status (23:7). See Carter, *Matthew and the Margins: A Sociopolitical and Religious Reading*, 254–55.
68. Ibid., 306.
69. See my analysis on 10:42 and on the crowds in 15:29–39 in chapter 9 of this study.
70. So, 25:35 and the interpretation that those providing food are both Jews and Gentiles.
71. Sahlins, *Stone Age Economics*, 210.

Chapter 9: Food from God's Earth (15:29–39)

1. Initially characterized as the twelve in Matt 10:1, 2, 5, the disciples are bold as they go out to the lost sheep of the house of Israel to act upon the world, to proclaim, heal, raise, cleanse, and cast out. Yet in 10:9–15, the disciples are characterized as day laborers in need of a place to stay, as dependents that are acted upon by the world.

2. Approach (προσέρχομαι) is used 52 times and often linked with προσκυνέω (to worship or fall down) (8:2, 9:18, 20:20, 28:9) to suggest that approaching Jesus is to approach a king or god with reverence. In this context, the crowds are probably not recognizing Jesus as a god but are certainly showing some respect for his authority. See Davies and Allison, *The Gospel According to Saint Matthew*, 1:360. See also Carter, *Matthew and the Margins: A Sociopolitical and Religious Reading*, 573, n. 4.
3. See the use of "feet" in 5:35, 22:44, 28:9. See Carter, *Matthew and the Margins: A Sociopolitical and Religious Reading*, 326; Davies and Allison, *The Gospel According to Saint Matthew*, 2:568; Gundry, *Matthew*, 318.
4. See 5:16, 9:8, 16:27, 19:28, 24:30, 25:31 as examples of glory in the sense of reverence. See, however, 4:8, 6:2, and 6:29 as examples of the misplaced glory of "this world" and humanity as opposed to God.
5. Davies and Allison, *The Gospel According to Saint Matthew*, 2:569.
6. Ibid. Philo, *Leg.* 3.1.86; *Fug.* 208; Clement of Alexandria, *Paed.* 1.9; Origin, *De prin.* 4.3; Eusebius, *Praep. en.* 11.6; On the Origin of the World 105.24–25.
7. See (βλέπω) can take on a variety of meanings according to Louw-Nida: (1) to see as a sensory event, to become aware, to take notice (domain 24), (2) to be able to see, to have the faculty of sight (domain 24), (3) to notice carefully, to be ready to learn about and to be prepared to respond to future needs (domain 27), (4) to process information, give consideration (domain 30), (5) to recognize, perceive, understand (domain 32). I contend that "see" (βλέπω) in 15:31 is interpreted according to numbers 3 and 4 above and the beginnings of number 5—they notice Jesus' healing, are learning about and processing information and beginning to understand his work as part of God's work. See Louw and Nida, eds., *Greek-English Lexicon of the New Testament Based on Semantic Documents.*
8. Ibid. Domain 30 is the same domain that see (6:26) and consider (6:28) can be located in the 6:25–34 passage.
9. In 6:25–34, the Matthean community looks (ἐμβλέπω) at the birds of the air, considers (καταμανθάνω) how God clothes the lilies of the field and seeks (ζητέω) the kingdom of God and his righteousness. All three verbs have in common the idea of thinking and learning as well as acquiring, processing, and manipulating information. "See" and "consider" have in common the semantic domain of thinking (30) which involves the idea of processing and manipulating information. "Seek" is in the semantic domain of learning (27) and primarily refers to the acquisition of information, probably referring to the step before processing and manipulating information. In 6:25–34, the Matthean community has moved beyond asking and praying for food (6:1–21) and is now learning about where one might find food. Louw and Nida, eds., *Greek-English Lexicon of the New Testament Based on Semantic Documents.*
10. Davies and Allison, *The Gospel According to Saint Matthew*, 2:560, 661. See also L. Ruppert *Jesus als der leidende Gerechte?*, SBS 59, Stuttgart, 1972, 63–65. Ruppert is referred to in Davies and Allison, *The Gospel According to Saint Matthew*, 2:661. Another interpretation for the three days suggests that it was a long enough time that a crowd would have run out of provisions. See Carter, *Matthew and the Margins: A Sociopolitical and Religious Reading*, 327; Davies and Allison, *The Gospel According to Saint Matthew*, 2:570. See Gen 40:12–13, Gen 42:16–17, Exod 10:22,

Exod 15:22, Josh 2:16, 1 Sam 9:20, 1 Sam 30:12, 1 Chr 21:12. See also Matt 12:40 (Jonah), 27:63 (Jesus).

11. Those Gentiles whose suffering is relieved after three days include the chief cupbearer in Egypt (Gen 40), all the land of Egypt (Exod 10), and an Egyptian (1 Chr 21:12).
12. Przybylski, *Righteousness in Matthew and His World of Thought*, 1.
13. See my discussion of righteousness in chapter 4 of this study.
14. For a discussion of 5:6 and 6:33, see chapter 4 of this study.
15. Cousland, *The Crowds in the Gospel of Matthew*, 87.
16. Ibid., 89; Levine, *The Social and Ethnic Dimensions of Matthean Social History*, 40.
17. Cousland, *The Crowds in the Gospel of Matthew*, 134–35.
18. See also 5:16 where glory is to be given to the Father not to Jesus. Ibid., 135. "Approach" (προσέρχομαι) can take on several meanings according to Louw-Nida: (1) to move towards with the intent of a reciprocal relationship (domain 15), to take the initiative to seek association with or join someone (domain 34), or to agree with someone, to believe or trust or hold the same view or opinion as someone (domain 31). In this context, "approach" is interpreted primarily in line with number 1 with some intent to seek association with Jesus but not to join his group or advocate his teachings. Louw and Nida, eds., *Greek-English Lexicon of the New Testament Based on Semantic Documents*.
19. Cohen, "Crossing the Boundary and Becoming a Jew," 17.
20. "Righteous outsiders" are also apparent in the Matthean narrative. Those Gentiles "outside" the Jewish and Matthean communities would include the Magi, Pilate's wife, and the centurion at the cross. Those Jews who are outside the Matthean community would include the women from Galilee and Joseph of Arimethea. See Levine, *The Social and Ethnic Dimensions of Matthean Social History*, 262–65.
21. Malbon, *Narrative Space and Mythic Meaning in Mark*, 101–03.
22. Ibid., 84–85, 102.
23. Terence L. Donaldson, *Jesus on the Mountain: A Study in Matthean Theology* (Sheffield: JSOT Press, 1985), 41–50.
24. Zion theology in the first testament and Second Temple Period included both a present religious and political reality as well as an eschatological perspective. In both perspectives, Yahweh was seen as king over all the nations. Two traditions exist of the nations, one as the defeated nations who are cast in a subservient role (e.g. Isa 42:23) and one with a more constructive view of the nations as processing forward to worship Yahweh and sharing in the eschatological blessings of feasting, healing, and the abolishment of death (e.g. Isa 2:2ff, Mic 4:1ff). See Ibid., 36–70.
25. Ibid., 26, 39, 45, 59–62. For traditions that emphasize the cosmos and creation in relation to Mt. Zion, (1) Zion as center of the cosmos (pp. 26, 59–62): LXX Ezek 38:12; Jub 8:12, 19; 1 Enoch 26; (2) Zion as new Eden (p. 45): Ezek 41:1, 6b–12; cf. 28:12–16; (3) Mountains as places of fertility (p. 39): Joel 3:18, Amos 9:13.
26. Claassens, *The God Who Provides: Biblical Images of Divine Nourishment*, 66–67. Claassens contends that God is feeding all of creation in these texts which speak of the abundance in the time of restoration.
27. Ibid., 70–71.

28. Ibid., 80–82.
29. Ibid., ch. 4. Claassens interprets the dripping wine as the result of so many grapes that mountains shall drip with newly pressed grape juice and the hills will flow with it. The cattle now give milk in such large quantities it flows from the hills (p. 68).
30. The image of wine flowing down the hills, in light of the images of God nursing and mountains as places of fertility, suggests that the mountains might be viewed as God's breasts from which milk is supplied for God's hungry world. See D. Biale, "The God with Breasts: El Shaddai in the Bible," *History of Religions* 21 (1981): 240-56.
31. Davies and Allison, *The Gospel According to Saint Matthew*, 2:566–67.
32. Carter, *Matthew and the Margins: A Sociopolitical and Religious Reading*, 325–26; Davies and Allison, *The Gospel According to Saint Matthew*, 2:566–67; Donaldson, *Jesus on the Mountain: A Study in Matthean Theology*, 129–31.
33. Carter, *Matthew and the Margins: A Sociopolitical and Religious Reading*, 328; Hare, *Matthew*, 167. Carter suggests it is a sign of abundance but Hare argues these few leftovers are hardly the sign of abundance compared to the number of people present.
34. Carter, *Matthew and the Margins: A Sociopolitical and Religious Reading*, 92; Davies and Allison, *The Gospel According to Saint Matthew*, 1:290; Malbon, *Narrative Space and Mythic Meaning in Mark*, 72; Ulrich Mauser, *Christ in the Wilderness: The Wilderness Theme in the Second Gospel and Its Basis in the Biblical Tradition* (Naperville, Ill: A. R. Allenson, 1963). The wilderness is a place of danger: (a) where demons and wild beasts reside (Lev 16:10; Isa 11:6–9, 43:20, 34:9–15, 35:7, 9), (b) and a place without food and water (Exod 16-17). It is also a place of providence and redemption and refuge: (a) in the exodus from Egypt (5:1, 3; 7:16; 13:18, 20; 14:3, 11, 12; Hos 2:14, 9:10, 13:5) and (b) the new exodus from exile (Isa 40:3, 41:18, 43:19–20).
35. Malbon, *Narrative Space and Mythic Meaning in Mark*, 102; Mauser, *Christ in the Wilderness: The Wilderness Theme in the Second Gospel and Its Basis in the Biblical Tradition*. Malbon refers to Mauser and discusses the link among the sea, wilderness, and mountain together as various isolated areas.
36. Carter, *Matthew and the Margins: A Sociopolitical and Religious Reading*, 326; Davies, *Matthew*, 109; Hagner, *Matthew 1–13, 14–28*, 1:419; Harrington, *The Gospel of Matthew*, 241–42; Senior, "Matthew," 127. These scholars all make the connection between the feedings and the Exodus story (Exod 16:13–35; Num 11:7–8, 31–32).
37. Carter makes the connection between 14:13–21 and 14:22–33 (Jesus walks on the water) and the Exodus but does not include 15:29–39 and the scene on the mountain. Carter, *Matthew and the Margins: A Sociopolitical and Religious Reading*, 308–09. While the wilderness experience in the exodus story is understood as a time of testing, the experience here is one of danger and need.
38. Isa 41:18, 43:19–20, 48:21, 51:3 (like the garden); Ezek 36:33–38 (inhabited again). See Ibid., 92.
39. Exodus motifs are often intertwined with creation motifs in Jewish thought, Davies and Allison, *The Gospel According to Saint Matthew*, 1:345.
40. See my analysis on 7:7–11 for the connection made between *The Life of Adam and Eve*, Matthew 4:11, and 7:11.

41. Brown, *The New Brown-Driver-Briggs-Gesenius Hebrew and English Lexicon: With an Appendix Containing the Biblical Aramaic.*
42. Hare, *Matthew*, 167. See Hare on 14:13–21.
43. Betz, *The Sermon on the Mount: A Commentary on the Sermon on the Mount, Including the Sermon on the Plain (Matthew 5:3–7:27 and Luke 6:20–49)*, 397. "'On earth' means not only the space where bread is made but also the resources of the earth in the sense that the earth provides the grain which feeds humanity." See BAGD, s.v. "ἐπί," for the use of ἐπί with the genitive.
44. BAGD, s.v. "ἀναπίπτω." Two Greek words for recline, ἀναπίπτω and ἀνακλίνω, are used in 8:11, 14:19, and 15:35 to refer to reclining or leaning while eating a meal.
45. Betz, *2 Corinthians 8 and 9*, 100.
46. Jesus looks to heaven (14:19) and gives thanks (εὐχαριστέω, 15:36) as a way of expressing gratitude to God for the provision of loaves and fish.
47. I will compare Matt 14 and 15 with Exodus and Numbers here but see my description of how the Matthean community is fed in 6:1–21 and 6:25–34 in chapters 3 and 4 of this study.
48. This characteristic is one of Theissen's features of a gift miracle. Theissen, *The Miracle Stories of the Early Christian Tradition*, 105.
49. Theissen claims that in gift miracles, which he classifies these feedings, the miracles are initiated by the miracle-worker with no requests from those receiving the miracle. "No help is expected from the wonder-workers" (104). There are, however, some implied requests and expectations from the crowds. See Ibid., 103–04.
50. The use of "heaven" subtly connects the view of God in Matt 14 with the "heavenly Father" in 6:1–21, 6:25–34, and 7:7–11. This provides some continuity with the view of God in the narrative but also leaves open the movement in the narrative toward a God who is seen as creator and provider for all creation and not only as a parochial Father.
51. Looking to heaven implies thanksgiving to God and not the blessing of the food. See Davies and Allison, *The Gospel According to Saint Matthew*, 2:491; Luz, *Matthew 8–20: A Commentary*, 314; George T. Montague, *Companion God: A Cross-Cultural Commentary on the Gospel of Matthew* (New York: Paulist Press, 1989), 167.
52. See chapter 4 in this study for a fuller discussion of this idea and its use in 6:25–34. See especially Pss 104:27, 145:15; Isa 40:26; *Pss. Sol.* 5:10.
53. McFague, *Models of God: Theology for an Ecological, Nuclear Age*, 20, 65ff. See McFague and her critique of the monarchical model of God and discussion of a "parental" model.
54. Hanson, *Palestine in the Time of Jesus: Social Structures and Social Conflicts*, 124–25.
55. See Carter, *Matthew and the Margins: A Sociopolitical and Religious Reading*, 325–26; Davies and Allison, *The Gospel According to Saint Matthew*, 2:566–67; Donaldson, *Jesus on the Mountain: A Study in Matthean Theology*, 122–35.
56. Davies and Allison, *The Gospel According to Saint Matthew*, 2:569. See Exod 5:1; 1 Kgs 1:48; 1 Chr 16:36; Pss 41, 59.5, 68:35, 69:6, 72:18 ,106:48; Isa 29:23.
57. Ibid.

Chapter 10: Conclusion

1. In 6:1–21, God is in secret and sees in secret, yet this "secret God" is one that sees all and is God of all. So, while in secret, God is active and present—a paradox. In the narrative, God becomes less and less visible, but with this initial image of God in secret yet active, the reader is led to believe that God continues to be active through the narrative albeit through other human communities.
2. McFague, *Models of God: Theology for an Ecological, Nuclear Age*, 68–69.
3. Hanson, *Palestine in the Time of Jesus: Social Structures and Social Conflicts*, 113.
4. Mary Ann Tolbert, "A New Teaching with Authority: A Re-Evaluation of the Authority of the Bible," 174-175.

Bibliography

Abrams, M. H. *The Mirror and the Lamp: Romantic Theory and the Critical Tradition*. New York: W. W. Norton & Company Inc., 1958.

———, ed. *A Glossary of Literary Terms*. 7th ed. Orlando: Harcourt Brace College Publishers, 1999.

Adams, Edward. *Constructing the World: A Study of Paul's Cosmological Language*. Edinburgh: T&T Clark, 2000.

Allison, Dale C., Jr. "Matthew 10:26–31 and the Problem of Evil." *St. Vladimir's Theological Quarterly* 32, no. 4 (1988): 293–308.

Althusser, Louis. *Essays on Ideology*. London: Verso, 1984.

Andersen, Francis I., and David Noel Freedman. *Hosea: A New Translation with Introduction and Commentary by Francis I. Andersen and David Noel Freedman*. Edited by William Foxwell Albright and David Noel Freedman, The Anchor Bible. New York, New York: Doubleday, 1980.

Anderson, Bernhard W. *Understanding the Old Testament*. Fourth ed. Englewood Cliffs, New Jersey: Prentice-Hall, Inc., 1986.

Anderson, Gary A. "Sacrifice and Sacrificial Offerings (OT)." In *The Anchor Bible Dictionary*, edited by David Noel Freedman, 870–86. New York: Doubleday, 1992.

Bailey, James L. and Lyle D. Vander Broek. *Literary Forms in the New Testament: A Handbook*. 1st ed. Louisville, Kentucky: Westminster/John Knox Press, 1992.

Bakhtin, Mikhail. *Problems of Dostoevsky's Poetics*. Translated by Caryl Emerson. Minneapolis: University of Minnesota Press, 1984.

Bal, Mieke. *Narratology: Introduction to the Theory of Narrative*. Translated by Christine Van Boheemen. Second ed. Toronto, Buffalo, London: University of Toronto Press Incorporated, 1997.

Balch, David L., ed. *Social History of the Matthean Community: Cross Disciplinary Approaches*. Minneapolis: Fortress Press, 1991.

Barbour, Ian G. *Myths, Models and Paradigms: A Comparative Study in Science and Religion*. New York: Harper and Row, 1974.

Barton, Stephen C. "Can We Identify the Gospel Audiences?" In *The Gospels for All Christians: Rethinking the Gospel Audiences*, edited by Richard Bauckham, 173–94. Grand Rapids, Michigan: William B. Eerdmans Publishing Company, 1998.

———. *Discipleship and Family Ties*. Cambridge: Cambridge University Press, 1994.

Bauer, David R., and Mark Allan Powell, eds. *Treasures New and Old: Recent Contributions to Matthean Studies*. Atlanta, Georgia: Scholars Press, 1996.

Berger, Peter L., and Thomas Luckmann. *The Social Construction of Reality*. Garden City, NY: Doubleday & Company, 1966.

Betz, H. D. *2 Corinthians 8 and 9*. Edited by George W. MacRae. Philadelphia: Fortress Press, 1985.

———. *The Sermon on the Mount: A Commentary on the Sermon on the Mount, Including the Sermon on the Plain (Matthew 5:3–7:27 and Luke 6:20–49)*. Minneapolis: Augsburg Fortress, 1995.

———. *Essays on the Sermon on the Mount*. Translated by L. L. Welborn. Philadelphia: Fortress Press, 1985.

Biale, D. "The God with Breasts: El Shaddai in the Bible." *History of Religions* 21 (1981): 240-56.

Bohannan, Paul, and Mark Glazer. *High Points in Anthropology*. 2nd ed. New York: Knopf, 1998.

Brooks, James A. and Carlton L. Winbery. *Syntax of New Testament Greek*. Washington, D. C.: University Press of America, 1979.

Brown, Francis; Edward Robinson; S R Driver; Charles A Briggs; Francis Brown. *The New Brown-Driver-Briggs-Gesenius Hebrew and English Lexicon: With an Appendix Containing the Biblical Aramaic*. Peabody, MS: Hendrickson Publishers, 1979.

Brueggemann, Walter. *First and Second Samuel*. Edited by James Luther and Patrick D. Miller Mays, Interpretation: A Bible Commentary for Teaching and Preaching. Louisville: John Knox Press, 1990.

———. *Genesis*. Edited by James Luther Mays, Interpretation. Atlanta: John Knox Press, 1982.

Carrier, James G. "Exchange." In *Encyclopedia of Social and Cultural Anthropology*, edited by Alan Bernard and Jonathan Spencer, 218–21. London & New York: Routledge, 1996.

Carter, Warren. "The Crowds in Matthew's Gospel." *CBQ* 55 (1993): 54–67.

———. *Households and Discipleship: A Study of Matthew 19–20*. Sheffield, England: JSOT Press, 1994.

———. *Matthew and the Margins: A Sociopolitical and Religious Reading*. Maryknoll, NY: Orbis Books, 2000.

Cartlidge, David R., and David L. Dungan. *Documents for the Study of the Gospels*. Philadelphia: Fortress Press, 1980.

Chatman, S. *Story and Discourse*. Ithaca, NY: Cornell University Press, 1978.

Claassens, L. Juliana M. *The God Who Provides: Biblical Images of Divine Nourishment*. Nashville: Abingdon Press, 2004.

Cohen, Shaye J. D. "Crossing the Boundary and Becoming a Jew." *Harvard Theological Review* 82, no. 1 (1989): 13–33.

Collins, John J. *The Apocalyptic Imagination: An Introduction to the Jewish Matrix of Christianity*. New York: Crossroad Publishing Company, 1992.

Corley. *Private Women, Public Meals*. Peabody, MA: Hendrickson Publishers, 1993.

Counihan, Carole. "Bread as World: Food Habits and Social Relations in Modernizing Sardinia." In *Food and Culture*, edited by Carole Counihan and Penny Van Esterik. New York: Routledge, 1997.

Cousland, J.R.C. *The Crowds in the Gospel of Matthew*. Leiden/Boston/Cologne: Brill, 2002.

Crosby, Michael. *House of Disciples: Church, Economics, and Justice in Matthew*. New York: Orbis, 1988.

Davies, Margaret. *Matthew*. Sheffield: JSOT Press, 1993.

Davies, W. D., and D. C. Allison. *The Gospel According to Saint Matthew*. 3 vols. Vol. 3, *I.C.C.* Edinburgh: T & T Clark, 1997.

– – –. *The Gospel According to Saint Matthew*. 3 vols. Vol. 2, *I. C. C.* Edinburgh: T & T Clark, 1991.

– – –. *The Gospel According to Saint Matthew*. 3 vols. Vol. 1, *I. C. C.* Edenburgh: T & T Clark, 1988.

Donaldson, Terence L. *Jesus on the Mountain: A Study in Matthean Theology*. Sheffield: JSOT Press, 1985.

Douglas, Mary. *Purity and Danger*. London: Routledge & Kegan Paul, 1966.

Duling, D. "Matthew and Marginality." In *Society of Biblical Literature 1993 Seminar Papers*, edited by E. H. Lovering Jr. Atlanta: Scholars Press, 1993.

Durrenberger, E. Paul. "Economic Anthropology." In *Encyclopedia of Cultural Anthropology*, edited by David Levinson and Melvin Ember, 365–71. New York: Henry Holt and Company, 1996.

Edwards, Richard A. *Matthew's Story of Jesus*. Philadelphia: Fortress Press, 1985.

Elliot, John H. "Temple Versus Household in Luke-Acts: A Contrast in Social Institutions." In *The Social World of Luke-Acts: Models for Interpretation*, edited by Jerome H. Neyrey, 211–40. Peabody, Massachusetts: Hendrickson Publishers, 1991.

Esler, Philip F., ed. *Modeling Early Christianity: Social-Scientific Studies of the New Testament in Its Context*. London and New York: Routledge, 1995.

Evans-Pritchard, E.E. *The Nuer: A Description of the Modes of Livelihood and Political Institutions of a Nilotic People*. Oxford: Oxford University Press, 1940.

Exegetical Dictionary of the New Testament. Edited by Horst Robert Balz. Vol. 3. Grand Rapids, MI: Eerdmans, 1990.

Feeley-Harnik, Gillian. *The Lord's Table: The Meaning of Food in Early Judaism and Christianity*. Washington; London: Smithsonian Institution Press, 1981.

Firth, Raymond. *Symbols: Public and Private*. Ithaca: Cornell University Press, 1973.

Flesher, Paul V. M. "Bread of the Presence." In *The Anchor Bible Dictionary*, edited by David Noel Freedman, 780–81. New York: Doubleday, 1992.

Fowler, Robert M. "Reader-Response Criticism." In *Mark and Method: New Approaches in Biblical Studies*, edited by Janice Capel Anderson and Stephen D. Moore. Minneapolis: Fortress Press, 1992.

Friedman, Harriet. "The International Political Economy of Food: A Global Crisis." In *Food in the USA: A Reader*, edited by Carole M. Counihan, 325–346. New York: Routledge, 2002.

Garbarino, Merwyn S. *Sociocultural Theory in Anthropology: A Short History*. Prospect Heights, Illinois: Waveland Press, Inc., 1977. Reprint, 1983.

Garland, D. *Reading Matthew: A Literary and Theological Commentary on the First Gospel*. New York: Crossroad, 1995.

Garnsey, Peter. *Food and Society in Classical Antiquity*. Edited by P. A. Cartledge and P. D. A. Garnsey, *Key Themes in Ancient History*. Cambridge: Cambridge University Press, 1999.

Goldschmidt, Walter. "Functionalism." In *Encyclopedia of Cultural Anthropology*, edited by David Levinson and Melvin Ember, 510–12. New York: Henry Holt and Company, 1996.

Goldsmith, Dale. "'Ask, and It Will Be Given.' Toward Writing the History of a Logion." *New Testament Studies* 35 (1989): 254–65.

Goody, Jack. *Cooking, Cuisine and Class: A Study in Comparative Sociology*. Cambridge; NY: Cambridge University Press, 1982.

Gottwald, Norman K. *The Tribes of Yahweh: A Sociology of the Religion of Liberated Israel, 1250–1050 B.C.E.* Maryknoll, NY: Orbis Books, 1979.

Goulder, M. D. *Midrash and Lection in Matthew*. London: SPCK, 1974.

Gowler, David B. *Host, Guest, Enemy and Friend: Portraits of the Pharisees in Luke and Acts*. Edited by Vernon K. Robbins. Vol. 2, Emory Studies in Early Christianity. New York: Peter Lang, 1991.

Grenholm, Cristina, and Daniel Patte, eds. *Reading Israel in Romans: Legitimacy and Plausibility of Divergent Interpretations*. Harrisburg, Pennsylvania: Trinity Press International, 2000.

Gudeman, Stephen. *The Anthropology of Economy: Community, Market, and Culture*. Frome, Somerset: Blackwell Publishers Inc., 2001.

Gundry, R. *Matthew*. 2nd ed. Grand Rapids: Eerdmans, 1994.

Hagner, D. *Matthew 1–13, 14–28*. 2 vols, Word Biblical Commentary. Dallas: Word, 1993, 1995.

Hanson, K. C. and Douglas E. Oakman. *Palestine in the Time of Jesus: Social Structures and Social Conflicts*. Minneapolis: Fortress Press, 1998.

Hare, D. R. A. *Matthew*, Interpretation. Louisville, KY: Westminster John Knox, 1993.

Harland, Philip A. *Associations, Synagogues, and Congregations: Claiming a Place in Ancient Mediterranean Society*. Minneapolis, Minnesota: Fortress Press, 2003.

Harrington, D. J. *The Gospel of Matthew*. Vol. 1, Sacra Pagina. Collegeville, MN: Liturgical Press, 1991.

Hasel, Gerhard F. "Sabbath." In *The Anchor Bible Dictionary*, edited by David Noel Freedman, 849–56. New York: Doubleday, 1992.

Hauer, Christian E. and William A. Young. *An Introduction to the Bible: A Journey into Three Worlds*. 5th ed. Upper Saddle River, NJ: Prentice Hall, 1886.

Heifer International. "Cornerstones Make Heifer Unique,"Heifer International. http://www.heifer.org/Our_Work/Our_Approach/Cornerstones.shtml (accessed May 22, 2008).

Henaff, Marcel. *Claude Lévi-Strauss and the Making of Structural Anthropology*. Translated by Mary Baker. Minneapolis: University of Minnesota Press, 1998.

Hengel, Martin. *Judaism and Hellenism: Studies in Their Encounter in Palestine During the Early Hellenistic Period*. First American ed. Philadelphia: Fortress Press, 1974.

Hicks, John Mark. "The Sabbath Controversy in Matthew: An Exegesis of Matthew 12:1–14." *Restoration Quarterly* 27 (1984): 79–91.

Howell, David B. *Matthew's Inclusive Story: A Study in the Narrative Rhetoric of the First Gospel*. Sheffield, England: JSOT Press, 1990.

Iser, Wolfgang. *The Implied Reader; Patterns of Communication in Prose Fiction from Bunyan to Beckett*. Baltimore: Johns Hopkins University Press, 1974.

Jencks, C. *What Is Post-Modernism?* 3rd ed. New York: St. Martin's, 1989.

Johnson, Elizabeth. *She Who Is: The Mystery of God in Feminist Theological Discourse*. New York, New York: The Crossroad Publishing Company, 1992.

Kelber, Werner H. *Mark's Story of Jesus*. Philadelphia: Fortress Press, 1979.

King, Philip J., and Lawrence E. Stager. *Life in Biblical Israel*. Edited by Douglas A. Knight, Library of Ancient Israel. Louisville: Westminster John Knox Press, 2001.

Kingsbury, Jack Dean. *Matthew as Story*. 2nd ed. Philadelphia: Fortress Press, 1988.

———. "The Verb Akolouthein ('to Follow') as an Index of Matthew's View of His Community." *JBL* 97 (1978): 56–73.

Klosinski, Lee E. "Meals in Mark." PhD diss., The Claremont Graduate School, 1988.

Koenig, John. "Hospitality." In *The Anchor Bible Dictionary*, edited by David Noel Freedman, 299-301. New York: Doubleday, 1992.

Koester, Helmut. *Ancient Christian Gospels: Their History and Development*. Philadelphia and London: Trinity Press and SCN Press, 1990.

Kramer, H. *Exegetical Dictionary of the New Testament*. Edited by Horst Robert Balz. Vol. 1. Grand Rapids, MI: Eerdmans, 1990.

Lauer, R. H. *Temporal Man: The Meaning and Uses of Social Time*. New York: Praeger, 1981.

Lévi-Strauss, Claude. *The Elementary Structures of Kinship*. Boston: Beacon, 1969.

Levine, Amy-Jill. "Matthew." In *The Women's Bible Commentary*, edited by Carol A. Newsom and Sharon H. Ringe, 252–62. Louisville, Kentucky: Westminster/John Knox Press, 1992.

———. "Second Temple Judaism, Jesus, and Women: Yeast of Eden." *Biblical Interpretation* 2, no. 1 (1994): 8–33.

———. *The Social and Ethnic Dimensions of Matthean Social History*. Vol. 14, Studies in the Bible and Early Christianity. Lewiston, NY; Queenston, Ont.; Lampeter, Wales: Edwin Mellen Press, 1988.

Longstaff, Thomas R. W. "God." In *Harper's Bible Dictionary*, edited by Paul J. Achtemeier, 350–51. San Francisco: Harper & Row, 1985.

Louw, Johannes P., and Eugene A. Nida, eds. *Greek-English Lexicon of the New Testament Based on Semantic Documents*. New York: United Bible Societies, 1989.

Luz, U. *Matthew 1–7: A Commentary*. Minneapolis: Fortress, 1989.

Luz, Ulrich. *Matthew 8–20: A Commentary*. Translated by James E. Crouch. Edited by Helmut Koester, Hermeneia—a Critical and Historical Commentary on the Bible. Minneapolis: Fortress Press, 2001.

Malbon, Elizabeth Struthers. *In the Company of Jesus: Characters in Mark's Gospel*. Louisville, Kentucky: Westminster John Knox Press, 2000.

———. "Narrative Criticism: How Does the Story Mean?" In *Mark and Method: New Approaches in Biblical Studies*, edited by Janice Capel Anderson and Stephen D. Moore, 23-49. Minneapolis: Fortress Press, 1992.

———. *Narrative Space and Mythic Meaning in Mark*. San Francisco: Harper & Row, Publishers, 1986.

Malbon, Elizabeth Struthers, and Janice Capel Anderson. "Literary-Critical Methods." In *Searching the Scriptures*, edited by Elisabeth Schüssler Fiorenza. New York: Crossroad, 1993.

Malina, B. J. *The New Testament World: Insights from Cultural Anthropology*. rev. ed. Louisville, KY: Westminster/ John Knox Press, 1993.

Malina, Bruce J. "Christ and Time: Swiss or Mediterranean?" *The Catholic Biblical Quarterly* (1989): 1–31.

———. "Hospitality." In *Harper's Bible Dictionary*, edited by Paul J. Achtemeier, 408–09. San Francisco: Harper & Row, 1985.

Malina, Bruce J., and Richard L. Rohrbaugh. *Social Science Commentary on the Synoptic Gospels*. Minneapolis: Fortress Press, 1992.

Malinowski, Bronislaw. *Argonauts of the Western Pacific: An Account of Native Enterprise and Adventure in the Archipelagoes of Melanesian New Guinea*. New York: Dutton & Co., Inc., 1961.

Martin, Dale B. *The Corinthian Body*. New Haven: Yale University Press, 1995.

Matthews, Victor H., and Don C. Benjamin. *Social World of Ancient Israel 1250–587 B.C.E.* Peabody, Massachusetts: Hendrickson Publishers, Inc., 1993.

Mauch, T. M. "Sojourner." In *The Interpreter's Dictionary of the Bible*, edited by George Arthur Buttrick, 397–99. Nashville: Abingdon Press, 1962.

Mauser, Ulrich. *Christ in the Wilderness: The Wilderness Theme in the Second Gospel and Its Basis in the Biblical Tradition*. Naperville, Ill: A. R. Allenson, 1963.

Mauss, Marcel. *The Gift*. New York: Norton, 1967.

McBride, S. Dean. "Polity of the Covenant People: The Book of Deuteronomy." *Interpretation: A Journal of Bible and Theology* 41 (1987): 229–44.

McCracken. "Character in the Boundary: Bakhtin's Interdividuality in Biblical Narratives." *Semeia* (1993): 29–42.

McFague, Sallie. *The Body of God: An Ecological Theology*. Minneapolis, Minnesota: Fortress Press, 1993.

———. *Metaphorical Theology: Models of God in Religion Language*. Philadelphia, Pennsylvania: Fortress Press, 1982.

———. *Models of God: Theology for an Ecological, Nuclear Age*. Philadelphia, Pennsylvania: Fortress Press, 1987.

McKibben, Bill. *Deep Economy: The Wealth of Communities and the Durable Future*. New York: Times Books, 2007.

McKnight, Scot. *A Light Among the Gentiles: Jewish Missionary Activity in the Second Temple Period*. Minneapolis: Fortress Press, 1991.

Meeks, W. A. *The First Urban Christians: The Social World of the Apostle Paul*. New Haven, CT: Yale University Press, 1983.

Meier, John P. *The Vision of Matthew: Christ, Church, and Morality in the First Gospel*. New York: Paulist Press, 1979.

Meigs, Anna. "Food as a Cultural Construction." In *Food and Culture: A Reader*, edited by Carole Counihan and Penny Van Esterik. New York: Routledge, 1997.

Mendenhall, George E., and Gary A Herion. "Covenant." In *The Anchor Bible Dictionary*, edited by David Noel Freedman, 1179–202. New York: Doubleday, 1992.

Mennell, Stephen, Anne Murcott, and Anneke H. van Otterloo. *The Sociology of Food: Eating, Diet and Culture*. London and Newbury Park, CA: Sage, 1992.

Merenlahti, Petri, and Raimo Hakola. "Reconceiving Narrative Criticism." In *Characterization in the Gospels: Reconceiving Narrative Criticism*, edited by David Rhoads and Kari Syreeni, 13–48. Sheffield, England: Sheffield Academic Press Ltd, 1999.

Milgrom, Jacob. "Leviticus." In *The HarperCollins Study Bible*, edited by Wayne Meeks, 151–53. New York: HarperCollins, 1993.

Miller, Patrick D. *Deuteronomy*. Edited by James L. Mays, Interpretation: A Bible Commentary for Teaching and Preaching. Louisville: John Knox Press, 1990.

Mohrlang, Roger. *Matthew and Paul: A Comparison of Ethical Perspectives*. Cambridge, London, New York, New Rochelle, Melbourne, Sydney: Cambridge University Press, 1984.

Mol, Hans. *Identity and the Sacred: A Sketch for a New Social-Scientific Theory of Religion*. New York: Macmillan, Free Press, 1977.

Montague, George T. *Companion God: A Cross-Cultural Commentary on the Gospel of Matthew*. New York: Paulist Press, 1989.

Moore, Stephen D. *Literary Criticism and the Gospels: The Theoretical Challenge*. New Haven and London: Yale University Press, 1989.

Mowery, Robert L. "God, Lord and Father: The Theology of the Gospel of Matthew." *Biblical Research* XXXIII (1988): 24–36.

Murcott, Anne. "Sociological and Social Anthropological Approaches to Food and Eating." *World Review of Nutrition and Dietetics*, no. 55 (1988): 1–40.

Neyrey, Jerome H. "Body Language in 1 Corinthians: The Use of Anthropological Models for Understanding Paul and His Opponents." In *Social-Scientific Criticism of the New Testament and Its Social World*, edited by John H. Elliot. Decatur, GA: Scholars Press, 1986.

———. "Ceremonies in Luke-Acts: The Case of Meals and Table Fellowship." In *The Social World of Luke-Acts*, edited by Jerome H. Neyrey. Peabody, MA: Hendrickson, 1991.

———. "The Symbolic Universe of Luke-Acts." In *The Social World of Luke-Acts: Models for Interpretation*, edited by Jerome H. Neyrey. Peabody, Massachusetts: Hendrickson Publishers, 1991.

———, ed. *The Social World of Luke-Acts: Models for Interpretation*. Peabody, Massachusetts: Hendrickson Publishers, 1991.

O'Connor, Kathleen M. "Crossing Borders: Biblical Studies in a Trans-Cultural World." In *Teaching the Bible: The Discourses and Politics of Biblical Pedagogy*, edited by Fernando Segovia and Mary Ann Tolbert, 322–37. Maryknoll, NY: Orbis Books, 1998.

O'Day, Gail R. "John." In *The Women's Bible Commentary*, edited by Carol A. Newsom and Sharon H. Ringe. Louisville, Kentucky: Westminster/John Knox Press, 1992.

Oakman, Douglas E. *Jesus and the Economic Questions of His Day*. Vol. Volume 8. Lewiston/Queenston: The Edwin Mellen Press, 1986.

Ortner, S. B. "Theory in Anthropology since the Sixties." *Comparative Studies in Society and History* 26 (1984): 126–66.

Osiek, Carolyn, and David L. Balch. *Families in the New Testament World: Households and House Churches*. Edited by Don S. Browning and Ian S. Evison, The Family, Religion, and Culture. Louisville, Kentucky: Westminster John Knox Press, 1997.

Overman, J. Andrew. *Church and Community in Crisis: The Gospel According to Matthew*. Valley Forge, PA: Trinity Press International, 1996.

———. *Matthew's Gospel and Formative Judaism*. Minneapolis: Fortress Press, 1990.

Pace, David. *Claude Lévi-Strauss: The Bearer of Ashes*. Boston, London, Melbourne and Henley: Routledge & Kegan Paul, 1983.

Patte, Daniel. *The Challenge of Discipleship: A Critical Study of the Sermon on the Mount as Scripture*. Harrisburg, Pennsylvania: Trinity Press International, 1999.

———. *Discipleship According to the Sermon on the Mount*. Valley Forge, PA: Trinity Press International, 1996.

———. *Ethics of Biblical Interpretation*. Louisville, Kentucky: Westminster John Knox Press, 1995.

———. *The Gospel According to Matthew: A Structural Commentary on Matthew's Faith*. Philadelphia: Fortress, 1987.

Patte, Daniel, Monya S. Stubbs, Justin Ukpong, and Revelation E. Velunta. *The Gospel of Matthew: A Contextual Introduction for Group Study*. Nashville: Abingdon Press, 2003.

Perdue, Leo G., Joseph Blenkinsopp, John J. Collins, Carol Meyers. *Families in Ancient Israel*. Edited by Don S. Browning, Ian S. Evison. First ed, The Family, Religion, and Culture. Louisville, Kentucky: Westminster John Knox Press, 1997.

Pitt-Rivers, Julian Alfred. *The Fate of Shechem or the Politics of Sex: Essays in the Anthropology of the Mediterranean*. Cambridge, London, New York, Melbourne: Cambridge University Press, 1977.

Plummer, Alfred. *An Exegetical Commentary on the Gospel According to St. Matthew*. Grand Rapids, Michigan: Baker Book House, 1982.

Polanyi, Karl. *The Great Transformation*. New York: Rinehart & Co., Inc., 1944.

Powell, Mark Allan. "Expected and Unexpected Readings of Matthew: What the Reader Knows." *The Asbury Theological Journal* 48, no. 2 (1993): 31–51.

———. *What Is Narrative Criticism?* Minneapolis: Fortress Press, 1990.

Przybylski, B. *Righteousness in Matthew and His World of Thought*. Cambridge: Cambridge University Press, 1980.

Resseguie, James. "Reader-Response and the Synoptic Gospels." *JAAR* (1982): 411–34.

Rhoads, David. "Narrative Criticism and the Gospel of Mark." *Journal of American Academy of Religion* (1982): 411–34.

Rhoads, David and Donald Michie. *Mark as Story: An Introduction to the Narrative of a Gospel*. Philadelphia: Fortress Press, 1982.

Richards, Audrey I. *Hunger and Work in a Savage Tribe: A Functional Study of Nutrition among the Southern Bantu*. Cleveland and New York: The World Publishing Company, 1932.

———. *Land, Labour and Diet in Northern Rhodesia: An Economic Study of the Bemba Tribe*. London: Oxford University Press, 1939. Reprint, 1952, 1961.

Robbins, Vernon K. "Plucking Grain on the Sabbath." In *Patterns of Persuasion in the Gospels*, edited by Burton L. Mack and Vernon K. Robbins. Sonoma, California: Polebridge Press, 1989.

———. *The Tapestry of Early Christian Discourse: Rhetoric, Society and Ideology*. London and New York: Routledge, 1996.

Russell, D. S. *The Method and Message of Jewish Apocalyptic, 200 BC–AD 100*. Philadelphia: Westminster Press, 1964.

Sahlins, Marshall. *Stone Age Economics*. Chicago; New York: Aldine-Atherton, Inc., 1972.

Saldarini, Anthony J. *Matthew's Christian-Jewish Community*. Chicago: University of Chicago Press, 1994.

Sanders, E. P. *Judaism: Practice & Belief: 63 B.C.E.–66 C.E.* Philadelphia: Trinity Press International, 1992.

Schneiders, Sandra M. *The Revelatory Text: Interpreting the New Testament as Sacred Scripture*. San Francisco, California: HarperSanFranciso, 1991.

Schottroff. "Human Solidarity and the Goodness of God: The Parable of the Workers in the Vineyard." In *God of the Lowly*, edited by W. Schottroff and W. Stegemann. Maryknoll, N.Y.: Orbis Books, 1984.

Schweizer, Eduard. *The Good News According to Matthew*. Translated by David E. Green. Atlanta: John Knox Press, 1975.

Segovia, Fernando. "Introduction." In *Reading from This Place: Social Location and Biblical Interpretation in the United States*, edited by Fernando Segovia and Mary Ann Tolbert. Minneapolis, Minnesota: Fortress Press, 1995.

Segovia, Fernando F. ""and They Began to Speak in Other Tongues": Competing Modes of Discourse in Contemporary Biblical Criticism." In *Reading from This Place: Social Location and Biblical Interpretation in the United States*, edited by Fernando F. Segovia and Mary Ann Tolbert, 1–32. Minneapolis: Fortress Press, 1995.

———. "Cultural Studies and Contemporary Biblical Criticism: Ideological Criticism as Mode of Discourse." In *Reading from This Place: Social Location and Biblical Interpretation in Global Perspective*, edited by Fernando F. Segovia and Mary Ann Tolbert, 1–20. Minneapolis: Fortress Press, 1995.

Senior, D. "Matthew." In *Abingdon New Testament Commentaries*. Nashville: Abingdon, 1998.

Sheffield, Julian. "The Father in the Gospel of Matthew." In *A Feminist Companion to Matthew*, edited by Amy-Jill Levine, 52–69. Sheffield: Sheffield Academic Press, 2001.

Simkins, Ronald. *Creator and Creation: Nature in the Worldview of Ancient Israel*. Peabody, MS: Hendrickson Publishers, 1994.

Smith, D. "Greco-Roman Meal Customs." *ABD* 4 (1992): 650–53.

Smith, Dennis E. "Table Fellowship as a Literary Motif in the Gospel of Luke." *JBL* 106, no. 4 (1987): 613–38.

Smyth, Herbert Weir. *Greek Grammar*. Cambridge: Harvard University Press, 1956.

Stambaugh, John E., and David L. Balch. *The New Testament in Its Social Environment*. Philadelphia: The Westminster Press, 1986.

Stanton, Graham N. *A Gospel for a New People: Studies in Matthew*. Louisville: Westminster/John Knox, 1992.

———. "Revisiting Matthew's Communities." *SBLSP* 33 (1994): 9–23.

Stewart, Claude Y., Jr. *Nature in Grace: A Study of the Theology of Nature*. Macon, GA: Mercer University Press, 1983.

Strecker, George. *Der Weg Der Gerechtigkeit: Untersuchung Zur Theologie Des Matthaus*. 3rd ed. Gottingen: Vandenhoeck & Ruprecht, 1971.

Suleimann, Susan. "Varieties of Audience-Oriented Criticism." In *The Reader in the Text: Essays on Audience and Interpretation*, edited by S. Suleimann and I. Crossman, 3–21. Princeton: Princeton University Press, 1980.

Tannehill, Robert C. *The Narrative Unity of Luke-Acts: A Literary Interpretation*. Vol. 1: The Gospel according to Luke. Philadelphia: Fortress Press, 1991.

———. *The Sword of His Mouth: Forceful and Imaginative Language in Synoptic Sayings*. Philadelphia, Pennsylvania: Fortress Press, 1975.

Tauxe, Caroline S. "Exchange." In *Encyclopedia of Cultural Anthropology*, edited by David Levinson and Melvin Ember, 469–73. New York: Henry Hold and Company, 1996.

Taylor, Nicholas H. "The Social Nature of Conversion in the Early Christian World." In *Modeling Early Christianity: Social-Scientific Studies of the New Testament in Its Context*, edited by Philip Francis Esler. London; New York: Routledge, 1995.

Theissen, Gerd. *The Miracle Stories of the Early Christian Tradition*. Philadelphia: Fortress Press, 1983.

Tolbert, Mary Ann. "A New Teaching with Authority: A Re-Evaluation of the Authority of the Bible." In *Teaching the Bible: The Discourses and Politics of Biblical*

Pedagogy, edited by Fernando Segovia and Mary Ann Tolbert, 168–89. Maryknoll, New York: Orbis Books, 1998.

Tompkins, Jane P., ed. *Reader-Response Criticism: From Formalism to Post-Structuralism*. Baltimore: The Johns Hopkins University Press, 1994.

Torjesen, Karen Jo. "Reconstruction of Women's Early Christian History." In *Searching the Scriptures*, edited by Elisabeth Schüssler Fiorenza. New York: Crossroad, 1993.

Trilling, Wolfgang. *The Gospel According to St. Matthew*. Translated by Kevin Smyth. Vol. 1, 2. London: Burns & Oates, 1969.

Turner, Jonathan H., and Alexandra Maryanski. *Functionalism*. Menlo Park, California; Reading, Massachusetts; London; Amsterdam; Don Mills, Ontario; Sydney: The Benjamin/Cummings Publishing Company, 1979.

Waetjen, Herman C. *The Origin and Destiny of Humanness: An Interpretation of the Gospel According to Matthew*. 2nd ed. San Rafael, CA: Crystal Press for Omega Books, 1978.

Wainwright, Elaine Mary. "Matthew." In *Searching the Scriptures Vol 2: A Feminist Commentary*, edited by Elisabeth Schüssler Fiorenza. New York: Crossroad, 1994.

———. *Shall We Look for Another? A Feminist Reading of the Matthean Jesus*. Maryknoll, NY: Orbis, 1998.

———. *Towards a Feminist Critical Reading of the Gospel According to Matthew*. New York: de Gruyter, 1991.

Wallace, Scott. "Last of the Amazon." *National Geographic*, January 2007.

Weaver, Dorothy Jean. *Matthew's Missionary Discourse: A Literary Critical Analysis*. Sheffield: Sheffield Academic Press, 1990.

Weiner, Annette. "Reciprocity." In *Encyclopedia of Cultural Anthropology*, edited by David Levinson and Melvin Ember, 1060–68. New York, New York: Henry Holt and Company, 1996.

White, L. Michael. "Crisis Management and Boundary Maintenance: The Social Location of the Matthean Community." In *Social History of the Matthean Community*, edited by David L. Balch. Minneapolis: Fortress Press, 1991.

———, ed. *Social Networks in the Early Christian Environment: Issues and Methods for Social History, Semeia 56*. Atlanta, GA: Scholars Press, 1992.

Williamson, Clark M. and Ronald J. Allen. *A Credible and Timely Word: Process Theology and Preaching*. St. Louis, Missouri: Chalice Press, 1991.

Wire, Antoinette Clark. "Gender Roles in a Scribal Community." In *Social History of the Matthean Community: Cross-Disciplinary Approaches*, edited by David L. Balch. Minneapolis: Fortress Press, 1991.

Wood, Roy C. *The Sociology of the Meal*. Edinburgh: Edinburgh University Press, 1995.

Wren, Brian. *What Language Shall I Borrow? God-Talk in Worship: A Male Response to Feminist Theology*. New York: The Crossroad Publishing Company, 1989.

Wuthnow, Robert, James Davison Hunter, Albert Bergesen, and Edith Kurzweil. *Cultural Analysis: The Work of Peter Berger, Mary Douglas, Michel Foucault, and Jürgen Habermas*. London and New York: Rutledge & Kegan Paul, 1984.

Index

F

G

H

I

J

L

M

N

O

P

R

S

T

V

W

Z

Studies in Biblical Literature

This series invites manuscripts from scholars in any area of biblical literature. Both established and innovative methodologies, covering general and particular areas in biblical study, are welcome. The series seeks to make available studies that will make a significant contribution to the ongoing biblical discourse. Scholars who have interests in gender and sociocultural hermeneutics are particularly encouraged to consider this series.

For further information about the series and for the submission of manuscripts, contact:

Peter Lang Publishing
Acquisitions Department
P.O. Box 1246
Bel Air, Maryland 21014-1246

To order other books in this series, please contact our Customer Service Department:

(800) 770-LANG (within the U.S.)
(212) 647-7706 (outside the U.S.)
(212) 647-7707 FAX

or browse online by series at:

WWW.PETERLANG.COM